H.G. Wells on Science Education
1886-1897

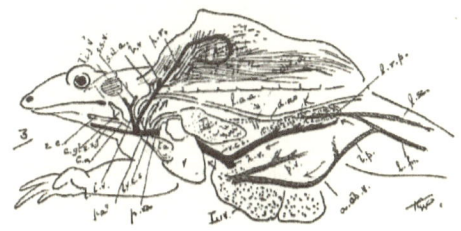

Edited by Lisa M. Lane

Published by Grousable Books, Encinitas, California
ISBN: 979-8-9869845-0-6
Library of Congress Control Number: 2022914999

Contents

Preface

"Would you like to take it back to the table and do it yourself?" he offered, holding the knife out to me.

The Bodleian Library at Oxford University is a warm, inviting space, and the knife-wielding the result of me struggling with uncut pages. It was my third time at the desk to ask that a page be cut for me and no, I declined the offer to slice pages that had been sealed for over 125 years.

The bound volume of the *University Correspondent* was hardly, by this standard, a coveted item at the Bodleian. How was it possible that no one had opened these pages in all this time?

Victorian educational periodicals, I have since discovered, have been somewhat neglected. And despite the fame and popularity of H.G. Wells, some of his early writings have suffered the same fate.

H.G. Wells, born in 1866 to a lower-middle class family, had ambitions to be a school teacher. His mother Sarah, however, wanted her sons to be clerks in shops. She had been forced to return to domestic service, and she would not let the same happen to her children. But Herbert George was a terrible tradesman, and he failed as both a chemist's assistant and a draper's apprentice. What he really wanted was to learn and to teach.

Wells was in the first group of children to benefit from the Forster Act of 1870, which established mandatory elementary education. He would belong to a generation of readers. His month as a chemist's apprentice in Midhurst, West Sussex, provided an opportunity to attend Midhurst Grammar School. There he would study in the evenings for examinations from the Science and Art Department, where high scores could bring grant money to the school. After another failed apprenticeship, he would return to the school as a pupil-teacher, teach himself using the available books, and make more money for the school. He was particularly good at teaching himself science, and would pass certificate exams for teaching.

Such cramming would stand Wells in good stead, then and later. In 1883 it secured him a scholarship to the Normal School of Science (now Imperial College). He studied under T.H. Huxley and determined to become a teacher of biology. He wrote articles for the *Science Schools Journal* there, and joined debates. It was an exciting time. The scholarship he'd won was part of a government program to expand science education. Wells studied for College of Preceptors exams to earn teaching certificates. After Huxley left, however, Wells failed his London University exams, which would have led him toward a Bachelor of

Science degree.

He found work as a low-paid schoolmaster. Although he suffered illness and injury during this time, he kept up his self-studying. In 1890, while working at Henley House School in Kilburn, he was offered a post as tutor for the University Correspondence College. For the next several years, as he passed his Bachelor's exams, taught a biology laboratory class in Red Lion Square, and marked papers through the post, Wells published over 35 articles in the educational press.

These articles, in such journals as *Science and Art*, *The Educational Times*, *Education*, and *The University Correspondent*, critiqued science teaching. They were part of a major debate in the educational press about pedagogy, the examination system, and the role of scientific learning.

Unlike many of the educationists and bureaucrats writing letters and articles, Wells had experienced the entire system from the inside. He had attended a dame school as a small child, and the grammar school at Midhurst. He had been a pupil-teacher. He had studied independently for College of Preceptors exams, during a time when teaching was being professionalized, and had won a Doreck scholarship for his thesis on Froebel's educational theory. He had sat at the feet of T.H. Huxley. He had studied formally for London University exams at the Normal School, and independently after he left. He had taken Matriculation, Intermediate, and Bachelor's Exams in several scientific subjects. He had taught at a school in Wales that had hardly any scientific supplies, and a better school in London that had no unbroken lab equipment. He had taught students through distance education, and had written and published his first book, *Text-book of Biology*, for students to use in their studies. He had taught practical biology in a brand-new laboratory at the University Tutorial College (the London branch of the University Correspondence College).

Despite detractors who saw him as an upstart (since he had attended neither Oxford nor Cambridge), I can imagine few people more qualified to critique science education in the 1890s.

And yet his writings on science teaching have been neglected, or merely mined for signals of the science which would underlie his fictional works. When read at all, they are searched for the early sources of *The Time Machine* (1895) and other "scientific romances".

So why recover them, at the risk of being stabbed by a paper knife?

Our schools and universities today, as in the 1880s, feel pressured to expand their science education. As England did when compared to the continent during the Victorian era, America and Europe fear falling behind. Now, as then, the methods of encouraging such education include government funding, privatization, and distance education. Now, as then, the pedagogy is controversial. Is it best to allow students to self-select science, or better to encourage them into particular programs? Are examinations the best way to test knowledge?

We also feel the need, as the Victorians did, for greater social equality and opportunity. The best scientists needn't come from the most advantaged sectors of society. They can be found and nurtured anywhere, with the right political will. And when this will fails, as it did also during the 1890s, there will be private ventures to fill the gaps.

In this collection is a wealth of knowledge that can inform today's discussions and debates about the role of science, how it is taught, and why it matters. And there is no better person to bring this knowledge forward than the author of *The Time Machine*. Even at the risk of a paper knife.

Introduction

H. G. Wells's work continues to be available in many languages around the world, and the popularity of his work has spawned many anthologies. But of his early, more journalistic work, only three are used by scholars of Wells: Robert M. Philmus and David Hughes's *H. G. Wells: Early Writings in Science and Science Fiction* (1975), Patrick Parrinder and Robert Philmus's *H. G. Wells's Literary Criticism* (1980), and John S. Partington's *H. G. Wells in Nature, 1893-1946: A Reception Reader* (2008). There are no anthologies of his many early works on science education, eighty of which are reprinted in this volume.

As Philmus and Hughes noted in their collection, anthologies provide access to sources which "are to be found scattered among a variety of publications".[1] They also tend to be scattered among various libraries, and listed in various bibliographies. The most important of these is *The Journalism of H.G. Wells: An Annotated Bibliography* (2012), created by David C. Smith and Patrick Parrinder. Two of the items appearing in this volume ("The Too-Ambitious Textbook", and "The Theory of Evolution") were not listed in any published biography, and were therefore re-discovered.

The articles are presented in five parts:

Student and schoolmaster (1886-1890)

Wells's journalistic writings began in 1886, in the *Science Schools Journal*, a publication of the Normal School of Science and Royal School of Mines. Wells was 20 years old, and had earned his scholarship to the Normal School of Science by studying independently and taking examinations at Midhurst Grammar School, where he had been a pupil-teacher. The exams, given by the College of Preceptors, were designed not only to earn grants for the schools, but to call attention to students likely to become good science teachers. In his first year at the Normal School, Wells studied under T.H. Huxley, from whom he adopted his own principles of science teaching. Examinations were at the center of education for many students. This preoccupation is the focus of **To the Average Man**, with a humorous description of fellow students "fraudulently cramming" and being unable to write, thus dooming the entire enterprise of examinations. His piece on **Socrates** introduces some of his early ideas of education. In 1890 the

---

1. Philmus, Robert M, and David Y Hughes. *H. G. Wells: Early Writings in Science and Science Fiction*. Berkeley: University of California Press, 1975, p ix.

I

journal would become the *Royal College of Science Magazine*, and later *The Phoenix*. According to the biography by Geoffrey West, H.G. Wells, later ashamed of his work in the *Science Schools Journal*, claimed to have bought all the back numbers and destroyed them.[2]

Despite an excellent start studying under T.H. Huxley, Wells became bored and distracted after his mentor's retirement. His other professors (Guthrie for physics, Judd for geology) were far less inspiring. Wells's plans had been clear. He very much wanted to be a science teacher, and to get a Bachelor of Science degree, and he was good at studying on his own and passing examinations. Obtaining numerous passes in biology, mathematics and physics had been no problem, and he had passed the Matriculation Exams at the University of London. But in his third year he began failing, first astronomical physics, and then geology. He resigned as editor of the *Science Schools Journal*, and left the Normal School, taking a job as a poorly paid schoolmaster at Holt Academy near Wrexham in Wales in summer 1887. After an injury forced him out of this position, he returned to London and did some coaching in the sciences, but had trouble making ends meet.

Wells was hired as schoolmaster at Henley House School, Kilburn, in 1889, at the age of 22. The headmaster was J.V. Milne, a qualified teacher with interesting pedagogical ideas. Unfortunately, the school had little scientific equipment for Wells to teach practical science, so instead he used his drawing skills as a demonstrator. He also wrote for the school journal, the *Henley House School Magazine*, which had been founded by Alfred Harmsworth (later a famous publisher) in 1881. The two pieces from the *Magazine*, **Holiday Science** and **The North Sea**, were written for students, and are clearly instructional. The journal itself includes hints about him as a teacher, featuring a description of a trip to the zoo, and good wishes for his health when he became ill. At the same time, Wells prepared for Intermediate Examinations at the University of London, and studied pedagogy. At the end of the 1889, he submitted a thesis on Froebel to the College of Preceptors, won awards for his work, and sat exams to receive his diploma as a Licentiate.

At the beginning of 1890 Wells took a job as biology tutor with William Briggs of the University Correspondence College. Reducing his hours at Henley House, he taught at the UCC's branch on Booksellers' Row in London, as well as tutoring biology by post. He also worked on getting elected a Fellow of the Royal Zoological Society, to which he had been recommended by J.V. Milne. In February of 1890, Wells began writing for *The Educational Times*. His **College of**

---

2. Geoffrey West, *H. G. Wells: A Sketch for a Portrait* (London: Gerald Howe Ltd, 1930), p. 287.

Preceptors: **Conversazione at University College, London** was mere reportage, and only in **Registration**, a letter to the editor, does he begin to reveal his criticism of the education system and join in the debates about educational reform. Later that year he sat his Bachelor's exams at the University of London, earning a First in Zoology and degrees in Physical Geography and Zoology. His goal when he entered the Normal School was now fulfilled.

Tutor and scholar (1891-1893)

In a January **Letter to the Editor of the** *Educational Times*, Wells began a debate with a well-known scholar, Reverend Quick, over a book by Herbert Spencer. **The Value of Science** continued this debate, and Wells also began writing for the organ of the University Correspondence College, *The University Correspondent*. His **Subtle Examinee** was the first humorous piece Wells wrote about the contradiction between learning and doing the examiner's bidding, which would become a theme in a number of his writings. Making a decent living working for the College, Wells was able to leave Henley House School, but he still read the Magazine, and in August 1891 contributed **That Problem!** A month later, his criticism of the focus on facts, rather than concepts, in science began to take form. **School Zoology**, written as a letter to the *Educational Times*, used actual College of Preceptors' examination questions to demonstrate the continual focus on facts. His first piece for the *Journal of Education*, **The Too-Ambitious Text-book**, was a criticism of the text-book displacing actual teaching. In attributing to the text-book "ambition, a divided aim, treachery", Wells continued the style of using humor to make his point.

For the short-lived journal *Education*, which was only in print 1890-91, Wells contributed **The Problem of Sympathy in Teaching**, which humorously claimed that young men were generally unsuited to teach young children. It was one of the first articles he signed "H. G. Wells, B.Sc." *Science and Art* provided a more practical and serious venue, as the organ of the Science and Art Department providing scholarships to students. Wells's **Drawing and Art** began his argument about being too practical in instruction, his byline incorporating not only B.Sc., but also F.Z.S. (Fellow of the Zoological Society) and L.C.P. (Licentiate of the College of Preceptors). Drawing should benefit the learner, by teaching better observation, rather than striving for perfection. It was followed by the more significant **Natural History in Schools** for the *Journal of Education*, which complained against the expansion of curricular subjects which Wells considered accessory to the main goals of education. In promoting the role of Natural History, drawing was not related to art, but rather the ability to render either scientific subjects, or natural subjects scientifically. Art was, he felt, derivative of nature anyway; art was simply "nature working upon the mind of man".

With his next piece for *The University Correspondent*, Wells began a multi-year tirade of the examination system that had structured his work as a biology tutor. In the satirical **Hints to the Subtle Examinee**, he advised scholars on how to fail an examination: write long papers, take no particular stand, and leave questions unanswered. **A Plea for the Study of the Teacher**, written at the beginning of 1892, opined that teaching training should focus on the teacher rather than the study of children. The **College of Preceptors' Science Examination** built on his earlier letter for *The Educational Times* but emphasized the need for proper preparation for the practical, or laboratory, portion of the College of Preceptors' examination, an issue to which Wells would later return. He was, at the time, in the process of writing the *Text-book of Biology*, which would include advice on creating a kitchen-table laboratory for such work.

Wells's focus broadened in the spring of 1892. In a not very veiled criticism of contemporary educational reformers, Wells's **Comenius** was a response to the increasing popularity of celebrating that 17th century figure. This was followed by his first article about the University of London. This institution had been an examining body since its inception in 1836, but various attempts had been made to reform it over the years. It served primarily students who, like Wells, could not afford Oxford or Cambridge, and who had to learn on their own or through private entities like the University Correspondence College. Beginning in 1889, various commissions had considered proposals to make U of L a teaching university, with King's College and University College, London considering forming their own "Albert University". Wells, having obtained his coveted B.Sc. as an external student, was one of many opposing any plan that might disadvantage those of his class and circumstances, thus **The University for London**.

In **The Future of Private Teaching**, Wells framed his support for the examining university in the context of private students and teachers, who although necessary were frequently maligned. With **The Use and Abuse of the Text-book** he returned to pedagogical critique—textbooks are necessary, but it is the teacher that brings their information to life. Wells was at this stage called upon to review science books, often anonymously, and in **Apodidae** he not only displayed his deep knowledge but also denigrated a book that didn't demonstrate any knowledge of its own. His reviews of books on education, such as *The Science of Education*, further demonstrated his own study of the discipline. His **On the True Lever of Education** was so popular it was reprinted in the American journal *Educational Review*. He vehemently criticized educational reformers who behaved as if teachers could simply change everything they did, without regard for the examinations to which their teaching led. **The Miscellaneous as**

Educational Curriculum, written with his friend A.T. Simmons, humorously lambasted a new curriculum based on the already disjointed manner of teaching various subjects. Wells's letter **Professor Laurie on Herbert Spencer** supported the usefulness of Herbert Spencer's ideas against attack by a respected figure. His interview, **Dr. Collins Upon the Educational Outlook**, gave voice to one of the opponents of restricting the University of London. But Wells was still, primarily, a biologist. His fairly brutal review of **A New Book on Evolution** castigated the author for flights into "fantastic romance" in his story of evolution. But his **Biology for the Intermediate Science and Preliminary Scientific Examinations** was a lengthy and useful set of instructions for students engaging the practical demonstrations of the exams, and would be reworked into his own *Text-book of Biology*. In **What is Cram?** Wells detailed the use of the term as epithet, and set it within the context of the times.

Critic and pedagogue (1893-1894)

H.G. Wells was always challenged by health problems, in particular a kidney injury when young and a recurrent lung condition that was misdiagnosed as tuberculosis. He had a recurrence of the latter in May 1893, and was forced to recuperate before doing much work. His *Text-book of Biology* was published as his first book, and he continued to write about science and teaching. In **Against Being Too Practical in Teaching** he lauded not only the enthusiastic teacher, but the use of theory to provide meaning to the facts one learns. This theme continued in **Biological Teaching**, which noted sharp delineations between facts and theory, and theory and demonstration, which would need to be dissolved to create good teaching of biology. For **At the Royal College of Science**, Wells chose to hide behind the pseudonym "Z." which allowed him to relay his own experiences as a former student. His descriptions would later be seen in a number of his fictional works, which often featured characters attending practicals at South Kensington. The letter **Scholastic Isolation** provided a heart-felt tribute to teachers who were misunderstood by society. In September 1893, the first of several unsigned **Science Notes** appeared in *The Journal of Education*, the first marking despair at how new knowledge of science rarely made its way into the curriculum. **The Examiner Examined** returned to Wells's old bugbear, creating a fictional place where examiners were humble and thoughtful.

In **The Academy for Young Gentlemen**, Wells chose to revisit his earlier years at Morley's Academy in Bromley to describe the abuses of late Victorian private schoolmasters. But in **The Teaching of Geography**, he offered specific examples of pedagogy, from chalkboard drawing to textbook study, in which he "keeps the schoolroom in mind". This was followed by **On Certain Defects in**

English Public Schools, signed as An Outsider. Here Wells lashed out at everything from the lack of female influence on young boys, to the expense of food at boarding schools, to the overemphasis on classics in the curriculum. In **Mr Churchill: The Dreamer as Schoolmaster**, he examined the fictional character in Longfellow's novel *Kavanaugh*, a "schoolmaster against his will", who would rather dream than teach well.

Educationalist (1894-95)

By the beginning of 1894, Wells was no longer working for the University Correspondence College. He had published two textbooks, and was writing for the *Pall Mall Gazette* under its editor Henry Cust, which provided a steady income. At this point, Wells's fictional stories would become more numerous, and he was writing well. At the same time, the volume of science and science teaching articles vastly increased. **The Very Fine Art of Microtomy** was a light piece that nevertheless celebrated an overlooked aspect of science, the preparation of specimens. Spring of 1894 saw serious **Science Notes** for *The Journal of Education* interspersed with a satirical series, **The Scholastic Frame of Mind**, for *The Educational Times*. The first of these (**I: Self-Satisfaction the Necessary Groundwork**) considered that teachers needed to have unswerving faith in themselves. Part **II: Its Lack of Sympathy** continued with the idea that teachers must be wholly unsympathetic, and **III: The Passion Pedagogic** covered the extremes to which people will go to instruct other people, even to the point of screaming and shouting. The more typical **Science Notes, 1 March 1894** entry directly criticized "bogus science teaching", with the column of **April** attacking both laboratory drills and unsound examination methods, and the piece in **May** arguing for the external student at the University of London. Among other critiques was **Jellygraphia**, Wells's only direct examination of educational technology, which ridiculed the use of mechanical reproduction of documents as a kind of teaching mania. **The Science Library, South Kensington** mocked the organization of books on the library shelves. This was followed by **The Theory of Evolution**, written for *The University Correspondent*, which derived from his text-book and featured one of the clearest explanations of the evolutionary ideas of the day. Wells's writings for *Nature* are best exemplified by **Popularising Science**, which caused some controversy. His scathing review of an educational book in **Pestalozzi** also demonstrated his deep knowledge of pedagogy, and is a good example of some of Wells's harsher writings. I consider **Science, In School and After School**, also from *Nature*, to have been one of his clearest and most through critiques of science teaching and the examination system that supported it.

In the autumn of 1894, at the same time as he was working on *The Time Machine* (his first popular novel), Wells's science journalism took a pessimistic tone. **A Specimen of American Pedagogics**, another review, provided one of his few examinations of the American faith in educational science, which he saw as heavily promoted but poorly demonstrated in the perused book. His **The Problem of Sympathy** declared that young men were the least perfect teachers of children, by reason of their own insecurities. This was followed by a series called **The Sins of the Secondary Schoolmaster** for *The Pall Mall Gazette*. With sarcastic humor, the failings of schoolmasters were considered to include **His Technical Incapacity**, **His Remarkable Examinations Results**, and **His Absurd Technical Teaching**. Intended to show the shortcomings of teacher training, and sympathetic at all times to the teachers themselves, it also spawned comment and controversy. **The Biological Problem of Today** marked Wells's return to the *Saturday Review of Politics, Literature, Science and Art*, this time by request. **The Darwinian Theory,** a review, showcased his deep scientific knowledge, and at the end of 1894 he was invited to speak to the College of Preceptors, whose pupil examinations had begun his ambitions to be a schoolteacher many years before. This talk, called **Science Teaching: An Ideal and Some Realities**, returned to his favorite subject, and although published in *The Educational Times*, received a response in the journal *Nature*. **The Science and Art of Education** picked up on earlier themes about whether a science of education either existed or was useful.

A Man of Science (1895-1897)

As he began to focus more on fiction writing, Wells's articles on science and science teaching dealt with broader interpretations and new discoveries, and he continued his work for the *Saturday Review*. He explored the idea that art and culture might be **Bye-Products in Evolution**, created accidentally as a result of evolutionary changes needed for survival. His review **The Palmy Days of the Universities** was an early historical effort, analysing the ways in which universities had changed over the years, while in **The South Kensington Revolution** Wells undertook a deep analysis of new reforms in science schools. His view of popular science culture was more disparaging. The tone of his book review **Scientific Research as a Parlour Game** was hostile to popular science, and clearly distinguished it from the real thing. Similarly, **Variorum: Of the Fallacy of Museums** derided natural history museums for the disorder of their exhibits, and their inappropriateness for teaching science to young people. As issues arose over new teaching ideas for the University of London, Wells submitted letters to the *Saturday Review*: **The Threatened University** and **The London University Question**. The first defended correspondence classes and the external students who took them, and both were part of an argument with Silvanus P. Thompson, an educational leader, over the possible exclusion of private students from the new schemes for the university. But there was praise too. In **Elementary Science Teaching**, Wells shared his hope for better equipment and support for science classes, and lauded his friend's text-book in **Mr. Gregory's "Physics Exercise-Book"**, a friendly review. Provoking an argument with microscope vendors, **Cheap Microscopes and a Moral** claimed that expensive and inferior equipment was holding Britain back in its competition with other countries for superiority in science. His articles for the Daily Mail continued a theme of Britain's science education as dangerously behind that of Germany. In **The Root of the Matter: Some Reflections on the British Schoolmaster** he blamed the lack of education in those doing the education, and in **Sums: The Fine Art of Not Teaching Mathematics** he attacked poor mathematics education. With **"Stinks": The Cheerful Game of Teaching Science Without a Balance,** Wells returned to his earlier criticisms of science education in Britain, including the lack of equipment.

H. G. Wells continued writing about education beyond his success as an author of scientific romances. The novel *Joan and Peter* (1918) would be a conversation about education. He would write *The Outline of History (1920)* and *A Short History of the World* (1922) in response to dull and repetitive history teaching, and *The Story of a Great Schoolmaster* (1924) to show his admiration of schoolteachers like Frederick William Sanderson. Although he left the realm of professional teaching, he would consider himself a life-long educationalist. His work never stopped instructing his readers. In a sense he would transition his didacticism from journalism to fiction to political treatises, from direct to indirect and back again.

A note on editing

I have tried to avoid articles published or reprinted in previous collections that are readily available, unless they correspond directly to the issue of science teaching. In transcribing the documents for annotation and ease of use, I have corrected publication spacing, removed first word capitalization, and standardized indentation. I have left unchanged Wells's name as printed, spelling errors/differences, and idiosyncratic word usage and sentence structure.

"I am an old and seasoned educationist; most of my earliest writings are concealed in the anonymity of the London educational papers..."

H. G. Wells, *The Salvaging of Civilization* (1921)

Student and Schoolmaster
(1866-1890)

Preface. To the Average Man.

Science Schools Journal, vol 1, no 1, pp1-2, December 1886.

This torturously written piece introduced the Science Schools Journal, *which Wells edited while a student at the Normal School of Science. Even in this very early work, he notes the cramming of scientific facts as a factor in learning, although here it is an excuse for the poor writing that may occur in the journal.*

Respected Sir,

It was, in a more learned and less educated age than this present, the law that literary eruptions should be preceded by a sonorous dedication, by a moving appeal to some eminent person whereby his judgment might be distorted or overthrown, and the fiery flood of poetry, or scoriaceous shower of facts, or dense vaporous arguments, came upon him while disorganised and helpless.

This phenomenon of a dedication is imagined by many not to occur in the current epoch, save as an aborted, a complimentary, thing; but *this* is an error of some bigness. It is true the dedication is no longer, in many cases, a distinctly separable part, but it is equally true that it vigorously survives in the main portion of the Preface now always prefixed to papyrean perpetrations. *Why* this modification has occurred is easily explained.

This Land has, unfortunately, become in spirit, democratic, whereas it *was* utterly aristocratic.

The appeal for favour has no longer to be made to Eminences, but to the Average Flat, and has undergone much adaptation. The eminent love open flattery, while the vulgar an elevated confidence is more effectual. The dedication has become a prefatory dedication; no longer is it *"De profundis,"* but *"Attendite, popule."* Nevertheless, the adamantine foundation, the fundamental, characteristic, dishonest object of the disarmament of justice, immutable remaineth. The Author no longer, with sheet and candle, bewails his frailties, but, like Cleopatra in the presence of Cæsar, garbed in the thinnest veil of modesty conceivable, poses to suggest unprecedented gifts: yet the guilty consciousness is there still.

We merely mention these facts. We do not contemplate such an introduction to you, O Excellent Average Man; for we know full well you feel as superior to the vulgar herd as we do, and are confident of awakening a twang of sympathy in that Catholic Diapason, your mind, without such artifice. What we would here say is merely a dry indication of why this paper is established. The *personnel* of the Normal School of Science and Royal School of Mines is emphatically *recherché*. Every May the myriads of science students in the British Isles undergo gravimetric sorting. The noblest specimens reach this building.

Here, from north, south, east, and west, are gathered minds specially capable of acquiring, retaining, and displaying systematic knowledge. Clearness of perception, imagination, and order are alike *the* mental requirements of the scientist and the writer. We may, therefore, reasonably expect that our pages will be filled with right opinion well expressed.

If not, it seems to us that some such absurd explanations as these which follow will have to be accepted:—

That our fellow-students have no time for writing, which implies that they are committing to memory classified facts without opportunity for exercise in the re-sorting and displaying thereof; that, like athletes who, professing to train, merely eat, they are fraudulently cramming; or, that they are incapable of writing, which (as above hinted) condemns the whole magnificent examination fabric of the Science and Art Department.

It is thus hard for us to imagine how anyone can deny that this periodically will contain great things.

Anticipating, therefore, your entire satisfaction, we would here record our sense of obligation to the compositor for his valuable aid in setting up our Magazine; to the boy who brought round the proofs for us to look at; to the compiler of "Nuttall's Dictionary," to whom which we owe much, if not all, of our material; to the young lady (next door) who is practising "Scales," and to whom is due much of the praise for the euphony of this introduction; and to the four fellow-students who, at a great sacrifice, *refrained* from offering us advice as to our duties. Less conventional and more sincere thanks must be expressed to those who have contributed matter to this issue. We hope that the number of the contributors to No. 2 will be greatly increased, and shall be glad to receive help of *this* sort from all quarters.

I conceal from every eye beneath this calm, hopeful, even proud, exterior, the devastation of the furies, the fierce, ceaseless assault of fear, remorse, and despair. Like the Roman sentinel at Pompeii, or, better, like the responsible public official before an election,

> I remain,
> O Average Man,
> Your faithful servant,

THE EDITOR

Socrates

Science Schools Journal, vol 1, no 1, pp18-21, December 1886

While clearly writing to fill the pages of the Science Schools Journal, *Wells's discussion of Socrates contains early evidence of his concerns about teaching, an activity which both expresses and influences conceptions of societal progress. Many other elements – a disdain for useless wealth, a poor opinion of religion, an acknowledgement of history, and a connection to scientific thought – would be motifs throughout his work.*

The study of men in the past is in almost all cases a difficult undertaking, and is often of little apparent utility save as a source of material for the mosaic of the historical fictionist. There are exceptions, however, which we can discuss with some certainty and consequent profit, as for instance, when a participator in past occurrences is the reporter and an observant man. It is in this way that we are able to form, frequently clear, and sometimes vivid conceptions of many of the men who made Athenian history, while the splendid Pericles administered, and while tyrants and demagogues alternately sapped the magnificence of the commonwealth. Especially is the figure distinct of the great founder of the Academics—Socrates.

The world in which Socrates lived presents on the moral and mental side many resemblances to this present world of ours. It was a time of unusual mental activity of free enquiry into everything in and around men, of excellence rather than grandeur in art, and of true, rather than emotional thought. There was much setting up and pulling down of gods and oracles, and leaders of men. Wealth and knowledge derived from an extensive commerce with the rest of Greece, and with Italy, Sicily, Cyprus, Lydia, and Pontus had increased leisure and widened discussion. And the like results had followed the internal developments which Pisistratus and Hipparchus had initiated. The sciences of magnitude and form were being studied. Astronomy and philosophical history were developing and microphysical and metaphysical speculations were eagerly discussed. Painting, sculpture, architecture, and music flourished. Dramatic art was especially excellent. The stage had, at that time, much of that influence upon opinion which now the press exercises. The Athenian mind seems indeed to have been specially adapted and inclined to arts which involved observing the forms and actions of men. Even the philosophical thought of Plato was imparted in dialogues of inimitable dramatic merit. It is from those dialogues chiefly, and from the apologetic memorabilia of Xenophon, that we derive a clearer portrait of the man Socrates than we have of any other of the giants in those days.

His personal appearance was grotesque, "worthy to represent the voluptuous Silenus," but beneath this was a mind of an extraordinary nature.

His panegyrists have ascribed to him superlative degrees of qualities in which, to our limited intelligence, it seems he was deficient. That he possessed an intuitive insight into the nature of the Universe, or into the mind of man, that he was sublimely virtuous or profoundly wise; seem to us to be assertions inharmonious with inferences from undeniable facts. His dubious connection with Aspasia, the nature of the prosecution that destroyed him, many of the sayings which his friends quote, should at least modify the first member of these assertions; while his intercourse with Critias and Alcibiades, his proverbial uncleanliness, and certain features of his system to be speedily examined, militate against the second.

It requires no doubtful assertion of attributes of this sort, however, to enforce the justness of the prominent placing of Socrates among men. He had the extraordinary development of those faculties of the mind which constitute love of truth in opinion. It is this that we should respect in him; for it is this that has ever distinguished reformers and originators from the mass of men that has moved the feeble to defy princes, and common men to re-shape the world. Identical with this is that love of independence which induced Socrates to remain contentedly in poverty when his widespread reputation, if he had chosen to teach for money, would have speedily placed immense riches at this disposal.

Another, almost equally marked feature of this man's character was his adoration of beauty. Beauty was to him the Fact in the Universe. What was beautiful was Good. This was the foundation of his teaching; the assumption to which his reasoning was ever turned. In "The Banquet" he discourses on love. There he states, in the form of the narrative of a conversation, what is in his own mind. First with personal, then with other physical, then with moral, beauty, he endeavours to show that love is the desire to possess and perpetuate the beautiful; simultaneously with this, he indicates a conception of the development of the perception of beauty in the mind of man until he attains *the* Beautiful, absolute beauty, which is everlasting happiness.

It is not our intention in this paper to criticise assumptions, our design is to call attention to methods; still we cannot avoid pointing out here how entirely unsound is this idea of love, how the recognition of superior strength of mind or body, and the sense of being beloved, which things are not identical with the sensation of the beautiful, may produce passionate affection, and that the desire to perpetuate can only by a gross image and a gross mind be identified with love.

The way in which Socrates sought to establish truth was such as naturally obtains in thinking.

A sensation is the perception of a difference; whether that difference is of the perceiver or not, is immaterial in the connection. An idea of a thing is the memory of a sensation or a group of sensations, the definition of a thing should be the verbal indication of the idea. Imagination is the mingling of ideas; thought, the comparison of definitions. It is impossible for a man to think a *new* thing. He has a certain number of sensations, which he can classify and intermingle, and with which he can form more or less fair structures, but possibility of other sort of material is there none; he is a maker but not a creator.

Opining, rather than knowing this, Socrates, in the dialogue on virtue, argues that all truth is *in* man. Calling to him an altogether uneducated slave, he, while ostentatiously avoiding imparting information, questions him on certain geometrical points. In a little while, the slave is led to perceive clearly that the square of the diagonal of a square equals twice the square of the side. "All this," says Socrates, "I have *drawn out of the man.*"

This conception, that truth is in the mind of man, being established, it becomes evident that truth is merely the statement and correlation of definitions, and that upon the initial definition depends the truthfulness of an investigation. This is what Carlyle means when he says: "What is science but the right naming of things!" This is what the dialogue with Meno seems intended to display: "Socrates," says Meno, "can virtue be taught?" and straightaway Socrates falls to questioning and suggesting until the puzzled sophist confesses that he knows not what virtue may be, and they start together searching their minds for a true definition.

Although the *method* of Socrates is natural and correct yet he erred in his opinion of the origin of ideas. It appears that he believed in the transmigration of souls: and thinking out a definition appeared to him to be the recollection of the knowledge of a previous, and presumably more perfect, state. This misconception crippled the Academic philosophers, since it prevented experiment. Vague memories rather than drilled sensations, constituted the foundation of their thought, and consequently only those departments of mental exercise were fruitful under the Platonists, whereof the first principles are almost universal properties of matter. Of all the learning of the philosophers before the age of Bacon, only their mathematical science seems in these days sound.

Macaulay,[3] in a panegyric upon Bacon, seems to depreciate Socrates, insinuating that his philosophy was a playing with words, and stating that the ancient philosophers disdained utility. In this latter connection he quotes Seneca to illustrate the ideas of Socrates, as one might quote a cheap popular scientific periodical to exemplify the thought of Darwin. But this accusation of disregarding utility harmonizes little with the tone of the original Socratic

---

3. This would be historian Thomas B. Macaulay, "An Essay on Francis Bacon", Edinburgh Review, 1837.

teaching. It is true Socrates denied that the philosopher should be an encyclopædia of useful and entertaining knowledge, that he slighted the enthusiastic investigation of complicated mathematical relations, and underrated material comfort; yet in a hundred places we may read how he above all desired his teaching to be useful. It was to show that men should be virtuous, and not virtuosi, that he raised his voice against geometrical and arithmetical subtilties being esteemed philosophy.

In the primary principle—the desire to benefit men—Socrates is in perfect harmony with Bacon. But while Bacon sought to increase material comforts Socrates sought to instil just thought and elevated sentiments; and to call the former fruitful and the latter fruitless, is to show an utter disregard to the necessary difference of the results accruing from such divergently directed efforts. The teachings of Bacon were the seed that presently produced the Royal Society and the "Century of Inventions," and in the fulness of time, the railway, the telegraph, and the factory system. The teachings of Socrates shaped the minds of Xenophon, Plato, Euclid, Euripedes, and a host of as excellent, if less famous, men.

It has been pointed out that the era of Socrates was one of great material comfort. And with that material comfort the majority of men had become practically materialists. Religious service was merely the excuse for gorgeous display: the gods were scoffed at, even actually represented on the stage. The people regarded politics as the science of winning tribute and the distribution of doles. Wealth was the key to power; and the pleasing of the coarser senses, bodily desires and the love of power, was the end of living. No wonder then that a man zealous to see things real and true, a man with an intuitive hatred of shams, yearning to see men leading the lives of men, resolutely turned his back on the study of extraneous matter and pointed to ideal things, to virtue, and to beauty.

And in this age, which so resembles his, when religion is the recreation of the rich and the annoyance of the poor, when the whole fabric of society is boasted to be a struggle for existence, such teaching is sorely needed.

In one matter we are at once better off and worse off than the Athenians. We are better off in having a great number of men among us specially set apart to exhort us to turn from the husks that the swine eat, and to guide us to what is good. We are worse off because these men, as a body, utterly neglect their work. They preach platitudes to women and children, they shine in the administration of hospitals, doles, soup kitchens, flower shows, fancy bazaars, and primrose league habitations. Meanwhile the bitter struggle among the multitude of men goes on, and the selfish cruelty of the clever and rich is sanctioned by the silence of their putative teachers.

HERBERT G. WELLS.

Holiday Science

Henley House School Magazine, vol III, no 33, p. 217, August 1889

Almost three years after Socrates, Wells would leave the Normal School unable to complete his degree. After working in Wales and suffering an injury, he returned to London and became a schoolmaster at Henley House School. J. V. Milne, who ran the school, introduced Wells in the 1889 issue of the school magazine, as replacement for the previous science teacher:

> *"His successor, Mr. Wells, now takes the Science and Drawing throughout the school. Mr. Wells holds advanced certificates from the Science Schools at Kensington in Zoology, Botany, Geology (Mineralogy and Palæontology), Physics, Chemistry, Mathematics, Practical Geometry, and Drawing (Freehand, Model, Geometrical, and Perspective). He has already awakened a thirst for science and a spirit of inquiry."*

The pieces Wells wrote for the magazine were designed to interest the pupils, and in the first article he achieved this by using abbreviations of what were undoubtedly his students' names. He also makes an argument for spontaneous scientific observation of nature, rather than just collecting specimens and learning names, to gain knowledge about the world.

There is a suggestion abroad of the dawn of a great epoch in the history of science. Our eminent school-fellow B. i. has expressed a determination to "go in" for insects; G. iv. is already hard at work treacling the trees on Primrose Hill; and F. iii. has spent one and sixpence at least in test tubes and dangerous explosives; P. ii. and Z. xvi.—the insurance companies are warned—have found out how to make a fire balloon, and will most certainly do it; while M. i. has consecrated his life to the vertebrata, and invested all his worldly belongings in a fishing-net and a fish globe. Knowing the ability and energy of our men, we can scarcely imagine a limit to the impending discoveries. Rare species!—*Hipparion* or a living *Ichthyosaur* in Maida Vale! Rare variations!—an adult insect with abdominal legs (some of the third-class boys have found *that* already)! or a flower with compound eyes!—these will be only every-day incidents when the holidays begin. Perhaps among all our *savants* the natural history specialists and professors will get the best innings this vacation. Chemistry is the fun for the winter. It has to be done indoors, and in the cold weather. The window must be shut, and you get the full value of your chemicals in stinks—a thing you lose in summer. Natural history, on the other hand, begins on the other side of the door, and goes right away to the woods, the river, and the sea. I cannot imagine how any fellow can avoid being a naturalist in the summer holidays. The insects flutter round him and buzz into his face; the gnats even get to biting to call his attention; every wayside plant flaunts the secret of its existence, in the shape of a flower before him; the thickets are bursting with natural science, and you cannot dip your hand into a pond without catching some interesting thing; while, at the sea side, old Ocean comes every day and piles up billions of specimens for the boys of this fortunate island to pick from. It is everywhere for those that have eyes to see; and it is difficult indeed to account for the eyes that cannot. They *do* exist though. Some even are artificially blinded. N. ii., for instance, recognizes the existence of nothing in this universe but butterflies; even moths he rejects as "vermin;" and the whole science of natural history is to get rows of his one creature pinned out on cork, with its crowning triumph, the capture of a great Copper. A. iii. has a vicious inclination to long words, and feels satisfied about a thing when he has got a phrase for it. Ask him what a glow-worm is, and he tells you it is a "vermiform animated creature." Now, this sort of thing is not science. *Science is the understanding of things,* not the collecting of them merely, and certainly not the naming of them. The first thing to find out about a living thing is, *How it gets its living.* It may not have occurred to all that every creature has to work for its living somehow; but that is *the* fact of natural history, and makes almost all the peculiarities of creatures plain. *Why* has a caterpillar claws to its numerous feet? and *why* is the proboscis of a butterfly longer than that of a fly? *why* has a caterpillar legs throughout its length? The answers to these questions are in every hedgerow. The best sort of collection undoubtedly is the one that suggests and answers questions like these. Two or three cast skins; a bit of gnawed wood that you found a willow-eating caterpillar in; a gnawed leaf, and the creature that gnawed it; a flower you have watched a butterfly on, pulled to pieces to find why the butterfly was there; a toad dissected to show his supper; a ladened bumble bee;—these things are worth a whole museum-full of *imago Lepidoptera.* Moreover, they do not involve a monstrous outfit of museum-cases and killing bottles. They can be made the diversion of any walk, and need only a sharp pen-knife, a pill-box, and a magnifying glass as the utter most outfit—these, that is, with eyes and brains. It is well to bear this in mind, because often just the most observant boys are kept away from natural history by the atrocious unreasonableness of the *Young Collector* style of handbook, and by the idea that natural history is only to be "done" properly by making a collection of things and finding out those specific names which vituperative naturalists with a classical bias have affixed to them, calling a harmless sunflower, for instance, *Helianthus annus,* and fixing *Lepus cuniculus* on the inoffensive "bunny."

H. G. WELLS.

The North Sea

Henley House School Magazine, vol III, no 34, pp. 227-228, December 1889

As a teacher at Henley House School, Wells took part in the Henley House School Debating Society, and led field trips. J.V. Milne wrote in a letter of recommendation for Wells in 1891[4]:

> *"Mr. Wells did his work here in a painstakingly and thorough manner. I have particularly admired his teaching of science, where his extensive reading and his power of expression enabled him always to handle his subject in a manner at once exact and humorous . . . The proof of his success was the enthusiasm aroused in his classes which was not dependent upon mere experiment."*

J.V. Milne's son, A.A. Milne (the future author), does not seem to have performed well at the school compared to his siblings, when looking at the student standings in the Magazine. Wells did teach A.A., and one can't help wondering whether the field trips to the London Zoo might have introduced the boy to bears. Here Wells teaches about the North Sea, first by critiquing an examiner's question about islands, then expanding the story into a pupil-pleasing tale of seafaring history in the lively manner he would later exhibit in The Outline of History.

Homer nods at times, we are told, and really we believe that we have caught one of our Association examiners napping. If so, there is still hope that the proverbially difficult exploit of discovering a somnolent weazel may be brought within the record of things achieved.

The question was meant for small boys; four islands were wanted in the Mediterranean, three in the Baltic, and three in the North Sea. What are the three in the North Sea? Texel and those other little islands by it are not *in* the North Sea, they mark it off from the Zuyder Zee; Sheppy is in the Thames; Thanet has ceased to be an island: that leaves Heligoland, Nordstrand, Pelrorm, Fora, Syltoe, Fanoe, Schiermonik, Bommel, Oe, Sulen, Holy Isle, and one or two others of about equal importance, of which list we can expect the best of small boys to know only the first and last. We have a shrewd suspicion therefore that it was in the mind of our examiner that Great Britain, or Ireland, or the Orkneys and the Shetlands, and the Loffoden Isles came in the question—which they don't in spite of the fact that the sea is called North.

Why is it called the North Sea?—there is a small problem for you. And Zuyder Zee means South Sea;—that raises another. The explanation is that the sea people who named these parts lived in Friesland and along by the mouths of

---

4. From the Wells Archive, excerpted in Norman & Jeanne MacKenzie, *The Life H. G. Wells: The Time Traveller*, revised, The Hogarth Press, 1987, p 80.

the Ems and Weser, the land of our ancestors, the Saxons. When the Frieslander wanted either herrings or British plunder, he sailed northward; therefore, he called the sea he sailed through the North Sea; when he went southward after the flat fish, and so on, he called the water he navigated the South Sea, on the same principle. And we English, who are the descendants of colonists from Friesland, stick to the old name, though the North Sea is now due east of us, and we know of boundless waters south of the Zuyder Zee.

It is wonderfully shallow sea, this North Sea; you might take St. Paul's and drop it in anywhere and nearly half of it would be out of the water. Geologists tell us that, once upon a time, all this shallow sea was dry land—the Rhine must have been a huge river then!— and animals, and perhaps even men went to and fro from France and Germany. *The Thames, then, and the Poole river were tributaries of the Rhine.* The country was ever so much colder than it is now; there were huge glaciers on the Welsh and Scotch mountains; and the great elk, the mammoth, and bears wandered over the site of Henley House School and were hunted by, and probably occasionally hunted, those primitive men who used to live in caves, and fight with flint weapons.

What a lot of finds we should make if this shallow sea were to be raised above the level of the water again! If we could only just raise a little bit of it off the coast of Kent we should find enough to set us thinking for years. The wrecks we should find, the big modern ships, warships, passenger ships like sea hotels, trading ships, pleasure boats, fishing smacks, that the Godwyn Sands have swallowed up! Then when we got lower among the wrecks that have been there longer and are almost covered by sand, weed, and drift, there would be ships of the type of the "Adelaide," "Royal George," and "Victory," of the grand old times of Howe and Nelson; and now and then very likely a French privateer, sturdy wooden ships, with guns of gun-metal. Then the ships would get broader in the beam, "tubby" almost in shape, with gorgeous galleries and figure-heads, ships of the brave days when Blake and Albemarle fought the Van Tromps, and the Dutchmen almost took London. Then perhaps a lank Spanish galley or so, with its iron beak; and queer sailing-ships that rose high at stem and stern, like the "Great Harry." And then the long series of wrecks would gradually dwindle down in size. We should come at last on long "Sea Serpents," "Fire Drakes," and "Black Ravens" of the Danes, here and there among the smaller fishing boats; and then the gilded Imperial galleys in which the sailors of the Roman Count of the Saxon shire went out after the Sayons. Finally, perhaps, might be found, deep buried under the accumulations of centuries, a wickerwork tub, hide covered, in which the woad-painted savages of Celtic Britain ventured out for fish; and beneath that, no human trace, for the strata then would be of the ages before men went down to this sea in ships. Though, indeed, for all we know to the contrary, some venture-some Phoenicians from Tyre, in Syria, or Carthage, in Africa, *may* have crept along these shores in those far distant ages when the Children of Israel came pouring across the Jordan to conquer the Holy Land. For in those days Tyre and Sidon, Carthage and Marseilles, were new cities, and the Phoenicians were, in their trading, their colonizing, and their naval enterprise, the English of that old world.

College of Preceptors. Conversazione at University College, London.

The Educational Times, vol XLIII, no 346, p66, 1 February 1890

The Educational Times *was the publication of the College of Preceptors, of which Wells was a recent Licentiate. In this piece, unsigned but claimed as Wells by David C. Smith, it is evident that Wells is performing the duties of a mere reporter. Likely assigned because of his experience with science, Wells here exhibits an unusually detached style, and he seems to be padding the article, with only the phonograph technology creating much interest in a poorly attended event.*

A Conversazione of members of the College of Preceptors and their friends took place at University College, London, by the kind permission of the Council of that College, on Tuesday, the 14th of January.

This was the first time that a Conversazione had been given by the College, and care had been taken by the Committee appointed for the purpose to make the programme as varied and attractive as possible. The visitors were received by the officers of the Council at the entrance to the Flaxman Gallery, whence they distributed themselves over the extensive buildings of the College, according as their respective tastes led them to prefer science, or music, or the seeking out of friends and acquaintances, for which such a gathering affords opportunity.

The principle assembly room was the handsome and spacious General Library, which was abundantly provided for the occasion with objects of scientific interest, in the shape of microscopes, graphoscopes,[5] &c., as well as a large collection of autotypes[6] of celebrated pictures.

In a neighboring room was exhibited a collection of pictures supplied by the Art for Schools Association, a society recently founded for the purpose of awakening and cultivating the artistic faculty in the young by the selection and publication of copies of suitable pictures and engravings for the adornment of the too frequently bare walls of the schoolroom.

In the Botanical Theatre, a room possessing excellent acoustic properties, there was a concern of vocal and instrumental music, under the direction of Mr. Sidney Hann, consisting chiefly of shorter pieces selected from the works of some of the best known composers of chamber music, interspersed with songs, which were admirably rendered by Mrs. Helen Trust. The performance, both instrumental and vocal, was much appreciated and heartily applauded. The

---

5. a portable device with a magnifying glass for viewing pictures
6. copies or prints

programme was divided into two parts, with a sufficient interval between them to admit of the audience attending an entertainment of another character in the Physical Theatre, which is situated immediately over the Botanical Theatre.

In the Physical Theatre a very interesting lecture on the Moon was delivered by Dr. A. H. Fison, illustrated by very striking and beautiful selenographs,[7] and photographs of Nasmith's models of lunar mountains,[8] shown by the lime-light lantern.[9] The theatre was crowded before the time fixed for the lecture ; and many who were unable to obtain admittance, consoled themselves by listening to the phonograph, which was exhibited continuously throughout the evening in the Ladies Reading Room.

This latter part of the programme excited the most lively interest. The phonograph used was one of the most recent type, with Edison's latest improvements, and the wonderful powers of the instrument were skilfully exhibited by Mr. Steytler.[10] The "loud records" were exhibited alternately with the "low tone" records, the former comprising specimens of instrumental music, barking of dogs, spoken dialogue, and phonograms made on the spot by the operator. One of the most popular "records" was the performance of a village band in Edison's laboratory a year ago, followed by the cheers and clapping of hands of the boys of the factory, the whole being heard by every person in the room with the greatest distinctness, though it had been repeated by the same instrument several thousand times. The "low tone" records were still more extraordinary, as showing the power of the instrument to reproduce the most varied shades of inflection of the human voice.

Of more practical value, from an educational point of view, was the Engineering Laboratory of University College, which was exhibited by Professor Beare and his assistants, and attracted a good deal of attention, in face of the competition of the more popular forms of entertainment provided.

About seven hundred ladies and gentlemen were present during the evening, not a few of whom came from distant parts of the country, and had it not been for the prevailing influenza epidemic,[11] which kept many away, the

---

7. photographs of the moon's surface, usually taken through a telescope

8. Also spelled Nasmyth, James Nasmith was an engineer and inventor who built his own telescope to study the moon, then created plaster scale models and photographed them.

9. Also known as a magic lantern, this technology used bright calcium light to project images.

10. Mr C.R.C. Steytler, of the Edison United Phonograph Company, London, would have been demonstrating the new wax cylinder, an improvement in sound recording longevity over tinfoil cylinders.

11. A flu pandemic was occurring at the time this article was published. According to a letter he wrote to his father, Wells himself would come down with it in May.

attendance would have been much larger. There was a general expression of satisfaction with the arrangements made by the Committee and it was hoped that the Conversazione might become a regular institution.

Registration. To the Editor of the Educational Times.

The Educational Times, vol XLIII, no 350, p264, June 1890

In March 1890, a Bill for the Organization and Registration of Teachers was introduced in the House of Commons. This measure proposed a board to establish requirements for teachers to be on a Register, including being 21 years of age and being certified by examination or the Board as being qualified. In May, The Educational Times reported on the meeting at Cheltenham of the Third Annual Conference of the Teachers' Guild, which proposed creating a Council to register teachers, making sure to separate the performance of the individual teacher from that of the school. Wells objected to the "grandfathering" in of incompetent assistants.

Sir,—While admiring the hopefulness of the numerous registration schemes that have lately been advanced, there are two points upon which I feel tempted, in the absence of any more authoritative voice, to offer some remarks. The first of these, which was incidentally mentioned at Cheltenham, is the want of restriction on the employment of totally incompetent assistants. It was pointed out in that debate that an unqualified assistant would no longer be able to recover salary. Without wishing to question the great convenience and practical efficacy of this provision, based undoubtedly on a keen appreciation of the business relations of private schoolmasters, it may yet be asked if some further guarantee would not be required—as, for instance, making continuance on the register dependent on the maintenance of the proper staff. Otherwise, there is an apparent unfairness in inflicting a serious risk on the unqualified assistant, and none on the master who may decoy him from board, counter, or plough, by the promise of munificent pay.

The unconditional admission to the register of all unqualified persons now engaged in misleading the young of the middle classes, seems to be a condition common to all the schemes proposed. The idea is too strongly established to encourage opposition now. It is interesting, however, to point out that registration will be accepted as a satisfactory guarantee of a teacher's capacity by a very considerable section of the public. Many a dubious prospectus, at present mainly dependent for its attractiveness upon a poetically treated view of Hevingly House, Mr. John Kidd's exotic diploma,[12] and the airy indication of visiting and foreign masters and a resident cow, will be endorsed by that solid-

---

12. This may refer to the Bachelor of Medicine, required for physicians following reforms which were advocated by Kidd in the first half of the nineteenth century.

looking guarantee, "Registered Teacher." That will be the immediate and most actual fruit of the register.

To make qualification within a definite time one—and not the only—condition of permanent registration, is not only perfectly reasonable, but would probably give many masters an enviable intellectual stimulus for which they would, I am sure, be ultimately very grateful indeed.—Obediently yours,

H. G. Wells

Tutor and Scholar
(1891-1893)

Correspondence: To the Editor of the Educational Times

The Educational Times, vol XLIV, no 357, pp30-31, 1 January 1891

Reverend W. H. Quick lectured at the College of Preceptors on the topic of Herbert Spencer's recently published book Education, *a collection of Spencer's late-career articles on the topic. Quick's speech, reprinted in* The Educational Times, *appeared in November 1890. It was highly critical of Spencer as an educational expert, and objected to Spencer's replacement of classical education with the many disciplines of science. Quick disliked Spencer's characterization of science and religion as being twinned, an idea brought forward from T. H. Huxley, and his claim that science is "religious". He had accused Spencer of putting science at the forefront of all human endeavour, displacing art and beauty. Wells responded that Quick's view of science was fragmented and antiquated. Further, Wells was disturbed that reactions like Quick's might prevent the expansion of science in schools.*

CORRESPONDENCE
To the Editor of the "Educational Times."

Sir,—Every teacher who is interested in the welfare of his profession will be grateful to Mr. Quick for his polemical treatment of Herbert Spencer's *Education*. The student who may be contemplating the servile assimilation of that work must almost inevitably be set thinking, even against his will. With this in view, it may possibly be simply the expression of Mr. Quick's own intentions to protest that he is too severe upon his author, and, through him as a representative, on science.

In the first place there is an initial doubt, of which Mr. Spencer is not allowed the benefit, regarding the meaning of "education." Throughout he seems to use that word in its popular acceptance of "schooling"; and this opinion is verified by the absence of any special and technical definition. This deficiency Mr. Quick counts as a blameworthy omission, and supplies by "a judicious supervision of the development of an organism," which is certainly an excessive amplification of the meaning in the vulgar tongue. These amplified meanings are a prominent feature of recent discussions: Mr. Ruskin inverts our ideas of "riches"; Mr. Buchanan explains that most people called Christians are not, and most who are not are; while "we are all socialists now-a-days" is almost proverbial. In this case education is stretched to cover the purchase of feeding bottles, and patent egg incubators are brought within the purview of pedagogics.

When we recognise the different standpoints taken by author and critic in this matter, and remember that *Education* was written less for schoolmasters than for a public which identifies the word with "book-learning," the objection to the order of Mr. Spencer's topics loses much of its force.

Mr. Quick, with perfect justice, objects himself to an unjustifiable amplification of the terms religion and science, whereby matter of fact is made to invade and blot out matters of faith. But, while it is not desired to defend the passage criticised in detail, it may be pointed out that its tenor is not so much the immediate confusion of the two as the assertion that, granted science and religion are true, science followed faithfully will lead through wider and wider causes to that incomprehensible Cause of which we are assured by faith. The only alternative is an unthinkable dualism. That wide realm, which science can never enter, of "wild realities" *outside phenomena*, cannot possibly be defined from the realm of hallucination, so far as I can see; and Mr. Spencer's statement that art and religion are amenable to scientific analysis no more destroys their distinctness and value than does the discovery of hydrogen and oxygen the integrity and necessity of the ocean.

It is, however, certain that science can be made extremely interesting and comprehensible to the young, while the results of direct school teaching in religion and art are, at least, extremely dubious. This latter does very probably involve a loss of spontaneity, a precocious piety, sentiment, or amativeness, learnt by heart. It is this kind of instruction above all against which Mr. Quick's charge of giving the child what is good for the man should be directed. The gist of Mr. Quick's argument in this matter is, however, to make the existence of the essentially adult religious and æsthetic interests a reason for grudging science a predominant share of the child's school course.

Throughout, the tone of Mr. Quick towards science is one which the meanest pretender to purely scientific teaching may very justly resent. He speaks of "all the sciences" as one might speak of such incoherent and heterogeneous things as the Latin classics, and complaining that Mr. Spencer wants them *all* taught, proceeds to speak of specialization and of the varying states of life to which men are called. Here, again, while Mr. Spencer speaks of the educational groundwork of sound judgment and universally necessary knowledge, Mr. Quick points to adult needs, and he entirely ignores the intrinsic unity of science. The great doctrine of energy binds together the phenomena of physics, chemistry, and biology into an inseparable whole. The teaching of physics, for instance, without mixed mathematics and chemistry, can only by a corruption of courtesy be styled science teaching; but Mr. Quick appears to be under the impression that one may take a science and teach it exactly as three or four discontinuous literary fragments are sometimes taught to a boy as literature.

Finally, objection may be taken to Mr. Quick's opposition of "theoretical knowledge," in the sense of scientific knowledge, to "practical skill." Scientific knowledge, as the term is used in *Education*, is a more intimate knowledge of things and deeper appreciation of their inter-relationships. Whenever possible, as at the Universities, the method of instruction is by dealing with the things themselves—the knowledge is the knowledge of eye, and ear, and finger-tip. At the South Kensington Royal College of Science the students spend four hours or more experimenting, surveying, dissecting, assaying, or analysing, to every one spent in the lecture theatre. Even the widest laws of science are not theories, but continually verified facts. The student of science is, above all, the systematic student of tangible things—the eminently practical person. The distinction between theory and practice is notoriously a provisional one in favour of those unfortunates who are obliged to extract their knowledge laboriously from woodcuts and letter-press—fact at second-hand. Yet Mr. Quick, in the face of modern science teaching, misinterprets all that Mr. Spencer says of science in relation to men's callings, and charges him with "attributing success to a knowledge of theory in cases where it depends far more on practical skill." The science Mr. Quick contemplates evidently smells strongly of the midnight oil, while Herbert Spencer's is the science of spectroscope and scalpel, balance and slide-rule, the museum, the workshop, and the open air. Few, I think, will disagree with Mr. Quick's unmistakable aversion to the speculative, hearsay science he has in view, but there are many who will fail to find in his remarks the quietus to the claim made by the science teacher for a generous increase of his share of the school time.—I remain, Sir, obediently yours,

H. G. Wells.

The Value of Science

The Educational Times, v XLIV, no359, pp154-155, March 1891

In a continuation of the discussion in The Educational Times, *Reverend Quick responded to Wells's letter. Among other arguments, Quick defended his remarks about "theory", and reiterated the idea that general knowledge does not make one equipped to handle specifics. Wells replied with another letter to the editor, noting that "generalizations of physical science are exact and immediately applicable", and affirming the laws of science.*

To the Editor of the Educational Times.

Sir,—Mr. Quick's reply to the somewhat disconnected remarks I made upon his paper, narrows our differences down to three matters, and contains a very definite statement of his position regarding them. As they are things of fairly wide interest, I will venture, with your permission, to continue this discussion, the more readily since I have found more to dissent from in Mr. Quick's reply than in his previously expressed opinion.

The first and least of the differences raised was the question of a definition. I do not think I have any ground for the charge of suggesting that Mr. Spencer would have us read "book learning" for "education" ; I said "schooling," which is a very much wider thing. Still, if Mr. Quick prefers his own rendering, and makes a point of adhering to it rigidly, there need be no objection if he will only tolerate a narrower use on the part of other people. But he read *Education* in the light of his own definition, and that is not following the indisputable maxim that "people who want to get at the truth cannot be too careful to understand one another." Under the circumstances, it is simply my duty to press him gently, but firmly, to take that egg incubator, in addition to the feeding-bottle and the perambulator he has accepted, as a pedagogic property.

The next point at issue is of much greater importance. I am glad to hear that Mr. Quick does not consider the difference of theory and practice the difference of fact at second-hand and fact at first-hand, and that he intends by "the study of theory" (and, I presume, "science") the "study of generalizations," because it brings us into agreement at the starting-point, at any rate. But the word "generalization," like most other of those treacherous tools we have to use to get at one another's thought, may convey several meanings. I can best illustrate my idea by an instance. One may see in Mr. Galton's Anthropometric Laboratory certain multiple photographs of students and others, obtained by superimposing individual portraits in such a way that a vague, foggy, collective face resulted ;

such a face would be an instance of a *blurred* generalization. In the same laboratory, upon the same persons, certain definite facts of proportion and average, of immediate value to the railway director, detective, doctor, artist, hatter, and ready-made tailor, had been ascertained, and were of the nature of *exact* generalization—they fitted all the cases. Now, if physical science, like the science of education, is yet in a stage of blurred generalization, I will admit all that Mr. Quick said against theory or science in relation to practice, but I hold that the generalizations of physical science are exact and immediately applicable. An enormous mass of human duties and actions are application of scientific generalizations, as Mr. Quick points out, and to me it is certainly not so obvious as it is to Mr. Quick that the more a man knows about these the less skillfully can he employ them.

Of course, if Mr. Quick chose to assert that the laws of physical science *are* blurred generalizations, his position so far would be good as mine, if it were not that he has already written, "we cannot value too highly the laws of science," and so, I take it, subscribed to their truthfulness. Either a scientific law is to be compared to a picture or photograph—a something *like* the phenomena represented, but getting away from them—it is like the mirror of or laryngoscope that brings us nearer to the source of outer symptoms. The alternative is not to be decided in half-an-hour's thinking or by discussion ; the answer must arise from habits of though—from the educational influences of a lifetime. There are authorities who find the maximum of truth, beauty, and mental value in the Greek classics, and who regard science as the fermenting soil from which spring such matter as Eiffel towers, aerial advertisements, and heterodoxy. To such minds the suggestion that art and literature are things of the market-place, and that science is the veil of the temple, appears absurd. Curiously enough we owe it to Mr. Quick that the attention given to Froebel by educationalists has been largely increased, and Froebel before all things was the prophet of teaching, through perceptions of phenomena, and by implication and in fact, by direct, statements, of the religiousness of science.

H. G. Wells.

The Subtle Examinee

The University Correspondent, vol I, no 8, pp9-10, 15 April 1891

One of the few stories contained in this volume, "The Subtle Examinee" explores with humor the student who has trouble continuing his studies beyond his Matriculation. His paralysis, caused by reading a magazine article of the hard life of an examiner, seems to be a result of overthinking the role of the scholar in the system. The student ends up avoiding answering examination questions properly in an effort to entertain the examiner. By this point Wells was a correspondence tutor and biology laboratory instructor for the University Correspondence College, and was writing for their journal. He had completed his own examinations for the Bachelor of Science the previous October.

Many of us have wondered why Q. "stuck" after his Matriculation. He is by no means thick, his talk is endurable, he has read a good deal; he has, it is true, a little, a very little touch of one of those elusive brain disorders that make a man say "black" when his whole mind is full of the idea "white," but that could not happen times enough in an examination to fail him. We wondered vainly, until Q. one night, in a mood of subtle disquisition, volunteered an explanation.

"Before knowledge comes the beautiful flower of innocence, which dies under facts, like the daisies in an eligible building plot under the contractor's bricks. That is why I keep on failing at the Inter., you know." We saw no earthly connection ourselves, so we smoked on silently and waited for Q. to explain. "When I passed Matric. I was as innocent, as perfectly simple, as Adam before the Fall. I smile now, with a pensive melancholy, to think of it; how I trotted out my little bits of facts in answer to the questions—*à la* Master Harry Sandford, really feeling that I was giving useful information needed and asked for—never dreaming of the caustic learned one behind the veil of paper. How shameless I was, and yet how happy, before the fall came! Ah, Paradise!— Eva was laughing, I read the magazine over her shoulder: we ate, one may say, of the tree of knowledge together. The article was by a professor, jeering, scoffing horribly at the answers of examinees! I was suffused by a lively shame. Had I really strutted through an examination, exhibiting all my self-complacent ignorance before a man of this calibre? It was a horrible revelation. I entered for my Inter. in a curiously mixed frame of mind. I was keenly ashamed of myself, profoundly awe-stricken at the thought of *him* behind the veil. I read over my first answer; it seemed indecent, insulting to tell such things to *him*, things he knew before I was born. In a spirit of grim, self-deprecatory humour I added to my impertinent little statement of familiar, hackneyed facts, as they must have seemed to an expert,

'Queen Anne is dead.' I meant no reflection on the examination—none whatever—though my coach seemed to fancy it may have been construed in that sense; it simply expressed my feeling of the mutual relationship of examiner and examinee. I longed to tell him something new; I carefully eluded the gist of his subsequent questions, and racked my brain for novelties; once even I deliberately lied. For that, possibly, he failed me.... Yes, perhaps I am *too* subtle.—I was made so. Ever since that magazine article I have been incapacitated by self-consciousness from doing justice, as you would say, to my work. Other men saw a paper to answer, sheets of paper to fill, and they carried in a puerile stock of facts and fooled away happily. *I* saw through these flimsy devices. The mighty soul of the examiner bowed over me. I crouched, awe-stricken and paralysed, at his feet. While other men repeated Mnemonics, and scrawled and passed, I failed—to my honour. For two years I failed through shame; last year it was through pity. Some remark suggested a vision to me of the reality of an examiner's work—its treadmill repetitions, countless piles of papers, the same old fact, the same old error, that ever-recurring diagram. He shall not suffer so from me, I thought. I risked my pass last year out of charity. I tried to enliven his dulness, joked to him, drew caricatures of the things he asked about. 'Come,' I said in effect, 'sorrowful Titan examiner, here is an interlude; come, gambol and smile.' I meant my paper to be a ray of light in a sunless cavern of monotony. It may have been, I still hope it may have been, though he failed me. This year I shall face him in the mood of one bitten by ingratitude; satire, irony, will sting him——"

"But, Q., is not your real object to pass the examination?"

And Q. answered with his most crushing saying: "You are elementary."

H. G. Wells

That Problem!

Henley House School Magazine, vol III, no38, pp259-260, August 1891

Although Wells had left Henley House School in June 1890, J.V. Milne continued to follow his career, and Wells maintained an interest in the school. He responded to a mathematical question in the school magazine, thus continuing to educate the boys.

[I gave a problem in the last number (Examiners are not obliged to answer their own questions. This law is made for the preservation of the species). For the sake of those who have not a copy, I repeat it. "There are two animals exactly alike, except in size; one is simply a large edition, and the other a small. Call the big one A, and the little one B. B (i.) can jump 5 feet; (ii.) has 20 square feet of skin; (iii.) requires 1 lb. of meat a day; (iv.) and takes half an hour to masticate it; (v.) can run a mile for five minutes; (vi.) can lift 200 lbs.; (vii.) takes 10 minutes to rub himself down; (viii.) requires 8 hours sleep; (ix.) weighs 300 lbs; and (x.) can hear a watch tick at ten yards distance. What are the corresponding figures in the case of A?" Our late science master, who always takes a lively interest in the school, has been kind enough to answer it. When it is remembered that Mr. Wells took his B.Sc. degree last year in First Class honours, his contribution will be read with interest." —J. V. M.]

1. B can jump 5 feet. A's mass is 27 B's, and his muscular force –if the force of a muscle *is* as its sectional area—9 B's. Hence the acceleration A can give his carcass is ⅓ B's and the distance therefore about 5/3 ft.* {F=ma.}

2. B had 20 square ft. of skin. A has 20 x 9 = 180 square feet.

3. B required 1 lb. of meat. A, 27 lbs.

4. B requires 30 minutes for mastication. A would required 3 times this.

5. B can run a mile in 5 minutes. A takes a *stride* 3 times as long, and with a ⅓ acceleration. Hence he also takes a mile in 5 minutes. (?)

6. B lifts 200 lbs. A, 200 X 9 = 1,800 lbs.

7. B takes 10 minutes to rub himself down. A can (from 5) make his hand travel at the same rate as B, and has 9 times more surface. ? 90 minutes.

8. The length of time required for sleep is the same for both. Sleep seems to be a repair process adapted to the recurrence of night and day. The ratio of repair time to active time would be about the same, subject to the remarks at end.

9. B weights 300 lbs. A, 8,100 lbs.

10. B hears a watch tick at 10 yards. A, with ear tympanum, &c., 27 times more massive, would only have these parts stirred at 1/27 the distance.

I have done my best with the problem, which is certainly an atrocious one. The funniest things are 5 and 8. By 5, an animal microscopically small may race an animal infinitely great. By 8, an animal must sleep always to repair the waste when it is not sleeping. As a generalization on the problems, they are impossible. There are size limits for blood corpuscles, blood capillaries, and so on. An animal 27 times the mass of another would probably have 27 times the blood-vessel surface. If not, such a matter as § 8 becomes the *reductio ad absurdum* of the proposition, because given 27 times the mass and 9 times the repair surface, the animal must needs rest 24 hours per day, to repair a proportionate loss that occurs (?) when!

The problem establishes no comparison between large men and small, because large men would have a more intricate blood-vessel network, and their histological elements would not be proportionately larger.

H. G. Wells.

School Zoology

The Educational Times, v XLIV, no 365, pp400-402, 1 September 1891

In this letter, Wells characterizes the College of Preceptors' examinations in science as merely an examination of facts, using specific exam questions to prove his point. Students who cram will do well, while those who understand "the interdependence of structure and mode of life, and the bearing of systemic position and habit upon structure" will do poorly. The "type" classification system promoted here was that popularized by T.H. Huxley, whose methods guided Wells throughout his career. He closes by claiming to be only an "irritant", that others should create a teaching syllabus, but then follows with his own suggestion for examination papers.

To the Editor of the Educational Times

SIR,—May I call your attention, and that of your readers, to a matter a little off the main line of school work—to the troubles of some of the science masters who prepare pupils for the College of Preceptors examinations? It has been repeated so often, that any one repeating it again must need apologise in doing so, that examinations, for good or evil, are the preponderating influence in the determination of what shall and what shall not be actually taught in schools. Doubtless the fancies and prejudices of parents have their effect upon the prospectus and time-table; but the working schoolmaster knows full well that the verdict of the examiners is universally considered as the final verdict upon his work, and, far more than anything, is the maker or destroyer of his prosperity. In thousands of schools, therefore, examinations guide the teaching, and the responsibility for the character of that teaching devolves upon examiners, who indirectly direct it. Undoubtedly, for instance, the want of insistence upon oral tests and retranslation into English, in the language teaching of the immediate past, has done much to confine such work to the easier exercise of simple translation, with a cram, when the examination approaches, of the accidence; and there are thousands, as a consequence, in the position of the writer, who can read French easily without being able to speak or understand a spoken word of it. In this matter the College has recently set an example in the foundation of an, at present, optional test of conversational ability. The College has also recently lightened the yoke of obligatory subjects, and these indications of a liberal spirit are an encouragement to those who imagine that room for improvement exists in other directions, and notably in the department of science.

The great objection made by many adverse critics of the claims of the science teacher is that much of what goes under the name of science is merely "information," and that of what Mr. Herbert Spencer himself would call the "unorganizable" kind. Now, an unfortunate difference of opinion exists as to how far scientific facts are organizable, how far they can be built together into one coherent and independent structure. Those who have specialized along the scientific line assert a wonderful unity in diversity exists in their field, and belittle the harmonies and allusions of literary study; and it certainly appears to the writer that the opinion of scientists in this question is of slightly greater value than that of literary men, for there are few scientific men so illiterate as not to be familiar with the beauties of some literary masterpieces, while there are many men on the classical side who know little or nothing of science. But leaving this wider question, I think that all teachers will be agreed that a subject that is so taught as to be merely an information accumulation, without any mental exercise except that of the memory, is of very little value, and should either be mended or ended as part of the school curriculum.

Now, if we ask whether Natural History, and especially the branches of Zoology, Botany, and Geology, as the examination papers of the College of Preceptors determine and exhibit it taught, is anything more than an accumulation of information, I am afraid that our answer must be, No. And, in order to justify this statement, an examination paper in Zoology, set this last midsummer, may be called as a witness, and itself examined. The first Zoology paper has been selected, but the others have much the same character, and, as the writer considers, faults.

VERTEBRATA.

ELEMENTARY SECTION.

1.   Give a classification of the *Mammalia*, and indicate the differences of structure whereby the Divisions you enumerate are distinguished.

2.   Describe, and show by diagram, the circulation of blood in a Mammal and in a Fish, respectively.

3.   What are the *Rodentia?* Why are they so called? Mention some that live in Britain.

4.   Make a list of the chief kinds of Lizards (*Lacertilia*), and state where they are to be found in a state of nature, and anything particular that you know about them.

5.   Give the proper names to the difference kinds of Fish that are brought to market, and state whereabouts in the British seas and rivers they are severally caught.

ADVANCED SECTION.

1.   Classify the *Monkeys*, and point out in what respects the *Chimpanzee*, *Ourang*, and *Gorilla* respectively present the nearest approach to human structure.

2.   Enumerate *either* (i.) the freshwater Crustacea of the British Isles; *or* (ii.) the Birds frequenting the rivers, marshes, and coast of these Islands; and point out in either case the localities most abounding with the species or kinds that you mention.

3.   In what respects do Birds differ in their organization from Mammals? What are the chief Orders and Families of Birds?

4.   Give an account of the *Ophidia*. *What are they?* What are their structural characteristics? What are the habits of different kinds, and where are they met with?

5.   On the Outline Map of the World mark the areas where different kinds of Crocodiles, or Bears, and of Sirenia and Cetacea are respectively known to exist.

Where praise is due it should be given, and the second question in the Elementary Section is certainly a good one: it demands a knowledge, and something more than a verbal knowledge, of wide and important facts; but here our praise must end. There are two fundamental objections to this paper: in the first place, over an immensely wide subject, containing endless departments complete in themselves and capable of independent study, there is apparently no choice of questions; and in the next place, it is a paper that directly encourages "cramming." If any one had tabulated the classes, orders, families, and genera of vertebrata, and given that and some thirty or forty definitions to a class of boys to learn by heart, and had drilled them a little with an atlas of blank maps, questions 1 and 2 (imperfectly), 3, 4, in the Elementary, and 1 (in part), 2 (?), 3, 4, and 5 of the Advanced would have been done, and they might even have got a "special" or so; while the success of pupils familiar with the museum and zoological garden, and to whom the interdependence of structure and mode of life, and the bearing of systemic position and habit upon structure had really been rendered clear, would have been, to say the least, doubtful. It is difficult to imagine any explanation of the inclusion of "freshwater crustacea," in the vertebrate paper, that is not a little uncomplimentary to the examiner. Finally, attention may be called to the vagueness of Question 4 in the Elementary— "*anything*...you know!" and do the disproportionate difficulty of 5 in that section and 1 in the next. It seems to me that for a teacher to be very successful upon papers such as this, a gallop through a zoological miscellany, coupled with a cram such as I have suggested above, would be the only possible course. Now this is the character of the College of Preceptors' Natural History at present. Need it remain so?

There is one thing that can easily be done, and that is to give a wide choice of questions; at present, the country schoolmaster who has tried to show an animating and unifying soul in hedge-row, river bank, and moor, and the London teacher who has availed himself of his vast resources in museum and zoological collection, are equally "out of it." The suppression of "classify," "enumerate," and "refer to their orders" from the papers will alone suppress the process of unintelligent list-cramming. But there are wider possibilities in Zoology yet, and more sweeping changes to be suggested.

Almost alone among examining bodies the College of Preceptors ignores the "type" system of teaching biological science. The first great exponent of this method was Professor Huxley, and it is now the one recognised by the Cambridge and London Universities and at the Royal Colleges of Science. Instead of a scramble over endless unmeaning names, ending in a vague, inaccurate, and often misleading knowledge, a few types are dissected, the dissections drawn, and comparisons instituted and homologies traced between them. This is really an intellectual and manual training combined; it interests almost all boys and fascinates some, and it leaves a permanent effect in after life. The dissecting instruments need not cost 5s. per head, and among the most instructive types are the rat, the sparrow, the frog, any fish, the cockroach, crayfish, worm, and amœba. But the College of Preceptors, instead of promoting this kind of work, raises an obstacle in its examination papers. I do not by any means wish to suggest that the "type" system is the only one, but simply to point out that at present an indubitably excellent way of going to work is entirely disregarded, and thereby discouraged.

In view of all these things, it seems not unreasonable to ask that the College should reclassify its Natural History subjects, and offer some kind of syllabus for the guidance of teachers. No one could be more willing to confess incapacity than the writer, but with a view to provoking those who are abler to action, he ventures to suggest his own ideas—not, be it understood, as a standard, but as an irritant. Five papers are suggested, each carrying one hundred marks, and of which—to prevent schoolmasters giving a disproportionate time to Natural History—no candidate should take more than two. They are :—

(1) Vegetable physiology, as illustrated by such a type as the bean plant, and the compared structure of such typed as the pine, the fern, the moss, and any common fungus and alga. (A science properly speaking.)

(2) General morphology of the flowering plant, and the study of the common British natural orders. (A training in observation and drawing for rather younger boys.)

(3) Comparative Anatomy of the animal types mentioned above.

(4) Descriptive Zoology, with especial reference to the relations of form and

habit; classification and distribution. (For younger pupils.)

(5) Physical Geography and Geology, with a number of questions (of which one only must be done) with the stratigraphy of different selected districts defined by a syllabus. Questions on the names and horizons of fossils should not occur. Palæontology, requiring, as it does, for its proper comprehension, a sound and advanced knowledge of Zoology, and being largely a memory subject, can hardly come into the scheme of a well-planned school, where the mind is developed and the memory dulled with better things.

Trusting sincerely that my remarks may lead to some discussion, and eventually be of benefit, I remain, Sir, very obediently yours,

H. G. Wells.

The Too-Ambitious Text-book.

The Journal of Education, vol XIII, no266, pp468-469, 1 September 1891

Wells's first piece in The Journal of Education *was a clever, but pointed, tale of the ambitions of the printed text-book, which was taking over the teaching. In particular, he blames the lack of proper science teaching for this problem, because the book is used as a substitute when there is no science teacher. This article was discovered by the editor, and has never been reprinted or indexed in any of the common bibliographies.*

It may seem impertinence or boredom—one is always open to criticism—or an insistence upon "shop" in the weeks of relaxation, but to the writer it seems anything but needless or wanton to take the earnest schoolmaster aside to buttonhole him gently, and to whisper in his ear: "Come, we have talked of registration, we have conferred and contemplated our high moral mission, we have discussed pension schemes, and debated a teaching degree, and now it is holiday time. We cannot always live in altitudes. Let us talk about the little text-books we deal with every day."

We would begin with him sunnily, let him meander among his eyot likes and dislikes, speak at first of varied type and other vast improvements, convenient bindings, lithographed diagrams, and cheap maps. We would try and get at it gradually, very gently and slowly, at that sinister suspicion we have engendered, and which we contemplate dropping in his ear as he lies like Gonzago in the sunlight.

At last out it would come, the fearful truth! The little text-book, the close companion of every day, is showing vices—ambition, a divided aim, treachery. Its accusation unrolls—the little text-book is an insidious rival and a foe. It would disturb him, no doubt, but the thing must sooner or later be done; and we should, of course, have to prove our case.

And once, alas! the school-book was as faithful a companion as a shepherd's dog. The teacher taught; the school-book was an unpretending and useful collection of declensions, principal parts, and exercises "subject to approval." It was, as it were, an armour-bearer to the warrior who eloquently fought against ignorance, and "let daylight through" a class. Or, again, it was as pages, bearing the train of a peer—helpful in triumph, necessary, but without honor. A certain mutual trustfulness, and affection grew, and sometimes grew to romantic proportions, between the teacher and his handbook ; but alas! these pleasant idylls are becoming rarer: the text-book, once so faithful, we assert, rises against its master. It is an age of selfish insubordination, and the very inanimate paper intrigues, usurps, and betrays.

It began in the "outcast" sections of our schools, among the science and modern language books. The fact is, that when all that talk about teaching science began, plenty of headmasters found themselves disinclined to add a competent science master to their schools—they were rarer then—and so, little recking of its effect upon the thing's vanity, these heedless heads asked the text-book to take the classes. That is really what it amounted to. They got a master, of course, to sit in the room while the thing was teaching; but he simply said, "Page 45 to page 60 to-day, boys," and saw that they attended.

Now the text-book, abruptly, and, we must confess, recklessly, enfranchised, did its work neither well nor loyally ; it neglected a lot of the boys—we may put it that way, for action and reaction are always equivalent—and intrigued with the rare few who had a taste for science. It told them things the master did not know, prompted them to ask impossible questions, and behave like the proverbial beggar on horseback. This was the beginning of the demoralization.

The text-book, despite its actual want of success, like many commonplace, well-meaning persons one might think of, was bitten with the idea that it was born to be a teacher. It displayed initiative, and, taking advantage if the linguistic deficiencies of many of the smaller schools, boldly made the modern languages teaching his own. Other teaching, the oral teaching that can alone avail in this department, vanished. The text-book arranged the work, set the exercises, and had them corrected through the medium of a Key, while a pitiful usher undertook the drudgeries of discipline.

Ah, schoolmaster! the vacation sunlight is browning your face to the hues of health, but can you hear this little suggestion and keep your vacation-peace? The text-book, for instance, is steadily invading literature. You ought to read the classic "set" for Christmas Examinations with your pupils. It is for you to give it life, and help out their limited experience, but the text-book intervenes. Geography, again, has been snatched from you, and made so luminous, so attractive, so readable, that you are out of it—you know you never teach geography now. Need one expiate? Does no inkling of the future turn your strawberries and cream to gall and wormwood, your boyless tranquility to a convict expectation?

For, unless you gallantly face this ominous revolt, I am convinced that the fate of the schoolmaster is merely a question of time. The prospectus of the future will run, perhaps, as follows: "The school is managed in strict accordance with the directions in Professor Jimjams's scheme of study, and his celebrated text-books are alone used in the establishment. All the masters are members of the corps of Commissionaires, and no effort is spared to ensure the punctual delivery and exchange of text-books and keys to the pupils. The diet is impeccable, and the site of the school one of the healthiest in England."

The traitor text-book—the insidious foe he cherished in the soft folds of his academic gown, will squat, guiltily triumphant, in the seat of the headmaster. And as for the schoolmaster—all schoolmasters—the place that knew the schoolmaster will know him no more. He will have gone after the postboy, the crossbowman, and the dodo, into the mysterious shadows that surround existence, not perhaps improved upon but inexorably superseded.

I am no baseless alarmist: I say there is a certain measure of hope, but I earnestly warn the schoolmaster to keep his eye on the ambitious, wordy, and explicit text-book. It attacks through indolence and incapacity, it renders possible the economy of the pitiful usher at nothing a year; but it does away with all the excellencies of teaching. At the best it is lifeless, rigid and unsympathetic; and that readily adaptation of statement to mind which is the duty and virtue of the teacher, is impossible. Let the teacher teach, and let the text-book be a compilation of maps, lists, vocabularies, diagrams, propositions, and maxims, or the author studied, as the subject requires. With the text-book presented and explained a subject one way, and the teacher with his almost certainly different presentation of the case, there can be nothing but confusion; and the text-book triumphant is even worse than confusion. For where is the teacher then?

H.G. Wells.

The Problem of Sympathy in Teaching

Education, v 2, no 10, p307, October 1891

This humorous piece arose out of Wells's experience teaching boys of several ages when he was quite young himself. Here he claims that although everyone says teachers should have sympathy, in truth some pretend and some try vainly to cultivate it. Young men are too involved constructing their own knowledge to be patient and sympathetic, and most education of children should be turned over to women, who have natural sympathy and are the original teachers. Only once a young man can provide military or scholastic inspiration to children should he be teaching; in the meantime junior schoolmasters should be replaced with mothers and female teachers. The journal Education *was short-lived, in press for only a year before becoming the* Educational Review *for a decade.*

By H.G. Wells, B.Sc.

"Sympathy is essential." That is an assertion to which no one dealing in matters educational ever fails to subscribe; and yet one may believe that in practice the essential is still dispensed with. Sympathy is a flexible word, like charity, and may cover a multitude of things—Lady Bountiful's motives; the sympathy of the sound analyser; the sympathy of DuMaurier's imported violinist, who was "zo zorry" for the deaf old gentleman; and the sympathy of that decorated address to the widow of the man you neither knew nor cared for, and which you signed under the impression that it referred to the Jews in Russia. Very many things, over and above these, are sympathy, just as very many things are happiness, but some would be undesirable, and even inconvenient, in a schoolroom. The sympathy one needs there is a kind of thought-reading, or, rather, *sensation*-reading—a telepathic knowledge of what is going on in certain unattainable cubic inches of immortality below a curly pate; and it is a thing no more to be acquired by human endeavour than that hypnotic power the curious antiquarian student reads about in the superannuated fiction of last year. This last is a sad consideration for some of us. Some schoolmasters live in the belief and hope that sympathy may be cultivated like a beard, or learnt like the game of draughts; some think it may be taken like the measles, and, getting some book infected with it—Dickens is infected with sympathy—sit down solemnly to *catch* it; and some, knowing better, abandon the impossible, but nevertheless keep the school open. Others, vainly striving, like blinded souls, to see, conceive a counterfeit sympathy, and so, out of their very desire for what is right, begin with self-deception on the broad way of humbug—the broad way of humbug that yawns wider and more fatally for schoolmasters than for any other kind of sinful men. *Miserere!* Others—happy ones!—*really feel* the working of the little brain that is so near and yet so far away.

Yet the severe psychologists who refuses all possibilities of artificially and conscientiously becoming as little children again, though with resolute straining and panting, and who grimly define such interference with our own emotions as sha——, as disingenuousness (bless their sweet impudence!), still give us a grain of hope. They base it on strictly scientific grounds, which wakens a faint distrust immediately choked by that grain of hope. The schoolmasters who, in fits of frankness, confess how profound the mystery of the curly pate is, are mostly young men. Have the older teachers become more sympathetic, or only more discreet? Positively they answer, "More sympathetic."

In boys—I speak from my own experience and for my circle of confidential friends—there is a lively hate of babies and a dislike for children, while in the young man there is at least a sharp impatience. Between twenty and thirty-five is the militant time; home is left behind and the young man faces the universe. He first powders his carefully learnt opinions to chaos and builds them up afresh, labels himself, like the celebrated individualist, "agin the Government anyhow," and then, seeking opposition in act as well as thought, beholds presently, with joyous emotion, wigs upon the green. Scientific persons tell us that an individual life repeats the development of the species, and that the young man at this stage is going over the lessons of the predatory epoch. It is perhaps best to keep him clear of children under twelve, of any immature and delicate mental plants, till this Viking reminiscence has faded away. It will. Sooner or later silken cords will bind him, he will be led back to gentleness of life, and the aureole of paterfamilias will be his; the more mature man returns in harmony with natural law unto that harmony with children from which he had first to separate. One of the pleasantest figures in the history of teaching is that of Froebel, grey-haired, in a long greatcoat, leading a double file of little children singing up a winding hillside way; but before that there come stories of less successful starts, of pupils who disagreed. It is impossible to stuff zeal and patience into one soul, and as in the meantime the children may not spoil, we must look to the women. Countless centuries of natural force have been training them as teachers of children—a training to which science subject, "hygiene," and Kindergarten are small, though perhaps quite necessary, additions; but the great thing, the sympathy, was drummed in by schoolmistress Dame Nature ages ago. Older men cannot be spared to teach children; counsel and government are the uses for their experience and patience. Besides, even against wise men women have the prior claim to do the teaching; they were thinkers—of a kind—while men were still savage brutes; and it was the necessities of the family, the feminine realm, that turned, in the course of ages, hunter and warrior into law-abiding citizen. The selfishness, passionate violence, and feeble self-control of the child remind us, in individual development, of the old savage phase of human history—they are spiritual antiquities. The archæological interest of the militant young man is, however, sometimes too feeble to keep him from the raving pitch. The sooner, then, that we hand over our preparatory schools and lower forms to the ladies, who, as the miserable little clerk says, "oust us everywhere," the better for us all.

When the boys begin to think those "long, long thoughts" of the poet; when they frequently and earnestly seek to drink the delights of battle; and when hero-worship arises in their souls to grapple with the love of sugar-plums, then the young man may be utilised, bringing his own fresh manliness to make men of them, or of his scholarship, scholars, turning then towards duty, right, and interminable series or Greek particles, as his special training may decide. Before that, in spite of a successful junior master here or there, it is respectfully, but firmly insisted—mother, if possible, and otherwise *school marm.*"

Drawing and Art.

Science and Art, v V, no 56, pp182-183, November 1891

The beginning of this article seems to describe Wells's own experience as a pupil at Midhurst Grammar School, teaching himself through textbooks in order to pass examinations to earn grants for the school, a "grant-earning automaton". The policy known as "payment by results" had been adopted in 1862, increased with the Education Act of 1870 which provided for elementary schools, and expanded with compulsory elementary education in the year this article was published. It would be abolished in 1902. Wells claims to criticise the system rather than the teachers, through a questioning of the ends and means of teaching drawing as part of the curriculum. As always, Wells's primary interest is in science, with drawing both the result of close observation and a means of expression for the non-artist. He argues that the Science and Art Department is "too thorough and finished in its methods, and too narrow in its selection of things to draw, for the needs of a common education", and should encourage variety rather than precision.

By H. G. Wells, B.Sc., L.C.P., F.Z.S.

One of the greatest dangers in the way of the acting teacher is to become too "practical," using the word in its most offensive sense, and to teach for the sake of teaching, with no end in view, all aspirations forgotten, and by dint of inertia, with an all-pervading scent of dinner as the only stimulus to keep him going. It is a danger, subtle as it is imminent, and it finds its most acceptable lair and ambush on the narrow paths of code and syllabus, where indeed one may at last become altogether a grant-earning automaton, with the persuasion of being a successful teacher big in one's mind. The syllabus interpreted by examination is the law and automatic will that replaces the living initiative of the teacher, sometimes indeed crushing an "educational reformer," but on the whole securing a higher standard than would be possible from the indolent and sinful creature, the average man, if left to himself. We say this that, though we may criticize teaching methods, we would have it understood that our criticisms are not aimed so much at the teacher who pursues them—though we court his opinions—as behind him at the regulating influences that make such methods successful—as measured by the "results" standard—and therewith practically necessary.

We propose in this paper to discuss the ends to which the teaching of drawing in schools, not primarily schools for the production of artists, should tend, and then to point out how far the first and second grade drawing of the Science and Art Department appears directed to these ends. This paper, be it noted, is written not in the spirit of one having authority, but as the scribes; and we present our conclusions for critical consideration and mental germination, rather than entire acceptance. For an uninspired mortal to do otherwise savours of the wisdom of the agricultural amateur who wanted "young potato plants" for his garden.

What is

THE END IN VIEW

when a child or embryo science student is taught to draw? If we listen to educational authorities, our answer must be that the end is too complex for expression in one brief answering phrase. Most people will be ready enough to say, "In order that he may be able to draw in the future"; but, in the first place, this saying requires very considerable modifications of how? and what? before it means anything; and secondly, there are subsidiary ends as well. Among the chief of these subsidiary ends, there is a general agreement that a training in observation is desirable, and a quasi-moral influence toward neatness and patience.

There is a class of schoolmaster, middle-class schoolmasters chiefly, who—being persons of such sorely neglected education that they are unable to draw—assert of drawing, as Dogberry did of writing and reading, that it "comes by nature," and wait therefore for its advent, reverentially, but in most cases unavailingly. Few of our readers, however, will share this opinion; no drawing teacher will subscribe to it; and the writer's own experience in encouraging students of zoology to draw their dissections witnesses that "Perfectly hopeless, you know," who "hasn't the ghost of an idea how to do it," will make passable enough sketches with a little showing and practice. Hence we put this initial objection, that drawing is a subject for the few, on one side, with some confidence, and proceed to the question of what and how a human being who is not to be any kind of pictorial artist should be able to draw.

Will it be that we shall soar at once into the region of raised, expostulating eyebrows and hands, if we assert that drawing, even rough drawing, is

A MEANS OF EXPRESS

—communication—exceeding speech in value, or has a sufficiency of our readers discovered this for the thing to be palatable? A psychologist, to the extent of knowing the meaning of realization, or a student of science who has been "bogged" for want of illustrations once or twice in a text-book, will indorse this readily enough. However, we are anxious not to slip into the unacceptable, and a more lowly and practical tone should perhaps be adopted. If a human being draws at all, we will say then, he will draw to indicate how he wants a shelf erected, a machine mended, a garment cut, or as a guide to a network of streets; but even this may be too much. For a great majority of those who are taught to draw are not expected to draw anything except an easy freehand copy—such cleverness would cause surprise, and even alarm—and their drawing stops with the last collection of pencils they witness at school.

Dropping lower again, shall we say that pupils are taught to draw, not in order to draw, but for the subsidiary effects—to give a keener observation, a juster sense of form and proportion? Nothing we imagine could be more thoroughly practical than this. What things will there be need of observing—we are not Utopian enough to say drawing—in after-life? Chiefly, we imagine, irregularly-shaped things, or regular bodies seen obliquely and askew, and effects of illumination and shadow. One thing will never be seen—except on an "urgent" wall-paper, growing, we hope, old-fashioned—and that is a bilateral form, balanced exactly on a middle line, like

THE TYPICAL SOUTH KENSINGTON LOWER-GRADE COPY.

In these lower-grade copies, with their one symmetry and stereotyped trick of balance lines, there can be no denial that the incentive to any exercise of the observation upon real things is reduced to a minimum. It is tacitly suggested to a child who is brought to draw in this way that the common things round him are beyond the sphere of drawing—they are crooked, and don't balance; and one of the uses of the subject, as a stimulus to further excursions on his own account, disappears. This objection applies to all freehand from the flat. There may even be detrimental prejudice created. We heard, recently, of a teacher who took a drawing class of small boys, for whose instruction the conventional freehand had been, perhaps, too exclusively patronized by his predecessor. He began operations by saying, "We will draw a cat." The little boys seemed rather astonished at this undignified proposal, but they began promptly. He was surprised at this start without any copy or further instructions, and went round to see what they were doing. In each book a faint vertical line was appearing—for a Blondin[13] cat to balance on!

This does not apply so forcibly to model drawing, but that usually comes some time after freehand,* sometimes never ; and here, too, there is a peculiar insistence by the Department upon neatness and correct lining-in, and an antagonism to any premature attempts at shadow, that is probably excellent for the future artists, but very undesirable in the education of the ordinary person. A

---

13. Blondin was a famous French tightrope walker.

teacher can, and ought to, insist upon neatness and precision in the writing lesson; and if the accent is put upon these qualities in drawing, it is at the expense of others which must go unaccented. The Departmental drawing is too thorough and finished in its methods, and too narrow in its selection of things to draw, for the needs of a common education. What is needed is a

MORE SKETCHY TREATMENT OF A WIDER RANGE OF OBJECTS,

and a subordination of drawing *from the flat*.

For instance, is it impossible in practice to distribute leaves, sprays, or flowers among children, to be drawn after the teacher has been given an example of the "way to do it" on the blackboard, instead of giving them copies on cards? or to start the subject with attempts at sketching "models"? Does not this involve a far greater element of interest and mental exercise than the present plan? Another method that is of the greatest educational value is memory drawing, the reproduction of a copy that has been exhibited and removed, or of some common object previous appointed for observation. A teacher drilled on the old lines will sneer, "You will get some pretty drawings that way!" Undoubtedly we shall—and

GROTESQUE AND MISERABLE PERFORMANCES

at times—possibly even on the blackboard itself; but the question arises, Do we teach drawing for the sake of the drawings or for the sake of the drawer?

The end of the old-fashioned school drawing was a triumph of painful copying, framed and glazed in the best parlour. Have we altogether changed all that? The theorizing educationalist carefully distinguishes between drawing as a mental and quasi-moral discipline, and drawing as an art; the former is for everyone, the latter for the budding artist. Now, the drawing of the second grade of the Science and Art Department was evidently arranged chiefly as an introduction to artistic work, and is doubtless fitted to that end; while the Department has grown to far wider influence and responsibilities than its projectors foresaw, and is yearly examining vast numbers of students who have, and will have, nothing to do with technical art. The Department not only controls the drawing in elementary, but overshadows and influences that in middle-class schools, and it is time that attention is called to this shifting of its influence.

The main point we are trying to enforce is expressed in the title of this paper, that it is possible to consider drawing and we would add that this does not appear to be sufficiently appreciated by the Department. As a direct result of this discouragement of rough and educational sketching, we find many people who hold drawing certificates, and yet confess a remarkable want of practical drawing ability. First and second grade drawing are with many necessarily an abiding-place, but in the art scheme they are evidently only the janua and atrium to the third grade studies. It does not seem unreasonable, then, to ask that now these lower grades have become part of the general education, they should be more adapted to this new end, and made educationally complete. We are not asking the Department to change its character, or to desert any tradition; we are simply pointing out that it has grown into new relations, more especially with regard to its second grade art, and that these new relations need expression in a wider syllabus.

It has been asserted that the current freehand copies cultivate æsthetic appreciation, but this is too ridiculous for serious discussion, for it amounts to the identification of bilaterality and beauty.

Another objection to the disproportionate share of freehand drawing from flat copies, in Government education, is the ease with which it lends itself to the ways of the incompetent drawing-master, who distributes copies and "loafs"—a genuine critic, among his scholars for the rest of the class time. The fact that this passes for a drawing lesson in numberless schools shows the need of the emancipation of drawing from "freehand," for which we are pleading. The remark I once heard a scholastic agent make to an aspirant to the handle end of the ferrule, "Stick down drawing—*anyone can teach drawing*," is worthy of every art teacher's earnest consideration in connection with our other suggestions.

* There is no model drawing in Standards I., II., III., and IV.

Natural History in Schools

The Journal of Education, v XIII, no 268, pp581-583, 1 November 1891

This piece was one of young Wells's most extensive explanations of the place of natural science in the curriculum, but there are several other elements here as well. Wells's critique of English literature and history, which he claimed were introduced solely to turn students away from academic subjects and toward commercial studies, is interesting given his later writing of a history book. In listing bookkeeping as one of the minor subjects, Wells was likely remembering his childhood learning the subject at Morley's Commercial Academy. The bulk of this article consists of Wells's advice on the pedagogy of science education, the process from the particular to the general, from samples to theory. His emphasis on the word "tell" mark the places where direct instruction is more appropriate than observation and experimentation, and imply that such instruction should be subsidiary to actual experience with the samples and demonstrations by the teacher on the chalkboard. His discussion of pedagogy also notes a separation of boys and girls in their methods of understanding, and the view that if science cannot be taught properly, it shouldn't be taught at all.

NATURAL HISTORY IN SCHOOLS.

At the best Natural History can claim but a subsidiary place in education; the staple, the main body, of the school curriculum must necessarily be an intellectual and quasi-moral training, and that must be furnished, as things are at present, by a grammatical course, "corrected" by mathematics, though in the near future it may be that the backbone of school work will cease to be linguistic, and the teaching of physiology, physics, chemistry, mathematics, and mechanics may be organized into a coherent educational course. We are not concerned now with the schoolmasters' main battle against ignorance, however, but rather with one of the numerous flanking, advanced skirmishing, or covering, detachments of his work. Such accessory detachments have multiplied very considerably of late years—as some think, to the pitch of disorganization—and we have, sharing with natural history what at any rate *should* be a lesser half of the school time, such diverse subjects as English literature, commercial geography, bookkeeping, shorthand, typewriting, Italian, logic, political economy, hygiene, agriculture, drawing, fine art criticism, land surveying, carpentering, plumbing, weaving, dogmatic theology, and basket-making. Of course these various branches of human knowledge and exercise are of very unequal importance. Drawing, when it is regarded as a means of expression, and not foolishly made into a fine art and mystery, is the absolutely essential right wing to the teacher's centre of intellectual training—far more necessary than even the universally studied French. English literature and history, whatever their actual merits may be, are, on the other hand, apparently merely introduced into many schools in order to give a sometimes superfluous distaste for such studies, and to turn the pupil from the unprofitable road that leads to Grub Street into the golden way of some trade or profession. Other subjects play a greater part in the prospectus than in the school, on the principle of answering a foolishly exacting parent according to his folly. Shorthand—of which the pretended teacher has, in nine cases out of ten, no adequate knowledge—is one of these, and wastes in most schools a ridiculously insufficient allowance of two or three hours a week, that can, nevertheless, be ill afforded from other subjects.

Where schools are encumbered with a host of subsidiary subjects in this way, natural history may, with advantage, be used, like Jonah, simply as a relief. But in a school where, in addition to the main course of work, linguistic or scientific, and the drawing, little is attempted or professed, its claims for retention in the work of the school may reasonably be considered. It has, however, no urgent claim, and since the amount of material and of knowledge and special aptitude required for the efficient teaching of most of these additional subjects are considerable, it would be well for a head master to consider his staff, and the available resources of illustration, before he decides upon the competing candidature of natural history, literature, history, or of some other science, in cases where the main work is in classical or modern languages, for a share in the school time. But where a capable teacher is at hand, and where the school is sufficiently solvent to spend a few pounds at rare intervals upon museum cases, a microscope, dissecting and other appliances, then there is no doubt that natural history may be made very interesting, and educationally very valuable indeed. It is beyond dispute that boys, as a class, have a natural proclivity for the work, and the pains and labour boys will put themselves to through their inborn interest in animals and plants, without sympathy and even under discouragement from some dead mind of a master, is at times even pathetic. The intellectual value of the work, properly done, in substituting a conception of order in diversity for the simply heterogeneous, is certainly very high. If it is asserted, furthermore, that the germ of æsthetic pleasure and capacity may be better nursed by the handling of leaves and twining stems, and the contemplation of mountains, hills and valleys, than by all the paintings of Turner and all the photographs of Greek sculpture that have ever been taken, then universal assent cannot be expected, though that is the persuasion to which a naturalist arrives; for the beginning of art was not a teaching, but nature working upon the mind of man. Still, without this, the considerations of interest and aptitude recommend the subject highly.

No single agriculturalist can plough a continent, and no teacher can cover the whole field of natural history. But everywhere there are two headings under which the subject falls, namely, forms and functions; and the teaching must, in all cases, be essentially the explanation and correlation of the forms of natural objects by their causes and uses. Unfortunately, however, in too many cases the teaching of natural history becomes a mechanical classification subordinated to names. This is particularly the case with botany, one of its most commonly taught branches. To illustrate how this subject might be taught, an imaginary course may perhaps be briefly described.

Let us say that the teacher decides to direct attention, at first, particularly, to the most immediately attractive side of the subject, to the flower and its meaning. His first lesson would be on the formation of the fruit and seed in some common and simple flower—a buttercup, a pea, a wood anemone, or a hyacinth. Each pupil would be provided with a buttercup, and with the head of achenes which constitutes its fruit, or with a pea-flower and pod, or with any other flower and fruit selected, and the teacher, drawing on the board, would call attention to the carpel or carpels, the position of the ovule, the change of the carpels to form the fruit, and of the ovules to form seed. He would then *tell* his class of the necessity of fertilization, and call attention to the sticky stigma, and describe on the board how the tubes of the pollen grains reached the ovules. The anther lobes would be crushed or artificially dehisced, and the pollen seen. The attention of the pupils would be called to its stickiness. The pupils would sketch the carpels and fruit, the stamens, and a section of the flower, and compare them with other simple cases.

In the next lesson, the teacher would *tell* his pupils the general necessity for cross-fertilization. No flower brings home the method of cross-fertilization better than the violet or pansy—the little trap-door stigma appeals at once to the intelligence. And now the root of the nectary, the coloured corolla, and the sweet scent may be developed and the whole flower of the violet understood. The buttercup and pea could then be reverted to, and compared. The mechanism of the scarlet-runner is a handy and "pretty" instance for comparison. In the note-books, the violet, together with the pansy, if possible, should be sketched—the teacher will show the way on the board.

After this, attention should be called to some anemophilous type—the nettle is an especially convenient instance. The small inconspicuous flowers, crowded together, become at once intelligible, now that conspicuousness and insects are correlated, and the catkin and fruit of any ordinary amentaceous tree may be compared. The pupil now begins to appreciate the fact that flowers are not stuck wantonly over the world as they are over a wall-paper, or designed like the adornments of a lady's hat, with no design at all, but have a causative connexion with other things, and an end for which they are fitted.

Systematic botany should follow, to elucidate the bearing of relationship upon form. Let us see that in the next lesson each pupil has specimen flowers, and, if possible, fruits, of a pea, a bean, clover, vetch, and laburnum, and of a primrose, poppy, and rue, for comparison. From the comparison of these, the deductive features of the order leguminosæ may be made out. The cruciferæ form an equally distinct and suitable order for beginning, and proceeding from these, in perhaps twenty or thirty lessons, the flowers and fruits of the leading natural orders of flowering plants are systematically arranged.

After or during this course, the male, and green female, and ripe cones of a pine might be produced and examined, and the fact of plants without true flowers, but with pollen and ovules, might be shown, and a bracken frond with sporangia, or a moss in "fruit," used to elucidate the fact of quite flowerless plants. But ordinary work with the cryptogams is more difficult and much less attractive than with the phanerogams, and their recognition as a great group outside the work of the class is all that is advisable at first. Meanwhile the collecting spirit, that is usually more or less wasted upon stamps and crests, might be set at work in forming collections of dried and flattened plants; and a half-holiday or so given to a botanical expedition, *when the systematic knowledge justifies it,* would do a great deal in deepening the intension of the names of the orders.

Vegetable physiology cannot go far without some chemical knowledge. Attention should be called, first of all, to the leaves spreading their begging palms out to the sun, and the roots seeking food assiduously through the soil. The competition for sunlight explains many forms of stem, the tall woody stem, the mean trick of climbing and creeping, the bare ground round a tree stem, and a whole regiment of facts of that kind. Storage and the competition for the soil explain tuber and rhizome, and the varied forms of root. In the diversified shapes of leaf, our systematic study of relationships will occur. As a discipline in these facts comes description. And at last the elements of morphology are reached, and the wide generalization that all the forms of leaf, thorn, stamen, tendril, sucker, tuber, rootlet, hair, sting, pitcher—an endless category of shapes and appliances—are all reducible to four primary groups of organs. With this, a first botanical course might very well close.

The school museum should grow, and to a certain extent perish, with the course of study. First would come flowers and fruits together, whole and dissected, carefully displayed, and with explanatory labels. Then the school herbarium, in which each new specimen accepted would bear the name of its discoverer. Then specimens to display morphological points; the sunflower capitulum and the green fig, the mulberry flower and fruit, the arum, the red berry of the yew, the apple, side by side with the peach and cucumber, a collection of typical stems, and so on. The school museum on a magnificent scale is to be found in the educational cases in the great hall of the South Kensington Natural History Museum. But so far as the school museum consisted of common objects, it might reasonably be swept away (saving perhaps the labels) and replaced by the next class again.

Entomology may be worked over in a similar manner; it is almost the only division of zoology in which a sufficient diversity of forms is attainable for satisfactory systematic study. The vertebrata do not present, close at hand, a sufficient variety and representation of groups for *systematic* work, unless a menagerie or museum is accessible; but comparative anatomy on the type system, with dissections, is possible anywhere. On the sea coast, general invertebrate zoology becomes possible, and indeed almost unavoidable, unless boys are to waste their leisure and curiosity through the want of teaching. Dynamic and structural geology, with, of course, elementary mineralogy, constitutes another attractive branch of natural history. But the teaching, in schools, of palæontology, with its endless names, frantic reconstructions and general dubiety and inconsecutiveness, cannot be too strongly deprecated.

None of these subjects are indispensable in a school. They are far better left out than taught badly. Nothing, among all the atrocities committed in schools, can be much worse than natural history taught by an ignorant or incompetent teacher. There is reason to believe that this nadir atrocity is, however, not infrequently attained.

I have been told by a young lady that she was taught systematic botany at a school of fair repute by having placed before her a schedule of the characters of the principal natural orders, after a course of preliminary instruction in terminology—"*syngenesious, gynostemum,* and *hypogynous,*" and all that kind of thing. I have before me the note-book in geology of a girl whose teacher began instruction in that subject with a statement about the problematical nature of *eozoon,* and the information that the *trilobates* were crustacea (which is wrong), that the *grapholites* were like *sestularia* (of which organism her pupils, and probably she herself, had not the remotest idea), and that all the Cambrian fossils were 'lowly' forms, which is untrue. It is the usual thing to begin zoology with tigers and dromedaries, condors and pythons, instead of cats and dogs and sparrows and slow worms, and the reason is, I uncharitably believe, because the teacher can blunder more securely when he blunders out of the sphere of childish verification. And we find elementary school books in botany sometimes beginning with a description of *parenchyma*. Now natural history is much better left alone than treated in ways that were exploded—theoretically—years ago.

The really responsible person in this matter is the examiner. It is his place to "hall-mark" teaching, and it is a painful thing to observe that in this province of natural history he is too often hall-marking useless and worthless rubbish. In no branch of science can a fictitious knowledge be sooner acquired from text-books and the loose talking of a teacher than in natural history. Girls, especially, have a fatal knack of catching phrases quickly, and resting satisfied. In no subject, therefore, should there be a steadier insistence upon evidence of practical work, and a steadier refusal to accept mere names, however neatly tabulated, as proofs of knowledge. Let anyone consider how easily the following questions could be answered by phrases got off by rote, the impossibility of teaching the matter of some of them by means of the actual thing, and the altogether disproportionate value attached to names and terms—and the reason for the wide discrepancy between the common practice and the accepted theory in the teaching of natural history becomes at once apparent. They have all been set during the last three years in middle-class examinations, mostly those of the College of Preceptors.

Give the popular names of the following Animals—*Sus scrofa, Bos taunts, Equus caballus,* and *Canis domesticus* ; and mention their nearest allies among their respective Natural Orders.

(In this way pig, cow, horse, and dog become fit for "scientific" treatment.)

Give the scientific names of the following Plants, and refer them to their Natural Orders:—Dodder, Mallow, Leek, Eyebright, Heath, Wheat, Hemp, Melon, Hawthorn, Meadowsweet, Foxglove, Groundsel.

Describe a Jelly-fish (Sea-nettle), and *give the scientific (classificatory) names* of that and the nearest allied animals.

Mention the different kinds of Birds that live by or on the Water, whether sea, river, or marsh, and refer them to their respective Orders, *with their Latin names,* if possible.

Give a Tabular View of the divisions of the Protozoa, and indicate the chief characters of the several groups which you mention.

What are following fossils zoologically, and in what groups of strata do they occur?—Ammonites, Baculites, Ceratites, Lituites, Nautilus, and Orthoceras. Give some details of the structure of one or more of them.

The student must know the *horizon, order* and *phylum* of each, but an idea of the *form* of one is sufficient.

Define at least six of the following:—sarcode, cilia, trachea, siphon or siphuncle, polypidom, nervure, pupa, goniophore, endoderm, odontophore, operculum, and larva.

Define what is meant by any six of the following terms —acephalous, acalephs, abranchiate, bilateral, cephalo-branchiate, cœlenterale, cœnenchymatous, coleopterous, dibranchiate, equilateral, equivalved, helminthoid.

Define the meaning of any six of the following terms:— viviparous, ungulate, carnivorous, marsupial, ratitæ, raptores, rasores, quadrumana, præmolar, phalanges, plastron, heterocercal.

Name and succinctly describe one or more members of each of any *six* of the following groups:—Chondropterygii, Urodela, Passeres, Didelphia, Insectivora, Dibranchiata, Brachiopoda, Hemiptera, Araneidea, Decapoda, Ostracoda, Hirudinea, Stellerida, Sclerodermata, Hydroida.

State what you know of the *Bathymetrical Range* of the *Protozoa, Cœlenterata, Echinodermata*, respectively.

What is meant by "Morphology"? In explanation, *describe the morphology* of the *Echinoidea, or* of some other Order of the *Echinodermata*.

Define what is meant by *Annuloida* and *Annulosa, Mollusca* and *Molluscoida*, respectively, and give the origin of these words.

Into what groups have modern zoologists divided the "Pachydermata," formerly so-called ? Give the reasons for such division.

These are specimens—not exceptions. Now what can it profit a boy or girl to know the "scientific name" of the pig or groundsel, or the "Latin names" of all the aquatic birds in the universe, or the misconceptions of the ancients regarding "pachydermata" and "molluscoida," or that "bathymetrical range" is simply the depth at which they are found? What school has a microscope for every pupil, and how else can the divisions of protozoa, or even the meaning of protozoon, be clearly conceived? Yet that question has recurred thrice. What conception of order in diversity will a boy get that is just pelted with *polypidom, sarcode, goniophore, coenenchymatous, equilateral,* and *helminthoid*? If this is natural history, let us have it out of the schools at any cost, and the sooner the better.

But there is a better natural history than this, as there has been an endeavour to suggest in the earlier part of this paper. Within its limits, and soundly taught, such sane natural history is desirable in schools—as desirable as, or more desirable than, any "artistic" drawing or literature, or even history, since it is a subject in *harmony* with the youthful mind, for which these contrasted branches of work are more or less premature. And boys especially will still get at it, without a teacher, with a waste of energy and loss of profit, if the benefit of a competent teacher's direction and advice is denied them. But *acalephs* and *polypidom!* and, as it was recently pointed out in a letter to the *Educational Times*, that elicited no explanation, "*crustacea*" in a paper on *vertebrata!* If we wish to give our born Darwins and Wallaces a distaste for their fate, we could not do it more effectually than by treating them to such "science" as this.

H. G. Wells

Hints to the Subtle Examinee

The University Correspondent, vol II, no 15, p13, 15 November 1891

Geoffrey West refers to this as a work where Wells "gave free rein to an engaging whimsicality".[14] In advising the student to write a lot about nothing, and avoid difficult questions, he appears to be criticizing the examiners as much as the examinees. The salutation means roughly, "from an indignant tutor".

The following hints may be of use to those perverse souls who are bent upon failing in examinations, and conceiving therewith a noble distaste for "cramming." Very considerable experience with "tests" and examination papers has convinced us of their soundness and value, and we submit them to the earnest consideration of all who still move towards the goal of a degree. It is "the way not to do it"—a way that should also be known and avoided by those who mean to succeed.

First, then, before you enter an examination room, get firmly hold of the idea that you enter it to *write*. Write as much as possible—and write big. There is no pleasure keener than boasting of the sheets that you have filled to your friends outside. Begin writing at once, if possible with a squeaking pen, when you are seated in the room, and waste no time in any foolish ticking off of questions. The men sitting round you cannot see your paper, and they will think you are doing one-hundred-per-cent. of the answers—they will envy you, and being envied is mainly what we live for.

Avoid abruptness. Examiners, as a rule, mark so much to a line. Always begin your answers with irrelevant remarks; for instance, if you are asked for the chief provisions of Magna Charta, you can write that it is the "keystone of an Englishman's liberties," and other variegated metaphors of that kind for a page or so, and then you can give a picturesque biographical sketch of King John. The examiner will see that you know something about it, will probably not read your answer through and will mark you highly, even if you do not give any of the provisions.

Examiners, you must bear in mind, are a most gullible class, they know little or nothing of the subjects, as a rule, and rarely appreciate the drift of their own questions. The examination question is to be regarded not so much as an enquiry as a suggestion for an essay. And examiners are easily touched by literary graces of the voluble kind; you can dazzle them and confuse them and make them doubt

---

14. West, Geoffrey, *H.G. Wells: A Sketch for a Portrait*. London: Gerald Howe Ltd, 1930, p92.

their own authority and forget entirely what a question is about.

Still, sometimes, they add to their simplicity a certain cunning. Always suspect "catches." What a question looks easy and seems to demand one short explicit answer, *do not give it!*—it is probably a "catch."

A question or so left unanswered increases your chances of passing, because you cannot possibly lose marks upon a question you have not attempted. If there is one which you can answer one portion only, leave it altogether—the examiner will then not be able to tell what it is you do not know.

The aim of the examiner is not to find out what you know, but to catch you making blunders. Therefore, above all things, be equivocal. Keep away from diagrams, tabulated answers, numbers, anything that commits you definitely. Adopt the tactics of the cuttle fish, and clothe yourself in darkness.

In this way you may hope to defeat your enemy; and if your name should, after all, not appear upon the pass list, you will know that he has failed you, not so much through your errors or ignorance, as through his own intense chagrin at your skilful fence to his questions. "He did not kill me," you can say; "he simply could not get at me. That is the list of the wounded who were nevertheless not slain. *I* remain intact, and he in malignant fury would have me dead." Nevertheless

"Saevit Indignatio Tutori."

TUTOR.

A Plea for the Study of the Teacher

The Journal of Education, vol XIV, no 270, pp 29-30, 1 January 1892

In this article promoting the study of teachers, Wells notes that so much scholarship has gone into studying the pupils, but so little in looking at the lives of teachers. They, too, have needs and ambitions. He is also explicit in connecting low salaries to the quality of schoolmasters, and arguing for reform within that context. Although female teachers are mentioned in earlier articles, in this one Wells seems to acknowledge more directly the equivalent role women have as teachers, without romanticizing their character.

There has grown up, during the present century, a really very respectable literature, at last, upon the child, and how to educate the child. It would even appear that some of the most earnest teachers read this literature, and that the knowledge of educational conditions and method is slowly and steadily increasing. Pestalozzi's resolution, to "psychologize" education, has had its effect, and the study of the thing we cultivate has begun in earnest. No one—in an educational paper, at least—need plead with educationalists for the psychology of the child. But the question of the psychology for the teacher is in an altogether different position; for it is not at all clear in educational literature that such a study is needed. Yet it is, we contend, the most urgently.

One finds that, in the books of pedagogic literature, the gentle reader is more or less overtly assumed to be "one of us," and there is a polite tendency on the part of the author to avoid personality. Your methods, my dear friend, are bad, even very bad, your ideas are rudimentary or wrong, but you yourself, he hints, are Better Nature, pure and simple, and needing only the light. The adoption of this tone enables us to read him in an easy chair, and without any great searchings of heart. He convicts us of mistakes, plentifully enough, but of limitations—never. "To-morrow we will alter our procedure, all will be well."

Teachers who read books on pedagogics, and others too, who have caught it from them, understand now pretty clearly what is meant by the comparison of the pupil's mind to a plant. We have in the pupil not an inert thing, but a centre of forces; we have something obeying certain inexorable laws of development, which we can stand outside of and affect, but into which we can introduce no new motive influence. We are dealing with growth, a matter as much beyond our immediate control as creation; we may plant, we may water, but the increase is not in our decision. And, consequently, our success is proportionate to the adjustment of our teaching to the intrinsic constitution of our pupil. We know now the import of that childish restlessness that the old type of schoolmaster identified with original sin. Inattention is now, by a veritable revolution of opinion, not a crime of the child's, but a verdict. In fact, all educational matters have, in theory at least, been brought to the test of the child's psychology, and appraised by its laws. And the teacher has been forgotten.

Every advance in our knowledge of educational laws has made a greater demand upon the teacher. In the first place, upon his character: the need of patience and self-restraint has been enormously increased by our wiser views of discipline. In the good old rough-and-ready days, a schoolmaster might "give himself away" half-a-dozen times in a day and recover the position with the cane. But now he must needs be watchful, careful, dextrous, introspective, planning his praise and blame, and manipulating the minds under him with the skill of a Jesuit, while, at the same time, preserving a contagious cheerful openness that must defy youthful scrutiny—a difficult combination. And then, upon his intellect : how thorough is the preparation of lessons in the theory of the educationalist compared with those given—let us say, in the distant past! The fertility of illustration, the richness of the iridescent side-lights of the New Teacher, need only compared with the lessons we grown-up people actually suffered, to realize the difference. And then, finally, one must consider the huge requirements of "preparation" and "correction" now made upon him—or her. The conscientious examination and correction of exercises, the skilful utilization of errors, in such a subject as English composition, for instance, involves not only a powerful intellect, and taste enough for a minor poet, but a colossal, a superhuman conscience. When we think of all these things that a modern teacher *must* have, and in the literature of education is politely assumed always to have, our self-respect grows like Jonah's gourd. While we are eating the apple of knowledge we become like gods.

But the real teacher is not like this. I speak not in the spirit of Mephistopheles, but of Mrs. Betsy Prig. On earth, such serenity with such subtilty, such avoidance of all but righteous anger, such impartiality, such innocent and æsthetic intellectuality, as the theoretical teacher needs, is not to be attained. Perhaps some member of the Brotherhood of the Common Life, perhaps some odd exceptional Jansenite or Jesuit, has clambered as near as earthy gravitation admits to this celestial dream. But it is a great obstacle, a great gulf, as it were, between the school of the theorist and this everyday world in which we would realize his doctrine.

It is possible to misinterpret the agricultural comparison of teaching. People forget that in agriculture we not only study the needs of the plants we grow, but the nature of the things we bring to bear upon them. We investigate, for example, the properties and peculiarities of soils, and the origin and idiosyncracies of various manures. And we find in the nature of agricultural appliances and stimulants as rigorous a set of possibilities and limitations as we do in the intrinsic conditions of the growth and prosperity of the things cultivated. Wheat may grow with exceptional luxuriance on certain old battlefields, or in certain alluvial valleys, between narrow limits of latitude, or on virgin soil, but an agricultural writer who quietly assumed these conditions, and who indulged in incidental humorous allusions to those who cultivated it elsewhere, would be subverting practical necessities to an ideal—in itself an excellent thing—rather too unreservedly. Before educational science can be completely recognised as a branch of technical education, the laws of the mind that plays upon the mind of the child—the limitations and necessities of the average teacher—must be exhaustively formulated, and the demands of the educational writer corrected after the process.

The mind brought to bear upon the mind of the child is anything but divinely comprehensive. The economic conditions of teaching render it probable that, in ninety-nine cases out of a hundred, this mind will not be even exceptionally powerful. At the most, the taste for teaching, and the desire to honourably earn a salary, are only two among many other impulses of the human heart. As young men and maidens—so many of our teachers answer to that description—grow into men and women, their thoughts go out of themselves, and not altogether into their teacher. Since the schoolmasters of a civilized country must, on the most obvious economical considerations, be necessarily numerous, and in receipt of an average salary not greatly in excess of the average wages of the citizens, it is apparent that these limitations of average intelligence and moral fallibility are not merely transitory circumstances of this age, but permanent considerations in the educational problem. The whole tenour of education reform, for a hundred years or more, has been the substitution of a sane acceptation of the actual facts of a child's being for an absurd and pedantic ideal. Is there not some necessity for a smaller but parallel movement in respect to our ideas of a teacher? The claim of a child to ample air, to play, to patient guidance and to tolerant encouragement, to sweetness and light, in its surroundings, is abundantly, almost redundantly asserted. But that education must necessarily be a mere beginning, and even then half a failure unless the teacher has leisure, athletic relaxations, the refreshments of music and leisurely social intercourse, freedom from the avoidable anxieties of life, and, in the case of assistant teachers and employed headmasters and mistresses, social recognition and confidence, is by no means so keenly insisted upon, and, in the practice of too many schools, it is quite evidently not understood.

In fine, the nexus of all mental existence is compromise, and it is submitted that, in their devotion to the child's needs and to educational ideals, pedagogic writers are too often impracticably uncompromising, and ignore the fact that the teacher is, after all, like the child, of fallible clay, a bundle of instincts and desires, of small power and finite horizon—a consideration which would profoundly modify very many of their prescriptions.

H. G. Wells.

The College of Preceptors Science Examinations

The Educational Times, vol XLV, no 371, p 140, 1 March 1892

The Educational Times was a journal that frequently hosted exchanges of letters, creating a forum for the debate about educational reform. Here Wells refers back to his School Zoology letter of September, noting that it had no response, and turns his critique toward the lack of preparation for, or delivery of, a practical (laboratory) portion of the College of Preceptors' examinations in science in middle-class schools. Also noted are the inconsistencies of examiners themselves: some may want only facts, others only analysis. Wells's argument about text-books ("the mere rote learning of a text-book, however well written, cannot be science at all") will be refined in later articles.

To the Editor of the Educational Times.

SIR,—Some few months ago I called attention to certain weaknesses of some of the Science papers set at the Pupils' Examination. May I trespass again upon your space to discuss the same subject further? My original letter, I regret to say, led to no reply in your columns, but I remain, nevertheless, persuaded of the necessity for some ventilation of the matter. To attain this end I shall now lay down certain propositions, and I propose, unless they are previously sufficiently disposed of, to embody them in resolutions to be put before the next General Meeting of the College.

It is simply stating the unanimous agreement of all educational writers to say that book-science is, perhaps, as useless and objectionable a department of school work as it is possible to imagine. I believe I am outside the realm of controversy altogether, when I express the opinion that the mere rote learning of a text-book, however well written, cannot be science at all. That is, indeed, simply a paraphrase of your conclusion in your January issue. The College of Preceptors, which has always exercised, as modern teachers must gratefully admit, a directive, as well as a representative function in middle-class teaching, should, I take it, do nothing to recognise such teaching, and all that is within its power to reform or destroy it.

I attempted, in my previous letter, by instancing questions actually set, to demonstrate that, so far from doing this, the College is really encouraging the objectionable method, and, I may now add, it is discouraging those who walk in the right way, but setting no stamp of approbation upon better taught pupils through the medium of practical examinations. I am afraid my criticisms may have appeared to the reader—if there was a reader—as levelled mainly at the

College Natural History examiners; but, excepting that they appear to be steadily set against the doctrine that in such subjects as theirs, without a syllabus of recognised order of teaching, a choice of questions is advisable, I fail, on further consideration, to see what they can do to produce any change without the prior action of the Council of the College. All that an examiner, under the present conditions, can do, in the way of thorough examining, is done in, for instance, the "Sound, Light, and Heat' papers of Mr. Loewy; and the next steps necessary to improve the present condition of science teaching in middle-class schools appear to be (a) the establishment of a directive syllabus, and (b) the institution of practical examinations.

With regard to (a) it may be pointed out that at present the teacher and examiner are entirely in ignorance of each other's ideas and methods. It is only by a careful examination of the College chemistry papers, for instance, that the fact comes to light that the chemistry in question is almost entirely the chemistry of the non-metallic elements, excluding the carbon compounds, that experimental demonstrations of the orthodox type are advisable, and that analytical work by boys will be thrown away. And there is no guarantee that a new examiner may not recast the subject to his liking, put all the stress upon replacement and quantivalence, for instance, and practically insist upon analytical work. Such a state of affairs as this renders teachers of higher capacity in considerable anxiety as to their final section of success.

With regard to (b) there is no doubt that a dextrous teacher may, by clear explanation and plentiful note-book drilling, prepare quick boys to pass any *written* examination without practical work; while, one the other hand, many boys may have a great deal of really useful knowledge, and may be even sound thinkers, without the gift of luminous exposition. But it is late in the day to plead for the absolute necessity of practical work in science teaching, and for what goes with it, and indeed often precedes and stimulated it, practical examination. Four or five years ago I anticipated with easy confidence the immediate advent of practical tests in the College examination scheme, and it is largely as a reminder that I am now making these proposals.

H. G. Wells.

Comenius

The University Correspondent, vol II, no 19, 15 March 1892, pp11-12

Seventeenth-century Czech bishop John Amos Comenius is still often called the father of modern education. Here Wells attacks his revival, despite the fact that many of Comenius' reforms were similar to those Wells suggested, including learning through actual objects. Simon Laurie of the University of Edinburgh (the Professor Laurie mentioned below) had recently republished his 1881 biography of Comenius, and lauded him in Oscar Browning's Educational Review.[15] *The Mr. Quick was the same with whom Wells had disputed the year before in* The Educational Times *over Quick's lecture on Spencer, and who had died the previous March. Wells had studied Pestalozzi and published his thesis for the College of Preceptors on Froebel, and he posits both educationists as more deserving than Comenius. Other than Comenius' religious predilections, it is unclear why Wells felt obligated to denigrate his life and work in this article.*

Just three hundred years ago, this month, Comenius, the "First Realist," according to the classification of our educational writers, was born at Niynitz, in Moravia. His works, since his death, have experienced many fluctuations of popular favour, but now it seems that he is reinstated in the esteem of educationalists, though certainly not with that eminence his contemporaries accorded him, He was a voluminous writer—a thing in itself detrimental to immortality— and he wrote in Latin, as Professor Laurie, who has had to read it all, says pathetically, "good, bad, and indifferent." So that the reawakening of his fame is a matter in which his translator and Professor Laurie, the late Mr. Quick and Mr. Oscar Browning, have had a share. And this is an age of revived reputations.

He was, they say, the "First Realist," and, of course, since Carlyle's historical epic, writers have felt in duty bound to give him some pithy title of this kind. It is a convenient practice for the writer: it gives an air of powerful precision, and drives the connotation of the epithet deep into the reader's mind. So that literature and the overtaxed human memory profit, even if it is untrue. As in this case, where the factors in the man's making would seem to have been singularly complex and diversified.

It is, indeed, hard to find, in his history or writings, the gospel put in a nutshell in this smart epigrammatic way, by saying he is a Realist and deriving

15. S. S. Laurie. *John Amos Comenius: Bishop of the Moravians: His Life and Educational Works.* Reading Circle Edition. Syracuse, N.Y.: C. W. Bardeen, 1892, p iii.

him right away from the current legend of Bacon. He was a great man undoubtedly as Luther was great, in his simple devotion to and labour for a cause—in his case the cause of man-manufacturing—but he was not great in the luminous discovery and steadfast enunciation of a principle, as was Darwin, or even Pestalozzi. He preached no central doctrine that one can call "Realism," but he went about with ideas voluminously vague—a cloud of the suggestion of something better possible about him—and stirred up people. His endless publications, his self-contradictions, retractions, changes of front, indicate how active and important he was, and how his gift of expression and persuasion outran the search after truth, and the thought that would justify the epithet we condemn. The title of one of his Amsterdam books, "Wisdom's Winnowing Machine, or the Art of Wisely Retracting One's Own Opinions," says as much for his want of unity as it does for his perfect honesty.

There came to the making of him two, at first parallel, but diverging, factors: a perfervid evangelical Christianity, and that new spirit of clarified common-sense that the modern writer has christened with the name of "Lord Bacon." He was born in the former, and caught the latter from books. He suggests to one's mind one of those common-sense upright tradesmen we sometimes meet with, who spend their Sabbaths in edifying a sect, and their weeks in prosaic usefulness. Perfect honesty, clear penetration, were moulded to the form of a theological philosophy that had been stamped upon his mind, beyond all tampering, before doubt could arise in it. The conditions of compatibility with the tenets of the Moravian Brethren were the intellectual limits of Comenius. It is absurd to write of the man without considering these moulding prepossessions; it is, indeed, ignoring the very foundations of the house. He was born in persecution, his library and MSS. were burnt at Fulneck in 1621, he was proscribed as a Hussite pastor in 1627, he became a bishop of his sect, and he wrote upon Prophecy; and yet there are writers who deal with Comenius as though his educational project sprang out of a soil of advanced liberalism, and were sown there by the "Novum Organum," whereas, as he clearly intimates, his whole scheme aimed at a final graduation in heaven. He deduced his doctrine of universal education from the fact that all children are the children of God. The belief of Comenius in this wide and simple proposition is the essential factor in his greatness. Sturm, using the precious years of youth to perfect Latin style, Ascham, trailing his pupils backwards and forwards over a book of Latin prose— all the oil-lamp teachers—are dwarfed by that assertion. We are taken, as it were, out of the study into a high place in the open air, from which we see city and river, wide landscape, plains, and mountains, and, above all, not blue space, but the ruling hosts of heaven.

But when we seek to trace this inspiring idea through the life and writings of Comenius, it eludes us again and again. It is amply in evidence in the pansophic scheme of education—a progression of philology (or language), philosophy (or science, logic (or reasoning), politics (or men), and theology; but the appearance of unity vanishes as we examine into the details of his plans. It is an extrinsic unity, holding these parts together, and not an intrinsic unity, of synthesis, that we find in Comenius. He set a crown upon education rather than gave it a new foundation; he pointed men to an end they had forgotten, rather than showed them a way. His educational ambition was vast, but his proposals of method—as a comparison of the various editions of the "Janua" will show—were chaotic. He left behind him chiefly books and a dwindling reputation, and yet, in Sweden, Hungary, and Amsterdam, he had had great opportunities.

It is hard to trace any fruit in educational advance from his career. Far more justly does the title of the First Realists belong to Rousseau, Pestalozzi, and Froebel, for they, and not Comenius, first turned from books to things, and from corrupted and cramping traditions back to nature and to natural method. But of his exalted honesty and his wide influence upon his contemporaries there can be no denial. And, as special claim upon the consideration of our readers we may add that, just two hundred and fifty years ago, he was almost instrumental in giving London a teaching University, but, the first gust of the coming storm, the Civil War, sent him away disappointed.

H. G. Wells

The University for London.

The University Correspondent, vol II, no 20, p 19, 15 April 1892

The previous article may have inspired Wells to write separately and at length about the controversy over a teaching university. In 1888, the first royal commission had been set up to determine whether changes were needed to the structure of the University of London, which until that point had been only an examining body. The University College London and King's College had proposed to form a teaching university called the "Albert University" and the later inclusion of Gresham College transformed the idea into the "Gresham Scheme" or "Gresham University". Proposals for creating a teaching university had been refused by either the Senate or the Convocation, but in 1892 the idea was raised again. But to Wells and many others, the University of London examinations were less biased because of their independence, and comprised a "court of vindication for private students and private teachers" like himself. Arguments against its examinations, he claimed, were because they were rigorous. If cooperation among the colleges is to occur, public-minded individuals must lead it, or the plans will continue to fail.

The rapid progress of the Albert University proposals has been effectually checked. The growing voice of disapprobation rose at last to a cry that could not be ignored, and the unhappy scheme fell finally by its own inherent weakness when the weight and responsibility of the Gresham funds were placed upon it. A new Commission will sit, and a new scheme will be advanced. A period of many months will doubtless intervene before this is elaborated, but there can be no doubt that it will depart as widely as possible from the inadequate and dubious proposals of Sir George Young and his associates. That there is room for a unification of higher teaching in the metropolis no one can doubt; that there should be such another and invidious failure to include numberless institutions where teaching of a high order is given, is highly improbable. The Albert scheme erred on the side of a disingenuous narrowness; it is possible that its successor may be too freely inclusive. Certainly the problem is far too complicated for the haphazard listing of institutions as admissible or inadmissible, and the wholesale elevation to University status of the staff, teaching, and students of those preferred. And the question is again reopened as to what relation the present University of London should hold to the University in London that must inevitably arise.

The peculiarities of the circumstances of London University were brought out in a very striking manner by the series of incidents that culminated in the rejection of a former scheme by Convocation. It became evident then that

London differs from any other English University in its entire disregard of teaching establishments as establishments; it simply meets the candidates who come to its judgement, and, without any enquiry as to the source, examines and weighs their knowledge with singular severity and precision, and gives or refuses the guinea-mark of its certificates and degrees. Where teachers are necessary to the proper mastery of a subject, their existence is tacitly assumed, and the proof of their influence demanded by the examiners; but the University deals with the student as a man and not as a *protégé* of Professor This or the Council of That College, and it has, in the emphatic voice of the Convocation vote, refused to depart from this attitude of judicial impartiality. London University has now been for long, and we trust will always remain, the touchstone for colleges, and the court of vindication for private students and private teachers. It might be a source of pecuniary gain to many an endowed and pretentious home of dull or preoccupied teachers, but it would be a distinct loss to the cause of higher education, if the independence of the University were destroyed, if it were barred in any way to the poor student over the usual scholarship age, to the teacher in the day-school, or to the believer in Carlyle's dictum that the modern University is the University of books, or if any unfair advantage were given to those who had sacrified [sic] time and money at the feet of some privileged college lecturer. The University of London is, and is firmly resolved to remain, an open and an impartial examining board. This must always be borne in mind by those who would endow the new University with the name and prestige of the old. Does it, however, necessarily place Burlington Gardens[16] outside the scope of the proposed University altogether?

It certainly does, if a University of the good old sort is hoped for; if an impressive imitation of Oxford or Cambridge, and especially of their defects, is desired, with "special" degree examinations, *ad eundem* and honorary degrees, the M.A. refinement, and the like venerable attributes, which add so much to the national pride in these grand foundations. The London Matriculation and degree examinations are too exacting, the pride of London graduates in the severity and integrity of these tests is too great, to admit of any proposal of concessions in the direction of degree-selling. But otherwise, admitting the value of London examinations, there is no particular reason why a new examining and degree-granting board should be created in the metropolis, and why the students and teachers of a new University should not avail themselves of the neighbourhood and reputation of the older foundation. In other words, one must either show how the London examinations are objectionable, or admit the reasonableness of a Teaching University, with no facilities for conferring degrees additional to those of the existing University.

---

16. Burlington Gardens was the first purpose-built location for London University.

No doubt, objections may be made in plenty to London examinations—and answered. Schoolmasters complain that the Matriculation is too rigid for them, and that the span of subjects is too extensive. There is no room, they say, for specialization and, if it is premature specialization, that involves the omission of a really very elementary study of other subjects essential to a liberal education, the objection is doubtless true. B.Sc.'s, who have reached the commencement of original work, complain, on the other hand, that they have not been required to learn a sufficiency of German. Medical students cannot, for the life of them, see the value of the Preliminary Scientific; but that is only a survival of these schoolboys objection to the particular work upon which he is engaged. Such objections are matters of detail; the real, the sweeping complaint of many London "Reformers" has never been quite openly formulated, and is that the examinations are too severe. Many a teacher, now in possession of a degree won during this teaching period, can testify that, in his own case, this assertion is not correct. In his paper in the current number of the *Educational Times*, Mr. J. Spencer Hill puts this objection in euphemistic style—"In the case of the University of London, which, as the chief examining board of the country outside the older Universities, has naturally had a great influence in determining educational standards, this desire for greater freedom and for wider scope has chiefly found expression in loud and lengthy complaints against the stereotyped methods on which the examinations at Burlington House—[17]so unfortunately miscalled the examinations of the University of London—have been carried on. These complaints found their first and their fullest expression in the North of England. The teachers of the now rapidly growing corporation of the Owens College, full of young and energetic life, and, therefore, munificently supported by the citizens of Manchester, loudly expressed their dissatisfaction at the inelasticity of the trammels by which they were fettered and bound by Burlington House. . . . An Association for the Promotion of a Teaching University for London was established, mainly through the efforts of Sir George Young, together with some of the chief leaders of medical education in London, who found the high standard exacted for the degree of M.D. a serious hindrance to the prosperity of the London medical schools."

The relative value of the Victoria B.Sc. or of a Scotch M.D. and of the same London degree needs consideration before we decide upon this arraignment of London examinations. And, even if it is possible to impeach London examinations, this is rather an argument for reform of the examinations in question that for the establishment of an experimental rival in the metropolis.

It may be urged that a Teaching University which does not grant degrees is practically what exists in London at present—that in University College, in the

---

17. Burlington House was the administrative address of the University of London.

Medical Schools, in the University classes of the Birkbeck, King's College, and the Working Men's College, in the University Tutorial College, in the training colleges for teachers, in the Science Laboratories at South Kensington, we have the somewhat motley colleges of such a University, and that the proposal of their union is simply the suggestion of a linking name. But if it were possible to bring all these institutions and others together into harmonious co-operation, there would have been a great deal more than a simple linking effected. The South Kensington schools, for instance, entirely ignore literary culture, and its students matriculate in the University at the expense of their current scientific work. In the words of the *Quarterly* reviewer, these institutions "are isolated and unrelated, they work independently, in ignorance of each other's doings, and not unfrequently as rivals and competitors rather than as helpers in the performances of a public duty."[18]

It has also been too often forgotten in this discussion that the work of teaching men and women up to the level of a pass degree is by no means the highest function of a University—in fact, only its lowest work—that the crying need of London is not graduation courses and means of graduation, which indeed are plentiful and cheap enough, but post-graduation courses, and the stimulating and originative factor of University life. No one, except perhaps a medical practitioner here and there, or a F.S.Sc., will assert that a degree is inaccessible to an industrious London student who is not specializing prematurely; but many will be prepared to admit that the absence of any Honours schools in London, except where the energy of a particular teacher may have raised the standard of work to that level, and the want of University—not collegiate—laboratories, wherein research work may be conducted, is in striking and humiliating contrast with the condition of things in the older Universities.

We have, then, an examining board; we have a most painfully heterogeneous collection of institutions systematically preparing students for the pass examinations of that board; we have, not only the need, but, in the Gresham College and elsewhere, the possibility, of University teachers, fellowships, and honour schools, and the problem, which still defies solution, is the establishment of the latter, and the coordination of all three into one great University worthy of the Imperial city. The difficulties that have wrecked the former schemes arose from the attempt to include or exclude institutions, as institutions, in the organization of the University governing body; and, reasoning from the experience of these attempts, and from what has arisen in controversy we may

18. "ART. VIII.-1. Minutes of Evidence Taken before the Royal Commissioners Appointed to Enquire Whether Any and What Kind of New University or powers is or are required for the advancement of Higher Education in London, 1889. 2. Draft Charter of the Albert University, 1891." *Quarterly Review* 174, no. 347 (January 1892): 251.

say, with confidence, that any scheme involving the direct representation of the governments of "constituent colleges" upon the controlling body of the new University is foredoomed to partial or entire failure. The representation of such bodies as the Incorporated Law Society is, of course, an altogether different matter.

It would also be impossible for the existing Senate of the London University to remain as at present, if there is to be complete co-operation in educational work and influence. A new Council, having the new responsibility of the University professoriate, must be created, and faculties erected, but not by the method of electing two members to represent and guard the financial integrity of High Street College, two to forward, in and out of season, the particular ambitions of the Civil Service (and University) School, and so on. The men upon the Council must represent not instructions, but departments of learning—not the interests of an endowment, but the cause of science and culture. Whether those who are in control of the destinies of the various London colleges, are educated to the pitch of such self-effacement as this involves, time alone can show, but so long as they persist in their demands, so long will the prospective University remain an incomplete and disappointing scheme, and so long will the present educational chaos of the county of London endure.

H.G.W.

The Future of Private Teaching

The University Correspondent, vol II, no 21, pp 12-13, 15 May 1892

Continuing his monthly contributions to The University Correspondent, *Wells here answers critics of private teaching ("good liquor often comes from an illicit still") by focusing on secondary schools. Earlier in the year, two bills for the Registration of Teachers had been introduced in Parliament, but with no agreement.*

The distribution of £60,000 among Scotch schools engaged in secondary education is imminent, the organization of secondary education in Wales proceeds apace, and here and there in English localities the technical-education funds have found their way to secondary schools. The Associated Chambers of Commerce demand "the reorganization of secondary education" in England, and "returns of the supply of schools above the elementary," and, sooner or later, the organization of middle-class education in the country appears to be inevitable. There seems to be a tendency on the part of many men, with inelastic and methodical minds, to anticipate a revolution in secondary teaching—to cast horoscopes of a pedagogic constitution, and of a drilled and disciplined, a rigid and pedantic, organization of secondary teachers in the future. There is to such men something particularly provoking in the existence and prosperity of numerous private schools—"illicit stills of learning," as one indignant speaker styled them, mindful of the revenue of "legitimate" teachers, and forgetful of the fact that good liquor often comes from an illicit still. And there is a by no means guarded attempt to bring all private schools under one common stigma of incapacity, and to exclude them altogether from consideration in the schemes of organization that are growing up in the minds of men.

Now we should be sorry to hold a brief for all private schools, in this discussion. No doubt private schools do graduate insensibly into the *crèche*, the cheap boarding-house, and the dumping ground for undesirable children; but, for this, registration might be a remedy. Such facts do not destroy the truth of the statements that private schools far more thorough and efficient than many public ones exist, and that the great majority of the members of the College of Preceptors, its active members—if not its figure-heads—are private schoolmasters, and that this college was the first to initiate local school examinations, and to endow lectures on the "Theory and Practice of Education." Indeed, it is scarcely too much to say that private enterprise has also been an important agent in whatever improvements have taken place in public schools in the direction of sounder educational work. The army crammer, for instance, is still the necessary complement of the fine torso of a public-school education, and makes the running for, and even, it is whispered, sometimes takes the prize from, the modern-side master of the endowed institution. One has only to inspect the class-lists of such an examination as the half-yearly one of the College of Preceptors to see how efficient, numerous, and important private schools are in this country, and how unique, therefore, the conditions are under which secondary education—if no rank injustice is to be done—must be organized here.

In fact the same complications are to be found in this question as arise in the Gresham University problem; the difficulty of drawing a sharp line between efficient and detrimental institutions, and the same objection follows to the policy of subsidizing this or that highly favoured school. To propose to establish a series of inspected, ruled, trained, and drilled "educationalists" throughout the country, side by side, and competing with, the efficient private teachers who already in many places amply meet the local requirements, is not only a wild disregard of public economy, but also scandalously unjust. The organization of secondary education in England will do more harm than good if it fails to recognise, assist, and encourage, efficient private enterprises, equally with those having a public of quasi-public character.

This can only be done by avoiding hard and fast discrimination between institutions, and any attempts to exact a uniform regulation of hours of teaching and choice of subjects. Possibly a capitation upon efficiently educated pupils, subject to their payment of an adequate fee, would furnish a means of aiding, without destroying the internal freedom or general initiative of, private establishments. Again, much might be done in urban neighbourhoods by the establishment of science and technical-training laboratories, lectureships, and the like, to be shared in common by all efficient schools, public or private, in the district. One thing must be insisted upon. Inspectors of secondary schools, if such inspectors are unavoidable, must be drawn from the ranks of experienced secondary teachers, and be advisers and reporters rather than judges, and the entire organization must be independent of the Education Department, and its government more representative and immediately accessible and responsible than that body. The distribution of the Scottish £60,000 by the hands of the existing Department is indeed the least satisfactory of all the signs of the impending organization of secondary education in England.

The Use and Abuse of the Text-book

Science and Art, vol VI, no 63, June 1892

This was written for the Science and Technology section of Science and Art, *and references the same topic as Wells's "The Too-Ambitious Text-book" of the previous year. Here the emphasis is on the teacher's relationship with the text-book, as well as the suitable elements of such a book for teaching science. Because teachers are not paid well and teach too many subjects, the text-book can provide help. But text-books for the private student (as Wells often was, as well as the students he taught by correspondence) must be different than those used in the classroom, where the teacher's interpretations should be primary. Wells's distaste for the rote learning in geography and history textbooks foreshadows his later writing about history.*

H.G. Wells, B.Sc., F.Z.S., L.C.P.

Beyond all question, the most difficult, and even dangerous, piece of apparatus to handle in class teaching is the text-book. Its use is as hard to learn as that of a bicycle; its abuse is as immediate and frequent as that of strong drink. To give directions of its full treatment would be presumption, but we may perhaps endeavour to point out a few of the conditions of its employment. The problem is complicated by many little weaknesses the text-book displays.

In the ideal world we visit seeking a rest from realities and finding discontent, the text-book scarcely exists as such. In that sublimer sphere, where there is a class there is an adequate teacher; there we also find a well-fitted class-room and laboratory; there are diagrams—beautiful, plain, and eloquent; there are museums with just what is wanted, and no incubus of parasitic curiosities; and, in short, there is everything to aid that adequate teacher's teaching. The students have ample leisure to elaborate their work, and their neat notes of his explicit statements, their richly observant copies of the well-displayed diagrams, and the suggestions of their own minds, working free from anxiety or hurry, constitute a text that grows with the growth of their knowledge.

First and foremost in the world of realities, among the considerations that stamp this dream as unreal, is

THE MISERABLE MATTER OF MONEY.

Only a University teacher can nurse just one class into knowledge; elsewhere, the popular ignorance of teaching necessities forces an attempt to teach several and even a great number of subjects upon teachers. No science teacher under the Education Department can afford to confine himself to one subject, and give his whole time to it. Hence the beautiful, plain, and eloquent diagrams we had imagined him creating, arranging, and using, the frequent personal help to individuals, and the other accessories to his lectures, sink in quality, diminish in number, and drop slowly, and at last altogether, out of the visions, as it approximates to the real.

The dream is even further shorn. We find a scale of payment that is barely remunerative for the time actually spent in teaching, and which certainly does not admit of the really adequate designing and preparation of diagrams and lessons, and the fitting-up and rehearsal of the necessary experiments. The teacher's demonstrations have often to be very unconvincing, and his incidental details may even be inaccurate; so that a text-book in which facts are stated with accuracy and precision, and in which the inevitable deficiency of diagrams is supplemented by numerous plain figures, becomes an absolute necessity in the earthly science class.

But even in the very ordinary science class, it should still be subordinate to the teacher. If the teacher is not at the head of the class, to introduce, to explain, and, above all, to

SET HIS STUDENTS' MINDS WORKING,

together with his own, he has no business to be there at all. The teacher's work it is, to build up the *ideas* of the science in the minds of his pupils, and to stimulate them to turn the facts over, to see them on many sides, to arrange them and rearrange them, and so make them their own. If it were not so, there is no reason why a teacher in London should not send off lessons to the whole of England, to be read aloud by the best reader among his pupils to the rest of the class assembled. Many a dreary hour of professorial monologue, however, testifies to the disregard of this consideration.

When, however, the conception is driven home, and the thing has been taught, then the text-book becomes useful, with its deliberately studied definitions and figures, and its carefully verified tables, to preserve the form and furnish detail to the lesson. That is evidently the primary function of the textbook in teaching.

There must, then, be

AN ESSENTIAL DIFFERENCE IN THE ORDER OF TREATMENT

of the text-book and the teacher. The teacher presumably starts with nothing in the pupil's mind, he calls attention to this phenomenon and that, gradually builds up a fabric of co-ordinated impressions, and works at last to the general law his lesson is to enunciate. His method must therefore be inductive; the text-book, on the other hand, will have the facts arranged in a more systematic way, with the wider law before, and embracing its branching manifestations and modifications. To be diffuse and explicit is a merit in a teacher, in a text-book there is a paramount need of conciseness and precision.

But such a type of book implies—imperatively requires, in fact—efficient teaching. What dangerous things quite useful hand-books may become in the hands of inefficient teachers is exemplified by the condition of affairs in middle-class schools with respect to lessons in geography. Dull, indolent, or over-worked masters long ago reduced this remarkably interesting subject to a horrible rote exercise, not through any intrinsic defect in the books, but in the teachers. Now there is a reaction, and we get such readable and picturesque—and from the class point of view impracticable—books as Prof. Meiklejohn's works.[19] These are models of

A SECOND AND ALTOGETHER DISTINCT TYPE,

the book for the unguided student: where there is an energetic teacher there is a discord of two voices, of two presentations of the subject, and like a badly arranged sounding-board they confuse rather than reinforce.

The treatise that is meant for reading and not for class use contrasts sharply with the hand-book—or should. It should be explicit, luminous, readable, and attractive, with diagrams as well as figures, and persuasion as well as facts. The want of recognition of this truth leads to a mongrel kind of production—here running into explanations, that are far better elucidated by the remarks and questions of teacher and pupil and which can only be of use to the solitary student, and there proliferating with questions that are of no earthly good to the solitary student because he cannot tell whether his answer may or may not be entirely wrong. And this must remain the case until authors and publishers recognize that the present division of aim is impossible, and restore to class-book, hand-book, text-book, and treatise, their etymological import.

The text-book would, from these considerations, appear to be liable to two serious abuses. The first abuse the author is guilty of when, instead of doing his work simply and precisely, he blazes into eloquence, and illuminates his pates with endless explanations and rocket-like figures of speech. Too often his coadjutor,

---

19. John Meiklejohn was a Scottish academic who published numerous books in history, geography, and literature, including several for Blackwood's Educational Series (1883-1887) and his own series beginning in 1894. He was known for his wit and humor.

in the figures and diagrams, and decorates them in the same festive spirit with glories of shading and triumphs of graceful line. So that the great pillars and beams of the science to be taught are masked under this doubtless attractive treatment, and the student never realizes the plain import of the fabric.

On the other hand, the teacher should be sensible that the textbook must be, after all, an unfurnished edifice, and that to place it in the hands of a class and expect them to find mental nourishment and comfort in it, without he invest it with such furniture, is absurd.

The exact converse to the proposition here advanced seems to be asserted in the late Mr. Quick's "Educational Reformers." "No epitomes," he says, and proceeds, as though the book was the teacher: "We will suppose that a parent meets with a book which he thinks will be both instructive and entertaining to his children. But the book is a large one, and would take a long time to get through; so, instead of reading any part of it to them, or letting them read it for themselves,

HE MAKES THEM LEARN BY HEART THE TABLE OF CONTENTS.

The children do *not* find it entertaining; they get a horror of the book, which prevents their ever looking at it afterwards, and they forget what they have learnt as soon as they possibly can. Just such is the sagacious plan adopted in teaching history and geography in schools, and such are the natural consequences. Every student knows that the use of an epitome is to systematize knowledge, not to communicate it, and yet, in teaching, we give the epitome first. . . ." Now this is altogether just, and yet the inference, "No epitomes," does not by any means follow. It does not seem to have occurred to Mr. Quick here that it is the duty of a teacher to teach, and he goes on, speaking of history—"What we want is a Macaulay for boys." Perhaps so, but Macaulay was a great talker as well as a vivid writer, and it is the teacher who should be the Macaulay, not the writer of class-books.

Possibly, in such a subject as history or even physiography a teacher may be unnecessary, or may teach best as a writer of readable books, but this does not apply to art, or to a great proportion of scientific work. There the too explicit text-book is an incompetent rival of the teacher, and an incumbrance instead of an auxiliary.

Apodidae

Educational Review, vol II, no 3, July/August 1892, pp226-227

It is in scientific analysis where Wells was willing to be most balanced, and also to split the finest hairs. His review of Bernard's book is highly technical, but acknowledges the contribution to knowledge of the scheme of biological relationships, even while its arguments don't hold. It is preceded in the issue by another review on Animal Coloration, but as David C. Smith acknowledges it is not clear whether that is also by Wells, so it is not republished here.

This new addition to the well-known "Nature" series has at least the merit of originality and capable treatment. It is full of suggestions, some of them of considerable merit, and is well worth the attention of the advanced student of Zoology, if only as an exercise in morphological discussion. Whether it has the same, or indeed any, value as a permanent addition to phylogenetic knowledge is an entirely different matter. The title appears to us to be singularly ill-chosen; instead of the systematic account of a group we anticipated, we find simply an argument for the worm-like character of that much debated type *Apus*, and some excursions into the wide subject of arthropod ancestry. That *Apus* represents most truthfully the foundation type of the various groups of true crustacea has long been on the whole the prevailing view of morphologists; that its nervous system is probably primitive in character, that its skeleton is imperfectly calcified, and that its hepato-pancreas is on the state of digestive diaticula and ciliated, have also been known. Hence to all who believe in the genetic connection of the annelids and crustacea its annelidan affinities followed. Mr. Bernard has attempted to establish this view upon the basis of a more exhaustive analysis. In doing this, he had especially to consider the following points which present difficulties, and in no case does it appear to us that these difficulties have been successfully attacked: the *Apus* coelom is, and its internal metamerism is not evident; there are no nephridia, there is an extensive proctodaeum; the ovum is centrolecithal; the spermatozoa are not filiform; there is no approach to the trochosphere in the nauplius, and the muscle is striated. In all these essential points *Apus* is typically crustacean, and does not diverge towards the annelid. Mr. Bernard describes a series of cavities through which the blood flows in *Apus*. He homologises the dorsal vessel (heart) with the similarly-placed vessel of the chaetopod, and the sinus containing the intestines and gonads with the chaetopod coelom. He assumes that the parietal coelomic epithelium has parted for the musculature of the body wall creating spaces comparable to lymph spaces. Yet the fluid which flows through this miscellaneous series of lacunae, he suggests, is equivalent to the pseud-haemal fluid of such a form as the earthworm, simply on the strength of its reddish colour. Mr. Bernard's attempt to show that the gonads are nephridia covered by peritoneal epithelium ("peritoneal" begging the whole question) because they branch, is perhaps the weakest point in the whole book. The other considerations we have advanced Mr. Bernard scarcely meets, or passes lightly over. The parallel figure of a polychaete parapodium and a phyllopod limb hardly needs serious discussion. By such figures and a little ingenuity any two things in the universe might be identified. Excepting the suggestion that the trilobites may be browsing annelids, and one or two others of minor importance, we find scarcely anything in this book that appears to us to be likely to become incorporated with the permanent mass of zoological knowledge. At the same time we would express our opinion that this volume has considerable value for the zoologist, perhaps more value than a rigorously correct text-book, inasmuch as it deals with anatomical facts in a manner that at once displays the relationships upon which their interest and importance depend. On this account, and with a warning against any hasty approval of any of Mr. Bernard's conclusions, we recommend this work to the student of zoological science.

H. G. W.

The Apodidae: A Morphological Study, By H. M. Bernard, M.A. (Macmillan.)

The Science of Education*

Educational Review, vol 1, no 4, September 1892, pp287-289

Geoffrey West's biography of Wells notes that in the autumn of 1892, Wells "was now at the climax of his career as a teacher".[20] He had made a favorable impression on his colleagues at the University Tutorial College in Red Lion Square teaching biology practicals in the laboratories, and had enough money to live on. In this review of a German book on educational philosophy, Wells uses extensive quotations to highlight the difficulty a reader might have reconciling the work's poor exposition with its excellent ideas. Johann Friedrich Herbart, who had died in 1841, promoted the idea that individual learning could be instilled as a foundation of moral character, encouraging a responsible contribution to society. His work was being revived in an age emphasizing moral character.

About the name of Herbart there centres, to the English reader, at first, an inexplicable contradiction. Here is an exponent of *Anschaung*, who leaves us sometimes in doubt as to his subject and meaning; a teacher to whom we go for instruction, and are given at first a headache. His works, to begin with, seem to raise the whole question of obscurity of style. Have we not here the ancient fallacy of education in the promulgation of a new educational gospel?—perfect precept as a heinous example? or is it that his message can have no clearer exposition? I think it is Canon Daniel who has remarked that the same laws should guide the teacher to consecutiveness, and the writer to readableness. Before everything else, an educational writer might be expected to be assimilable. But Herbart is, to say the least of him, crabby. If a book is written merely to preserve the tradition that in such a year a man reached certain altitudes of truth, there can be no objection to condensation and to carelessness of arrangement. But the conditions are altogether different if the work is to serve as a guide and help for feebler aspirants to the same altitude. For the toilers below there is little comfort in the name of Herbart written high up across an insurmountable hiatus. How did he get there is the absorbing question? "I studied; you must study too," appears, at first sight, to be the only answer proffered. If all the roughness is still to be climbed, the *Science of Education* is not a monumental road, but a roadside monument. We can appreciate its meaning by the time that we no longer need it. Treasure found and hidden again is as good as if it had never been discovered.

After all, though, we may be exaggerating the difficulties of Herbart.

---

20. West, Geoffrey. *H.G. Wells: A Sketch for a Portrait.* London: Gerald Howe Ltd, 1930, p90.

Repeated study of his book brings to light a certain formulated system. Much of the difficulty in grasping his suggestions at first arises from the nature of his fundamental views. Nowadays, the stronger tendency in educational thought is to regard child-mind and child-body as an organism together, to liken the educationalist to the gardener tending a plant. Like the gardener, the teacher adds no new thing to his plant's existence, supplies no developmental force, but simply guards it from frost, drought, and other deprivation. His work is with the accidentals. With the results of the incessant struggle for life of the generations of the past, with the destiny this past has impressed upon the individual career, he knows he has no power to interfere. His ideal is one of health and fulness, drawn from his experience of beautiful lives. But Herbart's writings are in a phraseology that jars with this. Apparently he considered that the mind, unlike the body, has no clearly defined possibilities of growth. As his translators express it in their singularly sound and valuable introduction— "To the true educator, he maintains, is given a vaster and nobler work, viz., *to penetrate the innermost core of the mind germ* entrusted to his keeping . . . . to inoculate it with thoughts, feelings, desires it could never otherwise have obtained." Herbart is of the school of 'creative' educationalists; he would make men, and he has a vision of humanity, power, fulcrum, and weight, all at once, raising itself by its own efforts in self-culture towards perfection. "Humanity," he says, "educates itself continuously by the circle of thought which it begets."

When this difference is clearly realized, then, and then only, this book begins to appear valuable to those who take the biological view, who accept the gardener image of the teacher's scope. We have found the clue to our author's language. Herbart was no mere theorizing professor of philosophy; he was always an earnest experimental teacher, and so soon as we begin to transpose into the key of our own thought, the value of his results becomes conspicuous. Having divested ourselves of the distressing idea that the philosophical secret of education is enigmatically hidden in the book, we are free to appreciate its merits. In recommending a psychological order of study it presents nothing very new to the English educational student, though, of course, at the epoch of its publication this must have been one of its most novel features, but we know of no work that contains anything like the discussions of moral development and discipline that we find here, as regards both precision and applicability.

Then here, for instance, is an intensely practical and suggestive passage:—

"Let every affected manner be banished from instruction! Catechising as well as dogmatising, fun as well as pathos, polished speech as well as sharp accent—all are distasteful, as soon as they seem arbitrary additions, and not to proceed from the subject and state of mind. But out of many things and situations there are developed many modes and turns of the lesson. Hence, that which teachers have discovered and so abundantly recommended under the high-sounding name of Methods, will increase more and more, and can be variously used without one or other gaining unconditional superiority. The teacher must be capable of many happy turns, he must vary with facility, must adapt himself to opportunity, and while playing with the accidental must so much the more emphasise the essential."

Then, again, what teacher may not learn something from such counsel as this:—

"The great activity of healthy children, which their need of movement expresses, the constant stratagems of inconstant natures, even the coarse pleasures of those who give indications of a wild manliness—all these apparent signs of future character do not reveal to the teacher so much as a single silent, well-weighed, compassed act of a settled mind, or as the single steadily maintained defiance of an otherwise docile child. And here therefore much reflection must be united with observation. Firmness, properly speaking, never exists in children; they cannot resist the *variation of the circle of thought* which is borne in on them from so many sides—among others it is to be hoped from the side of the teacher. But where an action of a child shows decided inclination, armed by deliberation, discipline can effect hardly anything, unless we reckon it something that, firstly, after opportunities have been cut off, capability can no longer be produced by exercise, in which case we need only take care to cut the opportunities entirely off; and that, secondly, the teacher can restrain the imagination by lively and attractive occupations of another kind, which again comes under the head of influence upon the circle of thought. Let this be taken to heart when any kind of ingrained perversity is to be exterminated, and discipline must mainly be used to that end. In such cases desist totally from severe punishments. Such are suitable when an isolated new inclination breaks out thoughtlessly as a fault for the first or second time, which, without fear, would be repeated, and engrave a wrong trait on the character. Discipline in such cases must interfere immediately and decidedly. Thus the *first* self-interested lie can hardly be too severely punished, hardly warned against too often by repeated admonitions gradually becoming gentler, hardly be made too hateful by pain penetrating deeply to the innermost soul. Such treatment would make, on the other hand, the deliberate liar even more deceitful and insidious. The false relation in which he places himself ought gradually to close around him with increasing pressure: this, however, is no good alone—the whole mind must be raised, the possibility of winning for himself respect, which is incompatible with lying, must be made perceptible and valuable to him. But can anyone accomplish this who does not possess the art of affecting the circle of thought from all sides? or do you think a few isolated speeches and admonitions will effect it?"

And so as we read, here and there Herbart's meaning takes hold of us, and the note of condemnation and dismay with which we commenced passes therewith insensibly into praise. In brief, this is a book for every teacher to read in with profit, but it is a book that few teachers will care even to read through. Sit down to it and you are dismayed, glance through it and you are delighted with the wisdom it contains.

H. G. W.

* *The Science of Education.* By Johann Freidrich Herbart, Professor of Philosophy in the University of Göttingen. Translated from the German, with a Biographical Introduction, by Henry M. and Emmie Felkin, and a Preface by Oscar Browning, M.A. (Swan Sonnenschein & Co.)

On the True Lever of Education

The Journal of Education, vol XIV, no 279, pp 525-527, 1 October 1892

One of Wells's most dramatic pieces on school examinations, this article was the first of his to be reprinted in an American journal, The Educational Review (U.S.). *His literary ambitions are evident in his depictions of the examiners as misguided, destructive entities in education, even monsters loosed upon the populace. Examiners, he writes, are subject experts, but forget that the object is to demonstrate intellectual processes rather than present pat conclusions. In the case of practical science, since the "examiner pipes and the teacher must dance", reform must happen first with the examinations, not the curriculum. Wells's first-person approach in the introduction is unusual, and indicates a new confidence.*

I shall never believe very much in educational reformers until they commence a vigorous mission to examiners. Indeed, I would almost say that the examiner is, under existing conditions, the educational reformer's only legitimate game. But such a generalization as that requires consideration. Whether it is true or not, there can be no doubt that the educational reformer neglects the examiner shamefully. Reviling "the fetish of examinations," be it understood, is an altogether different thing. In that the element of personality is eliminated, and this factor is really the gist of the whole matter. To eliminate personality is always the trick of a reformer who is eager for a cause, but not earnest for a fight. Then, you see, there is nobody in particular to hit him back. But the worth of the cause is affected.

Examinations may be anything, and indeed also almost, or even absolutely, nothing. "The fetish of examination," therefore, takes its particular character in particular cases through the intermediation of its priests. Where they are benevolent and wise, it is essentially a beneficent deity; and only where they are vain, weak, mean, or foolish, does it become a Juggernaut. The malignant and the misguided examiner are the real foemen of the teacher, and these we must carefully mark out, and then in due manner assail, if our world-mending enterprises are to be anything more than so much valiant defiance of windmills or mere beating of the air.

The teacher may as well dream of getting himself made exempt from gravitation, or altogether fireproof, as to think he will some day be free of examiners, good or bad. The teacher must, from the nature of things, be under the heel of the examiner all his life, as inevitably as he must face death at the end of it. In the happily dying state of affairs, the parent—rather *both* parents, worse luck!—were his sole examiners *ex officio*. Their syllabus was rigid, but peculiar.

Much attention was given to his personal appearance; he might, for instance, be ploughed for hats, or be distrusted, and lose marks, through his necktie. His wife, too, was a "compulsory subject," and he had to steer her a difficult course between commonness and uppishness. Practical—even ostentatious—religion was a *sine quâ non*, and social science, within limits. It was expected that he should sympathize with "little Georgie," be firm and kind in accordance with erratic and variable standards, and possess encyclopædic knowledge; but in this last requirement the examiners were anything but searching. Many of us have worked—and some are still working, some with special aptitude, and some with active protest, dying sullenly down to cynical acceptance in the course of time—to meet the requirements of this unwritten syllabus. Happily, nowadays, in many cases, the parent has seen fit to delegate his duties, and he will probably do still more in that direction in the future. At least one hopes so. Part of the bitter cry against set and definite examinations comes, I fancy, from the experts at the old requirements.

And, in the future, if the titular examiner be torn down from his present eminence and altogether done away with, it will only be that something more indefinite and less accessible to criticism will replace him. There must always be some discrimination between teacher and teacher, unless each of those who would teach is given his mathematical share of the great total of youth—his quota of

$$\frac{\text{number of pupils}}{\text{number of teachers}}$$

The teacher, if he does not prepare himself and his pupils for the sporadic or periodical inspection of a specially appointed and specially prepared authority, with some finality of decision, must work with an eye to a more informal judgment—to Governor A., who dislikes to hear boys about after meal-times; to Governor B., with Macaulay's ideal of omniscience; to Governor C, who takes his stand on Rousseau; and to Governor D., who detests sports. The examiner, in short, the teacher has always with him, the shadow is he that displays the teacher's material solidity, and from the desk of the junior assistant he is by us, even to the grave.

The teacher lives with the examiner as his dominant condition. But these educational reformers write as though the teacher had no conditions—as though he was as free as a Lamia to take whatever beautiful form he might fancy. They keep on writing for the teacher to do this and that and the other in the way of improvement, while they might as well preach perfection to the clay in the potter's hands. I suppose I have read in the last year in various publications more than a hundred new happy suggestions and incontrovertible criticisms of scholastic methods: how geography may be made a joy, science a discipline toward perfection, and history a dream of delight. And the old things go on. These improvements are no more than teachers' day dreams. The examiner pipes and the teacher must dance— and the examiner sticks to the old tune. If the educational reformers really wish the dance altered they must turn their attention from the dancers to the musicians.

Something perhaps might be done by instituting examinations for examiners. Examiners are, in nine cases out of ten, simply experts at special branches of knowledge or art; they have about as much special aptitude and training to sort students, when they begin, as a class, as they have to cut out suits of clothes, or act as tea-tasters. The typical examination, two or three hours of hard writing, which is so commonly reviled as if it were the only kind of examination possible, is the natural refuge of these unfortunates. In many cases, being simple-minded seekers after truth or beauty, they are less qualified than common people to detect subterfuge and specious vagueness. In many cases their interest is not in examinations at all, and they follow precedents—indolently. In many cases they live, as it were, in the border land of knowledge, and have forgotten the paths that led them there. They ask for conclusions that may be learnt by heart, and not for evidence of an intellectual process. Like worthy medieval householders, staff and scallop shell are evidence enough to them of a pilgrimage. In all these cases the examiners understand the subject of examination well enough, but the object not all. They seem to think that the examination is a genteel substitute for a raffle for places—or it is an inexplicable duty, like a Philistine's church-going—or it is an insistence upon orthodoxy, like the Inquisition. And they keep on at the tune that chance or the spirit of mischief has put into their heads, and the teacher, perforce, dances thereunto.

Perhaps the examiner who is an educational theorist is better than his peers. It may be. I believe indeed that if every examiner were forced to read something about, and think about, the theory of examinations, it would be very much better for us. But the great improvement needed is a moral one. Examiners examine so badly because they fail to appreciate their terrible responsibility. We want to awaken some inkling of this in their minds; to lift them out of their stupid moral insensibility. I believe if some examiners, complacent enough now, could be brought face to face with the mischief they are doing, in a concentrated concrete form, they would drop their brief authority forthwith and flee utterly away. What a terrible mass it would be in the aggregate—an inchoate horror wrought of minds that might have thought and were set to rote learning, minds that might have learnt and acted and were flattened out in books, souls that might have created, but instead they died, a Frankenstein monster of duty ill done, a living decay!

The examiner should in the first place be a philosopher. Instead, for our examiners we take specialists. He should have considered before all things the relation of his particular culture to the whole world of human thought and action. He should have asked himself why his candidates are studying in his particular realm of excellence; how they may study at the greatest permanent profit to themselves, and how at the least. He should know enough of their thoughts and feelings to know how he looks in their eyes and in those of the teacher. He must be able to plan his questions so that proper methods must, in the phrase of the coach and examinee, *pay* for the examination, and improper methods be a waste of time. He must be a philosopher, then, in the old sense of one having wide and comprehensive views, thinking of the scope of knowledge and of the aims and ends of things. After that he needs most urgently some actual experience of the kind of teaching he is to examine. And thirdly—essential, perhaps, but quite after these other things—comes an exhaustive knowledge of his subject.

These specialists, on the other hand, have no sense of proportion. Each candidate seems to them to be an aspirant to specialization in their particular branches; at least they treat them as if they were such aspirants. The end of a secondary school course in English one would imagine to be a sufficient command of that language to read and appreciate the shades of an author's intention and to write and speak discriminatingly. Perhaps English is also useful as an exercise in classificatory method. The specialist examiner, however, would make it a field for recondite learning, and sets youngsters, who could as soon fly as write pure English, investigating the value of the terminal-*t* in *that*. Again, in science, the specialist's ideal of a practical examination is to demand manipulation that will be useful for research. The London University examination in biology, which, if properly handled, might force upon every medical aspirant so much mental culture as a sound appreciation of organic evolution involves, is, among many excellences, disfigured by the extraordinary prominence given to certain tricks of dissection—the extraction, unbroken, of a very small organ (the ovary) from the earthworm, for instance, and the discovery of a minute branch of the tenth nerve in the rabbit. In training students to perform such dodges as these, the time of a teacher is necessarily taken from really educational work, and the mechanical crammer, endowed or unendowed, finds a sufficient excuse for his misdeeds in the examiner's weakness.

There is a certain type of examiner whose idea seems to be just to take as little trouble as possible. Now practical examinations are a bother. So much has been said of the necessity of practical examinations in natural science and (in the form of oral tests) in languages, that they need hardly be advocated here. The principle that, to test a knowledge of things, especially in the case of the young, whose descriptive powers are feeble, one must examine with things, is a truism of educational science. Yet withal these practical examinations are long in coming.

Examining bodies seem to be waiting for the schools to substitute practical for legendary teaching before they make any innovation—a policy which certainly has a powerful element of permanence. Sometimes a well-meaning examiner admits the weakness of his position. At the last London Matriculation examination, for instance, the examiner in one particular science asked his candidates to describe only experiments they had actually seen.

One can fancy what happened. Picture to yourself two candidates, A. and B.—A. from an experimental teacher, B. from the ideal mechanical crammer of the pedagogic fabulists. A. remembers the experiment distinctly, and the formulæ that represent it, piles up—in vast Cyclopean masses—his description, speaks of the pneumatic trough as a pan, calls flasks bottles, and beakers glasses, wanders wordily, losing his thread and finding it again, and ends his career in a dirty smashed-up drawing of what he fancies he saw, and the correct formulæ. B., fresh from the hands of a patent grinding and polishing mill, disregards, of course, the examiner's admonition, and turns out from his memory a sketch he has learnt—by repeated copying—of the experiment in question. Pithy words explain this: no verbosity, no wordy clouding, no evidence whatever of the thought obscuring the thing. Picture now the assistant examiner weighing the two papers! How else can it be when a knowledge of things is tested by purely verbal methods?

Unless they improve too rapidly—of which, at present, there is apparently no serious danger—teaching follows after examinations, formal or informal. There, then, is the objective point for the educational reformer. The teacher may be worried and made discontented, he may even "quarrel with his bread and butter," but the teaching will not be seriously affected, by any exhortations of the educational reformer in his direction. His answer—firm and, considering the provocation, remarkably inoffensive and quiet—to the reformer is this: "Will you, please, mind your own particular business—over there—and leave me, for the present, alone?" So far as scope and method go, the examiner is the educational lever; and when the educational reformer is not at that lever he is, I humbly submit, wasting his time.

H. G. Wells

The Miscellaneous as an Educational Curriculum

Educational Review, vol 3, no 1, pp 10-14, November 1892

Written with A. T. ("Tommy") Simmons, his friend from the Normal School of Science and editor of The School World, *this is the only article in this collection not written by Wells alone. According to David C. Smith in his biography of Wells, the hope was that satire about education would help examiners and educationalists change their ways. After this article was published, Wells's approach would shift to persuade more with reason than with humor, and would be better received.[21] Here the two satirize the common curriculum.*

Man plans but Destiny perfects. Men say let this or that be done, arguing logically, clearly, convincingly; objection is raised and battle joined, with opinions whirling and fierce invective succeeding, and all the time the loom of causation never ceases, the silent warp and woof of things mingle as men shout their little ideas of what ought and shall be promptly brought about. Wisdom, experience, all authorities differ widely in the reviews, and meanwhile in the background to their influential deliberate discussion, general folly, prejudice, and common sense strike the balance this way or that.

And so while educationalists talk of the merits of this scheme of education or that, and while some say that Greek is the highway to perfection, and some that science was appointed by nature before men began to be, while another argues that language is best but prefers German to Greek, and another sings the praises of pure mathematics, but less loudly—silently and inevitably the question is settled for us, and the *Miscellaneous* takes form among us as an educational curriculum.

The Miscellaneous is the natural expression of "liberal opinions," that want of conscience, that intellectual silliness that has a pride in believing in everything a little, and nothing much. We are "neither scoffers nor fanatics," indeed we are in earnest about nothing, and like yokels at a fair we gape at everything in turn, and think we are taking a fine impartial view of the world. And in the schools around us meanwhile the Miscellaneous arises and figures with Nature's grave sarcasm, our chaotic minds.

The nature of the new curriculum will be understood by a description of the course of a pupil up the ladder from the gutter to the university and what he knew after his education was complete. It will be perceived by intelligent teachers

21. Smith, David C. *H.G. Wells: Desperately Mortal.* New Haven and London: Yale University Press, 1986, p 41.

that he need be a person of powerfully discursive intelligence.

A. B. was born into an infinite and otherwise perplexing universe amongst people on a very low social level in a very ordinary English town, furnished with a quite ordinary board school. To this school he went more or less regularly and was under the charge of energetic board school teachers for seven years. Their sole endeavor was to turn him out sufficiently moulded to the code pattern to earn a grant. He learnt the three R's, and had it not been for a peculiar intonation in reading, learnt them well. On this foundation was erected what is called an elementary knowledge (but what Leibnitz[22] would describe as an obscure or confused one) on geography, algebra, mechanics (without mathematics) under the name of a specific subject, drawing and (after school) a little French, so that he could read a French book, with the verbs all regular and no idioms, without difficulty. He could draw a bilaterally symmetrical copy passably well, work out, like a slide rule, *s. g.* and other strange things if the questions were put in the right form, tell you that Pernambuco was off the coast of Singapore and knew his way with a little asking to Cotopaxi or Yakutsk.

Being a bright, intelligent boy, he passed the 7th Standard early, and succeeded in taking a scholarship at the local technical school, where a series of disconnected science classes in connection with The Department and the County Council was held. Here, with much persuasion and argument between the science teacher and the schoolmaster on the one hand and the parents on the other, he was allowed to stay for two years. His course of study was remarkably catholic. Hygiene, inorganic chemistry, steam, wood-carving and cheese-making, physiography, shorthand, mineralogy, mathematics, perspective drawing, were studied simultaneously. A. B. found it rather perplexing, but he struggled on, and was successful in earning payments for his teachers, and even in getting some knowledge for himself. At last his parents insisted upon his *doing something for himself*, as they called it, and to compromise with his schoolmaster, and because it was so respectable, he was made a pupil teacher in his old school, and revived his itinerary to Cotopaxi, his useful receipts for the *s. g.*, and his always wonderful teachings about *a + b*, yearly. On every hand the same advice was given him: "Study hard." But there were none who seemed able to advise him what to study. He prepared his work for his yearly P.T. exams; and to get enlightenment, of which he felt a need, beyond this P.T. work, he attended University Extension lectures in medieval history, commercial geography, Dante, and the colours of flowers. Being an earnest P.T. he secured certificated in these departments of knowledge. He also attended classes in Christian evidences under the curate, and was made a fervent atheist for a year of two.

---

22. Philosopher Gottfried Leibniz wrote in his "Meditations on Knowledge, Truth, and Ideas" in 1684 that knowledge is either clear or obscure.

But the evening classes at the Technical School took up most of his leisures. The idea of a scholarship at South Kensington was suggested to him by his grant-earning science teachers, and he forthwith began working for it. This meant a wonderful development of the Miscellaneous. The hint he received was, that he must take about twelve subjects in the May Examinations and do fairly well in them. This competition became his dominant idea, sleeping and waking. Machine construction, Geology, Hygiene, Human Physiology, Agriculture, Astronomy (without Mathematics), Botany, were all started in addition to those subjects he has begun before. Two years ceaseless grind with a result of some nine "advanced firsts," one "elementary first" and two "elementary seconds," obtained for him a National Scholarship at the age of 16, and he proceeded to South Kensington.

A.B. had now become a student at the Royal College of Science, and imagined he had obtained a haven of intellectual tranquility, and that, with steady study, he would soon be one of the leading scientists of the world—but disappointment awaited him. He began with chemistry, and, with the exception of a few hours at mathematics and freehand drawing, he did nothing else all day. This pleased him—it seemed so satisfactory to at least be studying something "thoroughly." But, ere long, contact with older students and teachers opened up new things to be worked for. In the future, they said, the associateship of his college, with no university degree, would be of very little use in obtaining a good appointment. One does not live by knowledge alone. He decided, therefore, to matriculate at the London University in order to take a Science degree. For this, Latin, French, English had to be acquired. His Latin composition was a wonderful thing indeed. These things were studied during hours when he should be taking exercise. He became an undergraduate, and continued his scientific work with physics, mechanics, and geometrical drawing. He decided to work more fully at physics during his third year, so that biology had to be taken privately, and, as it were, surreptitiously, for his university needs. He took his examination with honours in physics. Hearing of open scholarships at Cambridge, he entered and obtained one in natural science, and left London, after three years' stay there, an Associate of the Royal College of Science, and a London undergraduate.

At Cambridge he encountered the "little go," and found a difficulty with Greek. But by this time keen must have been the examiner and abstruse the "subject" to foil A. B. Greek was put away neatly with the "Matric." Latin and French, the University Extension Dante, the S. and A. Department Agriculture, in the ever-growing Miscellaneous stores of A. B.'s mind. After this he gave himself up to the science of physics, which he loved. And in the second year of his stay at Cambridge it dawned upon him that his mathematical knowledge was inadequate, that many excellent things are written about physics in French, which he did not read with ease, and in German which was unknown to him. Gallantly, but very unwisely, A. B. started into the remoter regions of the calculus, and began German in the fatal final year, and alas! there was no Fellowship.

So he—being more or less unfitted for the headship in a school where theological considerations might come in (the ill effects of the curate's well-meant Christian evidences class still rankling in his mind) became an assistant-master on the modern side, conceived a growing distaste for study, and decided to abide in this position, since there was no better open, all his days. There we met him, and in the course of a treacherous friendship sounded his knowledge and unfolded his story. Here is a truthful schedule of the mental equipment of a by no means lowly M.A., aged thirty, educated on the new Miscellaneous curriculum. Our notes are given as they were originally jotted down in odd intervals while we betrayed him.

ARTS

Art of Teaching—By the grace of Heaven, a little.
Wood Carving—Certificated; indifferent; cut his finger once.
Freehand Drawing—From copies, fair; from nature or memory—seemed to be unaware that ordinary people could do this.
Shorthand—Could construe the "correspondence" style slowly, and wrote well with care and attention.
Perspective Drawing—Had forgotten something about V. P., whatever that may be, and everything it seems hinges on V. P. in perspective drawing.
Geometrical Drawing—None.

LANGUAGES

French—Could read only; never saw jokes in this language.
German—Could misunderstand with the help of a dictionary.
Latin—Remembered much of the accidence, especially some mnemonic verses.
Greek—A lively hate and dread; soundings impossible.
English—Loose and inelegant; tendency to employ terms in a technical sense in ordinary conversation; difficulty with the subjunctive.

SCIENCES

Mathematics and Mechanics—An extensive knowledge, but insufficient for the higher physics.

Physics—A considerable knowledge.

Inorganic Chemistry—A considerable knowledge.

Organic Chemistry—Very little.

Astronomy—Nebular conceptions.

Botany and Zoology—Pour rire.

Animal Physiology—A store of facts, mainly erroneous.

Mineralogy—An extensive vocabulary.

Geology—An extensive knowledge; names, mixed; facts, faulted.

Hygiene—A passion for sitting in draughts, and strong opinions about drainage.

Agriculture—Abstruse knowledge, but did not know oats from rye.

Cheese-making—Expert knowledge, but mistook the smell of old Dutch for drainage. See under Hygiene.

Steam—Knew he had a Science and Art Department Certificate but forgot where it was.

Commercial Geography—Had very peculiar views as to the proportionate size of Genoa and the universe; seemed to imagine Genoa and commerce were synonymous terms. Something wrong with extension lectures here (?).

Science of Teaching—None.

Dante—Had real all this poet's works except the "Inferno", and knew most of the names and dates connected with him. Admired him greatly.

Shakespeare—Had never read the "Tempest."

Milton—Thought him a bore, but a great poet.

Colours of flowers—Identified them at sight.

Theology—Ideas vague but decided.

History of the Middle Ages—A considerable knowledge.

History of our own Times—Knew practically nothing.

ÆSTHETIC CULTURE

Music—Did "Sol-fa" (?) singing. Liked "Tiddy-Follol", whatever that may be.

Fine Art—Catholic tastes; seemed to consider any R.A. a great artist *ex-officio*. Admired old masters.

Decoration—Wore a bright green tie with a magenta barred hat-band.

Literature—Admired Dante, and Mr. Gladstone's style. Read little save the newspaper and Jerome K. Jerome.

Physique—Absent.

[What he would have been without Greek, heaven only knows!]

Now it seems to us—and we sincerely hope that A. B., M.A., will not penetrate the veil of our anonymity—that this man, considered even as a modern side master, is a poor creature. From the standpoint of the artist—musical, pictorial, or literary—he is not highly educated. From the standpoint of the old-fashioned scholar (and gentleman) he is not highly educated. No scientific specialist—not even a physicist now—would say he was highly educated in any particular branch of science. He teaches, just as a costermonger's boy sells cabbages, by imitating his fellows. From the old Roman standpoint he is certainly not highly educated. His training has done nothing to make him steadfast in the presence of misfortune and calm at the approach of death. From the Lord Chesterfield point of view he is not educated. He has little ease in the presence of his fellow man, and no courtesy. From the brutal point of view of the intelligent savage he is a lamentable failure. If he were left out all night on the downs in January he would probably be entirely spoilt as an organism by morning. It is only gradually that we have arrived at our own conclusion, and it is with some misgiving even now, and after leading up to it in this way, that we venture to propound the statement that A. B. is not educated at all. The man was not a powerful original genius, but he meant well. He was industrious, he was intelligent, to a certain extent he was ambitious. Now he is—what shall we say?—a graduate. Still, we would not have it thought that we are carping on the existence of a ladder from the gutter to the university, or, indeed, criticising unfavourably anybody or anything. We have written this little paper merely to call attention to The Miscellaneous as really the definitely-established higher education of the time, and to a typical product. A moral would be contrary to the spirit of the age.

A. T. S.

H. G. W.

Professor Laurie on Herbert Spencer

The Educational Times, vol XLV, no 380, pp 516-517, 1 December 1892

Simon Somerville Laurie was Bell Professor of Education at the University of Edinburgh. A well-respected expert in the field, the previous year he had testified to a Parliamentary committee in his role as president of the Teachers' Guild. He promoted consistent teacher education while emphasizing local control. To criticize this gentleman's work was rather daring, yet it is clear Wells felt obligated to defend Spencer against unfair criticism.

To the Editor of the Educational Times.

Sir,—The paper by Professor Laurie, which appeared in the November issue of the *Educational Times*, is one which arouses a considerable amount of dissent in my mind. I was, unfortunately, unable to attend the meeting at which it was read, and, even had I been there, I should not have greatly cared to have ventured a criticism upon it on the spur of the moment. Under these circumstances, I shall feel myself greatly indebted to you for your courtesy if you will permit me now to question his conclusions. I am strengthened in this request by the fact that Professor Laurie's paper is not merely a criticism of opinion, but a proposal—pretty plainly made—to remove Herbert Spencer's work altogether from the reach of young teachers.

We are told that Herbert Spencer's teaching is not Christianity. This itself is a very serious consideration to many, but to me it does not seem a very serious matter, so long as his premises are good and his arguments sound. If his testimony is true, though his profession may be agnostic or atheistic, he must, as far as he goes, harmonize with Christianity, if Christianity also is true. His limited wisdom will be better altogether, I hold, than the foolishness of the orthodox. If his testimony concerning education is false, it falls by its own defect. In either case the direct reference to Christianity, in a nation where the profession of Christianity is as good as all the virtues, lacks as much in fairness as it gains dialectically. To speak of Christ and Spencer as teachers diametrically opposed begs the whole question. It does not follow that a man who does not call himself Christian is Antichrist, or that he who saith, "Lord, Lord," is a soldier in the hosts of heaven.

And now, coming to the real arguments of Professor Laurie's paper, it appears to me that the case he has made out against Herbert Spencer rests chiefly upon the—to me—strange meanings he attaches to "proximate end" and "natural." Only allow that Herbert Spencer intended, by some strange aberration, the same things, in these words, that Professor Laurie conceives, and the whole of the vigorous chastisement of the paper is nothing more than Herbert Spencer deserves—yea, even to the holding of the comparison of his teaching to "Roman thought" an insult to the latter.

"Proximate end" Professor Laurie reads "end," simply. The word "proximate," however, has a certain qualifying effect. The end a soldier may be fighting for may be the liberty of his country, but the proximate end of his fighting may be simply to get a bayonet under another man's midriff. "Proximate" means, in fact, the more immediate, the nearest of a series. It is hard, however, to avoid drifting towards the conclusion—and harder still to accept it—that Professor Laurie regards it as a clipped form of "approximate." He writes : "The attainment of a proximate end in the *sense of an approximation to an ideal end* "! Is this a misconception or a misrepresentation; or how can Professor Laurie explain the thing away?

Unless the proximate end of education is simply a respectable livelihood for respectable people—a lowly thought that does not seem to have occurred to Herbert Spencer—is it not the preparation of a child for the "business of life"? Professor Laurie has not told us his own idea of the true proximate end, and it would be interesting to see wherein it differed from that of Herbert Spencer.

That Herbert Spencer has no place, in his philosophy, for high ideals, is altogether new to me. The chief impression the "Data of Ethics" left upon my mind, was the profound conviction of the reasonableness of self-sacrifice, and the folly and unnaturalness of individual selfishness. This man, Herbert Spencer himself, has been undeniably sowing truth with a single heart—which, I take it, is the intellectual part of the service of God; and to speak of him as the prophet of "beer and skittles," simply because he has not yet reached the same spiritual level as Professor Laurie, is distinctly hard. Professor Laurie, from his higher standpoint, has, as it were, hurled the crucifix at Herbert Spencer's head. I do not propose, in a discussion such as this, to follow this example and to deal too freely with sacred things, but I cannot resist calling attention to the consistency of the passage: "According to Spencer, Christ on the cross, and all the crucified and self-sacrificed martyrs, were enjoying the greatest sum of pleasure possible for them. . . . According to Spencer, it was foolish of Christ and the others; they were mistaken. They were blind to their environment." Either this is self-contradictory, or it contradicts Professor Laurie's statement elsewhere that Herbert Spencer regards pleasure as the only sane human end.

After this, it is not surprising to find that "natural" means, to Professor Laurie, "physical," and that the mutual affection of parent and child is unnatural. We are told: Poor " Spencer gets so muddled over his natural reactions that he begins, towards the end of this chapter, to see that he is somehow wrong, and says that the disapprobation of the parent or teacher is itself a 'natural reaction.'" I have carefully gone over the chapter, and I do not see, myself, that Spencer is "muddled"; and, even if he is, it would have more become Professor Laurie, as an exponent of the higher morality of the Christian, to have used a gentler and more charitable word.

These are my chief objections to Professor Laurie's paper. If it were not for these, I should be inclined to regard it as one of the most valuable, as it is certainly one of the most important, of recent contributions to educational science. Even as it is, I have read it with the greatest interest and benefit. But these objections, unless they are disposed of, completely destroy Professor Laurie's case for the addition of Herbert Spencer's "Education" to the *Index Expurgatorius.*—I am, Sir. very faithfully yours,

H. G. WELLS.

Doctor Collins Upon the Educational Outlook

The University Correspondent, Vol III, no 28, pp 9-10, 15 December 1892

Here Wells returns to the arguments about the Gresham University scheme by focusing on the efforts of Dr. W. J. Collins. William Job Collins had been the doctor staying at Uppark when Wells had arrived with lung hemorrhage five years before, and had treated Wells's condition. According to Wells's autobiography, he had been a "young heretic" of a doctor, and had refuted that Wells was a consumptive. Wells described him as a Positivist, a devotee of Comte's ideas of human progress. Here he promotes Collins's views on the University of London, and his own. Since Wells's main concern was the fate of the private student, he wanted to promote Collins's candidacy to the University's Senate. The classical dialogue format was an effective way to introduce a variety of issues.

The recent vacancy in the Senate of the University of London, occasioned by the death of Lord Sherbrooke, will shortly, as our readers know, be filled by the vote of Convocation, and among the candidates for the suffrages of the members of that body is Dr. W.J. Collins, who has long been recognised as the most prominent defender of the status of the private student. Dr. Collins has, in the past, taken a conspicuous share in the internal politics of the University; his was one of the leading figures in the stormy overthrow of the unhappy reconstruction scheme that preceded the "Albert" University proposal, and he distinguished himself in the brisk agitation that led to the arrest of the latter project at the eleventh hour. Only a few weeks since, he gave evidence before the Gresham University Commission as a representative of the views of Convocation. He is a Doctor of Medicine, Master of Surgery, and Bachelor of Science, a University Scholar and Gold Medallist in Obstetric Medicine, and he took, with a gold medal, in 1887, the now abandoned Diploma in Public Health. He is an active member of the London County Council, and in that capacity he is also— unless Mr. Acland[23] break his legislative promises—likely to have, before long, an influential part in certain other educational affairs. His sturdy efforts in their interest should appeal to all the private students among our readers, and it was

---

23. Sir Arthur Acland was a Liberal politician who was know for educational policy. An MP for Rotherham from 1885-1899, his achievements would include making elementary education mandatory, inspecting public elementary school facilities, and providing for adult education. In 1892 he was appointed Vice-President to the Council of Education. His name will appear in several more of Wells's articles.

with the view chiefly of elucidating his opinions upon one or two points for their consideration, that I called last week—in the character of the *University Correspondent* interviewer—at the pleasant house, overlooking Primrose Hill, in which Doctor Collins resides.

As a member of several committees, and as senior whip for his party in the "Parliament of London," Doctor Collins is a busy man, and I was fortunate to find him with a little leisure in which to answer my questions. The Doctor is a young man—as public men go. He is evidently blessed with a sturdy frame, and his broad forehead and clean-shaven face have about them a strong suggestion of reserve strength and determination. He impresses one with the idea that he has unlimited "staying" powers behind the animation and decision of his manner.

He laughs as I open the business of the interview by propounding a riddle.

"Can I guess the shape that the final scheme for a Teaching University for London will take? I am afraid not. You see there is abundant support for reconstruction and organization—until the details are reached; but then come the difficulties."

"The movement is not homogeneous?"

"It is distinctly heterogeneous. Somebody has said of the London University reformers, that where they are agreed they are not precise, and that where they are precise they are not agreed. I think that expresses the case to a nicety. There is the 'medical grievance,' an agitation to lower the standard of the M.D. examination; the aspirations, and also the rivalries, of would-be 'constituent colleges'; and the desire of the teachers to remove the check imposed upon their individual idiosyncrasies by an outside examination. All these are distinct and conflicting interests. First one party touches the balance, then the other."

"And you think it may continue to oscillate yet for some time?"

"Precisely."

"Has the present University of London, in your opinion, dissevered itself altogether from this movement? Must the new University arise, necessarily, beside it, and independently of it?"

"I do not see the necessity. I should be sorry to see a second degree-granting body arise beside our University in London, but I have no objection, of course, to inter-collegiate arrangements to systematize teaching under the University as head. The London University has not taught hitherto, mainly because of the understanding between the University and University College. The latter was to teach, and the former to examine. But, while the University has succeeded, and its graduates increase every year, University College has, financially, failed. The strength of the whole movement for an independent University now is in the revolt against the Verdict of the University examinations—the claim of the colleges and teachers, in fact, to brand their own herrings."

"You have, of course, a very high opinion of the London University examinations?"

"Decidedly so."

"It is claimed that the Matriculation covers too many subjects, and therewith that it prevents a very high standard of attainment in any one of these."

"It is a thoroughly sound test of elementary education. This objection really shows its value in tempering premature specialization. I am strongly opposed to any relaxation in the Matriculation requirements, either generally, or specially for the medical or musical degrees."

"And it is asserted that the severity of the Intermediate and Pass examinations checks originality in the teacher and in the student."

"They simply insist upon a sound general knowledge of the subject. If 'originality' comes in before this is attained, [it] is premature. The proper place for that is at the end of the academic course."

"But, except in the case of the D.Lit., and of the D.Sc. degrees, the University offers no great inducements to research and criticism among its graduates."

"That is a matter in which, I think, the University is open to considerable development. But research and criticism will not be forwarded by relaxing the introductory work. The University was formerly hampered by its tacit bargain with University College, but now I am strongly in favour of the establishment of University professorships by the University of London, and particularly in special branches of knowledge not covered by the ordinary graduation course, and of providing encouragement, as well as facilities, for postgraduate study."

"I think, also," added Dr. Collins, "that the London University should take up technology, and endow teaching in technical subjects. Such subjects should scarcely qualify for degrees—the essence of a degree is its implication of academic culture, over and above a professional qualification—but the courses might very well lead to diplomas. Indeed, in the teachers' diploma we already have one such recognition of technical study and attainment of an exceptional kind."

"And to that end the London County Council might very well work with the University?"

"Yes. And also, perhaps, in the organizing of secondary education that seems to be coming. There is also 'Extension' teaching. I am anxious to see the influence and usefulness of the London University enlarged in every way. I am only conservative in the matter of the fair fame of its degrees, though the charges of Toryism and mere obstruction have been made nevertheless."

"Reverting, for a moment, to the degree examinations, you do not think that, in any case, attendance at prescribed courses, and the teachers' certificate, can be accepted in lieu of any part of the examination requisite?"

"That point I regard as vital. If once this principle is admitted, I do not see what guarantee we have against a downward competition, to attract students, between competing professors or institutions. Uniformity would certainly disappear. The degree would mean one thing for one man, and something quite different for another, and the heaviest sufferer would be the private student, whom I regard as hitherto the distinctive and most honourable feature of London. The proposal strikes at the very root of the impartiality, uniformity, and invariable high standard, which give the London degrees their exceptional value. The knowledge a private student gets from a book or an unauthorized teacher may be as good, or better, than that obtained from a professor's lectures. If it is not, the examination should show it. The reputation of the London degree has been established upon these principles, and members of Convocation, I feel assured, will never consent to any 'constituent colleges' trading upon this good name. The higher teaching, that yet cannot stand a fair examination test, must be an extremely impalpable thing."

"You do not, I infer, regard correspondence teaching as objectionable, or inferior to professorial instruction, as such?"

"Certainly not objectionable. You are justified by your results. In any but purely practical subjects, I can imagine very efficient work being done by correspondence; and I understand that you are now also undertaking good practical instruction in oral classes."

"I would like your opinion upon one small personal matter here, and that is the exclusion of the names of correspondence institutions from the University lists. I have prepared, for instance, a student for a London examination in a certain subject, and in another subject that student studied at X. College. In the University list, the student is credited solely to X. College."

"I think that is extremely unfair."

"Thank you. There is one other matter about which I and others will be glad to hear your opinion, and that is the future of the private school."

"Well, you must admit that there is a tendency to collectivism in educational matters which does not promise very much for the private school in the future."

"I have a copy of the Bill for the Organization of Secondary Education, brought forward by Mr. Hobhouse, Sir Henry Roscoe, and Mr. Acland, and in that it is expressly provided that under no circumstances can the educational authority assist, or utilize, in any way, any institution conducted for private profit. Do you not think that is rather too sweeping?"

"I think so. Under special circumstances I can imagine that it would be more convenient to establish scholarships or special classes at private institutions, in preference to either completely absorbing them or establishing competing schools. In such a case—it might be an exceptional one—adequate examination and inspection would, of course, be an absolute necessity."

From this the Doctor and his interviewer passed to the more academic discussion of the principles of individualism and socialism, and the interview, as a formal interview, terminated.

H. G. W.

A New Book on Evolution

The Educational Review, vol 3, no 3, January 1893, pp159-160

In this review, Wells is highly critical of a supposedly scientific approach that begins with an invocation of the existence of God as intelligent creator. Scientists, instead, proceed from the evidence. The author also demanded proof of evolution in the form of a brand new species, which Wells finds preposterous. While his facts and conclusions may be correct, the method is full of scientific inaccuracies and must not be trusted.

This new addition to the Nature Series of Messrs. Macmillan embodies a course of lectures delivered last year in the Summer School of Art and Science, presided over by Professor Geddes.* It is therefore naturally in a popular and even diffuse style, and we find such things as an apology for speculative science, and a restatement of Paley's watch argument[24] for the existence of design in Creation, at the outset of the work. M. de Varigny, by-the-by, can scarcely be congratulated upon the latter, since he simply further accentuates, in his efforts to ignore it, the fatal fact that a mechanism can only be recognised as such by some apprehension of its object. And, moreover, it is not only not within the province of biological science to employ, as he does, such sham axioms as that "everything must have a beginning," but also a kind of treason to scientific method, to commence a work of this kind with assurances of a belief in a Creator. Let me not be misunderstood. The scientific worker builds an orderly edifice of material facts in obedience to a plan that is gradually revealing itself to him, and he has no justification in his science to say, as yet, *as a scientist*, that he is engaged upon either a factory, a prison, or a temple, whatever his individual persuasion may be. This impatience on the part of the writer to assail or aid the theologian is worthier of a young man in a debating society than of a biological teacher. Such an opening establishes a prejudice in the mind of the reader as to M. de Varigny's scientific sobriety, a prejudice which finds abundant confirmation as we proceed.

The book as a statement of results of the variation of conditions, no doubt, deserves a place in the library of those interested in biological questions, but M. de Varigny in his opening lecture very greatly exaggerates its importance. In a *résumé* of the various arguments for organic evolution we are practically informed that experimental evolution is the keystone of the proof. The palæontological, morphological, embryological, "pathological" arguments are given; the argument

---

24. 18th century philosopher William Paley had argued that God designed to world to run according to laws, just as a watchmaker designed a watch.

based on current modifications is ignored, and then with an appearance of brilliant logical continuity we are told that the only true test is the transformation of one species into an entirely new one! "They" (the Special Creationists, the hypothetical opposition to us Evolutionists—the reader and M. de Varigny) "ask for a proof of transmutation; we must secure that proof to meet the demand. How so? Through direct experiment, through experimental transformation."

This kind of lucidity is doubtless effective with the cultivated public, but it certainly simply creates objections in the mind of the thoughtful reader. Let us state a parallel case. The produced axis of the earth slowly describes a great circle in the heavens with the precession of the equinoxes. In the range of actual human experience, only the smallest arc of this circle has been traversed. Are we to regard any inference from this known part of the movement and our analysis of its causes as unsatisfactory until the whole cycle is complete? We know of cases of variation accumulating; we have absolutely no reason to suppose such accumulation has a limit, and this clamour for a new species on the part of M. de Varigny's Creationist is about as reasonable as a demand on the part of anyone who has heard the full proof of the earth's rotundity to be shown then the earth visibly round. The demonstration of (i.) fertile hybrids and (ii.) two varieties of a species which do not fruitfully interbreed is the sufficient experimental proof of organic evolution—the doctrine, that is, of indefinite species and unique individuals. So long as the proof is logically sufficient, it really does not matter very much, from the point of view of a scientist, whether or not it appeals with sufficient vividness to the man in the street to secure his approval. Why should we "secure" a proof to "meet a demand"? Science is surely not a propaganda!

Putting aside M. de Varigny's general case, we find much in his book to attract the biological student. The rest of the work, save the final appeal for funds and support for an institution wherein undeniable new species are to be manufactured by some method not clearly stated, is occupied with a number of cases of accumulated variation, many of them new to English students, and is useful and readable. M. de Varigny's style is light and pleasant, and he may well afford a sneer at Weismann's substantial heaviness.[25] This scientific pastry is the very antithesis of Weismann's indigestible but more nutritious fare.

It will be well for the student to be on his guard against a too literal acceptance of M. de Varigny's statements. This, for instance, is the most fantastic romance: "One may easily detect in the evolution of the human brain a stage corresponding to that of the brain of fishes; but while the fishes permanently

---

25. August Weismann, a German evolutionary biologist, rejected inheritance based on acquired traits. His work was a link between Darwin and Mendelian genetics. Scientists like de Varigny continued to promote Larmarkist arguments that external events acting on an organism could be inherited.

retain this brain-structure, an advance occurs in man, and the brain acquires the characters of the reptilian encephalon; later on it progresses again, and acquires bird characters, then mammalian characters, and finally it acquires those characters which are peculiar to mankind." It would be as true to say that a baby has scales, and then feathers, and then hairs before its pinkness is attained.

With this we may leave M. de Varigny. He had a good topic, and he has not, we think, handled it well. He has presented a great number of useful facts, the value of which depends entirely upon their perfect reliability, and he has given sufficient cause in his first lecture for a profound distrust of his accuracy and of his immunity from the rhetorical danger. There is no consolation to the reader after this in finding him on the same side in controversy with oneself.

H. G. Wells

* *Experimental Evolution.* By Hemy de Varigny, D.Sc, (London: Macmillan & Co.)

Biology for the Intermediate Science and Preliminary Scientific Examinations

The University Correspondent, vol III, no 8, pp 4-5, 25 February 1893

This piece shows Wells at his most pragmatic, recommending specific equipment for those studying on their own for biology examinations. He had been taught the "practical" (or laboratory) classes at the University Tutorial College during the previous three years, and wanted to advise on methods and materials for students studying independently. This selection would be expanded into a section for his Text-book of Biology.

HINTS FOR PRACTICAL WORK.

For the practical study of biology—and, without practical study, biology is a mere lore, of the most unsubstantial description—the student working alone will need, in the first place, suitable and suitably prepared animals and plants, and, in the next, certain instruments, apparatus, and reagents. The difficulty in ascertaining what these are, and where they may be procured, is no doubt in many cases sufficiently great to deter the would-be biologist from prosecuting his studies, and it is to remove this, as far as is possible, that the following notes have been written.

Among dealers in material we may mention the following names. Sinel & Hornell, Jersey, make a special effort to meet London University requirements, and are thoroughly reliable in every respect; they are particularly good for marine types, animal and vegetable. They supply not only the fresh material, but material hardened in various ways for section-cutting, injected specimens of the larger typed for special dissections of the vascular system, and microscopic slides. Mr. T. E. Bolton, Farley Road, Malvern, also undertakes to supply most biological types, but he is particularly good with living material for the microscope, supplying shilling tubes of all the microscopic forms that are required for the London Science courses. H. Meller, 27 Callender Street, Manchester, has recently submitted specimens to us of prepared skeletons, and embryological and other sections. His goods are prepared in a thoroughly practical spirit, and his charges are very moderate. From these dealers the student will be able to obtain most of the material he requires, except some of the stages in the life-history of the botanical types during certain seasons of the year. A reliable supply of suitably preserved botanical material is still a *desideratum*. Rabbits and frogs are usually to be obtained locally—the latter at most fishing tackle and bait shops for instance, the former from the dealers in puppies, rats, and the like. The London student will find several shops of both these descriptions in the neighborhood of Seven Dials.

For the preservation of his material, the student will require some wide-mouthed (pickle) jars, and methylated spirit (diluted 50 per cent.); whenever possible, however, *fresh* specimens should be studied.

For the dissection of the larger animals, he will need a set of instruments, a dissecting dish, blanket pins, and ordinary pins. He should also have a special note-book, and coloured pencils (*not* crayons). The set of instruments should contain—

(i.) Large scissors (2-in. blades), and small (1-in.), straight, tapering to the tips, and biting up to the very end of the blade;

(ii.) Forceps, gripping firmly;

(iii.) A small (1-in. blade) and two large (1 ½ -in.) scalpels;

(iv.) Two dissecting needles, set in handles.

A seeker is usually added, but no seeker supplied by a dealer is really so serviceable as an ordinary hair-pin. Bone forceps are quite unnecessary. Such a set as this is supplied by Clive & Co., Booksellers Row, W.C. for 10s. 6d.[26] When first brought out, this set was by far the cheapest in the market, but other dealers have followed their lead, and several other similar sets are now obtainable, at from half-a-guinea upwards. "Taxidermists's" and "histologist's" sets are to be avoided. In buying any of these, the reader will do well to test the forceps and scissors, of the particular set he is purchasing, for himself. The failure of his pair of scissors to bite to the very end will ruin nearly every dissection he attempts; and a pair of forceps that are continually slipping from their grip, if less disastrous to the dissection, are more so to the dissector's temper than even undecided scissors.

The dissecting dish may be an ordinary pie dish, with a bottom made either by pouring melted paraffin wax (loaded with shot) into it, or, better, of cork loaded with sheet lead. If the former is selected, the student must bear in mind that melted paraffin wax is highly inflammable. Or a piece of wood can be stuck in the bottom of the dish by means of marine glue.

A small syringe is useful for injecting blood-vessels. Any coloured fluid, at hand, may be used for this purpose, but Prussian blue, suspended in water, is the best.

For the smaller zoological types, and for botany, the student will need a microscope (with low power, 1 in. or ½ in., and high power, ¼ in. or ⅙ in.), a dozen glass slips, and ¼ oz. of cover glasses. I know of no microscope, except perhaps Beck's cheaper "Star," to rival, at the price, that supplied by Clive & Co. for £3. 12s. 6d. It has everything the student of elementary biology needs. Better

---

26. W.B. Clive, bookseller, was the publishing arm of the University Correspondence College.

and higher-priced instruments, from five guineas upward, are supplied by Swift (Tottenham Court Road), Crouch (Oxford Street), and Beck (Holborn), from whom illustrated lists can be obtained.

The student will also need, as reagents, in 2-oz. bottles, furnished with dipping rods, some 5 per cent. salt solution (for living animal tissues), some tincture of iodine, some dilute sulphuric acid, and some absolute alcohol; and, to mount his sections, he will also need glycerine. For cutting the sections, an ordinary shilling razor will be quite sufficient. A few watch-glasses will be found a convenient addition to his appliances, and he may also obtain solutions of eosin and magenta.

With the above-named apparatus, the student will be amply equipped for such a course in biology as that for the Intermediate Science Examination of London University. Without qualified advice, however, he will certainly meet with very considerable difficulty in his endeavours to use these instruments. To overcome these difficulties unaided, he will need either exceptional quickness or else very exceptional perseverance.

H. G. Wells, B.Sc., F.Z.S.

What is Cram?

The University Correspondent, vol 3, no 11, p 10, 18 March 1893

Writing for a sympathetic audience of auto-didacts and external students, Wells here explains how the word "cram" is used as an invective against those who succeed using self-study or state-funded schooling. While extravagant in his language describing the self-taught working man, at the same time the admiration is real. He was, of course, such a young student himself, emerging with "ideas cleverer, sounder, and stronger than many a student who has had all the advantages". For the shallower cramming undertaken for examinations, he blames the university lecturer far more than the private coach, whose goal is a thorough enough understanding to answer any question.

It is a pity that the word "cram," as applied to educational matters, has been allowed to degenerate into a mere scholastic curse. There was a need for such a word, for a thing hitherto unchristened that it hit off to a nicety. But quarrelsome teachers, feeling the need of expletives, and yet restrained from drawing upon the recognised stores of the language by their responsibilities of position, found something forcible and effective in it, and used it as other innocent words before were used by Mr. Robert Acres.[27] Did some board-school master presume to snatch a scholarship from the public school, "Cram!" said the public schoolman, and felt all the better for it. Did some self-taught scholar thrust himself before the heirs of the educational tradition of half-a-dozen centuries upon the honours list, and "Sheer cram!" gave the defeated candidates all the comfort that coarser colloquial consolations yield a disappointed cabman. The word is rapidly losing all meaning save one of offence. It is the genteelest bad word. The fellow-student who thrashes you, the teacher you do not like, the dangerous educational rival— you may call them all "crammers" unreproved, though your maiden aunt be in hearing.

Now, the pity of it is that the necessity of a polite missile for pedagogues has left the thing originally denoted by the word without its name. The poor monosyllable has been thrown all over the place. Mr. Wren had it last, I think, and aimed it—*hard* as is his wont—at the public school masters.[28] We may, perhaps, be allowed to pick it up, and to make some attempt, at least, to put it back in its original position.

---

27. Squire Robert Acres, of Sheridan's play *The Rivals*, was known for his absurd oaths, such as "odds whips and wheels".
28. Wren had written in journals about cramming, and was known for his frankness.

Obviously the original authority for the use of this word in matters scholastic must have had his mind running on sausages—young, poultry-fed perforce—trunks sat on again and again, all kinds of heterogeneous higgledy-piggledy, and indigestible filling frantically rammed home. "Cramming" is a word to indicate a method, or rather a want of method, in mental packing; and has, rightly, about as much to do with examinations as, say, the University side of King's College. Mental engorgement, learning without digestion; this is the true meaning of "cram."

The natural seat of the thing, the place where it flourishes most luxuriantly, is ——. As a matter of fact, the original home where cram is truly indigenous is not to be determined. But there are two rank expositions of it to be found now. First, there is your lonely private student, an uninstructed man possessed by the hunger for wisdom. He may be behind the counter, or at the desk, in the barracks or the mine, when the thirst for learning comes to him. Such men, of whom Doctor Smiles[29] quotes many successful instances, will attempt, in their little leisure, feats of mental assimilation before which a senior wrangler might quail—Greek, German, French, Latin, Italian, the mathematics, all science, all art, all literature; they will endeavour to make Ruskin lie down in peace with Herbert Spencer in their minds, and Pope and Plato. The educational ideal of an ambitious illiterate man does not stop short of omniscience. He toils incessantly and breathlessly at his growing heap of information. He gallantly strains his mind to comprehend an illimitable chaos. Either he strains it to the pitch of injury, or he learns in time the meaning of infinity, and devotes himself thoughtfully to some possible portion of the world of human learning.

There is something splendid and Titanic about these ambitious and self-taught men. They work in the dark and under a tremendous disadvantage; they have often to content themselves with few and insufficient books, second-hand books, and old editions; they begin subjects, haphazard, at the most difficult points, and yet withal they will often emerge at last with ideas cleverer, sounder, and stronger than many a student who has had all the advantages—and relaxations—of a University. There is, I believe, a great future before these pilgrims from the proletariat to wisdom. The free public libraries will certainly help them, the extension movement may. In the time to come they will cram less, and learn more, because guidance will be nearer at hand. Some self-taught men even now sit in Parliament and in other high places, the natural aristocracy of the democracy, and more will follow. But by that time they will no longer cram with the splendid vigour they display now. They will learn in that wiser time from the very beginning.

The other luxuriant bed of cram is—where? Under the very feet of the

29. Samuel Smiles, author of *Self-Help* (1859)

heaven-sent University teacher. There is the great Pawkins with his European reputation to maintain —or get; he "cannot be bothered with all this elementary stuff." He has an academic dread of "crudity." He opens profound gulfs of philosophy and information in his very opening definition, he coils an intricate maze of qualifying considerations about the simplest proposition. The pencil of the wretched undergraduate toils after him, panting and weary. Pawkins soars into the empyrean of the subject before his students have learnt to flutter. They must needs cling to Pawkins closely; they learn his every word by heart, fearful even of paraphrase. They even seek tutors and coaches to help them with the riddle of Pawkins. It is all clear and intricate and beautiful to Pawkins, but to the student it is blind cram. The student is, as it were, a trunk first packed anyhow by Pawkins in a fine frenzy as lecturer, and afterwards finished by the presence of Pawkins as examiner sitting on the lid.[30]

The only teachers who never by any chance cram are the "coaches" for examinations, the "crammers" according to the use of abusive pedagogues, those whose trade it is not merely to expound wisdom, but to build up knowledge that will stand a test. They may be drill masters, if you like, but to call them "crammers" is utterly absurd. Any coach of experience can witness that every student has his "Plimsoll line," a limit to the cargo he can carry, beneath which if you sink him is danger and disaster. Many a man comes to the coach corpulent and unwieldly with inefficient knowledge, and in such a case the secret of success is dietary and exercises. To the coach it is absurd for a man to have any fact lurking in his mind that he cannot get at easily and turn freely this way and that. This may be a reprehensible idea, but surely if the word means anything, it is the very antithesis of "cram".

H. G. WELLS

---

30. Wells also used the name Pawkins for the character of the entomologist in his story "The Moth—Genus Novo".

Critic and Pedagogue
(1893-1894)

Against Being Too Practical in Teaching

Science and Art, Vol VII, no 75, p 60, June 1893

In this piece Wells derides those who are so practical that it stifles their understanding of theory and their imagination. The style here is different from his other pieces, and he is careful to laud the Science and Art Department; the journal was directed at those benefiting from its programs. It marks a shift to a more authoritative tone as educational critic.

By H. G. Wells, B. Sc., Fellow of the College of Preceptors

When it is advanced that men may be too practical, it is, of course, 'practical' in an acquired and less worthy sense that is intended. The beginning and end of all human matters it to satisfy some human need, and not to be practical in its nobler sense it to cut adrift from humanity. But we very often meet with men calling themselves 'practical men' as an elegant covering for unsystematic and empirical ways, and with an idea of recovering a disadvantage against men of wider method and larger views,—of which viler practicalness there seems nowadays a mischievous excess, and we would therefore discuss it a little in an analytical and would-be destructive spirit.

This objectionable 'practical' finds its commonest expression in a noble scorn of words. The 'practical' man can use them freely for no other purpose than in their own scourging—as though they were Flagellants. He bears them a magnificent grudge, studiously misuses them, and shows by word and act this contempt for his birthright as a reasonable creature. And books, which are aggregated of words, are so much the more depreciated by him. The essential of his false practical need consists in an incapacity, disguised as an aversion, for symbolical methods. The practical man condemns mental, because they are not visible, material, means, protests at the interposition of mathematics in physics and astronomy, and is only really happy with knowledge that has no interdependence and no alarming possibilities of abstraction. He loves *facts*, especially curious and unenlightening facts ; and his loathing for 'theory' is unbounded. 'Theory' is the wide realm of human interest that the practical man, through neglected opportunity or mental insufficiency, cannot understand. To act upon an inference, to determine anything except by way of trial, is theorising, and therefore objectionable. He has a curiously narrow view of human power and possibilities, because he cannot imagine what he has not witnessed. In all matters of opinion he believes with the majority. In art he relies on the power of conscientious work, and thinks that faithful representation is the essence of a good picture. And in questions of morals, in cases for self-denial or generosity, his sordid practicalness trails across all his conduct. Rarely a professed doubter—from practical reasons—he is yet the typical and only absolute materialist. In short, in the worst case, his practicalness is something that cramps his imagination, defiled his conduct, and cows his initiative, and stands always at hand to remind him of the meaner things of life.

We are evidently following a common method of the moralist, and building up the evil tendencies we would deprecate into a type, giving them one form and head in order that we may seem to slay them. But there is, happily, no such human monster as the entirely practical man, and alas! conversely, no one is altogether free from some tendency to the practical fallacy. For instance, how often do we science students and teachers have an opportunity of seeing it in the form of excessive experiment? A lecturer will sometimes present a lecture in the form of a continuous string of experiments, forgetting how easily this method of illustration—for, at the best, experiments are only solid illustrations—may swamp instead of floating what it should support. Unless a lecture is simply a public opening-night display of scientific pyrotechnics and legerdemain, it is really open to question whether it should contain more than *one* experiment, or, at most, one group of related experiments with simple apparatus. So much has to be made clear, if the full value of an experiment is to be brought out; so much is involved, and so much has to be rightly seen, that the repetition of an experiment two or three times to a class is often advisable. Above all, how often do unmeaning experiments occur ! Chemical teachers, for instance, will sometimes simply *make* substances whose only bearing is, perhaps, on atomicity or vapour density. Here we have a very common instance of being too practical.

Just at present there is a strong tendency in some quarters to treat the Science and Art Department ungratefully, to ignore the really splendid groups of schools and the new class of teachers it has created, and to set up in competition with it technical schools, 'practical' technical teachers, and examining bodies of dubious capacity, by which a short cut to each of the skilled trades is to be presently opened up. We do not wish to deny the need for technical education, but there is no doubt that local practical men are here and there promoting the development of technical education schemed in a manner that will result in numberless boys and girls, attending classes in technical science for which they are unprepared, who might and would otherwise be far more profitably employed in studying the first elements of science and drawing.

And, further, as a third instance of being too practical, comes that sapient creature, the 'practical' teacher. He is the man who, when in a Board school, imagined the highest expression of a teacher's skill is in keeping his registers well. But he is really only found in his magnificence in the middle-class school. The secondary school variety despises method, despises and hates examinations. The fearful ignorance of their trade, due to a contempt of 'theory' among middle-class and public-school teachers, can hardly be exaggerated.

And here one may note, as, doubtless, the result of the 'practical' fallacy, that the Normal School factor in the Royal College of Science, which exists professedly for the training of science teachers, has no lecturer in education or method attached to its staff. Necessarily his employment would be mainly a dealing with the presentation of thoughts and words, and this would be heretical departure from the great gospel of 'things only,' that the practical man, inverting the old educational error with the idea of making it truth, incessantly preaches. So that the South Kensington *alumni* of a modest disposition seek method painfully elsewhere, while the bolder spirits trust to inspiration, or treat their scholars to imitations of their favourite professors, and are little Huxleys without wit, Boys without dexterity, and Judds without substance, and teaching becomes, through the influence of the practical man, not an applied science, but a tradition of manner.

Finally, we have the practical error in its simplest and worst form in the 'bread-and-butter' teacher, the man who goes through a prescribed performance before a class to secure himself food, raiment, and shelter. He thinks it wisdom to keep himself alive.

A wiser and wider practicalness would show him that these things, that he esteems ends, are but means; that his teaching is not for him to live, but that he lives to teach; that the reality worth striving for is not assimilation, but acts; that the end of science teaching is the propagation of truth rather than the multiplication of results, and that the end of art is beauty.

Biological Teaching

Science and Art, Vol VII, no 78, p 128, September 1893

In his next article for Science and Art, *Wells focused on newer methods of teaching biology. He updates the argument that teaching is more important than the content of a textbook, and expands on his views about practical laboratories being superior to lecture in the study of biological type. Specific pedagogical recommendations include choosing an animal for dissection and discussing theory during instructions. Drawing may be used instead of direct microscopic observation, but giving up dissection would "would render such biological teaching no longer an immediate vision of things but a legend".*

By H. G. Wells, B. Sc., Lond. First Class Hons. in Zoology.

The type system of teaching Zoology is still so comparatively recent that a really authoritative tradition of method has scarcely as yet come into existence. The character of such work is still tractably determined by the analogy of earlier-established sciences. At Oxford and Cambridge, and at South Kensington, for instance, the arrangement of the work has been clearly affected by that already found most convenient in the teaching of such a science as chemistry. A sharp line is drawn between the theoretical instruction given in lectures, enduring the traditional hour, on the one hand, and laboratory work on the other. The latter constituent of the courses is commonly conducted by subordinate demonstrators, sometimes with very little interference from the lecturing professor, and, in some instances, with the help of instruction papers, and 'practical' manuals that render the work considerably more mechanical than it need be. Biology does not yet admit of the same amount of separation between its generalisations and its concrete facts that is practicable in the case of physics or chemistry, and there can be little doubt that the existing method of presenting it, even at centers which are necessarily models to ordinary teachers, need to, and will, undergo very extensive modification before the best possible results are obtained.

At Cambridge the explicit instruction-paper method is at its highest possible development. Students for the Tripos Zoology are equipped with notebooks worth of a prominent place in the pedagogic museum of the future. These volumes have, at the head of each page, some such heading as this,—we take the example haphazard:—

'Dorsal view of sheep's brain, dissected to show the corpus callosus (*c. call.*);

c. c. h., convolutions of cerebral hemispheres; *c. quad.*, corpus quadrigemina; *c.b.*, cerebellum; *m.o.*, medulla oblongata.'

Opposite this inscription is a space of about half a page, in which it would appear to be anticipated that the student will draw the figure indicated from his dissection. Below comes the prescription from another figure.

In this way much of the charm of bookkeeping becomes wedded to biology. It is, perhaps, fortunate that this method obtains to this degree only at Cambridge or Oxford. Practised at a private establishment, it would long ago have been denounced as the quintessence of mechanical 'cut and excessively dried' cramming. However, it is quoted here not so much as an example as an instance. It is possible that, under the conditions obtaining at the Universities, it is as near an approach to efficient teaching as is practicable there.

At South Kensington explicit instruction books are also employed, but here, at least in practice, the demonstrator steps in front of the letterpress. The present writer does not remember, for instance, to have used his Parker or Bower except as works of reference, during his studies there.[31] A demonstrator, if he has the gift of teaching, can, with a few words, with a motion of the hand, and with two or three strokes on the blackboard, convey a far more vivid idea of what had to be done, than can be got from a heavy paragraph of letterpress, and that, as a matter of fact, was how the instructions were given.

During the particular year of the writer's studies at the Royal College of Science, both the lecturing and demonstrating were in the hands of the same man, and this unification—thought in many cases it is impracticable—appears to him to have very great advantages over the common severance of lectures and laboratory work.

Biological science has but few sections at all abstract in their character. It begins with anatomy, and it grown mainly by taking fresh anatomical arrangements into comparison with its initial type. Not only are the anatomical structures best studied in the laboratory, but there, and not in the lecture theater, is the best place for instituting the comparisons, and leading up to the wider laws. In fact, in this science, at present, the small school has a distinct advantage over the larger in the opportunity it offers of dispensing with the lecture. In the professional schools the laboratory work must either become mechanical, or the risk will arise of duplicate or conflicting teaching between demonstrators and professor.

In any school, any genuine biological study must be based at least on dissection. To commence with, in such classes as would prepare for the

---

31 These books are likely Thomas Jeffrey Parker's *Lessons in Elementary Biology* (1891) and Frederick O. Bower's *A Course of Practical Instruction in Botany* (1891).

Departmental Examinations, some type should be chosen which is not repulsive—a disadvantage under which the rabbit or dogfish suffers—not dear, since its dissection will have to be repeated, and not difficult, as the snail or mussel is at first. The best type to start with, particularly for evening class work, is the frog. Blackboard sketches should indicate each important phase in dissection, and in no case should ambitious students be allowed to push beyond their instructions. The over-energetic student, who can ruin a dissection before his next-door neighbour has begun, furnishes us with one of the strongest objections to the explicit instruction book in biological teaching. If you demonstrate to him from the blackboard, you are at least safe against his attempting step B before he has properly finished A, because he has no means of knowing what step B will be. The teacher must not confine himself to directing dissection from the blackboard; his instructions should be accompanied in the case of the first type studied by a running physiological commentary, and thereafter by constant reminders of comparisons with previously dissected types. In this way, the theoretical part of the work will grow in its natural connexion out of the actual facts of the science.

In no case should a class in biology meet for a lesser period than two hours. The time occupied in getting out, cleaning, and packing away appliances, changing water from dissecting dishes, and so forth, reduces a shorter period by such a considerable fraction as to render genuine study impossible.

One source of difficulty in departmental classes in biology, perhaps the great reason why they are not more abundant, is the microscopical work. Few local schools boast more than one or two microscopes, and the teacher has to weigh the alternatives of slurring this part of the subject or having his class spend an evening or so *en queue*, before the school instrument. There is a third course possible, though it is mentioned here with some hesitation. A teacher with a little artistic ability of the scene painting sort, may do very well without using his microscope at all, by means of big diagrams of what would be seen. But this suggestion is the thin end of the wedge. 'If one may dispense with the microscope in this way why not with dissection?' To this it may be urged, that it would render such biological teaching no longer an immediate vision of things but a legend. It seems to the writer highly probable that, as things are at present, with an examination entirely written, a teacher whose instruction consisted simply of a commentary on a series of diagrams enlarged and well coloured from Howes' Atlas,[32] might obtain as good 'results' as, or even better than, those of one who taught honestly in the right way.

---

32. George B. Howes, *An atlas of practical elementary biology* (1885).

At the Royal College of Science

The Educational Times, vol XLVI, no 389, pp 393-395, 1 September 1893

Unsigned but claimed by David C. Smith as written by H. G. Wells[33], this piece directly describes Wells's experiences at the Normal School of Science, instead of using them in service to other topics. The evocative, and sometimes harsh, descriptions were echoed in a number of his fictional works; several of the scientific romances and stories have scenes that take place in the classrooms and laboratories of Imperial College.

BY AN OLD STUDENT

That tall and stately mass of masonry in the Exhibition Road which formerly bore the title of the Normal School of Science and Royal School of Mines, was, a year or two ago, re-christened the Royal College of Science, and the change may be seen visibly effected in a handsome mosaic label on the right hand bottom corner of the building. The Students' Union and others protested against the implication that its science school was anything but regal, and its mining abnormal, and the associated alumni of its scientific members found something objectionable in their being written down A.N.S.S. But in the days of the writer the place still had its composite title; there was no Students' Union, and the miners went to lecturers in Jermyn Street, and kept themselves to a considerable extent apart from the new contingent. The awe-stricken teacher-in-training might then pass "Huxley" on the staircase every other day, and the science of physics was taught by Guthrie and chemistry by Frankland. Possibly, therefore, this article may not be strictly "up-to-date"; there may have been alterations that have escaped me since those days, though I have always had my eye affectionately upon the place.

My first impression, when, as a "teacher-in-training," in accordance with the minute instructions of My Lords of the Education Department, I presented myself, duly provided with a cheap shiny handbag containing a quarto note-book, coloured pencils, and a box of appliances, at 9:30 precisely, in the hall of that red-brick building, was Grummett. This bright and energetic person may be best described as the Angel of the Gate. He was flitting to and fro through a chaos of new arrivals, gently but firmly checking the general tendency to collect in impenetrable masses in the doorways, guiding all to the books they would thereafter sign daily, and then sending some to the lift and so up to the altitudes

---

33 Smith, D. C. (2012). *The Journalism of H.G. Wells: An Annotated Bibliography* (P. Parrinder, Ed.). Equilibris, p. 75.

of geology and biology, others to the depths of the metallurgical laboratory, and others again to the intermediate realms of chemistry and physics. He laid hands upon me in a swift, decisive manner before I could adequately survey my future fellow students and competitors, extracted from me my status, and I had signed a volume full of the vanity of self-conscious signatures, had navigated a lift for the first time in my life, and was sitting alone in a laboratory in a remote part of the building without any appreciable interval of time.

SIGNING THE BOOK.

This is one of the most remarkable features of our South Kensington Schools. You "sign on" every morning before ten, and forthwith you are under most explicit regulation; you may not, for instance, smoke, or whistle, or sing; your career, your conversation almost, is tenderly watched by demonstrators and assistant-demonstrators, and the sense of discipline enters into your soul. You may "sign off" as early as four; at five, unless you have special leave to stay in the building, you are chased out of any humble lurking place by a policeman, and you must do it. Your responsibility to the Department of Science and Art terminated with this second signature.

THE STUDENT'S LIFE.

Between "signing off" and delivering oneself into discipline again in the morning, no human being is so absolutely free as the South Kensington student, male or female, save that it is expected that lecture notes be copied somewhere in the interval. Where and how the student lives and lodges, what fare the student eats, and what company the student keeps, the Royal College takes no heed of. At Kensington we were and are "unattached", with a vengeance. It is perfectly open to a student from the provinces to have his or her lodgings on a seat in Hyde Park, or to spend the night in wandering about the metropolis, provided only that he or she returns with note-book, coloured pencils, and what other requirements are specified on the Departmental form, at or before ten o'clock the next morning. Considering that perhaps no great educational centre draws its pupils from such a variety of sources, or displays such contrasted types of students, as the Royal College, it might be expected that this entire disregard of extra-mural discipline would lead to "grave disorders." However, as a matter of fact—and I have known pretty intimately representatives of most of the sets among the students—Spanish, Japanese, the suburban young lady, the private students sent by their fond "guv'nors," the hopeful youth of the Yorkshire and Scotch elementary and technical schools, and *ci-derant* school assistants—there is a gravity and pervading sense of responsibility about even the golden youth of Kensington entirely lacking in the typical undergraduate. Your undergraduate is, perhaps, too evidently surrounded by the most delightful little regulations and suggestions of what he must not do, and the proctor, especially, is a constant provocation. When the dignity of the University is continually parading its purlieus, and asking whether any young gentleman will tread on the tail of its gown, there will be always some young gentleman found to oblige. But nothing stood between us at South Kensington and infinite possibilities of error. We were in our own hands, and the sense of that was a sufficient ballast for most of us.

TYPES OF STUDENTS.

The selection of students that presently dropped in to the laboratory whither the good Grummett had directed me on my arrival, will, with a little rectification, serve roughly to convey an idea of the diverse quality of our Kensington material.

Perhaps, however, I may parenthetically guard here against a natural misconception. There are student types, and, like Mr. Galton's student types, I have made them by combining the blurred negatives of several people. There are no personal portraits here.

Place aux dames, and in the foremost place, youth. Miss A. came to us straight from the celebrated —— High School, and at first she was possessed of that noble ambition engendered in High Schools, of beating men on examination lists. She sat apart, I remember, during that awkward interval in which the new-created class surveyed itself, and she read a text-book. I recall the fact so distinctly because at that time I was still a ferocious crammer, and the spectacle of her getting ahead in this way distressed me extremely. My own text-book was at home—an unpropitious oversight. Presently I was glad to see another girl arrive and interrupt her. The two made tentative conversation, and talked of Science and Art certificates and the Locals in an easy, superior way.

The second arrival was clearly a schoolmistress of some experience. That was the time of "art" costume, of which the essence was an extreme severity of skirt, emphasised, rather than corrected, by a vanity of puffed sleeves. The hair of Miss B. was brushed back and cut short, even to the point of harshness, exposing an ample forehead to the educational influences of the place. Her glasses were evidently tried instruments of discipline. Beside her Miss A., whose pretty hair, a widening experience tells me, must have been cultivated with curling-tongs and some affection, appeared at once in her true colours as a worldling, and I felt the disadvantage of the text-book page she had scored against us less acutely. Subsequently, the fundamental worldliness of Miss A. became more evident, and she even inaugurated afternoon tea, and did her best to refine the scientific atmosphere. But only two of the men students ever learned to manage a tea-cup properly.

Miss C. was the daughter of a Positivist family, and subsequently became a philanthropic medical practitioner. During our student time she had a steady glow of enthusiasm for electoral feminine emancipation, and divided a noble gift of scorn between mankind in general and Miss A.'s character in particular. She was a little peculiar among decidedly strong-minded women in being ungracious but not ungraceful. Indeed, the only approach to a romantic incident certainly known to have occurred at Kensington, happened to her. This was an anonymous gift of immaculate and fragrant white hyacinth that was found on her table when we returned from our lecture one morning. Miss C. with an expression of ineffable disgust, took the offensive thing with the tips of her fingers and flung it forthwith out of the window. That it fell at the feet of an Italian on his way to post in the life schools at the back of the science school, and that he bowed profoundly with a tremendous sweep of his hat, only illustrated the vexatious mixture of comedy with tragedy in all human affairs.

Miss D., the last of the feminine section that year, was a meek-looking, soft-voiced little soul in a plain black dress. I believe she lived quite by herself in apartments. The three other girls, by-the-bye, lived at their own homes. Subsequently, in another course, one of the demonstrators, so it is said, saw her notes of his demonstrations so beautifully, so methodically, and so fully written out, that the scientific severity of his life was suddenly irradiated by a glow of novel sentiment. At any rate they married, and, so far as one can judge by appearances, they are happy.

Next to the tables occupied by these ladies, sat Mr. MacE., a portly and florid old gentleman, bald and irascible, who had come to us, as had Miss D. and Miss B., as a State-aided science teacher-in-training. He did not approve of "cluttering up the laboratory with females," a disapproval only enhanced by their subsequent triumph over him in the examination. He sought occasion for quarrels with them in connexion with the opening and shutting of windows; he displayed a strong dislike to loaning them instruments of apparatus, objected practically to the reservation of the best seats in the lecture theatre for them, and maintained, in and out of season, on every possible occasion an absolutely scandalous assertion that none of them could cook a mutton chop. This last proposition was indeed Mr. MacE.'s great point against them. When he was found, an hour before lecture, squatting broadly on the seats sacred to Miss A. and Miss D., and we more youthful and chivalrous ones expostulated at the contemplated displacement, he punctuated every phrase in a lengthy argument with that mutton chop. And all his conversations with the "young females," however diversely they began, whether in the sky above or the earth beneath, ended in his insistence upon this crying wrong.

He shared his table with a small boy of fifteen, who had come from somewhere in the Hinterland of Sussex. Little F. was one of the most illiterate little wretches conceivable at that time, and knew nothing in the world but the contents of Messrs. Grind's Elementary and Advanced Text-Books, and the Science and Art Department Regulations. He had conducted his own education. He had worse than no manners—he had offensive ones, and notably a sniff. However, he got by his vulgar pushing within three marks of the head of our class, and is already a full-fledged professor at a provincial college. The laws of human development are dark and mysterious. I met F. at the Pantological Society a few weeks ago, and he struck me as having become emphatically the most gentlemanly-mannered man I ever met. But he did not understand an easy allusion I made to the "Merry Wives of WIndsor," and he deprecated my praises of his rival, Dr. Z., so that I have my doubts of the profundity of the change.

G. was a Midland schoolmaster, and wore spectacles, mutton-chop whiskers, a flowing frock coat, and a clerical hat. In an earlier stage of his history he had assisted in the education of one of our demonstrators, and he gained a certain factitious superiority over the rest of us by calling this distinguished person "Jack" on all possible and some impossible occasions. His companion was a Spanish Creole, who was chiefly remarkable for the conspicuous struggle that went on within him between an absolutely barbaric taste for gorgeous ornament and iridescent colour on the one hand and a desire to dress as the pink of European gentility on the other; sometimes he was over-gaudy and in manner abashed, sometimes excessively "neat" and assertive—he never hit the happy mean. It was discovered at the end of the course that the insufficiency of this student's English had prevented the slightest contamination of his mind by our science. He concealed his limitations in this respect with great tact during the session.

K., who was my companion, was one of those over-slender young men who eternally lean against things and droop into attitudes. He ought properly to have been one of the bundles of long grass that now form so constant a feature in æsthetic furnishing. He was one of the two men who would hand tea for Miss A., and his father, mother, and most of his relations had written books of undoubted cleverness. He read Shelley and needed a soul to understand him. J. did not understand him, being the product of a north-country mechanics' institute. J. was a thick-set youth who swore, and swore vulgarly, by Gladstone, John Bright, and Bradlaugh, and on the slightest hint of an argument, would put one foot on a laboratory stool, hold his arm out like a pump handle, and, addressing you with civility and frequency as "Sir," give you his views clearly, fluently, and at length, after his conception of the manner of those great men. Subsequently J. rather modified himself by reading Ruskin, and taking Art under his protection. He had a wonderful way of catching up tricks of style, and he used during his Ruskinian

art in the picture galleries, may have served already to give the reader some slight idea. We are approaching the limits of our space, and to give the conclusion its proper flavour of the Royal College we may imagine that Grummett's hand-bell is clamorously awakening the echoes of the great central staircase of the building. It is four o'clock, and forthwith from the various floors erupts a miscellaneous crowd of students, to form long queues at the books, "sign off," and vanish, north, south, east, and west, into the infinity of the metropolis, whence it will be concentrated again to-morrow, breathlessly, on the stroke of ten.

If we stay in the building much longer we shall have the elderly and portly policeman asking us for our permission to remain, so we had better gather our note books, coloured pencils, and apparatus together, and fare forth into the outside world without any further delay. And in the Exhibition Road we are swallowed up in a stream of country-town femininity coming from the adoration of the Royal Wedding presents displayed in the Imperial Institute close by.

Z.

Scholastic Isolation

The Educational Times, vol XLVI, no 389, p 390, 1 September 1893

Noting that schoolmasters are held to not only a different set of morals but of behavior, Wells here lays the blame on society's unreasonable expectations.

To the Editor of the Educational Times.

SIR,—With the possible exception of the minister of religion, no kind of man has been, and is, so exhaustively criticised as the schoolmaster. Individually and collectively he is worked over, no detail neglected, from his collars to his conduct of his immortal soul. The informal council of the parent, the pupil, and the disinterested relation is always in session, and to these has been added the educational writer. Beside the schoolmaster the general practitioner in a village is a free man. Even over the boundary of his professional duties he is pursued, and his behaviour in society, and his vacation employments , are the matter of well-nigh classical criticisms. He carries too much of the tone pedagogic into his lay conversation—that is an old complaint, and now there is added that he gathers himself together in his vacation in conferences, guild meetings, and the like, preferring his own kind to common humanity. Moreover, someone has discovered that he marries, with singular frequency, within his class. Doctors do not marry lady practitioners, nor the clergy sisters of mercy; masculine artists would sooner marry their models than their proper feminine equivalents—but statistics show that those who profess education mate within their calling more than any other kind of people. This is made a reproach to us. It is stated—and nothing could be more evidently false—that schoolmasters and mistresses are inflated by their schoolroom authority until none but teachers are good enough for them, that other adult humanity is to them merely so many fugitives, across an age limit, from salutary discipline, and the like.

But the truth of all this is, it is not the schoolmaster who has, in disdain, cut himself off from common men, but the general public which has, to a perceptible extent, put us in a class apart. It is the perpetual sense of criticism, and the absurd conceptions formed by the public of what a schoolmaster should be, that give so many of us the air of being consciously not as other men. The public *will* have its schoolmaster Sabbatical in garb, loving them best when they seemed to be clad, morally and physically, in ready-made mourning; its ideal teacher may not sing nor play nor dance. If he smoke at all, he smokes after bedtime up the chimney, and that mild tobacco. And their conception of our range of conversation is peculiar. We are supposed to delight especially in etymology, the verification of quotations, and nice questions of pronunciation; and talk in which we join is commonly politely wrenched round to these our topics. Moreover, it is expected of us that we should speak with language of unnatural polish, and our spelling and our handwriting must be devoid of the grace of variety.

As for wit, a witty schoolmaster is to the public eye clearly an immoral one, though a special kind of joking, as gay as the distant firing of great guns, is allowed him. These are some of the many conventions that are forced upon us. We must observe them, because no teacher can educate if he is not trusted with pupils, and so it is not of choice but necessity that many of us wear at least the exterior aspect of prigs. With the parent, that is, the public, the teacher is always on his guard, lest it be discovered that he is, after all, but a mortal man, and "the imagination of his heart only evil continually"—just as the parent's is. Of course where the parent is educated this isolation is at its least; the happy few in the upper ranks of the profession can almost afford to be taken for common men, and it is mainly upon the teachers of the children of the lower middle and working classes that this burthen falls, of being set apart in a deliberately "superior" class from ordinary humanity. Thus it happens that we are very much alone, and we must seek out fellow teachers in order to unbosom ourselves and let the bow of behaviour unbend. Teachers gather with teachers, and marry teachers, for no love of the teacher, but of humanity. Among ourselves we can set aside the armour of solemnity the public has made us wear, and taste the dear delight of human intercourse without pretence. That is the true and honourable reason of that isolation of which the critic unreasonably complains, and, indeed, no vain sense of superiority such as he suggests.

I am, Sir. &c.,

H. G. Wells.

Science Notes

The Journal of Education, vol XV, no 290, p 515, 1 **September 1893**

Science Notes appeared unattributed in the Journal of Education *between September 1893 and July 1894. In this first set, Wells reports on such varied topics as outdated geography, geology versus geography, and the disappearance of the Island of Sultana.*

We wonder how many schoolmasters are still accustomed to teach the theory ascribed to Dove of the Atmospheric Circulation. This theory is, roughly, to the effect that there is an upcast draught at the equator, and an overflow above the Trades, which, in the region of the *calms* of Cancer and Capricorn, *descends through the equatorially directed trade wind current* (in the old-fashioned diagrams the sceptic can still see these two currents flowing amiably at right angles through the same point) to become the "Anti-Trades" of the temperate latitudes. Now this theory was disposed of by the late Professor Thomson in 1858. Unhappily, the new explanation lacks the sweet simplicity of the older one, and that may account for its remaining in abeyance.

———

There is something inevitably conservative in things scholastic. One may find in two of the very best and most up-to-date of geographical text-books the venerable statement that all gneiss has the mineral composition of granite. Now, gneiss is really merely a coarser schist with well developed felspar, and even gabbro-gneiss is a possible thing. Speaking of lapsed science, how long will it be before the youth of this country ceases to hear of *Eozoon Canadense*, that spacious foraminifer, the "dawn of life"? Drs. Johnson Lavis and Gregory, however, have got beautifully perfect specimens in erupted blocks from Monte Somma, and there can be no further doubt of the purely mineral origin of this fossil. The oldest remains of life now known are the Radiolaria described by Barrois last year, from the Archæans of Brittany.

———

There is a comical printer's error in *Public Health* for August, by which Dr. Newsholme is made to expatiate upon the " Non-Participation of the Higher Ages in the Improved Expectoration (*sic*) of Life in England." His paper is devoted to an analysis of the belief, based on statistics, that, although the average duration of life has risen in the last two decades, the improved prospect does not apply to males over twenty, or females over forty-five. He considers that the present generation of adults was born in the pre-sanitary era, and that we may still hope to find, in the future, not only a diminished juvenile mortality, but also a lengthening out of the extremes of life.

———

America, which has long ago gone ahead of this continent in the matter of fossil reptiles, birds, and mammals, has now produced three new and great fishes of Devonian age from shales in Ohio, hitherto supposed to be unfossiliferous. They are huge placoderms of an antique type, with heavy armour, confined to the heads. The largest is styled *Titanichthys*, but the new genus, *Dinichthys*, is, perhaps, more remarkable, with its altogether abnormal "steel trap" jaw, having an unbroken cutting edge two feet in length. They find their nearest relative, among forms familiar to the English geologist, in the Devonian *Cephalaspis*.

———

Patents have been taken out in Germany and England for a new "artificial marble," formed by partially dehydrating gypsum, and immersing in a strong solution of alum and potassium sulphite. The imitation is stated (by the inventors) to equal the real thing, both in beauty and durability.

———

Mr. A. S. White expresses his objection to our current teaching of geography by saying that it is wrongly regarded as a *graphy*, whereas it is clearly an *ology*. It is made a "vehicle of description and not a body of thought"; and he pleads for a really scientific text-book still to come. He would base geography upon chemistry, physics, geology, oceanography, meteorology, biology, ethnology, history, and political economy, so leading up to the study of the "distribution and welfare of man as determined or affected by physical phenomena on the earth's surface." From this there would naturally spring cartography, demography, sociology, and philosophy. As a substitute for the existing curriculum, Mr. White's science of geography may very well pass muster, but as a two-hour-a-week school subject it seems a little too comprehensive. We have only heard of one person who could hope to get to that pitch of condensation, and *he* was in the "Arabian Nights." Genii that overspread the heavens he could seal down in little earthen-ware pots, but such educational skill as that is not given to everyone.

———

In the issue of the *Geographical Journal* containing Mr. White's views, there is a letter from Lieutenant-Colonel Leslie Ellis. All teachers, as the public is perfectly well aware, know the latitude and longitude of every island on earth. Now there are coins, he tells us, bearing the date 1835, and an inscription in English, "Island of Sultana." Here is a holiday task; where is this Island of Sultana? Or can a place have a coinage all to itself in 1835, and have passed out of human knowledge in 1893?

———

Fresenius recommends, for the separation of barium, strontium, and calcium, the following new method. The barium is first precipitated as chromate, the strontium and calcium are then converted successively into carbonates and nitrates, and the former is removed from the dried nitrates with ether alcohol. The strontium obtained in this way had a trace of calcium, but the barium and calcium precipitates examined spectroscopically were found to be quite pure.

———

J. W. Retgers has shown that red phosphorus is not amorphous. His argument is based upon the examination of this substance with the polarizing microscope, the difficulty arising from its high refractive index being got over by using methylene iodide as a matrix for its examination. The fact that yellow phosphorus is converted in to red under the action of sunlight is in accordance with its crystalline character, since no instance is known of the conversion of a crystalline body to the amorphous condition by such means.

The Examiner Examined

The University Correspondent, vol III, no 38, p 6-7, 23 September 1893

In his autobiography, Wells noted that scholarly examinations were "distortions of an educational process for which I felt dimly responsible".[34] He recognized, when he wrote for The University Correspondent, *that the college for which he worked benefited from and necessarily assisted students with, these examinations. He nevertheless found them pedagogically repellent, and attacking examiners had been part of his writing for a long time. Here he humorously creates a world where the examiners, experiencing the same problems as an ordinary examinee, cannot pass the exams.*

In the land of which I am writing they manage things very much better than they do here. For after they had determined that no man should practice any calling without being examined and found sufficient therein, they forthwith set about examining their examiners as a preliminary stop to their examination of other people. And there was thereupon visible immediately a distressing spectacle of examiners in a horrible stew, seeking kindly coaches and convenient rather than conscientious text-books, if such were to be found, and speculating about marking and what they might have "set." And many among them, in their sudden trouble, even avowed they did not believe in examinations—at least, so far as the science and art of examining was concerned. You would meet these Olympians in trains conning grubby little notebooks, and see them in public libraries reading three volumes at once, and in talkative knots in the street casting vain horoscopes of "what it would be," just as if they were not examiners at all, but only mortal men. It was indeed a terrible come-down.

They were given a syllabus to guide their studies—a syllabus of nine words, "The Science of Examining so far as is known." And they were also given little cards that threatened them with, rather than prepared them for, a practical examination. And none of them, though they bribed all the University porters, would get a tip, or an inkling of a tip, of what that practical examination would be.

You have only seen the examiner in his pride and vanity of power. He comes into the examination-room with scant civility to his assistants, sometimes forgetting to remove a brand-new silk hat, glares haughtily at us and the paper, fret-saws out a whispered remark or two, and so out again. His back is stiff, his

---

34. Wells, H G. *Experiment in Autobiography*. New York: The Macmillan Company, 1934, p. 361.

eye flashes, he is full of the pride and glory or life, and master of all he surveys. But in the land I am writing of, he bore himself very differently. He was meek, even as meek as *we* have been, when he gathered in his hundreds in the galleries outside the examination halls. He was bullied of commissionaires, and vulgar men in uniform bawled: "Not *that* way, STOOPID!" He worried his addled wits over well-thumbed note-books up to the last moment, even as those he tramples on are wont to do.

Then he filed in at the stroke of ten and took his seat. The seats were numbered anyhow, and most of the labels were on the floor. And oh! the written paper was a noxious thing. Seven-and-twenty questions were given him to answer in three hours, and I warrant you the quills shrieked aloud. The examination was, of course, by misprinted papers. He was asked questions, so far as he would make out, that he has never dared ask himself. For instance—

How would you mark a cleverly-written paper if the handwriting was practically illegible to you?

What is "difficult"? Which, in the absolute, is the most difficult question : "*Who was Beckett?*" or "*What is a fraction?*"?

In a choice between "south" and "north", a candidate drops a very natural-looking blot on the first three letters ; discuss this in relation to the Christian duty of charity.

"An examiner's function is simply to test knowledge."—How far does this apply in the case of a candidate who answers all your questions with absolute correctness, and then adds that you, personally, are an old fool?

How can you possibly mark "unseen" translations?

Mark the following answers to the question, "Where is New York?"—(*a*) "Not in the syllabus." [N.B.—This is correct.] (*b*) "In New York State." (*c*) "In New Yorkshire." (*d*) "In America." (*e*) "In the dark." (*f*) "My brother lives there."

It was written on the paper, "Some of these questions are worth many marks, and some worth very few; the candidate must use his judgment." And two examiners of examiners, with whispers like filing iron, walked up and down the room the while. It was a fine sight to see all these examiners writhing, knowing that, for once at least, their judgments on these problems would be judged over again. The temperature was 73°F., and the clock in the room ticked like a chaff-cutter, and outside were barrel-organs and a man grinding knives.

Better still was the practical exam. There was one question only:—

Conduct a *viva voce* with the candidates A., B., C., D., provided.

A. was a young lady who said she *must* pass because of her mother, and then she had hysterics.

B. was a panic-stricken little girl too scared to say *anything*.

C. was a chatty person who knew the examiner's aunts, and *would* talk about them. And

D. was an hot-headed, big man who answered volubly in an incomprehensible dialect.

And all the while the practical test lasted the examiners of examiners sat and glared and sniggered at their prey.

But the sweetest thing of all, to us who have suffered, was when the lists came out. They published them three weeks late and hung them upside down in the wrong place for fun. And when the examiners had bit and fought their way to them they beheld—

First Class.

None.

Second Class.

None.

For no examiner really knows his trade up to examination standard, as examinations go. And so they failed, and in the land about which I am telling you there are no examiners and no examinations to this day. And as they have determined that nobody shall do anything until an examination has been passed, nobody does anything there at all. That is probably why you have never heard before of this land about which I am writing now.

H.G. Wells

The Academy for Young Gentlemen

The Journal of Education, vol XV, no 291, pp 563-566, 1 October 1893

A hallmark of Wells's journalism at this time is the combination of criticism and storytelling. In his list of errata for David Smith's bibliography,[35] Patrick Parrinder corrected the schools discussed in this article: they are clearly Thomas Morley's Academy in Bromley, which Wells attended from ages 7–13 ("displayed a brass plate in a suburban High Street"), and Holt Academy, where Wells taught in 1887 ("adorned a little village at the foot of the Welsh hills") . The third ("had his seat by Thames' side"), schoolmaster Russell, seems to have a lot in common with both Horace Byatt at Midhurst or T.H. Huxley at the Normal School, but may be based on J.V. Milne at Henley House, where Wells had been a schoolmaster (although none of these were directly by the Thames). This piece makes evident what Wells believed to be the characteristics of the best private schoolmasters.

There is a stir in the air that bodes no good for private school masters. They are moving upon eventful times. Those sublunary astrologers who watch the greater and the lesser political lights, say that the ascendancy of Acland over Whitehall is a token of mischief and sore changes for the unchartered pedagogues in 'Ninety-three. The inspector will be after them, or, what is almost as bad, the registrar. Secondary education, it is even threatened, is to go into the furnace altogether, It is to be re-cast entirely, and when it is remodelled, the private schoolmaster will be with us no longer—or he will be pitifully changed. He will be a mere hanger-on of the sects and the select, we are told,—a conservator merely of such obscure creeds or gentilities as are incompatible with the public school.

If this is true, and it looks so, then it is only the long anticipated end of a quiet and steadily continued process of change. Things have been down-sliding with the private middle-class teacher, with ever increased velocity, for the last forty years. Time was when he could employ Dr. Goldsmith as an usher, and count Dr. Johnson, or even Milton, as his peer.[36] Those were the golden days of the "Academy"—literally its golden days. "Do any become bankrupts in trade," said "poor Goldie;" "they still set up a boarding school, and drive a trade this way, when all others fail; nay, I have been told of butchers and barbers who have turned schoolmasters; and, more surprising still, made fortunes in their new profession." And as it was in the days of Dr. Goldsmith, so also it was in those of

---

35. Parrinder, Patrick. "The Journalism of H. G. Wells: List of Errata." *The Wellsian* 36 (2013): 62–63.

36. The writer Oliver Goldsmith was an usher at Dr. Milner's Academy in 1757.

Messrs. Squeers and Creakle[37], and Dr. Blimber.[38] And then suddenly the world woke up and reorganised the grammar schools above, and established board and national schools below, and so prepared, all at once, an upper and a nether millstone, for the grinding of the Academies forthwith. And the mill, it must be admitted, has ground them exceeding small.

It would be hard to find many academies now; what survive are but poor stranded wrecks, breaking up visibly. Squeers and Creakle have long passed to dust, been ground to impalpable powder; we of the younger generation criticise the sketches of them severely, as gross caricatures. The existing private schoolmasters are the fittest and the best, surviving—men often of dignity, refinement, and originality, who can keep up a struggle, even on unequal terms, against the endowed and "public" schools. That is to say, most of them are. And these keep "schools" usually, sometimes "colleges," but hardly "academies" by any chance. What few academies still live, are like the comfortless leaves on a tree, after the nipping touch of many frosts. The shaking of the boughs that is coming, in 'Ninety-four, will doubtless be the winter of their discontent. The choicest specimens have already gone—perhaps it is for the best. Already, indeed, they are almost forgotten, though some are still dimly alive. And there is little articulate mourning as, one by one, these survivors die.

Under the circumstances, it may not be out of place to recall a few memories of three academies the prototypes of which were in existence in the last dozen years. Two of these, schools and schoolmasters alike, were of a type that the world has done with, and all of them have drifted now out of reach of any wounding by the critical shaft. One displayed a brass plate in a suburban High Street; the other dealt chiefly in boarders from afar, and adorned a little village at the foot of the Welsh hills; the third had his seat by Thames' side. But a common bond is found in the academic title, and, between the former two, in the inevitable silk hate, black coat, white tie, and ample display of shirt front, which their principals displayed as the recognised badge of their profession.

The suburban practitioner was a man of commanding urbanity, florid, portly with the portentous portliness of an encyclopædia, taking his ideals, it was suspected, largely from the great Dr. Samuel. He used "Sir" abundantly in conversation, and also as an instrument of discipline in school. Ever week-day night he took his chair—so our fathers have told us—at the gathering of the tradesmen in the "Golden Angel;" chair, and also church-warden, whiskey and water, and intellectual leadership. There they would discourse, through a haze of tobacco-smoke, of politics and science, investments and enterprises, medicine and social lore, after the manner of men: "You will admit, Sir, this—" "What I say

---

37. Squeers and Creakle were schoolmaster characters created by Charles Dickens.
38. Blimber ran an academy in Dickens' *Dombey and Son* (1848).

143

is that —" "If you was to ask *me*—." "Old Jimmy Reynolds" (that was the disrespectful name all male humanity in our town used for him behind his back, his boys being the sponsors) was pre-eminent at mathematical conclusions. "That, Sir, is *not* a matter for opinion; it is an A.P., an arithmetical progression, Sir, and I will work it out now, Sir, and show you you are wrong." Only Henbane, the undertaker ever had the temerity to face that clench. All the rest of our fathers bowed their heads until the Algebra had passed.

I wonder, sometimes, if anywhere now the chief tradesmen and the schoolmaster foregather and mingle a pleasant draught of whiskey, tobacco, and learning. It had its advantages. Home and school education gained in unanimity. "Look you here, Mr. Reynolds," said Carnegie, the butcher; "you tole my boys that Liverpool was a dirty city. Jus' set 'em right about that, will you, because my wife come from there."

Two glasses of whiskey and water, and anything that might be offered, that was old Jimmy's temperate rule. Punctually at half-past ten he would wish the assembled company good night, and walk with hands folded behind him—I do not remember him ever (indeed, I could not imagine him) with walking-stick or umbrella—up the silent High Street, as solemn in his manner as if he were a pompous plume-adorned funeral, instead of a single citizen simply going home to bed.

The schoolroom of the academy was built out over a scullery behind his house. We hung our hats in that scullery, and the disused rusty fireplace, the chimney, and the noisome darkness under the stairs, were convenient for hiding new boys' things. Greatly sculptured desks ran round the schoolroom, and two others stood in the centre about the stove. "Old Jimmy" sat at a desk in the corner, over which a gas bracket projected, and behind him hung the sole vehicle of discipline, the cane. From this point of vantage he hovered over us, as it were, throughout the morning hours, and there of a sunny afternoon, tamed by a substantial dinner, he would bow his head and sleep. This usually happened during our reading lesson—we read him to sleep, indeed, almost daily, out of the History of England, and then new readings, beneath the dignity of history, would begin to creep into the text. The monotonous somnolent hum of the reader would remain unaffected, but the sense would wander.

"In spite of these owdacious proceedings the king remained sunk in a profound lethargy and made no effort—(Old Jimmy's fair asleep now) who says kick post warning, day-boys against boarders, after school?—to protect his do-min-ions."

Orders, industry, interest—all were maintained by means of the cane. As a boy I used to think, and I think still, that that was one of the great advantages of our old academy. Sometimes we were sentenced to be kept in, but instances of the actual execution of this sentence were rare. The cane hurt at the time, but it left no ill effects—in our experience at any rate; and its smart followed so close on the crime that the dullest grasped the connexion. Then its ready infliction saved us from becoming "lawyers." Sometimes, for instance, Old Jimmy would thrash us promiscuously in the fulness of his heart—for like most heads of households he had his trials; or the wrong boy got the thrashing. This gave us early a philosophical view of life. A man who has grown up in the belief that all mischance should come from his own definite fault, and who cannot now and then take the lash across his clearly righteous shoulders without shrieking about injustice, has not begun to understand this universe at all yet, and he almost needs for his happiness to have another made for him. This arithmetical spirit is unnatural. None of us, I think, bore Old Jimmy any particular ill-will on account of his swishes going astray, and it even, I fancy, established a certain sympathy in some cases. The victim knew that he had committed no technical offence, indeed, but the feeling animating the thing was understood pretty well on both sides. The most pungent offensiveness, it seems to me, is always that which cannot be formulated. Men are not ostracized for indictable offences.

If our preceptor had not been consecrated to pedagogy, I fancy he was the kind of man who under due provocation would have found a relief in wicked words. But, following the profession he did, and being withal a conscientious man, he was driven back upon his invention for something vivid but irreproachable, and devised : "You *mis*—erable wobblers," "You *snivelling* chumblepumpenny," and many other such gracious reliefs, besides a terrible hard breathing and grinding of the teeth. He also gave many of us humorous or playful nicknames. "Come up here, Wiggle-waggle Wilson, come up here, you HOUND, and hold out your hand!" he would say.

Mrs. Reynolds was a motherly soul, resembling Britannia in personal appearance, and wore, I remember, those long curls at the side of the face that were *de rigueur* in the girlhood of our gracious Queen. She shone when headaches assailed us, or when our little interiors went wrong; but we did not like her. She was suspected—it is the common lot of schoolmasters' wives—of Machiavellian intrigues to our detriment. In the afternoon, after the vestiges of dinner had been disposed of, she would sometimes come up into the schoolroom and hear, with guiding forefinger, the little boys read. She used then to see things which we elder boys regarded as properly outside of her cognisance.

The curriculum of the school included reading, writing, the English language, arithmetic, book-keeping, mensuration, history, geography, and Scripture. The elder boys studied algebra, and even Euclid. French and drawing were "extras," and Latin a legend. Occasionally certain performances in experimental chemistry broke the even current of our work. The ordinary method of study was either to do sums to pattern out of a book, or enter items according to rule, or else learn things by heart. But in these chemicals lessons, we sat huddled together at one end of the room, pinching and pricking one another, and whispering and giggling, while Mr. Reynolds, at the other end, arranged and rearranged pans, tripods, flasks, and Bunsen burners, until either something fell down or blew up, or both, and the lesson came to an end.

The teaching of the academy was its weakest point—or rather, the absence of teaching. The worthy principal, I know now, knew no more of this essential of his business than he did of watch-making or the methods of creation. His idea seemed to be to set passages to be learnt by rote, and indicate sums to be done, and to maintain order, to a certain extent, while this was going on. We worked chiefly by tradition, surreptitiously showing one another how to do this or that. Then we would, periodically, be stood up in a wavering semicircle, to gabble off a lesson in rotation, or call out our answers to the sums we have been doing. Even if he had been a teacher of the greatest power, I do not see how Mr. Reynolds could have taught us much, with his unclassified assortment of boys between six and fourteen, at all stages in the educational process. As it was, we used to draw on our slates, tell one another fantastic stories, trade in stamps, play games with marbles, eat sweets and tarts, and bread and butter, while the process of our education was in active progress.

My happiest recollections of school hours are the rare intervals when relatives visited their "little friends," and Mr. Reynolds was called away from us. Then every boy, great or small, gave his mind with a simple earnestness to the manufacture of "shindy." Timid boys sat in their places and yelled and baa'd, bolder ones flung books and crumpled paper hither and thither, our leaders and heroes met in battle and rolled one another on the dusty floor. I can still, as I write, hear the din and smell the peculiar dusty odour that arose on those occasions. The delight was enhanced by the knowledge we had of our master's mind. He entered into the game thoroughly. His part was to steal upon us quietly, and then, in one stupendous pounce, smite down the hubbub at its climax into awful silence.

"*Cave*, you chaps! Here's Jimmy!"

And it has all passed away. Where now is there a schoolroom built out over a scullery, and a single-handed master of no particular education, who makes out his bills, and writes letters, or dozes, while his pupils, he fondly fancies, work sums to pattern, or drone away at reading-books. People have realized that teaching is an art, and the younger Universities have made the cultivated graduate cheaper. Little boys now-a-days do not bring home lists of the capes and bays of England to get off by rote, and they have their sums explained to them upon a black-board. Science is no longer a delightful episode of bangs and stinks, nor history just convenient matter for the reading lesson. At least, so they tell us in the educational publications. I wonder though, sometimes, if schoolboys whose teachers are always awake and active, and who never see the pedagogic back turned for a moment, can possibly have so much fun as we used to have in our academy, and whether that rough-and-tumble had not, after all, a very real education value of its own.

I must admit that we were happy enough with Old Jimmy, and that, after all, one or two of us have taken our places among educated people. But there is a darker side to the story of the unlicensed academy that this. For that we must visit the worthy pedagogue in Wales, whose staple was in boarders from homes far away.

Of Mr. Reynolds one can write with some pleasure. He was clean and wholesome, as honest as any man; his grave dignity he really felt—it was a delusion, perhaps, but not a pretence. His quick temper was not of his making, and his errors in educational method he shared with all his class. But it is hard to keep in the pleasant mood that is needful for easy writing when one speaks of Beulah Roberts. School-masters like Reynolds may be superannuated, but they did a useful duty in their time. I cannot see that there ever was a time when a man like Beulah Roberts would not conveniently have been dispensed with.

In brief, he and his wife were drunkards. The grimy streak of actual vice spears the story. Like his cockney compeer, the Welshman favoured the traditional chimney-pot hat, white tie, and black habiliments; but his yellow linen, dirty teeth, and unhealthy skin, hinted at the hidden plague-spot to any observant eye. He was a thick-set, bright-eyed man, speaking English with a Welsh intonation, loquacious, persuasive, at times almost eloquent. His wife had been even a pretty woman. They were not unpleasant people to meet, when they were sober. He had brought his school, once a prosperous academy of the ancient type, with some money that had come to him with his wife. Probably they were only just a little self-indulgent at first, but, when I knew them, the vice had won its way home. That, simply, was their story.

The house had once been the "Manse" of the sect, the schoolroom its chapel. There were, perhaps, twenty boarders and six or seven day-boys there. Some of these had friends and relations "abroad," two were step-children of people away in England, a few were the sons of small farmers in the district, men whose horizon was bounded by the market-town. Roberts himself rarely taught his pupils, and their entire charge, almost, was delegated to his assistant-master, a rejected pupil-teacher from the National Schools, and to a French *B.-ès-Lit.*, whom it suited, for some reason, to live in this remote district, and teach French, in return for board and shelter. In employing a discarded aspirant to the care of the working-man's children as his assistant, Mr. Roberts, I am afraid, did nothing unusual for an academy principal.

The schoolroom was a cheerless edifice, with dirt-dimmed windows (some of them broken and mended with wafers), whitewashed walls, and a brick floor. The trial of neglect, and all the marks of a nerveless control, were singularly evident in the house. The assistant master's sitting-room and study, for instance, boasted no serviceable chair. The meals were coarse and ill-cooked, served often an hour or so late, on bare tables. In the dormitories the boys were huddled three in a bed, and many in a room.

There was no time-table observed in the place. In wet weather the yard of the house became a morass, and the boys were kept in the schoolroom at their work for the whole day. The solitary usher had to prevent them disturbing his master by such method as he could devise. Corporal punishment was disowned in the school prospectus, but it was, administered on the sly, his sole resource.

When Roberts was sober, a certain fitful, aimless energy would at times be evident in the school. He would appear in the schoolroom, and, perhaps for a couple of days together, keep everyone hard at the Latin regular verbs, or he would inaugurate unaccountable half-holidays in the middle of his assistant's lesson. But periodically the boys would notice the coming shadow of his overwhelming vice. Abruptly, one day, he would enter the schoolroom, eyes glazed and steps solemnly uncertain, to make a rambling speech perhaps, before the boys, or quarrel incoherently with the usher. And then the whole household would for the next week slide steadily towards hopeless disorder.

"He is at it again," the boys would whisper. Woe betide the little unfortunate then who chose that time for an illness. He might whimper himself to sleep—to sleep for ever if he chose, without a solitary act of help in his discomfort, save such as sprang from the inherent tenderness of boys.

One might amplify this description, but it does not make pleasant reading. Sufficient has been said to show the character of this academy. The secret of its continued existence, for it lasted Roberts his lifetime, is not a pleasant one to formulate. Living, of a rough kind, was cheap in that village, his fees were remarkably low, and there are plenty of parents not too solicitous about their children. He was a figure in the pattern woven by unrestricted supply and demand; and sometimes that pattern runs into the grotesque. It will be a relief to turn to the brighter side of the fabric.

The strength, as well as the weakness, of the old Academy was its plasticity, its faithful reflection of the characteristics of its head. If he happened to be pompous, and not very energetic or able, the academy became a scene of humorous comedy; and if he was mean or vicious, the academy became sordid and miserable; but, on the other hand, a man of high aims, great capacity, and determination, could do things with an academy that would have been impossible in a school ruled by a great tradition. The pity is that while there was no tradition to trammel, there was also none to be created in a private school.

The splendid academy of Russell, for instance, to which many a distinguished man may confess himself indebted, has perished with him. No man ever realized more thoroughly than Russell the high calling of the teacher; and no one could have said less about it. But he showed his belief in his life. His school was to him no mere possession which yielded him a finite return of money for a finite amount of labour expended upon it. It was the one inspiring idea of his life. Looking at the list of his old boys that one might draw up, and seeing the exceptionally high proportion of famous and great names, one realizes at once that Russell was no mere tradesman, nor a simply capable head, whose idea of good work was his school's aggrandizement, but a teacher, a maker of men.

He infected his assistants. They presently forgot that they were hired for so much money to do so much work, that they must needs watch him suspiciously lest some extra burthen should be imposed upon them. The artistic spirit took possession of them. Young men, fresh from the Universities, came to him in a condescending mood to teach in his school as a stop-gap—and became teachers for life. He showed them that teaching had something in it that the ablest man might aspire to master without loss of dignity. By example, without a word of precept, he drove the suggestion home. Presently they would be going to him for advice in their work, freely owning to weakness here and incapacity there, and meeting always with the readiest help and encouragement. They did not feel that they were helps to an employer, but students, with him, of a great neglected art. His criticisms came not as an assault, but as a help and a favour.

Russell himself taught mathematics, chiefly in the lower forms. He believed strongly that the principal should come into that intimate personal contact with the boys that is possible only in school. None of his pupils, it is almost needless to say, regarded Euclid and trigonometry as the names of inconceivable mysteries. He appealed to our common-sense. He made us always see clearly that each new step we took was a reasonable—even unavoidable—sequence to the last. He always had something on the blackboard while he was teaching us, to hold our eyes. He asked a great many questions, all over the class. He seemed always to expect to meet a boy's eyes wherever he looked for an answer, and he always did. He never, I think had to tell a boy to attend, or interrupted his class to recall wandering thoughts. He was animated and happy while he was teaching, and we caught the suggestion of his manner, and felt all his delight in getting a thing clear and certain that was unknown or doubtful before. There was no boy in Russell's school without the "gift" for mathematics.

The discipline of the school was remarkably good. How he did it, I don't know, but he had managed to promulgate an idea among the boys that bad behaviour was just silliness. He never raged, never treated a rebel to pomp and splendour in his punishment. He really seemed only to feel contempt and a dash of pity for the delinquency. He knew the way, I think, to a boy's conceit of himself. If that was not his secret, then I cannot imagine what it could have been.

Russell was an educational reformer far ahead of his time. Many good methods and new and better ways, that have still to gain their footing in the public schools, were practised under him and, besides, advocated by him. It is here, indeed, if anywhere, that we shall lose by the disappearance of the academies, and the possible decay of all private schools. A mediocre teacher is inspired and upheld, perhaps, by the tradition of a long established school, but an innovator is fettered. There must be much that makes for rigidity and formalism, as well as permanence, in a school that is great, with a long and cherished history, and a board of governors that never dies.

These considerations must damp our congratulation at the fate of the inferior kinds of private school. It is good that the wretched dumping house for undesirable and neglected children should be competed altogether out of existence, as it very soon will be; but the crushing of all the private schools is a very different matter. Must Russell go, as well as Reynolds and Roberts? Because the field is full of weeds, must the wheat perish with the tares? But to wander into a discussion of the question whether private enterprises should or should not, under exceptional circumstances, be endowed, is outside the plan of this paper altogether, which was simply to record my memories of three typical Academies for Young Gentlemen.

H. G. Wells.

The Teaching of Geography

The Educational Times, vol XLVI, no 390, pp 435-436, 1 October 1893

Continuing to recommend and justify particular teaching styles, Wells here offers advice on the teaching of geography, especially to younger students. Geography can involve many other subjects, but at its base teaches where things are. The teacher drawing areas on the chalkboard while students do the same on paper can encourage a feeling of working together. A story, or fun fact, or pictures that seem to be spontaneously added can help the teacher prevent staleness. Assigning an in-class reading, where the teacher sits idly by, is to be avoided.

Perhaps no school subject has been written about so variously as geography, for the sufficient reason that no subject is capable of a more variegated treatment. Were it not for the examiner, who holds us all in a team together, at least as concerns certain cardinal points, it is open for one to imagine that geography would go altogether to pieces, but its own inherent tendency to differentiate, and there would be no longer one geography any more, but many. Geography, it has even been asserted, is of the nature of a gas, and takes its form altogether from the pedagogic vessel in which it is contained; for to the physicist it brings up a vision of isothermals, volcanoes, and the scour of tides; to the biologist, a struggle of this flora and fauna with that; to the historian, the growth of strong places at strategic points and rich cities on the water-ways; to the politician, an arithmetical problem of the balance of military power and productive activity; and to the philosopher, all these things and more. And one, in writing at one's ease on the subject, or in vacation plans, when the Lydian stone of practice has been left at home, is apt to follow those divergent suggestions too unreservedly, and to engender at last an ideal teaching of geography, beautiful indeed on paper, but requiring at its beginning the rare quality of omniscience in the teacher, and clearly aiming straight at omniscience in the pupil as its end.

School geography, or the geography of those that examine schools, is, however, an altogether different thing from the geography of pedagogic literature, and for a change it may not be uninteresting to consider this neglected branch a little, taking as our keynote for once low practice instead of high ideals.

Practically—this is written, without comment, as a matter of fact—school geography resolves itself into a knowledge of locality, the science of "Where is A?" This may be contradicted in the books teachers write for one another, but even among those who profess higher things on paper there may be found some who are worse—after the fashion of this world—than their words. This treatment of geography has at least the cardinal merit of being, when properly handled, well within the comprehension of small boys and girls, whereas physical and historical geography on philosophical lines, too often resolves itself in practice into an attempt to explain the half-known by appeals to the incomprehensible.

When, for instance, we teach a fifteen-year-old class the commonly accepted account of the atmospheric circulation, we begin with a description of quite hypothetical currents, and then pass tightly over an elaborate tangle of diathermancy, convection, radiation, expansion, and pressure, friction, inertia, and condensation, to explain how these currents (which, as a matter of fact, do not blow precisely as they ought to do to fit the reasons stated) originate. It requires either an exceptional memory of youthful experiences, or else an exceptional sympathy, to realize how the boyish mind feels as this day light falls upon it. On the other hand, a mere topography, that lapses into explanation only when it is or appears to be inevitable, rather than a teaching that deliberately strains after reasonableness, may be made very attractive to the immature mind.

THE PIGEON-HOLE METHOD OF TREATMENT.

School masters and mistresses in the past unhappily found a way of making such an intrinsically characterless thing as topography almost disgusting. They practised the list method of teaching and reduced the mental image of the world's surface to the form of pigeon-holes. I know one dear old lady, who was a proficient at that Georgian geography, and even yet she knows quite a respectable host of names, though many have in the course of years got into the wrong compartments. She has a kind of mental cabinet, England, with a pigeon-hole for each county, one for Europe subdivided into countries, and beyond large receptacles labelled "In Asia," "In Africa," and so on. Liverpool is in Lancashire, she knows, for instance, and Birkenhead is in Cheshire; but it has been elucidated that she is unaware whether these two places are one or a hundred miles apart.

Excellent people, by-the-by, within quite recent years have devised games of cards for the mystery of this valuable form of geography, and have modestly (or for business reasons) attributed the greater glory of their invention to Froebel. Each leading town has a card devoted to it, and there are county cards as well, with lists of towns, and the ideal George and Tommy sit round tables and make up complete counties in a mood of ecstatic enjoyment, as the picture outside the pack witnesseth to any that doubt.

However, the practical schoolmaster and parent are growing out of this kind of thing, and the next higher level is no doubt atlas teaching. Instead of having your list in books, your pupils find the places first on maps, and so construct their own lists. We go over the map in class together, dabbing our fingers on geographical features and intoning their names.

And here, by-the-by, one may notice an important matter for school masters inclined to this method. Our atlases vary flagrantly. In one atlas you may find a desolate plain where in a second there is one long ridge of mountains, in a third a radiating system of spurs, and in a fourth a system of parallel chains. Let the teacher who doubts this assertion compare the contours of East Anglia in half-a-dozen respectable maps by different publishers. Where your geographical teaching consists of the mastery of parts of an atlas, therefore, you must be extremely careful of establish a standard map, one authority of indubitable orthodoxy, to which all disputes may be carried ; otherwise children may become subtly infected with scepticism, and at last doubt together the sincerity of the educational process.

BLANK AND BLACKBOARD MAPS.

A little higher than atlas teaching is the blank easel map. With this it is customary, pointer in hand, to drill classes first collectively, and then with unexpected appeals to individuals; and no doubt much clearer and more refined conceptions of position are to be got in this way, and a skillful teacher can keep a class alive to its remotest corners; but a still better method is mapping.

By mapping is here intended sketch maps by the pupils, in pencil or ink, of the district studied, and not that elaborate imitation of atlas maps by which the sense of color is cultivated at the ragged ends of terms. These sketch maps must be done in class, and the teacher, it must be admitted, has to work hard to get them done. Perhaps this is best effected by the teacher's accompanying the class himself on the black-board. If he is, as all teachers of the subject should be, sufficiently expert, he can do this without depriving his pupils of the comforting sense of his watchful eye, and with a running suggestive commentary. "Let us begin here. The coast-line runs south, you see, for some way, then about twice the same distance eastward, and out into this jagged cape," and so on. In the same way he can call attention to the characteristic sinuosities of the rivers, and ensure the towns coming in their proper positions relative to coast and river and hill.

Thus far we have been tracing successive steps upward in the teaching of geography, but as yet it has been really simply an increasing refinement in the answer to the fundamental questions, Where is A? It has been, in fact, the teaching of maps pure and simple. But now, with the teacher half-face to class, and with a simple map growing under his hands, we begin to find openings for teaching something beyond this mere localization of place names. It is so easy to pass from a mere descriptive paraphrase of your map-drawing to other matters.

DESCRIPTIVE GEOGRAPHY.

Is it best, at any rate with boys, to let your declared object be merely to know the names and positions of places. But you lapse. You appear to be struck by a memory about a place, mention it involuntarily, glide into a reprehensible garrulity about this town and its people, tell of a siege, a difficulty of access, a local peculiarity, a remarkable product. The whole class listens, the bad boy best, and the good boy with a certain virtuous uneasiness. The general feeling of the class is a blissful consciousness of teaching being suspended.

And from such little slips from the path of rectitude one may lead on to the engraving and the photograph. In any heap of old illustrated papers there are dozens of suitable scenes one may clip and put by. It is perhaps a mistake to put pictures of places and peoples in geographical text-books,—pupils always look at them at the wrong times, they get "stale," and besides the suspicion is only natural that these things are intended to teach something. Such illustrations are looked at more keenly, and remembered far better, I think, if they seem to be no regular part of the school work, but genuinely accidental glimpses of the great real world outside beyond the pedagogic rule. It is ever so much more delightful to have the schoolroom door blow open for a moment and to peep through. Let your collection of scraps therefore seem to your class an amiable eccentricity of your own.

By such means a picture of this world may be made to grow in the most natural way in the pupil's mind. But it needs thought, time, and careful preparation. A teacher must like the subject for its own sake to do this kind of thing.

We need not stop at pictures and photographs. Almost every object has its geographical aspect and is available, if only the knowledge of the teacher is sufficiently wide. Even a collection of models and objects sold for the purpose might conceivably be utilized. The only absolutely indispensable requisites are wide knowledge and descriptive skill on the part of the teacher. Perhaps we should add a very considerable amount of leisure and energy, though these rare conditions seem to go without saying in all educational essays, possibly because most educational essayists are also enthusiastic educationalists, and do not realize, or have no patience with, the mortal nature of the teacher who does not write.

GEOGRAPHY AS SCIENCE.

In this way we rise from mere list, map, and diagram learning to genuine descriptive geography. Not only do we attempt to teach Where is A? but also, What kind of a place is A? Possibly if that is well done it should satisfy a reasonable ambition. But, as the average age of the class rises, a little thinking of the causes of things may be allowed to creep in rather than be designedly aimed at. It *must* do so if the teacher is to any extent geologist, physicist, or historian. We may incidentally discover why most towns stand on rivers, or why London is richer than Gloucester; why Liverpool distanced Bristol in the American trade, or why Scotland is poor. But beware of too much insistence upon the inevitableness of political geography and the positions of towns, or you may presently have pupils asking why Spain is poor, Galicia Austrian, or Babylon a desert. Sooner or later a question of this sort will crop up which it will either be inconvenient or impossible to explain.

The quality of the facts that may be chiefly considered in descriptive geography does not vary so widely as people imagine. A certain class of facts appeals most vividly to school children, and the next best is only the next best. I cannot imagine how "commercial geography" and trade details can possibly be anything else but boredom to any pupils but the precocious sons of self-discussing merchants. As a matter of fact, children have learnt the chief imports and exports of countries for years, and I think most grown-up people can recall their school days will agree that this part of the subject stood absolutely alone in its terrific dulness. Of course children like to know where things come from, how they are made, and so forth, and if that alone is intended by commercial geography, there is no harm in it. But jargon about the markets of the world, export of nitrates and barilla, and trade in calamine, is merely so much crackling of thorns under the pot of the enterprising rather than conscientious teacher.

Physical geography, except where the science master adds geography to his duties, scarcely grows naturally out of the ordinary school subjects. It is perhaps better regarded as being absolutely separate. An opinion has already been intimated in this paper that it is anything but an elementary subject. If it is studied at all in schools, it should clearly follow a sound and experimental course in Heat, and should indeed be simply a series of complex concrete instances of the principles of that science. Beyond this the subject becomes rather speculative geology than a natural development of what is called and studied as geography in schools.

So much for geography *virginibus puerisque*. There is, however, a suggestion of something altogether wider, a great and orderly body of knowledge centering about man in his relations to space. Such a comprehensive study might well form the body of one of the courses of the University of the future, standing based upon elementary physical and biological science, and embracing political economy and ethnography. It is however, an ideal altogether too wide for daily use in a boys' or girls' school, and the conditions of the teaching would be fundamentally different.

One method of teaching I have avoided mentioning, wherein the nominal teacher in charge gives out the portion of the text-book to be studied, and then proceeds to mark registers, toss with himself—it is always a man—left hand against right, for halfpence, or write letters to his private friends. It is really not a bad way if the text-book is well done, and it is—how common? There are some good text-books on the subject now. At the risk of being invidious, one might mention Professor Meiklejohn's. Certainly this is better than really bad personal teaching, this teaching of thousands of pupils all over the world by one clever man. But, for the young at any rate, a living present teacher to work with them, even if he is not above mediocrity, is a far better thing. Besides, logically, one should go one step further. There is no need why pupils should meet together merely to read books. That they can do as well or better at home. And, writing in a paper for schoolmasters, one naturally keeps the schoolroom in mind.

H. G. Wells

Science Notes

The Journal of Education, vol XV, no 290, p 536-537, 1 October 1893

Continuing from his column in September, Wells explores topics ranging from errors in drawing, to the contagious nature of consumption, the decentralization of London, trees, and Gilchrist lectures.

Nature last month contained an interesting paper by Mr. Haddon upon the Compulsory Laws of Error in Drawing, He does not consider that the chief mistakes of beginners are due to idiosyncrasy, but to certain universally applicable laws. All beginners, until instruction begins to have effect, display three chief tendencies. (I) Parallel lines which should converge to a vanishing point they make diverge. (ii.) Perpendiculars, except when in the direct line of sight, are never drawn perpendicular; if to the right, the line inclines from above downwards towards the central line, so as to be nearer to it at its lower end, and similarly on the left. (iii.) Perpendiculars to the picture plane, on either side of the central line, instead of converging on their vanishing point, are drawn as perpendiculars to the lower edge of the pictures. These tendencies, Mr. Haddon states, everyone who learns drawing will necessarily display, and he has traced them in Oriental pictures and even in the work of some of the great masters. It is open to any one who teaches model drawing to add a new interest to the occupation by verifying or overthrowing these conclusions.

———

There is in the current number of *Public Health* a brief and practical account of the conditions under which consumption is transmitted, which merits the careful attention of teachers. The hereditary nature of consumption is generally too much insisted upon; many people scarcely realize that this is a contagious disease for which, strictly, one can inherit only a predisposition. The commonest vehicle of communication is the expectoration, which may dry, become pulverized, and float in the air, without the germs losing their vitality. An ill-ventilated schoolroom may thus become a mere nursery of tuberculosis. The kiss of a consumptive person, again, may be literally the kiss of death. Clothing may serve to transmit the disease, and no doubt thousands of victims have died through sleeping with consumptive patients. We must also remember that the lower animals suffer, in these latitudes, with the highest. Household pets may be a danger in this way, if unduly fondled. Cows are a frequent source of contagion, and the milk given to children who may appear at all liable to this complaint should invariably be boiled. As a matter of fact, however, few of these precautions are observed even in the recognised presence of the disease, and it is even propagated, through ignorance, by people with the best intentions in the world.

——

Mr. Davison, in a series of observations communicated to the Royal Society, bearing upon the periodicity of earthquake phenomena, does much to confirm the supposition that the maxima of these coincide with seasons of low barometric pressure.

——

Herr G. Kassner has proposed a new method of preparing oxygen on a large scale. This is through the agency of calcium plumbate (Ca_2PbO_4), the compound which is formed by the action of lime upon peroxide of lead. This is exposed as porous masses to moist furnace gas at a temperature not exceeding $100°$ C. CO_2 is absorbed, forming $CaCO_3$ and free peroxide of lead. When the substance is saturated with CO_2, it is put into a strong retort and heated to redness. Very pure O is first disengaged, then O and CO_2, mixed together, and then CO_2. The CO_2 may be separated from the O, in the case of the mixed gases, by passing them over fresh quantities of Ca_2PbO_4. After the CO_2 is all disengaged from the calcium carbonate, the calcium plumbate may be reconstituted for use again by simply driving air through the retort. The suggestion seems a promising one.

——

We have read, with great interest, the thesis of Dr. Hume submitted by him in his recent candidature for the degree of D.Sc. (Lond.). It is a remarkably conscientious piece of work, upon the upper cretaceous rocks of the South of England. Samples of the washings from each zone have been examined, and the mineralogical, chemical, and zoological features exhaustively described. The work, as Dr. Hume indicates in his introduction, bears upon the question of the origin of the chalk, and through that on the discussion of the permanence of the great oceanic areas. He does not find any great support for the view of M. Cayeux that this rock was formed in comparatively shallow water and near land, and would rather ascribe it to an ocean of considerable if not of abysmal profundity.

——

This thesis is interesting as an example of the effects of the alteration in the regulations for the London doctorate. Previously a written examination admitted to that degree, but, as the standard of B.Sc. Honours rose, it became increasingly difficult to preserve a sufficient interval between the two tests. Now, no graduate can proceed to the doctorate without contributing his new mite to the heap of recorded facts. It certainly is well for the University student that he should spend his last years of study in the immediate presence of nature, rather than in a revision of the body of literature with which his B.Sc. work has already made him sufficiently familiar, but doubts have been thrown upon the scientific value of researches stimulated in this way. Unless Dr. Hume's work is exceptional, however, the new conditions will contribute not only to the advancement of the candidate, but also very materially to the advancement of science.

———

M. Bellet, in the *Revue de Géographie*, calls attention to the beginning of the decentralization of London. In 1801 London contained 10.78 per cent. of the population of England and Wales. From that date the proportion rose, but with a diminishing rate of increase, to 1881,when it reached its maximum of 14.63. It has fallen now to 14.52, and it would appear that the fall is likely to continue. M. Bellet also puts the relative alteration in population status of the three kingdoms in a convenient form by expressing it in percentages.

	England.	Wales.	Scotland.	Ireland.
1825	54.0	3.4	10.0	32.6
1893	72.8	4.0	10.7	12.5

In the *Journal of the Royal Society of New South Wales* Mr. Hamilton discusses the modification of the native flora due to the European settlement. He especially deplores the destruction of many valuable native timber trees, and especially of that group of eucalypts known as "iron barks," and he advocates state reforestation. The native flora is also being greatly impoverished by overstocking pastures. Old World seeds are being rapidly distributed, the railways having much to do with their quick extension. As a rule they seem better able to take care of themselves than the aboriginal flora, coming, as they do, from regions where competition is fiercer, but in some few cases native plants would appear to do more than hold their own.

———

At the British Association meeting, Sections C and E met in a charming discussion: "Does geography take precedence of geology, or geology of geography?" We were reminded that geology draws all its experience from physical geography; "But then," asked Mr. Topley, "who can understand the existing contours without a knowledge of geology?" It called to mind that other great issue: whether the hen came before the egg, or the egg before the hen. Mr. Henry Seebohm, the geographical president, in his remarks upon the contribution of Mrs. Lily Grove, one of those peculiarly honoured women who are F.R.G.S., to his section, administered a gentle reproof to the conservatives of the Society, in his wish that "other Fellows" would display equal powers of observation and descriptive ability. Mrs. Grove, by the bye, also favoured the anthropologists with a paper upon the ethnographic aspect of dancing, that was very warmly received. Canon Tristram's address to the biological section was essentially a field naturalist's paper, and very delightful. Professor Glazebrook (mathematics) was severe, and Professor Reynolds (chemistry) dwelt upon the *rôle* of silicon in the past. Professor Nicholson's theme, in the department of Economic Science and Statistics, was that the "dismal science" is not dead yet. In Mechanics Mr. Jeremiah Head took a rosy view of the prospects of the coal supply. Instead of the thousand years some pessimists have assigned as the period of its exhaustion, Mr. Head is inclined to give us, even without allowing for strikes, five times that time. So that he felt justified in a cheerful address, relieving the aridity of his subject, by a pleasant consideration of animal mechanism.

———

The Gilchrist Educational Trustees having granted a course of illustrated science lectures; they will be delivered, in connexion with the Bethnal Green Free Library, on alternate Thursdays in the Great Assembly Hall, Mile End. It is hoped that five thousand persons will attend each lecture. The first of the course was given by Prof. V. B. Lewes, on "Our Atmosphere and its Relation to Life," on September 28th. Other lecturers will be: Prof. Sir R. S. Ball, F.R.S., on "Other Worlds" (chairman, Sir Owen Roberts, F.S.A.); Prof. J. A. Fleming, F.R.S., on "Magnets and Electric Currents" (chairman, the Ven. Archdeacon Farrar, D.D.); Rev. Dr. Dallinger, F.R.S., on "Spiders: their Work and their Wisdom" (chairman, T. A. Bevan, Esq.) ; Dr. R. D. Roberts, on "The Evolution of the British Isles" (chairman, Mr. E. H. Pickersgill, M.P.); Dr. Andrew Wilson, editor of *Health*, on "Brain and Nerve, and their Work " (chairman, the Ven. Archdeacon Sinclair, D.D.).

Science Notes

The Journal of Education, vol XV, no 292, p 590, 1 November 1893

Wells here presents several separate but related notes, most interestingly in demonstrating how science works through the introduction of new ideas about the relationship between birds and dinosaurs. The theme is noting the passing of old knowledge (the Eozoön was originally thought be an animal), the success of new knowledge (Hurst's analysis of wing structure of pterosaurs and birds), and the failure of new knowledge to be implemented into the curriculum.

Prince Krapotkin, in his paper before the Teachers' Guild Conference, at Oxford, expounded a handsome scheme for the teaching of physiography, that had only one defect.[39] It was not true to his title. What he would have us teach was in fact not physiography but elementary omniscience. This was certainly a most desirable subject, and at a holiday gathering it was scarcely to be expected that we should be troubled with narrow practical objections. About half way through the paper its author appeared to grasp his own drift. He had asked for soundly taught mechanics, physics, chemistry, botany, and zoology, as a foundation. After this an attack upon the territory of the classics in the school time-table became a necessity, and this omitted foundation insisted upon its neglect. It is a pity the Prince did not deliberately undertake the case of natural science against literary studies, instead of selecting a narrow theme one's views upon which must be largely determined by one's decision upon the larger question.

———

Apart from this objection, we must congratulate the Prince upon a very valuable contribution to educational literature, and we are glad to find it reprinted in full in the *Geographical Journal* (October). His suggestion of regional types is especially good. That "the review and analysis of different types of scenery ought to be the leading feature of the teaching of geography in the secondary school"—the study, that it, of natural districts before artificial divisions—will be endorsed by every experienced teacher of geography.

———

In our September issue we warned geological teachers of the end of "*Eozoon*". Another alteration in the accepted teaching in palæontology must be noted. It has been customary, on the strength of Huxley's anatomical analysis, to assert that birds are descended, not from the pterosaurs of the mesozoic rocks,

---

39. Peter Kropotkin was a noted Russian geographer, scientist, and anarchist.

but from the kangaroo-like semosaurs. A fundamental difference in structure was supposed to exist between the wings of pterosaurs and birds. Dr. Hurst, however, shows very conclusively, in the October issue of *Natural Science*, that this difference is imaginary, and due to the careless examination and culpable drawing of the well-known fossil of *Archeopteryx* at Berlin. This most ancient bird, he proves, is quite intermediate between pterosaurs and modern birds, thus completely upsetting the received opinion.

———

The scholastic statistician is having a busy time. Mr. Townsend Porter has been weighing children by the thousand in the public schools of Saint Louis. He concludes that precocious children are heavier, and dull ones lighter, than the average child of the same age. This hardly seems in accordance with one's prepossessions in the matter.

———

There is always a chance of the young chemist, or amateur teacher of chemistry, making Iodide of Nitrogen (HNI_2 or NI_3), by adding excess of ammonia solution to a strong solution of Iodine in KI, and so entertaining an explosive unawares. Iodide of Nitrogen has apparently only one property—to blow up on the slightest provocation. By adding ammonia solution to powdered iodine, Dr. Szuhay has obtained a variety that detonated under water, and even when he contrived to get it upon a filter, it exploded violently—like an irascible valetudinarian—on the slightest draught. An attempt to ascertain its composition with sulphuric acid ended in the complete pulverization of the containing vessel. We recommend the compound to the careful attention of those who adhere to the principle of the "free and open" chemistry cupboard.

———

The examiner in geography for the Queen's Scholarship Examination (1893) we observe asked the stock question about the circulation of the atmosphere, and in the "Model Answers" published in a contemporary we find the stock answer— that venerable account that died in 1858, as we pointed out in our September issue—and certainly which now, in common decency, ought to be allowed to begin its rest. So slowly as this does knowledge advance. The successful candidates will doubtless inoculate the next generation with this error, and in the twentieth century the miracle of two winds blowing through the same point at right angles will still, in all probability, be solemnly taught.

On Certain Defects in English Public Schools

The Journal of Education, vol XV, no 293, pp 667-671, 1 December 1893

This is one of the strangest articles Wells wrote at this time, because it critiques the wealthy public schools. Since he never attended such a school, it is difficult to know how serious to take the criticism of meat at the table, additional expenses for tuck-shop food, or the role of the housemaster's wife. The comment that additional expenses may be difficult for the professional families to meet, and the implication that without these middle-class boys the intelligence level of the school would decline, seems satirical. But in criticizing the curriculum, Wells is on more serious ground, reinforcing the argument for science rather than classics education, and noting the lack of attention to pedagogy among public school masters. The list of defects at the end is particularly damning. He also emphasizes the importance of English composition and constitutional history, beginning an interest that will ultimately lead to him writing history himself.

BY AN OUTSIDER.

If the *Times* (whose editor is an old Wykehamist),[40] in its leader on the Winchester Quingentenary, felt justified in calling attention to the weak points in English public schools of which every good schoolmaster is perfectly aware, I hope it may not be thought presumptuous or ungracious in a foreign visitor to point out what seem to him certain other defects of which many good schoolmasters are apparently unconscious.

With regard to the ever-disputed question of boarding schools *versus* day schools, while much can be said on both sides, we have to recognise the fact that in many instances, owing to the business, political, and social engagements of the parents, and the lack of satisfactory schools near the home, most boys must go away from home for their education. In the houses of the masters they learn punctuality, prompt obedience, regular habits of study, and become accustomed to a wholesome method of living, which in these luxurious times is much to be desired. But is it well that, during the plastic years of school life, the boys should see so little of the influence of refined and cultivated gentlewomen, the grace of whose society would soften and humanize the roughish tendencies of the average boy? It is not pleasant for parents to find that often boys, after a term or two of school life, seem to have forgotten the German maxim, *Ehre die Frauen*. Masters' wives, of course, do what they can to counteract the roughening tendencies of too

---

40. A former pupil of Winchester College, after William of Wykeham, its founder.

exclusive masculine association, but it is to be remembered that the prior claim of their own families narrows the sphere of their influence.

It is much easier to point out this deficiency in the social training of school-life than to prescribe a remedy. But it is certainly desirable that matrons should not only be chosen for their executive qualities as housekeepers and economical managers, but that they should be gentlewomen of social tact and refinement, who are to carry out in the social life of the master's house the same relation as the mother in the home. The influence, day by day, of such women, whose attention would be given to the domestic interests of the house without distraction, would be a positive tonic for the moral and social life of the boys.

In discussing the food which boys have at the public schools, we touch upon a delicate but extremely important subject. Doubtless, matters have greatly improved since the days of the School Inquiry Commission, but it would be interesting to know of how many schools the statement would now be true, which Dr. Butler then said was true of Harrow, viz., that the boys had no meat for breakfast. The charge for board at all public schools is high enough to warrant the presence of meat on the table twice a day. The bill of fare at the homes of most of the boys always includes, at least, as much as this, and the parents always expect at least this at all hotels and boarding-houses, where they pay no higher price for board than the school charge amounts to.

That the profit made from boarding the boys is large, is patent. The fact is shown by the buildings and improvements which schools like Marlborough and Wellington, managed on the hostel system, are able to pay for out of their income, and from the large gifts made by the headmaster and masters of other schools for similar purposes. While this large profit is, undoubtedly, more defensible where it is used for the general improvement of the school than where it goes into the private pocket of the house-master, in either case, the patrons of the public schools have a right to demand that, considering the price paid for board, the boys should have an abundance of meat at breakfast as well as at dinner.

But the first meal of the day at public schools needs reforming in another respect. It should come earlier. With the exception of day schools, and schools, like Clifton, which have a large admixture of day pupils, morning chapel and first school come before breakfast. If we remember that not a few conscientious boys are accustomed to rise early in order to study, we can realize how injurious, especially to growing boys, is this custom of a late breakfast, which most medical men would most severely condemn. Dr. Clement Dukes, of Rugby School, one of the highest authorities on school hygiene, says that no boy should go to first school without having taken a reasonable supply of food into his stomach, and the hasty gulping down of a bit of bread and butter and a cup of tea or coffee, does not meet this requirement satisfactorily.

But any criticism of the arrangements for living at the public schools would be quite incomplete without a "fling" at that well-rooted institution, which many teachers look upon as more or less of an abomination, viz., the tuck-shop. It may here be pointed out that, in this case, as in the case of the high charges for food, an official tuck-shop, where the profits go to school uses, if carefully managed, and charging only a reasonable profit, is more satisfactory than a private tuck-shop; for the patrons, in paying their margin of profit, are contributing to the general good. The tuck-shop is unknown at girls' schools. Why should it be fostered or tolerated at a school for boys?

But to condemn it merely would not go to the root of the trouble. Do we not find that the *raison d'être* of the tuck-shop rests very largely upon the common law which prevails at public schools, that it is good form for a boy to supply the deficiencies of the bill of fare from his private purse?

Surely, nothing but a shabby defence can be made for this practice of supplementing the master's table out of the private purse, a custom which is wholly contrary to all principles of table etiquette, and sets a premium upon the carelessness of housekeeper, butler, or steward, whose conscience must be inevitably sapped by the solacing though that any deficiencies in the fare provided by the house the boys can easily make up by resorting to the pastrycook's or tuck-shop.

It is also a great injustice to a parent who has paid a large sum in advance for the support of his son at school, that he cannot consider this sum as inclusive, but must reckon on a considerable extra for the tuck-shop account. When a father desires to educate all his sons at a public school of high grade, these extra expenses, which have to be considered, will amount, in some cases, to a positive prohibition, unless the boys can win scholarships. Now the sons of professional men, who have limited incomes, form the best class of material, and the preponderance of them at Marlborough accounts in no slight degree for the prestige of that school. Eton and Harrow, with their large numbers of sons of wealthy and luxurious families, sadly need the tonic influence of this class of boys to raise the standard of intellectual work. The regular fees at these schools are exceedingly high now, and with these extra expenses, which custom sanctions, this most desirable class of pupils is more and more found on the lists of other schools.

Moreover, this custom, which permits a boy with a large allowance to supplement his table with extras, while a boy with a small allowance must be content with the ordinary fare of the master's house, inevitably leads to invidious distinctions, wholly out of harmony with the democratic spirit which we have been led to believe was the glory of the public schools.

But, perhaps, I have dwelt too long upon the material side of life at the public schools. The life is more than meat, and I pass on to the intellectual training of the schools. This phase of the subject naturally divides itself into two parts: the course of study, and the methods of instruction. With regard to the first point, the assertion can safely be made that the average amount of work now required of the public-school boy per week should not be greatly increased. From twenty to twenty-seven hours a week of school work, apart from preparation or pupil-room, is probably a fair estimate of the work required, and if this is thoroughly done it is all that can reasonably be expected.

It is not so much as the German boy does in the *Gymnasium*,[41] but, thank heaven, the public-school boy, on leaving the sixth, is much more of a man, physically, though less of the scholar, than the German youth when he takes his *Abiturientenexamen*,[42] and the English boy's school-life is richer in pleasant memories and health-giving sports. It is evident, then, that, if the course of study is to be reformed, it must be done not by retaining the present curriculum and making additions to it, but by limiting or excluding some of the present subjects, and by substituting others.

It is but thrashing old straw to say that the vulnerable point of attack in the present course of study, on classical sides, is the undue preponderance of time given to the classics, which, including divinity on the classical side, occupy, roughly speaking, two-thirds of the time of the boys. When the day of redemption from the bondage of compulsory Greek shall have drawn nigh, and the principles of Mr. Welldon's resolution[43] prevail at Oxford and Cambridge, this narrow curriculum will have given way to a broader one, wherein science, German and English literature will receive more attention than they get now.

When the old order changes, let compulsory verse-making be one of the first things to go by the board. In view of the many attractive fields of study which in the last fifty years have been opened to youth, we can well afford to be rid of this relic of mediæval Jesuitism, which Mr. Oscar Browning rightly characterizes as an attempt to play and juggle with the human mind, to make pretence at thought where there is no thought at all, to mark time instead of marching. Since Archdeacon Farrar's philippic against it in 1867,[44] it has slowly lost ground, but

---

41. Gymnasiums were German schools that prepared pupils for university.

42. The German examination indicating readiness for university.

43. Late in 1890, J.E.C. Welldon at Harrow had brought forward to the Conference of Headmasters at Oxford a resolution saying that Greek should not be a compulsory subject at Oxford and Cambridge. (*Journal of Education*, 1 January 1891, p 55).

44. Frederic William Farrar was a botanist, a teacher at Marlborough and Harrow whose lecture "Defects in Public School Education" denounced using classical verse construction in the curriculum. He considered the "non-achievement of this puny accomplishment" to be a huge waste (p 34).

still the practice dies hard. Let verse-making be required only of those clever boys who show a distinct aptness for it, as long as skilfulness in the art is necessary for winning honours at the University. The besom of reform we hope will soon sweep away that necessity, and then the elegant accomplishment of verse-making may be left as an avocation to those who are skilful adepts at it—for example, Mr. Gladstone and Pope Leo XII.

Repetition has a distinct educational value in training and strengthening the memory, but to confine it to Latin and Greek, as is commonly done on the classical side of schools, is not the best method. Let the rich heritage of our own tongue be utilized in this way. Which, one may properly ask, will be the richer experience in middle life for the schoolboy when he has reached that age—to recall, through the blessed power of memory, his Virgil and Horace, or noble passages from the Psalms and Gospels, Shakespeare, Milton, Wordsworth, Tennyson, and other singers, more humble, indeed, but still sweet? If this practice is followed merely to enlarge the vocabulary, then it is a poor use of a system which, properly utilized, would permanently enrich the æsthetic and literary nature.

To this end more attention should be paid to the manner of utterance in repetition, viz., to proper elocution. I do not mean by elocution the practice of artificial, self-conscious mouthing of speeches in public, but attention to such clear-voiced and varied utterance of ordinary speech as makes it easy to understand and charm the ear. English women are often complimented by foreigners on their melodious, distinct, and crisp utterance, so that it is said that the most commonplace phrases, falling from their lips, take on a new charm. But it is seldom that one hears English boys complimented in that way. The art of reading aloud well is no mean accomplishment, which our public schools should not consider beneath their dignity to encourage. Now the few boys who appear before the public on speech day are almost the only ones who get any specific training of this sort at school. A better system would give to a large majority of the older boys some simple elocutionary training, with especial view to voice-building, clear enunciation, and proper emphasis. In all work in the form room, dreary monotone in speech, and slipshot utterance, should be relentlessly scored by the master, who should remember to be a model to his pupils in this respect. To teach elocution in this simple sense becomes the duty of every form-master, and the opportunity for it comes with every lesson.

It is a most serious fault of the public schools that the study of English literature and the writing of English receive so little attention. While fifteen hours per week are given to the classics, seldom more than an hour a week, even on the modern side, is given to the rich heritage of our own literature. Sometimes a play of Shakespeare, or a poem of Scott, is added as a vacation task, and this represents all that the school officially does to make the pupil acquainted with English writers, and to awaken in him a taste for the best books, which will enrich all of his after-life. All honour to the masters who endeavour to supply this deficiency by private work in English with their pupils, but this does not excuse for a moment the discreditable fact that the regular programme of an English public school either entirely omits the study of English authors, or treats them with indifferent attention.

To the threadbare argument that to submit the English classics to the drudgery of the class-room will take the bloom off the peach, the fact that English writers are studied with delight at some schools is sufficient answer. No such complaint is heard from Harrovians who have studied English literature under the master of the modern side. Let the same enthusiasm and zest be given to teaching English authors as is often given to teaching the ancient classics. No essential elements of true culture of the boys will be lost if the time now given to Homer and Virgil, Cicero and Demosthenes, be lessened, and more be spent in intent study of Chaucer and Milton, Bacon and Burke.

The failure of many of the public schools with regard to English composition, is more glaring even than in the teaching of English literature. If some of the time spent on Latin verse composition were directed to training boys to express their thoughts in correct and forcible English, this great blot on public-school education might be wiped out. In this respect the English public school is distinctly inferior to the French *lycée*. The French youth at school not only obtains an appreciative knowledge of his national literature, but receives a definite and progressive training in writing his own language. Surely it is no mere accident, not wholly a result of the genius of the language, that a good literary style, crisp, lucid, and graceful, is much more common with French writers than with their neighbours to the east or west. The arduous training with the pen, under the unsparing eye of a critical master, which the late Guy de Maupassant imposed upon himself before appealing to the public, represents in kind, though not, of course, in degree, the method of training in the use of his own language which the State imposes upon the youth in the *lycée*.

How many public schools can show in their courses of study any such orderly system for training in English composition, where the pupil, beginning with simple sentence construction and paragraphing, goes on, through practice in narrative and description, to the more difficult work of exposition and argumentation? A few occasional essays, set by the form-master, with very little formal instruction in rhetoric, at most schools constitute about all the work in English composition. I do not forget that much incidental training in English is done by "live" form-masters, through construing, in the regular form work. Translation from a foreign language into English is one of the best methods of training in writing good English, if it is done properly, with an avoidance of foreign idioms. But this utilization of the construing lesson is by no means universal, and varies very much with the master. Many, like the late Headmaster of Fettes,[45] insist upon idiomatic vigorous English in translation, while many accept stilted and juiceless renderings, provided they are correct. Most admirable as the practice is, it does not give the broadest training in the use of English; for, while it cultivates dexterity in phrasing, and enlarges the vocabulary, the practice permits the use of metaphor only in a limited way, and gives the pupil little experience either in originating thought or in arranging his ideas in orderly logical sequence. It is a perfectly just demand that when so much time is spent in teaching boys to write Ciceronian Latin, much more attention should be paid to a study of the best English style, and to constant practice in composing English themes. It is to be hoped that some progressive schoolmaster will be disposed to try the experiment of taking one half the time now spent by masters and pupils— often so fruitlessly—on composition in Latin and Greek, and of devoting it with equal zeal and earnestness to the writing of English essays. Let the subjects be interesting to the boys, and in touch with their studies, reading, and life. Let there be equal care, in correcting, and suggesting improvements, as is now the case with verse composition. A well-planned and well-written essay should receive as high honour as any "fair copy" in Latin or Greek. Such as experiment as this, earnestly and faithfully carried out, would bring forth good fruit. It would show a great improvement among all the boys in the power to express thought, and would explode the absurd theory that the power to write well comes by chance, and that a good writer is born not made. In this, of course, as in other lines of achievement, natural gifts have much to do with the highest success. As we do not expect to make a silk purse out of a sow's ear, so one does not expect by any sort of rhetorical training to make an ordinary boy write like Macaulay or Newman.[46] But by constant practice under a wise system, he can be taught to write in a much better style than would otherwise be the case. Such an orderly and progressive system of training should be found in the English public schools as is found in the French *lycee* and the German *Gymnasium*.

Little space is left to consider the relative position of science in the course of study, especially on the classical side. In the last twenty years there has been great improvement. Physics and chemistry now have considerable attention at most schools. For general culture, as distinct from technical training, the former of these seems a more valuable study than the latter. Moreover, it would seem a fair questions whether natural science, in some form like geology, botany,

---

45. Alexander Potts, first headmaster of Fettes College in Edinburgh.
46. Cardinal John Henry Newman wrote extensively, not least about education. He died in 1890.

elementary biology, should not be adopted as a compulsory subject of study for the whole school, while chemistry remains as an optional subject for those preparing for the technical professions. The object would be to give a better opportunity for the development in early youth of a scientific habit and method of observation of nature than the public-school course now offers. Some schools, notably Marlborough, do much good work of this kind in a purely voluntary way. But the introduction of a boy to the study of nature should not be left to his mere volition or chance. The school course should require that at some time he should study closely the natural world that lies about him. He must learn the lesson that Agassiz taught his pupils, viz., to *look*.[47] Such work needs most stimulating teaching, to be sure, and a genius, like the master who directs the Natural History Society at Marlborough,[48] is not found every day. But when the value of nature study is once given hearty recognition in the curriculum, satisfactory teachers will soon be forthcoming.

It is sometimes remarked that few public-school men are to be found among our distinguished leaders in natural science and medicine. Whether this be true or not, it must be allowed that too much attention in the past has been given to words, and too little to things. The public-school curriculum has shown too much of the impress of Sturm,[49] and in it the spirit of Comenius[50] has not been heartily fostered. No school now is probably such a Sahara to the boy interested in the study of the animal and vegetable kingdom as Shrewsbury was to Darwin in his youth, but there is still much room for improvement in this direction. Through actual observation and practice, and not merely by text-book, every pupil in the public school should, at some stage of his course, be compelled to observe carefully the laws and phenomena of the material world.

While English history is generally well taught, the saying of Professor Freeman, "History is past politics, and politics present history," is often overlooked.[51] There is danger that too much attention be given to the centuries before the Elizabethan era, and to royal genealogies, and the details of campaigns and battles, while too little is given to constitutional development and a careful study of the frame of government under which we live. Elementary politics should have more recognition, at the sacrifice of special study of periods in English history, which have much less practical value for the training in

---

47. Louis Agassiz, a Swiss-American biologist who died in 1873, was a professor of natural history at Harvard. He emphasized learning through direct observation alongside instruction.
48. This is most likely Edward Meyrick.
49. Johannes Sturm was a 16th century innovator in public instruction.
50. See earlier article on Comenius, where Wells does not treat him as kindly.
51. Edward Augustus Freeman was an Oxford historian.

citizenship. Professor Bryce's noble plea for the teaching of civic duty, in the *Contemporary Review* for July, is a trumpet call to public-school masters, as well as to the audience before which it was originally spoken. While it is well that the public-school boy should learn through what heroic effort the heritage of civil liberty and constitutional government has come down to us, he should also, before he leaves school, become familiar with the civil institutions as they now exist, and some of the great questions that confront the voter of to-day.

It is true that the absence of a first-rate text-book on this subject will throw more work in lecturing upon the master, but this consideration ought to be a stimulus, rather than a drawback, to endeavour. Miss Buckland's "Our National Institutions" is a capital little book for lower forms, while Fonblanque's "How We are Governed" contains matter enough, but is not in form an ideal text-book. Mr. Raleigh's "Elementary Politics" could profitably be used with the sixth, but is hardly specific enough and sufficiently detailed to satisfy all purposes. There is need of a text-book for public schools, written with the same purpose as Mr. Arnold Forster's book "The Citizen Reader," for Board schools; though, in order to be successful, it should be less patronising and more accurate than that widely used publication. From our kindred beyond the sea has lately come a book that seems almost a model in this respect, viz., Mr. John Fiske's "Civil Government in the United States." That eminent writer on philosophical and historical topics, in this book has devoted his literary powers to explaining to American youth the details of their complex government, in such an engaging fashion that the book, supplemented as it is by stimulating questions, is full of interest from cover to cover. Will not some English writer render similar service to the youth of this country? Perhaps the present Chancellor of the Duchy of Lancaster, after winning such brilliant laurels by his exposition of the American commonwealth, may be disposed to do for the youth of his country what Mr. Fiske has done for those of the United States, or Compayré, in his "L'Instruction Civique," had done for France. For those who wish to enter upon this interesting study, Mr. Acland had "blazed" out a path in the new Evening Continuation School Code. The main outlines of the scheme there laid down, entitled "Life and Duties of the Citizen," might well be followed out in public schools.

With regard to methods of teaching, as distinct from the subjects taught, it will not be possible to go into detail; but what at once strikes an outsider is that many of the teachers seem to make little effort to find out systematic and scientific methods of teaching. The form-master is chosen chiefly for his scholarship and character, and, fresh from college, with no pedagogical training, is put in charge of his form to teach them as best he can. By painful experience he learns in time certain general principles of method which, under a proper system, he should have been taught before he took up his work. In most schools the headmaster, with his many duties, forgets that he should instruct the new teacher in the best methods of teaching. More than one famous headmaster could be named who were inspiring teachers themselves, but gave hardly a crumb of suggestions to the masters under them. These new teachers had to grope their way alone without any guidance; they could have learned very much by watching the methods of the more experienced masters in their class-room work, but custom does not permit this. Consequently, the variety of excellence in the teaching of different forms in the same school is very great; but if there were free opportunity for the less experienced masters to observe the methods of their most successful colleagues, the average quality of the teaching would be greatly improved. The lack of interest among public-school masters in improved methods, and in teaching as a science, is so marked, that a master who does show keen interest in the subject is viewed by his colleagues as somewhat erratic. Very many, satisfied with the present results, are disposed to look upon any careful study of method in education as food for the Board-school master, but of no value to the master in the public school. Much twaddle has occasionally been written under the name of pedagogy, and some talented writers on education, indeed, have been failures at the teacher's desk; but that is not a sufficient reason for neglecting the study of mental development and of the best methods of teaching. When we consider the number and position of the public schools in England, it is hardly a creditable fact that the permanent contributions to pedagogical literature which have come from them during this century can be easily counted on the fingers of one hand. Fortunately, there are some signs of improvement. Public-school masters are breaking away a little from the exclusive spirit which has held them aloof from keen sympathy with other teachers in studying the great problems of education. Let us hope that the day is not far distant when not only high scholarship, but a knowledge of the best methods of teaching, will be required of public-school masters before they are appointed.

With so much that is noble about the work of the public schools, it is unfortunate that the methods of stimulus are often ignoble and mechanical. Elaborate marking systems, which publish at intervals the standing of each boy, place-taking, prizes of all sorts, and constant exhortation to win scholarships—these are often the chief incentives to study, and are more in favour than efforts to persuade them to study for the love of the work, and to do their duty well. The slavish adherence to the marking system in certain schools, and the abject reliance upon it as a goad for boys, are sometimes pathetic. A marking system of some sort in large schools is essential, chiefly as a register of a pupil's attainments, and also as a spur to the laggard and shiftless. In the nature of things, it is a very imperfect register of attainment. Some masters mark high, some low. One master may mark high or low according to the state of his liver; he may mark a paper with the utmost conscientiousness when he begins to look over a pile of them, and with the utmost recklessness when his mind has become benumbed by the deadly monotony of the grind. Consequently, too much publicity and individual distinction in marking-lists are undesirable, because injustice is done and appeal is made to ignoble motives. Classification by groups according to excellence is a much fairer system than individual rating. When a marking system is made prominent in the life of a school, it not only absorbs much of the time and energy of masters in the tiresome work of accountants, there is a constant tendency to shut out from the sphere of motive in a boy's mind the play of the nobler impulses. The moment a teacher yields to making use of place-taking in order to keep his form awake, that moment his power and his will to make the subject interesting are being steadily sapped. There is a wide gap between the mechanical and the spiritual teacher. The first two essays in the "Lectures on Education," published by the Pitt Press, in their utterly diverse spirit illustrate these two types of teachers, and after reading them one realizes again how "the letter killeth, but the spirit giveth life."[52]

It is to be hoped that the principles embodied in the first essay are steadily gaining ground in the public schools, and that the ideas of the second will more and more recede. Whenever a master is ready to sweat blood, so to speak, in order to arouse and hold the interest of his pupils, then he will have a broader and nobler view of his calling, and these mechanical devices will more and more be put aside as childish things.

Space will not allow more than the slightest reference to certain other defects in the public schools, which have been more or less discussed in the last few years. The scandal of giving scholarships, which were intended for poor boys, to the sons of wealthy parents, the excessive use and abuse of examination, the particular attention paid to clever boys, to the neglect of ordinary boys, the spirit of exclusiveness among famous schools, whereby a proper feeling of *esprit de corps* degenerates into caste, the dangers of athleticism, the lack of co-ordination between the schools themselves, and between the schools and the Universities, the unwieldy size of some schools, and the fact that so small a portion of the youth of England are reached by the public schools—these are all questions which conscientious teachers need to ponder over.

In conclusion, the writer does not forget under what disadvantages headmasters labour in the struggle for reform. They must meet successfully the test of preparation for the Universities, in which the pre-eminence of classics is

---

52. This would be *Three Lectures on Subjects Connected with the Practice of Education*, Pitt Press Series, University of Cambridge, 1883. The first two essays are H. W. Eve, "On Marking", and Arthur Sidgwick, "On Stimulus". It is not surprising that Wells ignored the third, on Latin Verse Composition.

obstinately maintained by the authorities. He is aware, also, how the tremendous power of old traditions and of conservative subordinates can hamper the progress of reform. He knows full well that it is much easier to point out defects than to correct them. His criticisms may seem to some wounds, but they are meant to be the faithful wounds of a friend. He yields to no one in his admirations for the many noble features of the public schools. He appreciates the work of character-building which they have done in the past, and are still doing. But great success and prestige often breed indifference to progress, and pride not seldom blinds the eye to serious faults. Considering how imperfectly in this world ideals are realized, the best men in teaching, as in other professions, ought to be ready and eager for the summons "Forward."

Mr. Churchill: The Dreamer as Schoolmaster

The Journal of Education, vol XVI, no 294, pp 19-20, 1 January 1894

The character of Mr. Churchill, a schoolmaster in the novel Kavanaugh *(1849) by Henry Wadsworth Longfellow, is here compared with Wells's knowledge of the actual experience of being a schoolmaster. Interestingly, the fictional Mr. Churchill always wanted to write romances, which Wells was himself beginning to do at this time. The focus on fiction is evident in Wells's creative approach, as he redeems a character mostly ignored by its own author. The ending features a firm defense of the noble intentions of the "dreaming" teacher, over "showy, all-round success".*

Only desultory readers nowadays adventure into the prose works of Longfellow, or, perhaps, now and then, some admirer of his poetry makes of them a work of supererogation. For, to tell the truth, they are redolent of the golden age of the man, of the gay blossom days of the gifted person before the art of graceful self-abnegation is acquired. They have the offence of youthful monologue. "Hyperion" is a self-revelation of a florid young man, a Transatlantic rendering of d'Orsay, strictly proper and fairly orthodox, who lived in the days when men's hair seems to have curled more abundantly than it does now, and their sentiment, like their waistcoats, was mainly embroidery. And "Kavanagh" is just Hyperion, a little further sobered by the cure of souls.

It is, perhaps, a pity that "Kavanagh" comes second in the common editions of Longfellow's prose writings, for, on many accounts, it is a decidedly more readable story than "Hyperion." From our point of view especially is this to be deplored, because there is a really charming schoolmaster to be met with in the village of Kavanagh's ministry. This is Mr. Churchill, whom one may without much hesitation pronounce a real person. A living schoolmaster certainly sat to Longfellow for the portrait, though who the sitter was we do not know. Longfellow was not accustomed to portraiture, and there are sufficient indications of the transition from his familiar and characteristic "imaginative" to the "imitative." This classification of schools of art, by the bye, is Longfellow's own, and Hyperion founds on this basis the startling proposition of the æsthetic inferiority of Goethe. The surest indication, perhaps, that Mr. Churchill is a portrait, is the evident lack of sympathy between artist and sitter. You cannot invent what you do not fully comprehend. And Longfellow seems to us to miss the merit of this character altogether, to use him simply as a caryatid bearing a moral, an excellent moral, no doubt, about not wasting time.

Mr. Churchill is the foil of the energetic and able Kavanagh, who is, of course, like Hyperion, an avatar of his author. We meet with our pedagogue first, closing his school-house door behind him, thankful that the Saturday holiday has come. "All the bright young faces were gone, all the impatient little hearts were gone," and the master, casting a furtive glance at the last caricature of himself in red chalk on the wooden fence close by, entered with a light step the solemn avenue of pines that led to the margin of the river.

For this Mr. Churchill (master of the Fairmeadow Mixed School) is no educational enthusiast. "Nature had made Mr. Churchill a poet, but destiny made him a schoolmaster." He is an artist, but the knowledge of himself has come too late. His Pegasus is already bridled and saddled with a heavy harness and burthen of duty. "He was forced to teach grammar when he would fain have written poems." And, seeing how many literary artists have risen out of our ranks to success, it is not too much to suppose an even greater number have failed to break their professional prison. Mr. Churchill is distinctly a scholastic type, the schoolmaster artist, schoolmaster against his will.

One may doubt if the thoughts Longfellow ascribes to him were really his thoughts. There pass through his mind, we are told, a great variety of neat allusions and recondite figures; he even buys a discarded pulpit, whitewashed, upon which to write lengthy conceits. But such things of his as we read in the book are not the thoughts of a dreamer; they smack unmistakeably of the industriously compiled note-book of a professional poet. The figure of our artistic village schoolmaster lying under a sycamore by the side of a swift-running stream and spinning a tissue of pretty thoughts, is portraiture. But when we are told that he thought "of the Roman Consul, Lucinus, passing a night with eighteen of his followers in the hollow trunk of the great Lycian plane tree," we must respectfully intimate a doubt. Longfellow, there, has given our poet credit for some of his own literary "overmatter." Or, to use another image, he has fitted him up with condemned stores from his own intellectual commissariat.

We may very vividly figure to ourselves Churchill in that dusty schoolroom of his. He tried to relieve the aridity of mathematics by examples from the "'Lilawati' of Bhascara Acharya," until discouraged by his committee, who did not think it "sufficiently practical." The young lady whom Billy Wilmerdings, before his expulsion, used to annoy by peeping at her through a hole in his desk, relates in a letter to a friend, that "he gave us this question in arithmetic: 'One-fifth of a hive of bees flew to the kadamba flower; one-third flew to the Silanhara; three times the difference of these two numbers flew to an arbour; and one bee continued flying about, attracted on each side by the fragrant Ketaki and the Malati. What was the number of bees?' Nobody could do the sum."

Beside this incident, a vision of exercise-book correction, and an allusion to an ineffectual struggle to make Billy Wilmerdings—who afterwards became a whaler—love the dead languages, we hear very little of the scholastic side of

Churchill's life. However, we can imagine what the rest was like. No doubt teaching—even teaching Billy Wilmerdings what he neither needs nor desires—is a noble occupation. Yet even to those who are not poets it has its flavour of monotony and repetition. And what must it be when butterfly thoughts of beauty go fluttering ever and anon across the even hues of the scholastic cell, when in odd unguarded moments the door of the imagination opens, the horns of fairyland blow, an unearthly sunlight shines, and the clamour of the crowded realm of fantasie calls us out and away?

Longfellow, like Mrs. Churchill, takes a sensible view of the case. "Why not write your Romance?" says Mrs. Churchill—such an obvious solution it is! and he is always wrestling with himself, and really sitting down to begin, when some matter of cooking-stoves or patent needles, or Miss Cartwright, the poetess (for a preface), or Mr. Hathaway (blatant about a new magazine to contain American national literature commensurate with Niagara, the Alleghanies, and the Great Lakes, for which he wants gratuitous contributions), interrupts. The great romance never gets written, and Mr. Churchill is still the Fairmeadow schoolmaster at the end of the story.

Meanwhile our Kavanagh points the moral. He comes to Fairmeadow and preaches such eloquent sermons that Alice Archer pines away and dies of the love of him. He marries the beautiful and highly cultivated Cecilia Vaughan—an excellent match from any point of view. These two young people go off to Europe for three years to visit the picture galleries and the historical monuments, and do something towards Kavanagh's scheme for the reunion of Christendom—a project since advocated by Mr. Stead. A poem of great merit, and some other literary trifles, seem to have been accomplished in the interval. They return to find Churchill still stuck in his rut.

Greatness, on the theory of our author, cannot exist by itself; it is really entirely conditioned by publicity, and that Churchill has not attained. Hathaway has stolen his idea about obscure martyrs, and made copy and reputation. The romance has been anticipated by a brother author. It is clearly all very sad to Longfellow. Kavanagh does what he can to stir him up. "And you, my friend," begins this young leader of men, "what have *you* been doing all this while?" and he proceeds to enact the part of the candid intimate. All of which Churchill bears with almost divine fortitude and humility. And the story ends with Kavanagh, merged in Longfellow, trumpeting out some wisdom about staying the present instant, and the need of decision to begin and keep on with work. "Shall all these lofty aspirations end in nothing?" he asks. Possibly, if Churchill had been accorded the right of reply, a fitting one might have been given him—something after the fashion of Rabbi Ben Ezra's pleading:—

"Thoughts hardly to be packed

> Into a narrow act,
> Fancies that broke through language and escaped,
> All I could never be,
> All men ignored in me,
> That was I worth to God, whose wheel the pitcher shaped."

For there is a subtle flavour of vulgar materialism in all this outcry, simply because the man has nothing to show for his years of life. It is a tendency of thought that has increased mightily in the world even since "Kavanagh" was written, this persuasion that we come into being to score and break records. So many of us are lashing and spurring our poor selves to this high enterprise and that, that one is inclined to appreciate not simply the dreamer, but the dreamer in his scholastic position. He, at any rate, casts a peaceful shadow upon his pupils, and protects the place that would otherwise suffer under the arid glare of some energetic "practical" man. It is good that there should be some men to whom school work is an exercise which one may seek to invest with beauty, rather than a wily hunt for scholarships, and to whom cricket and football are games that develop graces of body and temper, rather than splendid ways of advertising a school. And one may even fancy that from a point of view a little higher than that of "The Public Schools Record," the results of the dreamer's teaching are not so sadly inferior to your energetic person's as the latter kind of verdict would make them appear. Boys and girls follow their teacher's eyes, rather than their teacher's precepts. They look where he looks. A good noisy energetic schoolmaster, keenly intent upon interviews, advertisements direct and indirect, scholarships, cricketing victories, shouting commemorations, and, in short, good palpable, showy, all-round success, will engender a fine, healthy, vigorous generation of boys, who will live in a lively fashion and die comfortably. But your dreamer, though he neglect this obvious opportunity and that chance of a really good thing, may, by the mere fact that his eyes are fixed upon something beyond and higher than all this pettiness, unwittingly plant seeds in the minds he influences that will come at last to such a harvest as the world would not willingly spare. For all we certainly know his negligence may be the noblest work and the failure we charge him with the great scholastic success.

H. G. Wells

Educationalist
(1894-95)

The Very Fine Art of Microtomy

The Pall Mall Gazette, vol LVIII, no 8998, p 3, 24 January 1894

H.G. Wells wrote to his father in August 1894, "About my work. The P.M.G. is still my bread and cheese. I do from six to ten columns a month and get two guineas a column."[53] This is a delightful description of the microtomist, the person who prepares slides for scientific examination. Again the tone of creativity, particularly the idea of the microtomist making slides out of his landlady's remains, showcases Wells's talent as a writer of lively fiction.

THE SUBTLE BEAUTY OF NEXT TO NOTHING.

The art of microtomy is really the finest of all fine arts. Indeed, so exquisitely delicate is it that it would seem to have hitherto escaped even the subtle appreciation of the amateur, who rangeth where he listeth, knowing all things and believing all things. The public is unfamiliar with the name of the art; the fame of the microtomist is not noised abroad. Those who appreciate the little glass slips with "Cole Deum" thereon, the quaint motto of the elder Cole, are less in number that those who gather walking-sticks or rejoice in the tracings of brasses.[54] Indeed collecting is almost unknown, though why people should collect stamps and leave these things alone surpasses our imagination. A day will come, however, when slides for the microscope of the early masters who are even yet living will be as eagerly sought and fondly treasured as were ever book-plates or violins.[55] Pity it is they worked in Canada Balsam, which has the trick of decay.

It is even possible that the reader needs to be told what his microtomy may be. It is, poor soul, the delightful art of cutting inconceivably thin sections of every conceivable substance. There is nothing one may not cut, save one's friends—your fingers always volunteer of their own accord sooner or later; but some things are unlawful (as, for instance, the coin of the realm), and some are not convenient (as the tail of a live lion). Moreover, the thing cut must be mounted cunningly on a glass slip, for the end for which the section exists is to be examined under a microscope.

If one would see some microtomist's work, let him seek a medical student possessed of a microscope. The same will show him a number of glass slips three

---

53. Wells, H G. *Experiment in Autobiography.* New York: The Macmillan Company, 1934, pp. 395-396.

54. Arthur C. Cole mounted high-quality slides, which featured a label with this motto ("Worship God"), for research and education.

55. A set of 50 Cole slides sold at auction for £384 in October 2019.

inches long, perhaps, by three quarters wide. These will be labelled: one, "Muscle;" another, "Sciatic Nerve;" a third, "Scalp of a Child;" and a fourth, "Cat's Liver." Such names do not lead one to anticipate art and beauty, and this makes the art and beauty all the more charming. In the centre of each of these slips, covered by an extremely thin circular disc of glass, he will see a little slice of matter the size, perhaps, of the head of a tintack, or smaller, and so thin as to be altogether transparent. This is, let us say, your cat's liver etherialized by the microtomist. Under the microscope it has the air of a circular stained glass window; the "cells" of the liver form an interlacing tracery of golden pink, and the diverse blood vessels, of which there are three sorts, appear, in injected, as branching shapes of crimson, blue, and other sweet and pure colours, even such as the Madonnas of the Old Masters wear. The scalp may be even more delightful, with its hairs like stout brown masts, a greenish cuticle, and sunset tinted sub-dermal tissue below. Or at Kew among the botanists they will show him what the microtomist can do with all kinds of vegetable litter—a cross-section of a little twig of bramble doubly stained is a lesson in circular ornamentation, and a splinter from a deal table cut down is amazingly dinty to see; and at the South Kensington Natural History Museum the geologists have a great collection of sections of rocks—which, it has even been supposed, they will someday sort and label—hidden away, which are even more delightful than these others.

THE TECHNIQUE OF THE ART.

It is obvious that with such an infinite variety of material the microtomist must needs have a great variety of instruments. Some things he cuts with a common razor in his hand; such must needs be of a firm consistency, neither flabby nor brittle. Some again—larger things—he cuts with a plane. Little things that he cannot hold he imbeds in wax or carrot, or the pith of the elder, and so gets a fingerful that may be grasped and cut. A soft substance, such as human muscle, he hardens by the immersion of a lump of it in a suitable fluid, or he takes it fresh and almost living and freezes it firm upon a metal slab by means of ether. A rock is cut in thick slices by a lapidary's wheel, a rotating disc of steel made keen by rubbing diamond powder on the edge, and these slices are stuck to a piece of glass and gradually rubbed thinner and thinner upon emery powder of increasing fineness, and finally upon rouge. Powdery things like sand grains the microtomist overcomes by imbedding in hard substances. He particularly dreads and rejoices over such brittle substances such as coal. One would expect mere blackness of coal even at its thinnest, but there are certain coals from Scotland, which, when cut, reveal myriads of little flattened cases of a streaky orange or lemon yellow color, the spores shed long since by the trees which perished to form our coal seams.

The Medical Microtomist and his Bottled Mysteries.

There are in London perhaps half a hundred or more human beings who live by this unknown art. One we know of plies his trade in a little den high above the roar of the Strand. He sits in his window facing the light, watch-glasses and little shallow dishes full of stains around him, microscope and micrometer ready at hand, sometimes amid a heavy aroma of ether from the freezing microtome, and sometimes reminding one oddly of pine trees and wide mountain slopes, with the resinous smell of his Canadian balsam. All about him are little bottles, innumerable little bottles, labeled "skin of toad," "orange pips," "pine inflorescence," "launcet," "kitten's lung" "tumour," and the like, or rather the unlike, some of them fit for the brew of a witch. One whole shelf presently catches the eye, labelled "Mrs. Webster," and in smaller letters the part of Mrs. Webster is specified. He relates a gruesome story in a tone of pathetic regret: how this Mrs. Webster was a landlady of his who died suddenly, "poor old lady," was "post-mortemed" by a confidential friend. "So I took these little mementoes," he says, waving his hand at the shelf. It is a grim and sordid fate for a landlady that she should be peculated by her own lodger and retailed at 6d., 9d., and 1s. a slice according to the choiceness of the parts. But there are those who suspect our microtomist of having obtained his human material in a legitimate way from the dissecting room, and having created his Mrs. Webster for literary effect.

Still the jumble of matters in the corpulent little bottles upon his shelves remains odd enough: pickled organisms from the deep sea are side by side with scraps of the plant, root, and stem, and the mortal remains of a pet puppy; while a fruit that grew and ripened in a jungle in Borneo shares a bottle with some cubic inch of substance that was once part of the vesture of a human soul in a London hospital. Sooner or later they all come to the knife edge and the glass slip. Our microtomist is indeed on the level of Shakspeare. All being pays its tribute to his art, he makes it clear and brilliant for us, using his stains and media not to hide but to display, making truth truer and the visible plain. His work is a veritable microcosm, a summary of the world.

Slices of Rocks and Stained-glass Windows.

The ordinary microtomist who cut sections for the medical student, as a rule, do little in the direction of cutting rocks. This is a special technique, and is practised chiefly at the greater geological schools—at the Royal School of Mines, for instance. It is almost impossible to convey an idea of the appearance of sections of some granite rocks when seen in polarized light. Let the reader think of the tints of a film of gas-refuse floating on water, of the spectrum thrown by a glass prism, of fire opal, of the mother of pearl, of old stained glass windows, of

Burne-Jones at his best.[56] All these, and more also, will he see in such a rock as Pierite or Dunite. A day will come when artists will seek these things and learn a thousand delights of colouring from their study. For microscopic sections may be collected for their beauty, for their technical excellence, thinness, and so forth, for their historical interest, and for their scientific importance. Few people have realized how our modern science rests upon them. At present it is probable there is not one serious collector of these wonderful things—collecting them for their own sake—at all in the world. This negligence cannot last. Before ten years are gone we venture to predict that a new species of virtuosi, and a new branch of criticism will have arisen. The art has not existed a human lifetime yet, but so far as the first works are concerned it may be that collecting, were it to come now, would still be too late to save them from neglect and destruction.

---

56. Pre-Raphaelite artist Edward Burne-Jones designed brightly colored stained glass work.

The Scholastic Frame of Mind:
I. Self-Satisfaction Its Necessary Groundwork

The Educational Times, vol XLII, no 394, pp 75-76, 1 February 1894

This may be the closest Wells came to confessing he was not a great teacher, but rather a reformer, because great teachers have certainty rather than a questioning nature. A. A. Milne, a pupil of Wells at Henley House School, wrote later:

> "H. G. is a great writer, and a great friend, and I am indebted to him for many things . . . but he was not a great schoolmaster. He was too clever and too impatient. He had the complete attention of his class once when vivisecting a frog (kindly provided by a day-boy), but school-life was not lived at that level, and on the lower slopes we lost him."[57]

In a semi-satirical series of articles, Wells distinguished those elements that make up the "scholastic frame of mind" necessary for good teaching. The first of these was that sense of certainty in one's own competence.

BY H. G. WELLS.

The temper is to the teacher what the voice is to the singer. Though your teacher be trained beyond the dreams of the most optimistic of educationalists, though his knowledge be as deep as the ocean and his will as strong as death, though the pedagogic passion, the love of teaching, glow white within him, if his temper be awry he is but worthless, and his gifts and training things thrown away. So that a teacher should cherish his temper even as a tenor cherishes that larynx of his. He should surround himself with the Jaeger's comforters of the soul, should ever be avoiding the little draughts and chills that ruffle the mind, and go nowhere without a sufficient supply of moral jujubes to keep his mood soft and sweet. Yet too often this paramount importance of the temper is forgotten, and the teacher, though redolent of the subtle necessary flavour of the Oxford or Cambridge, decorated with magic letters and mythical honours, and altogether charmingly wrought, proves but a brittle weapon when the test of service is applied.

No doubt the proper scholastic frame of mind, through which teaching is delightful and successful as a matter of course, is, in the first place a gift, just as the voice of the successful singer depends upon some subtle quality of the vocal chords that no man can bring about by design. But the gift in either case is but the seed of the power. If it were otherwise, one might stop this paper here for all

---

57. Milne, A A. *It's Too Late Now: The Autobiography of a Writer.* 3rd ed. London: Methuen & Co., Ltd, 1939, p 50.

the good writing it further could do. However, since there is something left to human care in these cases, we may, perhaps, enquire a little here what is the true scholastic frame of mind, and incidentally of some of the things that foster its growth or hamper its development.

Now possibly the very first requisite to successful teaching is that the teacher should be *self-satisfied*. This is written here with a "possibly," only because this branch of scholastic science is comparatively a neglected one, and it is becoming that our mood should be one of exploration rather than guidance. By both *a priori* and *a posteriori* methods one may arrive at this conclusion. For if a teacher is not absolutely at peace with himself, if he distrusts his will, his methods, his knowledge, or his personal fascination, his will vacillates, his methods change rather than grow, he shelters doubt in ambiguity, and he is nervous about discipline and jealous of respect. But with an inward assurance of his being infallibly right his rule is consistent, his procedure reliable, and his presence the presence of power. And by the inductive method, by the careful observation and experimental interrogation of experienced and successful teachers of both sexes, one may also arrive at last at the generalization that self-satisfaction is the fundament, the ground-work, of the scholastic frame of mind. We are not concerned here with the question how far this self-complacency affects the teacher's social charm; we are here simply asserting the absolute necessity of it to his or her professional success. The spirit of this present little paper is one purely technical and scientific.

Seeing how frail and weak all human beings really are, we may assume from this that one of the most detrimental things that can happen to the teacher is leisure and introspection. This may sound like heresy or paradox, but it is advanced in perfect good faith. Where there is no thought there is no scepticism; and the teacher should above all be guarded from that unpleasant experience that comes to some of us, of finding oneself out. The Education Department has tacitly recognised this danger in the making of the teacher; and the future administrator of elementary instruction, from the very beginning of his career in the infant school-room to the end of his days as a headmaster, is kept so strenuously satisfying inspectors and examiners, that the unwholesome habit of self-dissection finds no gaps of time unoccupied whereby it may creep into his character. Indeed such a really efficient fortification of certificates, diplomas, degrees, reports, "A.1's," "excellents," and so forth, arises at last round his self-esteem, as to defy any possible expostulation with his actual imperfections. The recent outcry against over-pressure was raised by those who overlooked this moral effect of continuous work. It is one of the disadvantages from which the middle-class teacher has hitherto suffered, that he has not had the same amount of stimulus to a virtuous—if useless and finite—activity, and he has been prone in consequence to look overmuch at the outer world, to speculate upon his place in the universe, and so arrive at last at that personal diffidence, that modesty, which, however becoming it may be in a drawing-room, is a serious weakness in a teacher.

It is probable that the success of certain of the great public schools—for in spite of the theory of education, which they are sometimes said to disregard, they are admitted by every critic to be successful—can be explained in the same way. The staffs of these establishments consist of men educated themselves in public schools, and returning to teach in them again after only a short course of higher education and athleticism in some Oxford or Cambridge college. They study classics and cricket, and the purest mathematics, and keep themselves unspotted from the world. They live in a charmed circle, an intellectual Eden, eating nothing of the fatal fruit that would teach them they were but naked men. The slightest doubt of there being anything possible in the world better than themselves and their methods is sedulously guarded against. The babble of the educational reformer goes on far below their Olympian feet. They possess to the quintessential degree that serene assurance of superiority that the foreigner finds so irritating in the Englishman. They do not boast, they do not depreciate, for they are certain of themselves. Now, this is a very enviable frame of mind—it is the perfectly efficient frame of mind from the scholastic point of view.

Practically a very large part of the motive power in the projected reorganization of secondary education is the desire to foster self-complacency in that part of the educational field where at present its growth is feeblest. There can be no doubt that the middle-class teacher not only need a better opinion of himself, but feels the need of it. In a few instances this craving is a little misdirected, and leads to such refuges as F.S.Sc., or a Ph.D. degree—clothed in vast parchments, mystic, wonderful. But the general tendency is towards Registration at least, and perhaps also to the final assumption of a quasi-official position in the State. These honourable ambitions have been deprecated even among private teachers, but on the score of increased personal efficiency alone they deserve support. Even the inefficient will become a little less inefficient if they have the assurance of a Register that they are not so at all. And the doubt that seems to trouble the private schoolmaster about his social position, and of the amount of respect felt for him by parents and scholars, is not simply an expression of personal vanity, as some would have us believe, but the clear indication of a grave subjective impediment to successful scholastic work.

Passing now from critical inquiry to a word or so of practical suggestion, it will be obvious that whatever tends to humiliate the teacher, or put him out of conceit with himself, the scholar will finally suffer for. Humiliation, the suffering of wrong, reacts in most unregenerate mortals in the desire to humiliate and inflict injustice. In Germany, where, in Richter's time at least, the schoolmaster was under the harrow of poverty and official contempt, the discipline was harsher than in any other European country. Respect the schoolmaster's profession, and he will respect his duties. In the case of assistants an overbearing headmaster or headmistress, or a headmaster's wife without the grace of tact, may do more by petty inflictions to ruffle the serenity and trouble the teaching of a staff of assistants than all the energy or scientific pedagogy in the world could do in the direction of improvement. Petting and flattery are less likely to spoil an assistant than one quarter the amount of snubbing or "staff discipline." Yet how many masters' meetings are, as it were, gatherings of the mere tools of Omniscience, to one that has its proper flavour of a Council of the Gods? A self-assertive assistant may be a thorn in a headmaster's private flesh, but an over-modest one is a weakness in the school. A self-depreciatory teacher, if he means it, deserves all his self-depreciation and more also. Away with him. He will follow this authority and that, fluctuate at a frown and speculate over a smile. One might as well try to cut down trees with a Japanese fan as teach with the loveliness of modesty.

The problem why so many educational writers in the past have been failures in practice—for we hear nothing in history of the human masterpieces of Milton, Comenius, Pestalozzi, and the rest of them—is no doubt due to that very philosophical turn of mind that makes their writings valuable. The educational reformer cannot possibly be a good teacher, because his necessary tone is dissatisfaction and change. The spirit of the reformer is growth, the spirit of the teacher consistency. The reformer makes war, the schoolmaster upholds the *pax ferulae*. That is why no pre-eminent educational reformer has been a woman, while yet women are the best teachers—because women have more faith, more steadiness of confidence in themselves and others, and an infinitely greater patience than men. Nearly all educational literature is the cry, of this instructor or that, that things are in a wretched muddle, that we need light, thought, and enquiry. How can anyone in that state teach serenely? Nevertheless, we hear a vast amount of complaint at the conservatism of teachers in matters of method and so forth, by those who fail to grasp this fundamental truth, that self-satisfaction is the groundwork of the scholastic frame of mind, and that without self-satisfaction teaching is an angry failure, and true teaching an impossible thing. Indeed so paramount is the teacher's need of being cock-sure of himself, that it is even open to question whether the study of the science and art of education by a teacher may not be regarded as a demoralizing pursuit. But it would be beyond our present scope to pursue this suggestion now.

In a subsequent paper, certain other of the chief characteristics of the scholastic frame of mind, of which this unswerving self-esteem is the necessary basis, will be considered.

Jellygraphia: A New Vice

The Pall Mall Gazette, vol LVIII, no 9028, p 3, 28 February 1894

In one of his few comments on educational technology, Wells humorously critiques the use of the jellygraph, also known as the hectograph, a means of creating copies using an ink and gelatin plate transfer process. According to the Mackenzie biography of Wells, Alfred Harmsworth had used a jellygraph machine to create the Henley House School Magazine.[58] *(See Wells's contributions to the magazine earlier in this volume.) In 1894 Harmsworth began publishing his first newspaper,* The Evening News, *so Wells was likely thinking of his new venture as he teased those using the machine to print things that would be better left unprinted. Harsmsworth later went on to become Lord Northcliffe, influential publisher of the* Daily Mail *and other newspapers.*

Among the minor vices that civilization has taught us is the art of reproducing our private writings by means of apparatus. It ranks, with the rubber stamp and the cheap camera, among the wild oats of the respectable young man. Oddly enough its victims do not seem to recognize the immorality of its use, and though the modern pulpit be always alive to a novelty, so far no beneficial thunder has proceeded thence to warn them that they are upon the magenta-coloured path to unspeakable sorrow.

The victim of the copying apparatus stands confessed to the diagnostic eye by his haggard and careworn appearance. A certain quality of aimless method and hurry may be noticed in his bearing. His face is picked out with patches and smudges of a violet hue, and his fingers are thickly coated with a metallic purple substance very characteristic of the disease. In the opening phases he is confident and even boastful, but as the disorder develops he becomes melancholy or very irritable. A certain bitter and painful unrest supervenes, and marriage, death, photography, record-breaking, or some similar great calamity carries him off from among the circles of sane and happy young men. Instances of *jellygraphia* among the nobility are rare, and it is curious that except among very strong-minded women indeed, the so-called weaker sex has a practical immunity from the disorder. And in such cases as happen among them it takes only the comparatively mild form of disfiguring the corners of notepaper with ornate renderings of "The Grange, Rotherhithe, Surrey," or

"THE COTTAGE, PUTNEY-HILL."

---

58. Norman & Jeanne MacKenzie, *The Life H. G. Wells: The Time Traveller*, revised, The Hogarth Press, 1987, p 80.

But with a man it is more deadly. To begin with, let us suppose he has caught his jellygraph. Commonly, men begin with those apparently simple expedients having a slab of buttery substance spread in a tin dish. You write your letter or draw your diagram with a viscous aniline ink—which clogs the pen, and opens hitherto unsuspected springs of blasphemy in the heart—upon a sheet of paper. Then you put this sheet of writing on your jelly, and presently peeling off the paper, leave a negative impression in thick violet ink thereon. From this, while the violet ink keeps moist, one may, by patience and grace, proceed to print off as many copies as one requires—up to a dozen or so. The first are dark, but they become paler and paler as your printing proceeds. Presently one portion of the writing wears away and then another, and your later prints are fragmentary. It is time to stop for your soul's health. Then take a sponge, and sponge off what is left of the aniline. (Some will remain with a wonderful pertinacity.) And to work upon yourself, change your cuffs and collars, do what you can for garments, and at fingers with pumice and a brave heart!

So having learnt the trick, you begin to cast about for some use for it. This is the most distressing part of the business. A schoolmaster will resolve to examine his class, and forthwith set to work upon examination papers. These he hands round with vast solemnity, and then still more solemnly reads out to his victims the questions that are symbolized by his violet smudges and broken hieroglyphics. In this way he will use half a day fighting a jellygraph to dictate at last the questions he could have dictated just as well without this. Your professor, too, will painfully copy notes out of a book for his class. And with your business man the mania takes the form of little unnecessary papers of rules signed "by order." The clergy "jelly" special prayers. Most unhappy is the quiet man of orderly life and few friends. Him we have caught hard driven and jellygraphing his name and address upon gummed paper, to presently stick the same into books, wherein his unimportant style and title were already quite sufficiently inscribed. And people have been known to get up private concerts in order to "jelly" the songs. Some foolish writing and sketching people are tempted by the insidious thing to little versicles, "skits," or quaintly sarcastic sketches, which they then reproduce and circulate beyond any possibility of withdrawal. By some, anarchism has been traced to this cause, inflammatory placards being the outcome of an otherwise useless jellygraph.

After some time your jellygraph hardens, and the ink of previous inscriptions that has escaped your most earnest scrubbing mingles pleasantly with your newer matter. The accidental juxtapositions thus brought about are always foolish and sometimes wicked. The ink displays an increasing tendency to abandon the apparatus and cling to the operator. And the sufferer is now in train for the next phase of the disease, which consists in an unreasoning discontent and furious research after and purchase of recondite forms of jellygraph. Hours and days are spent in this pursuit: business, social duties, moral ties are alike neglected. The friends of the victim are alarmed by increasingly confused forms posted to them or placed in their hands, until a distressing incoherency supervenes. There is a noxious species of the instrument wherein a thin skin is tightly stretched over glass paper and written upon with a steel style. If just the right pressure is used the style presses the skin down on the glass paper, and little bits remain adherent to the grains of glass, leaving small perforations along the course of the letters traced. Afterwards, with an inked pad beneath, one may take a series of impressions upon sheets of paper, the ink squeezing through the minute perforations. But the trouble is to get your pressure right. Press too little, and your print is an impressionist sketch of your writing. Press too hard, and instead of little dots you cut lines, each a little rift within the stencil, manifesting itself by a spreading speck of ink in garnered print, that slowly widening at last blots out words, letters, sentences, paragraphs in one ever-expanding destruction. It is enough to make one kick the cat. Consider the gamut of emotions your respectable young man must experience, and the gamut of language, the wide diapason of roaring wickedness it should lead him to.

But we have said enough to show the evil of the thing, its demoralizing effects on body and soul. Clearly the sellers of these abominable instruments should be placed under some restraint. And one might start by forming a league and "jellying" a code of rules.

Science Notes

The Journal of Education, vol XVI, no 296, pp 153-154, 1 March 1894

Although the format of the Science Notes section of The Journal of Education *was intended to present discrete items of interest, Wells instead used this forum to create an extended argument. He posits that for the previous five years, new models have encouraged the use of experiments in elementary science teaching, yet adoption has been slow. Wells spends much of this article lambasting book-based science teaching, parental gullibility, short-sighted concerns about expenses, and the undermining influence of examiners. New to the argument is the idea that science teaching is inherently different from teaching in other subjects. The new methods, proposing a syllabus of experiments and practicals at early ages, mark a turning point in the teaching of science.*

There is a vast amount of work to be done yet in the direction of reforming science teaching in schools. It is still in too many cases the mere methodical acquisition of a text-book, relieved rather than illustrated by the performance of experiments, a concession to the parent rather than a part of the headmaster's conception of the educational process. So far, science teaching is not science teaching at all. The method and the mental operation are precisely the same as they would be in teaching history or what passes for literature in schools, save that statements have to be remembered about oxygen and nitrogen instead of Cromwell or Milton. Scientific people are beginning to realize that such instruction is bringing science into disrepute, and they will echo Mr. Hugh Gordon's dictum that "science had much better be left alone altogether than be taught unscientifically."

———

Mr. Gordon is the author of an *Elementary Course of Practical Science*, now in course of publication, which embodies his own experience, gained under the London School Board, and the suggestions of Professor Armstrong's British Association scheme.[59] It is a genuine attempt to teach science "scientifically" from the very beginning, and the student is never allowed for a moment to become a mere passive recipient of the "wonders of Science." There can be no doubt that

---

59. In 1889 chemist Henry Armstrong presented suggestions to The British Association for the Advancement of Science, now known as the British Science Association, encouraging experiments for pupils in elementary science. See William Brock, "Founding Fathers of Science Education: In the Attitude of the Discoverer." *New Scientist,* September 1977, 678–79.

the child who has followed his course will be more observant, more accurate, have a little more manual dexterity than before, and have progressed some little way towards an inductive habit of thought. Is it necessary to say any more to recommend it to the teacher? Unfortunately it is. The teacher—such is the un-ideal tendency of the age—wishes to know whether the increased expense involved in individual experimental work, the increased share of the school-time table, the increased salary of the science master postulated by the greater educational skill required, the trouble of introducing new methods, is to have any other return than that of virtuous self-satisfaction. And we must regretfully admit that it cannot at present be said with any certainty that it will.

The painful fact is that there is really a premium upon what it is scarcely too severe to call bogus science teaching. The British parent does not know what is sound teaching and what is not. Let the school master put "science" upon his prospectus, dub his cheapest assistant science-master, and have a fortnightly explosion in the schoolroom, and the parent, who clamours for the modern and scientific, is satisfied. But scarcely any private schoolmaster, and possibly not all of those who rule over endowed or public schools, *dares* to equip boys with the requisite apparatus for adequate scientific study, unless at his own or the school's expense. So long as one will *profess* to teach science and art for nothing, well and good, but at the first genuine attempt to teach science the parent or the ratepayer arises and blocks the way. "Our fathers," they say, "bought the schoolmaster but one tool—a cane—and this man would have as many instruments as a cabinet-maker." It is at once imputed to us for want of skill.

This difficulty, arising from the relative expensiveness of sound science teaching, is one that can only be removed by the gradual progress of general education. But there is another obstacle in the way of the honest science teacher, that may be, and possibly some day will be, removed. It is bad enough to have teachers acquiescing in the parental misconceptions of the scientific method, but it is far more serious to find that examining bodies are willing to hall-mark their teaching. It is fully time that all who are interested in improvement in this matter, should lift up their voices against too complacent examiners and examining boards.

In the first place among the sinners is Her Majesty, in the form of the Science and Art Department. In the Elementary stage it is possible to get pure book-teaching "hall-marked," and indeed anything like practical instruction is a serious bar to good results in the evening classes. The skilful grant-earner drills his class for a purely written examination. A stock question of the physiography examiners in the elementary stage is: What is energy? How does a teacher of Mr. Gordon's type stand with regard to a man who has made his class learn that definition by heart, in the esteem of my lords of the Education Department, manifest in results?

————

The London Matriculation science is also a paradise for crammers, though there are now some signs of grace. The examinations are still wholly written ones, but a feeble intimation has appeared in the syllabus that "candidates in any one of the optional branches of science will find it an advantage to have obtained some elementary instruction in the practical use of apparatus." How they will find it an advantage is not known. Possibly it will affect their handwriting or grammar, for the character of the papers remains practically unchanged.

————

This journal has already animadverted upon the science examinations of the College of Preceptors. We had some hope that the body which instituted the first lectureship in education, and is acting as a pioneer in the matter of a practical test in languages, might also have been the first to insist upon genuine science teaching, but the financial aspect is the important one from the "members" point of view, and our hope is deferred.

————

The recent report of the Cambridge Local Examinations Syndicate upon the Higher Local results, shows that this unsoundness affects the whole body of school work. The candidates, who are in many cases destined to teach, show in their science a lack of practical instruction in zoology, and in chemistry insufficient experimental work. So, all round, we find our science teaching is science teaching "on paper," a cheap and nasty article, a thing made to sell. The examiner is the scholastic inspector of weights and measures, and it seems to us that he still has to learn either his art or his duty.

The Scholastic Frame of Mind:
II. Its Lack of Sympathy and Interest

The Educational Times, vol XLVII, no 396, pp 149-150, 1 March 1894

This satirical column continues from the first part, published the month previous, on the necessary scholastic qualities of a schoolmaster. Here he adds an unsympathetic nature to the requirement of self-certainty, encouraging the young teacher to be a distant task-master to his students, as his contribution to the "comparatively untrodden region of pedagogic psychology".

By H. G. Wells

Having concluded in our precious discussion that the necessary basis of the scholastic frame of mind is an unspeculative self-esteem, we have next to consider what may fitly rise upon this foundation; and here, at once, comes a subtle and even a delicate matter to consider and that is the range of the teacher's interests. Should he be a boy magnified, rejoicing in this football and keep after cricket— the class-room his city and the playing-field his field of nature—or should he care for none of these things? Or is it better if his work is indeed his work, and some harmless hobby—literature, politics, Selbornian natural history, decimal coinage, a violin, or water-colours—is the delight of his leisure and the lodestar of his dark house of toil?[60] And beside his intellectual interests are his emotional phases. May the teacher burn with conviction's fire, and may he have tender and animated affections? Or should he not rather have an unruffled serenity—a perfect evenness of surface, a superior indifference to all things? We have here to decide between the sympathetic and the unsympathetic dispositions; and, in spite of a common persuasion to the contrary, it must be maintained, in the interest of truth, that your ideal teacher is absolutely unsympathetic.

Now it may be that there are serious people who will controvert this. This sympathetic teacher is a favourite conception in our profession, as anyone knows who is acquainted with the literature of testimonials. The parent likes to think of this weakness as a quality in the master. Indeed, does not a sympathetic staff rank next to an unlimited dietary among the attractions we offer her? But the misconceptions of the parent, and the exigencies of advertisement, have nothing to do with this discussion. We repeat, the proper scholastic frame of mind is adamantine, and that the severest condemnation one can write of an assistant,

---

60. Gilbert White's *The Natural History and Antiquities of Selborne, in the County of Southampton* was a popular book at the time, although it was originally published in 1789.

next to the charge of modesty, is that of being sympathetic.

For sympathy is only another name for instability of mood. Your sympathetic flame flickers when a boy whistles, and shrinks and shudders at a note from the piano. The weather-cock is the type of the quality, and feels acutely any wind that blows. And your man of feeling is warmed by smiles, pained by silence, and washed from his purpose by a torrent of tears. But your successful teacher, to rule wisely, must have his movements unburdened by any fluttering emotions. How can a man mould and master a mind that moulds and master his moods? Not love but justice rules the school, and above all there must be an unchanging serene. And no man with cultivated and delicate sensibility can hope to be serene amidst the eddies and gusts of puerile exhilaration, jealousy, disappointment, and anger that work round him in the school.

And with the danger of a fluctuating mood comes the greater danger of favouritism. So long as you are at an infinite distance from your class any boy is just as near to you as any other boy. But so soon as the distance becomes measurable this ceases to be the case. There is no impartiality with sympathy. One boy is more open and human than another, becomes pleasant, exerts a nearer attraction. So one is caught by the currents of puerile politics and intrigue, takes sides, backs boarders against day-boys, helps persecute the exceptional youngster. From omnipotence and omniscience you descend to the level of a tribal god. And there are hopeless ones among your pupils who presently cease to call upon your name. No; sympathy is all very well in the poetical treatment of teaching, but in practice it is assuredly a most mischievous thing.

Now an unsympathetic disposition, like a colossal self-conceit, is in the first place the gift of the gods. But in either case we may increase or diminish our talent. And the young teacher who discovers himself wincing at a necessary punishment, sympathetic with Tommy's restlessness on a bright spring morning, taking an interest in Georgie's artistic aberrations on his text-book fly-leaves, or secretly agreeing with James that the *Principia* is a bore, had better watch himself carefully. A helpful thing is to take a severely technical view of your work. Put it to yourself: "Here are twenty or thirty scholastic units. Presently they will go into the examination testing room, and it behoves me to secure a good result. My predecessor would pass, so I hear, seventy-eight per cent.; how much over eighty can I carry this stuff?" Repeat this morning and afternoon on entering the class-room as a kind of grace before teaching. You will find it assist you wonderfully in taking a properly colourless view of the human item.

And of course there is Marcus Aurelius—or Epictetus—or Herbert Spencer. The severely scientific style perhaps is best. Try and see in your young charges so many organisms imperfectly adapted to their environment. Tears are but the overcopious secretion of the lachrymal gland through an irregular disengagement of energy consequent upon the nervous disturbances of an emotional phase. Laughing is a spasmodic reminiscence of an ancestral snarl. The whole life of your boy is only catastatic phases of a complex molecular apparatus. In this way one can at last forget the soul in it almost altogether and carve out human minds as serenely as one sets about a Sloyd model.[61] And this is the only way to carve minds, and to secure really satisfactory results for one's teaching.

So much for this matter in the schoolroom. But a school-master who lets a sympathetic or emotional disposition have play on his private leisure, will find it at last reacting upon him in the hours of duty. Your private life has no insurmountable barrier between itself and your life in school. Neither is an inland sea; both feel the tides, and away with the storms of the other. You cannot in private have a great grief or a great joy that will not send its emotional ground-swell into the school-room. So eschew the sources of deep feeling if you would be an ideal teacher. Smarting from the unkindness of Chloe, you are likely to deal harshly with Charles and his triflings. Delirious with her smiles, a certain passion for giving holidays, remitting impositions, and recalling all the golden age, except its virtues, may seize you. And that other strong passion, of worldly ambition, must have no sway. For the pomps and vanities of this world—some episcopal possibilities scarcely count her—come not in the teacher's way. Ambition spells discontent, and where is your serenity then?

Hence, though the thing may seem a harsh saying, we must infer that the perfect teacher cannot be a lover or in any way a fervent man. And as for hobbies, are not these among the minor passions? They ripple (if they do not billow) the smooth impartiality of your mind. They give the designing boy a handle whereby he may seize you. He too collects stamps, or writes sonnets, or hates Gladstone, or feels the craving for a tenpenny bit. The hobby rider cannot ride away from him.

Besides we sin against the light when we write of the school-master "out of school." The true teacher is in one sense never out of school. For the sculptor may put away his marble and it stops as he may leave it until he return again, the navigator may anchor his ship and trustfully go ashore, the trader close his shop for the night and regale him as he will, but the boy is incessant, the boy goes on. We never know when we may meet him, we never know when he may fall into temptation and go astray. Perhaps we need not always be actively edifying, but we must at least be always passively exemplary. And we must watch, watch indeed unobtrusively, but still closely. The school-master must therefore be always on his guard, maintaining the calm and watchful indifferences of his exterior presence.

---

61. Sloyd education, derived from Scandinavia and popular at the end of the 19th century, emphasized handicrafts for moral and educational development.

So we assert that not only must the teacher not be a magnified boy, or anything open to boyish contagion, but he must have no hobby and no distracting passions. Yet you object that a man without some desire is a man without a motive. The schoolmaster's desire is the desire to teach. But this brings us to what we may call the *pedagogic passion*, and that will be the better considered by itself in a subsequent paper. So far we have established this: that the true scholastic frame of mind is an utterly unsympathetic one, and its pedestal a powerful self-complacency. It is of course just possible that some flaw, some infinitesmal paradox, may have escaped our careful reasoning. However it is hardly reasonable to expect a writer to pick holes in his own production. Still, as explorers in the comparatively untrodden region of pedagogic psychology, it is well to be wary how we go.

Science Notes

The Journal of Education, vol XVI, no 297, pp 198-199, 1 April 1894

Again using the Notes format to write an argument, Wells continues here his criticism of the effect of examinations on practical (laboratory) science, giving a direct example of a chemistry examination at the University of London. Written examinations are far easier to develop than practical examinations, and easier to study for, so schoolmasters will always take the easier way. The solution proposed by Philip Magnus, the advent of an Examiner, has its own problems.

While our Science Notes of last month were in the hands of the printer, Sir Philip Magnus was discussing the difficulty to which we called attention, at the monthly meeting of the College of Preceptors.[62] So that the reproach we made, that the practical part of science-teaching is disregarded, and thereby discouraged, by this examining authority, was, to a certain extent, anticipated and met. However, there is a certain interval between proposal and action, and it will probably be some time before the College justifies the fear of this distinguished educationalist, that practical work may be ultimately over-stimulated, and laboratory "drill" swamp the intellectual culture of science-teaching.

———

Yet the dangers of laboratory drill are by no means to be disregarded. They appear to be peculiarly imminent in the science of chemistry. In this subject, indeed, the exigencies of examination have already, in some cases, developed a mysterious culture, curiously independent of the actual framework of the science. The candidate at the Intermediate Science Examination of the University of London, for instance, is popularly supposed to have his knowledge of chemical theory practically tested, but, as a matter of fact, the practical examination has assumed a stereotyped form, which tests nothing but his familiarity with an analytical table one might master in an afternoon. He is given two solutions—always solutions—containing, he is assured, at most one acid and one base. Find the acid and base, or acid or base, if both or either be present, is the invariable direction. To do so he adds a prescribed reagent and looks for a precipitate. If there is one, he has a choice of so many constituents, for each of which he has a recipe; if not, he passes to the reagent for Group II., and so through

---

62. Educational reformer Sir Philip Magnus was an authority on technical education, a fellow of the University of London Senate, president of the College of Preceptors, and an advisor to the government.

his schedule. A man with a good memory, and otherwise quite ignorant of chemistry, could, we assert, satisfy this test after a day's study. A man fairly conversant with elementary inorganic chemistry, on the other hand, need not necessarily know how to perform the prescribed operations in the right order. In fact, the business has nothing to do with the vital parts of theoretical chemistry. It has to be taught quite separately, and is, indeed, a mere excrescence on the subject.

———

There is no doubt that is in the heart and imagination of man to devise similar innocent and convenient employments in connexion with physics, geology, zoology, or botany, if it will satisfy a demand. But it is the fault of those who speak with authority on matters educational if it is allowed to satisfy the present very genuine desire for an endorsement of practical teaching by examining bodies.

———

The remedy Sir Philip Magnus proposes is Inspection, and the College, he suggested, "might keep ahead of the new movement by appointing special inspectors of schools in which science is taught from the beginning practically and systematically. Certificates and prizes might be given on the joint result of such inspection and examination, and such schools as feel the need of external recognition might in this way be encouraged to devote sufficient time to the teaching of science." And this they certainly would do if the easier way of a purely written examination be closed to them. But in the other alternative we must confess our belief in the Ohm's law of examination science, that, given two ways through which the desired end—an assurance to the parent that science is being adequately taught—may be obtained, one of which is long and difficult, the other broad and easy, the majority of mortal schoolmasters will walk in the broad and easy way.

———

And it is possible that new Inspector may prove to be only old Examiner with a change of name. The failure of the examiner is largely accounted for when we remember that a majority of the examiners of schools are apparently men who are not educationalists, and who are unfamiliar with practical necessities and innocent of educational ideals. If our inspector is to be drawn from the same class, he will display the same defects in inspection that are apparent in his papers. If it is proposed to draw upon some other class of the educational world, if the inspector is to be an educational expert rather than a scientific specialist, might it not be advisable to try first to introduce a few simple educational principles into our examining ?

———

For instance, there is one principle which appears to be fairly obvious. This is, that, given a sound educational course, an efficient examination will require the candidate to repeat, as far as the special conditions allow, some samples of the necessary exercises in that course. The proper performance of such exercises will be the most satisfactory guarantee that they have been done before, and that the educational benefit derived from them has been received. Moreover, a persistence in this course will render the energetic examination-coach a genuine teacher in spite of himself. This principle is already tacitly admitted in most mathematical examinations, in such examinations in language as are not overmuch alleviated by questions on gender rules, etymology, and history, in the typical practical examination in biology, and in such geographical tests as involve mapping from memory. How far can it be extended to practical science?

———

This question is a difficult one. In the case of physics the apparatus required is frequently expensive, and the arrangement of many of the experiments that constitute a satisfactory course consumes a considerable amount of time, but we doubt if the average experiment is more lengthy than a zoological dissection. So, too, in physiology or experimental chemistry, there are numerous countervailing considerations that demand attention. But it appears to us that between the existing condition of unsound examination methods, creating and supporting a "cramming" discipline side by side of, and competing with, sound instruction, and the supersession of practical examination by inspection, there is, probably, some more desirable intermediate way along the line of really scientific examinations in science, such as we have indicated in these notes.

The Scholastic Frame of Mind:
III. The Passion Pedagogic

The Educational Times, vol XLVII, no 396, pp 180-181, 1 April 1894

In the third installment of this series, Wells adds to his requirements of self-assurance and lack of sympathy the "passion pedagogic". Unlike the first two characteristics, such passion is not confined to teachers, but is inherent in everyone who cannot resist the act of instructing others. His great example is John Ruskin, whose teaching passion was such as to brook no opposition. The use of "his or her" near the end is unusual, as Wells typically used the male pronoun for teachers unless writing specifically about female teachers.

By H. G. Wells

And now, having made clear the ground-work of self-esteem, and established the pedestal of an unsympathetic firmness, we come to the crowning part of our discoveries —to the revelation of the passion pedagogic. This was promised in our concluding paragraph last month, and it was there stated that for the teacher this must be not merely the ruling but the absorbing passion. It must be the gold of his avarice, the glory of his ambition, the quenching of his thirst, the satisfaction of his hunger, and the dear lady of his love.

Now, this passion pedagogic is this: It is the something in a human mind that makes a man interrupt discussions with "Now, you listen to me." It snatches the distaff from the spinner's hand and takes the care of his vessel from the potter. Our psychologists, in their systematic account of the mind, seem to ignore this craving most unaccountably—one following in the footsteps of the other. Yet is there not a pleasure like no other pleasure is giving advice? Do we not yearn to give an opinion even when we have no opinion to give? Do not those who give way to this temptation parade before us in picture galleries, shouting crude criticism that all the world may hear? Do they not anger us at concerts, and render life a burden wherever art is practised and men gather together? It is indeed a most abundant and powerful motive in humanity. The old who have it bewail the decadency of the age, and the young with this passion teach the reluctant grandparent how eggs may be eviscerated. It is the twin of self-assertion, the irresistible impulse to assert one's own convictions so soon as they come to mind; or, failing conviction of one's own, the handiest, so long as there is stuff for assertion.

Two men much akin will serve us here to show clearly what difference a greater or lesser development of this passion makes. Both were clear-sighted men, both humourists, both saw what they conceived to be sinful error accepted as truth, and both had private reason for lamenting the results. But one had only the mildest of pedagogic passion, and was indeed an artist, content to write witty, graceful, and scholarly satire against the evil, and scarcely caring who saw his writing. The other was pedagogue in grain, forcible and noisy, and put his disbelief into fiery theses prominently displayed, that went far to alter the whole face of the world, gallantly risking a fiery death for himself in the doing of it. These two men, Erasmus and Luther, seem made for the exemplification of the passion we are discussing. The history of the sixteenth and seventeenth centuries is, indeed, one long battle of pedagogues.

Of all modern men the crowning teacher is Mr. Ruskin. High art was soon insufficient for his teeming impulse, he overflowed, and now where have the spreading volume, the flamboyant glories of his impeccable style not extended? Religion, politics, botany, geology, meteorology, the art of John Strange Winter[63] and Mr. Severn[64]—this life-giving and exuberant flood has rolled over them all, and left them all the richer and better for his touch. And mark, too, how essentially pedagogic is his style. Sometimes he reasons, but very rarely. Commonly he prophecies, as, for instance, that iron may be used in architecture as cement, but not as material. But he arms any utterance with such scathing scorn for dissent open or implied, with such whips of irony and satire, and such glories of indignation and sorrowful wrath, that we are dazzled and stunned, and take his prophecies even more meekly than we take his reasoning, lest worse betide. We are hushed in the presence of his passion, and close his books softly as we would a cathedral door. We feel that amid such grandeur debate is out of place, and withdraw, with our doubts, to some simple chamber, where a chairman and some rules of discussion give scope to the critical mind.

But here we are concerned chiefly with the evidently irresistible nature of Mr. Ruskin's impulses. He teaches because he cannot help it, because he was made to teach. What he teaches, I should imagine, is relatively a matter of indifference. But he must teach or die. If he writes of mineralogy even, the driest of all subjects, he must e'en be throwing quartz and calcite at your moral behaviour. Of such a passion as this, of its tolerance of dissent, its strenuous concentration of the entire being upon driving the conclusion—whatever that may chance to be—home, any teacher, to be a real teacher, must, to some extent at least, partake.

Now this is the ascending scale of the pedagogic passion; reasoning, witty advocacy, rhetoric, eloquence, satire, irony, mockery, stark assertion, flat contradiction, shouting, suppression of controversy, the ruler, the cane, the birch,

---

63. John Strange Winter was the pen name of Harriet Eliza Vaughan Stannard, who wrote popular stories of military life under that name. Ruskin admired her work greatly.
64. Joseph Severn was a popular painter, who was married to John Ruskin's cousin Joan.

Coventry, burning of books by the hangman, suppression of controversialists, the stocks, the penitentiary, the asylum, the hygienic cell, the crank, the dungeon, the noisome dungeon, the pillory, the thumbscrew, the scourge, the rack, the wheel, the lions, the axe, the halter, the bowstring, fire and sword, impalement, the stake, and the cross. All these implements have been used by men, pedagogic-minded men, for the vivid instruction of their fellows. Very red and very black in history are the mortal corrections of mortal exercises. But nowadays this passion, like all the other passions, seems better in hand, runs slower and steadier, with less froth of blood upon it, and less clamour in its flow.

Clearly no passion admits of more fatal perversion than the passion pedagogic. This it was that burnt the homes of the Albigenses and lit the fires of Smithfield. Paul was a great teacher, schooled in wise methods. But the unregenerate Saul, ravening after the Christians, shows the passion in its purity. This passion it is that sends good men and true, even in these milder days, out of their homes and into their neighbours' business, with the most enlivening and instructive consequences. It is the lust of conquest in the armour of right. The born teacher can no more have peace on his frontiers than the heaven-sent conqueror. He wants to spread his impeccable morals, his supremely right view of things—of everything—his little discoveries and great desires, over the whole habitable globe.

One cannot blame him. The teacher must be so, or be no true teacher. But these conditions we have laid down—it is to be hoped without offence—define his limitations and lead up to a clearer view of his particular difficulties, his stones of stumbling. The self-satisfaction swells easily into the quality of the prig. The righteous want of sympathy deepens into narrowness. The pedagogic passion blazes as aggressive intolerance and destructive persecution. Yet watch your going, teacher, carefully, and cling to your harshness rather than soften over-much. You walk in a narrow way. On one hand, indeed, a cliff, a severe, even repulsive, rigidity; but on the other, a steep, seductive slope with the rare wild flowers of sympathy and love tempting you to unbend and snatch at them. Better the stiffness than the gulf. Condescend but once—relax, admit, and you may topple headlong down to the level of common men, becoming *even as an uncle* in the eyes of those you teach.

It is possible, for we have met the phenomenon, for a teacher to have the true scholastic frame of mind, to be self-satisfied, concentrated, so far unsympathetic as need requires, and aggressive in all good—and some doubtful—things, and yet be a sweet and lovable being. Nevertheless, it is a wonderful equilibrium, a miraculous balance, that we may well have the grace to pray for, even with the assurance of its possession. Yet the queer contradictions of human nature, the subtle duplicity of the soul, come to our rescue. For a man may be this to one man and that to another, and, with congenial temptations, that teacher may happily forget himself. The bow cannot always be bent, nor the teacher straight and stiff. The teacher, like the respectable ancestral portraits in the story, may occasionally come out of his frame and disport himself, when the family, paterfamilias, materfamilias and the rest, are away. But these are holiday admissions, exceptional treats. Beyond any possibility of controversy this analysis of ours is true. A good teacher must be self-complacent, neither reformer, artist, lover, scientific investigator, nor philosopher, but teacher, having but one passion, the pedagogic passion, the passion of "Now-listen-to-me" ruling over his scholastic life. So far as he or she is modest, sympathetic, or distracted by other pursuits, so far will his or her work fall short of success, and his or her condition for the true scholastic frame of mind. Denial—even a warm denial—of these propositions, two correspondents have already shown to be possible, but a disproof that will carry conviction is still to come.

Science Notes

The Journal of Education, vol XVI, no 298, pp 254-255, 1 May 1894

Here Wells uses Science Notes in a more typical way, reporting snippets from science news. But he also makes the argument that the supposed contact with great teachers may amount to nothing more than saying good morning, so professor-student contact is not a good argument for a teaching University of London. Other issues include the latest on geological studies and teaching, and in particular the notion that geology is not only one of the cheapest sciences on offer, but it also is easier for the public to understand and support. To close, in reporting on the Smithsonian papers, Wells notes that the American language in science papers is drifting far from ordinary English.

A very large portion of the last published (Vol. I.) of the three volumes of Lord Kelvin's Popular Lectures and Addresses (Macmillan) deals with geological problems, and presents, in a convenient group, the entire series of papers by which Uniformitarianism in geology was demolished. Papers on the Sources of Mechanical Effect, on Beats, on Isoperimetrial Problems, and other questions in general physics are also included. We may perhaps notice a little point in physics that may be useful to a teacher here or there. It was stated by Tyndall that moisture in the atmosphere prevents degrees of cold obtaining that would be destructive to vegetation through radiation in the night, *by absorbing the radiant heat*, and this is still extensively repeated in elementary works. Lord Kelvin reinstates the view of Dr. Wells[65]. So far as invisible water-vapour in the air is concerned, its absorption is quite inadequate to prevent the blades of grass radiating away all their heat down to far below the zero point. The true agent in the preservation of the vegetation is the latent heat of the dew which condenses upon them. The limit to which the temperature can fall at any particular time is the dew-point of the air at that time.

———

The Address on the opening of the Bangor Laboratories bears closely upon that perennial London University question that is again upon us. The private student's degree, Lord Kelvin tells us, "is a splendid reason for the existence of the London University." But in properly constituted colleges he would have "an examination carried on by their own professors." The examination should be, in the first place, daily. No professor should meet his class without talking to them. He should talk to them and they to him. . . . Professors and students must speak

---

65. William Charles Wells, no relation to H. G. Wells, was a late 18th/early 19th century physician and scientist who did seminal work on dew.

to one another." Granted that ideal of intimate intercourse and we may well cry aloud for a teachers' University. But is such teaching the rule or the exception in the colleges that would be constituents of the London University Revised? I learn, for instance, that a student of the Royal College of Science, who studied for two years under Professors Huxley, Judd, and Guthrie, never spoke at all to the last named, and only once to each of the others. He told Professor Huxley that it *was* a fine day, and he acceded, "with pleasure," to Professor Judd's request that a window might be closed.[66] There is no guarantee that this is an exceptional state of affairs among "teaching" colleges.

———

The new semi-quarterly *Journal of Geology*, emanating from Chicago, contains a well written article by Mr. H. S. Williams upon the place of geology in the college course. He writes, happily, not only as geologist but as an educationalist, and presents his case simply and strongly. He calls particular attention to the value of geology in coupling observation with simple inferences, and reminds us that it is the one science among the natural sciences which may begin with the common language of the pupil, and by means of such language alone may build up ideas of precise phenomena in scientific terms. Physiography alone surpasses geology in this particular … but the very largeness and indefiniteness of the facts are in the way of the use of physical geography for the finer and more exact functions of observation. … So long as the object of the training is to teach the knowledge of ideas and how to use them, classics and mathematics are the simplest and truest means of developing a liberal education. The addition of sciences to the college course is not because of the usefulness of the knowledge of things thus to be gained, but because the language of the sciences is essential to call forth the observation and the exercise of the accompanying mental operations."

———

Mr. Williams also says some good things regarding the symbolic nature of geological facts. A battered lump of stone in a heap beside the road may gradually develop the richest and most fascinating view of some past epoch of the earth, may come at last to be a window in the present, from which we watch the long struggle of rain, frost, and sea against the hard rocks and the forces of upheaval, and amid which the stream of life ever struggles, broadens and deepens, becoming here exuberant with warmth and there narrow through arid conditions, until the record at last reaches and interprets the balanced variety of our own time.

———

66. This is clearly Wells himself, as he later notes in "The Threatened University" (December 1895), later in this volume, in defense of correspondence education.

Then Mr. Williams calls attention to the peculiar facility of geological study. "Chemistry must have its purified acids and reagents, test-tubes, and delicate scales for measurement of weight and volume. Mineralogy must have its chemical analysis or optical measurements so fine, that microscopes of the highest power are essential tools for the investigation. Physics must have the most delicate measurements of time and space and weight. Botany for the earlier stages of study is fully equal to geology in these respects, but its scope is much less general. Zoology requires dissection, calling for skill in manipulation, and in other respects is ill adapted to general classes. But precision in the intellectual processes of observation and reasoning can be cultivated in the use of geological facts to its highest and widest perfection with scarcely any aids to the normal faculties of observation. A couple of hammers, a pocket lens, a chisel, and a few pointed tools for revealing fossils, a tape line, compass, and clinometer, are the few equipments that will enable the geologist to carry his investigations to almost any degree of thoroughness."

———

We would add to the above that for school purposes one might teach geology to a very high level indeed, with appliances scarcely costing fifty shillings: a collection of rock specimens (10s., say), a collection of fossils (30s.), a geological map of England and Wales (5s), and a geological map of the district (5s.). That is a final outlay. It is not only the best school science, but next to botany it is the cheapest. In addition, in an age that clamours for something with the technical taint, something palpably practical, it has the advantage of very immediate practical bearings. It is the basis of an intelligent comprehension of soils, of mining, of the source and weathering of building materials; it illuminates a thousand engineering problems as well as a thousand industrial questions, and it is the sustaining substance to the superficies of geography. Thus, from its quality, its facility, and its applications, has geology a very powerful claim among sciences, if not a pre-eminent one, upon the attention of scholastic authorities.

———

The Smithsonian Report dated July, 1891, has just come to hand. Congress resolved to print these copies in 1892, and they were actually printed last year. The report is largely concerned with the enlargement of the United States National Museum, and the endowment of research in astronomical physics. The Appendix which forms the bulk of the volume is a miscellany of papers culled from *Nature* and other sources, English and American. It forms an interesting, though necessarily imperfect, summary of current science for the years 1889-90. The juxtaposition of English and American papers, apart from any patriotic complacency, brings out rather painfully the drifting apart of the two languages.

The temporary erection for "astro-physics," for instance, we are told, was "located near travelled streets." A time will, we verily believe, come, when American will need to be translated into the mother tongue, and *vice versâ*, and when the bodily transfer of papers of merit from English publications will no longer be possible. This will at least serve the purpose of an intellectual protection, and will save original writers upon scientific subjects in America from the present ruinous competition with the gratuitous and even involuntary contributions of English authors.

The Science Library, South Kensington

The Pall Mall Gazette, vol LVIII, no 9032, p 2, 3 May 1894

Wells continued to contribute to The Pall Mall Gazette *because they paid well, and his work usually appeared in the first few pages. Here he is creative in his critique of the classification of knowledge at the Science Library in South Kensington, detailing the absurdity of the catalogue.*

The mere newspaper man at a dinner party recently was drawn into a discussion about the winds. (It is really terrible how science is getting into ordinary conversation nowadays.) Some one asserted that the wind no longer bloweth where it listeth, but in the direction of the steepest barometric gradients, or some such nonsense, and this was flatly contradicted. Said the scientific talker, "You can see all about it in Ferrel's book. It is *the* book on the subject in English," and the newspaper person, being happily caught by a shower in the Brompton-road next day, determined to drop into the palatial Science Library of the Museum and read this Ferrel, and see what changes had recently been made in the order of nature.

Every one knows that spacious hall of books with its multitudinous little tables, long galleries, and array of busts. It is the second largest reading-room in London, and is entirely devoted to works on science and education. Entering, he accosted one of the dozen or so attendants who were watching a little man sleeping over an atlas, and asked for "Ferrel's Winds."

Assistant had never heard of such a book.

"Not heard of 'Ferrel's Winds' !" said the newspaper man, repeating what the scientific person had said to him. "My dear sir, it is *the* book on the subject. They are always quoting him in the *Meteorlogische Zeitschrift*, and they have just been printing some stuff of Müller's about him in *Nature*."[67]

"Is the book in the catalogue?" said the assistant.

The newspaper man had some little difficulty with the catalogue. " Let's see—it's about meteorology," said the assistant, coming to his rescue. "In this catalogue you find books on Meteorology under Physics. Is it a new book? This catalogue was printed in '91. There's a catalogue of newer books over there."

"I suppose," said the newspaper man, trying in his vulgar way to be sarcastic, "when your people had a catalogue like this printed and bound up they did not expect any more books would ever be published ?"

---

67. Wells likely means Prof. M. Möller (see "The Dynamics of the Atmosphere", *Nature*, 1 March 1894, p. 422).

Assistant did not know. "Oh! in *that* supplementary catalogue, by-the-bye," said he, "we put books on Meteorology under Astronomy."

But the South Kensington authorities, it would seem, had never heard of Ferrel. The assistant told some one else who told an official sitting on a throne at the end of the room, and he conveyed a promise to the newspaper man that he would tell some one else, and very probably if he would come again in a week or so, the book might be ready for him. The newspaper man then tried for another modern book on meteorology he had heard of by Dickens or Dickson, and failing that, and finding the rain continued unabated, he settled down to the studious consideration of the South Kensington catalogue.

It is one of the most astonishing catalogues in existence, and took, he hears, a numerous staff of librarians many years to bring to its present climax of badness. As a sample of scientific classification it is in all probability unique. Its merits are well displayed if we take the books upon zoology, which are divided into the following sections: (1) Protozoa, Cœlenterata, Worms, Crustacea, &c. (2) Insects. (3) Molluscs, Conchology, Tunicata, &c. (4) Fishes. (5) Reptiles. (6) Birds. (7) Mammals. (8) General Natural History. Now the beauties of this arrangement will be appreciated at once if we consider the case, say, of the scorpion, which is neither insect nor crustacean, nor under any of the heads specified. Clearly the scorpion is either "General Natural History," or "&c.," section 1, or "&c.," section 3. We try, accordingly, to find a book under these heads— vainly. Finally, we discover that, according to the library of our State centre of science, spiders and scorpion are insects. So, too, the locust shrimps are insects, and so is Latrille, whose portrait and memoir get classified here. We also find that Townson's "Travels in Hungary" comes under the same heading, which seems a gratuitous insult to the memory of Kossuth. Allman's splendid monograph on the Polyzoa comes under the " &c." of section 3, but Busk's Polyzoa, for some mysterious reason, belong to the other " &c.," the " &c." of section 1.

Clearly the South Kensington librarian has chosen a form of classification for his books not only quite unsuited to his readers' needs, but loose and defective as a classification. An alphabetical catalogue of authors, capable of, interpolations, after the British Museum model, and supplemented by bibliographies, would be far more convenient. Who is responsible for this catalogue the newspaper man does not know. As it is a Government affair, probably nobody is responsible. But he writes with a certain animus, nevertheless, for, at one time and another, he has wasted much time in his efforts to get at books by its means. At last his investigations were disturbed by a tall and slender official of respectable appearance, who, after sibilant whispering of some merry tale or other, in one of the little chapels in the corners of the library, had mild hysterics The little man woke up and took his head off the map of Sussex, and the newspaper man discovered the rain had ceased. So he gathered up his hat and stick and withdrew to the British Museum, where Ferrel was presently disinterred for his inquiries.

As he was leaving the South Kensington Library the newspaper man's eye caught the racks of new books recently received. It would be interesting if any one could tell the public who buys the books for this establishment. While Ferrel—his grievance still rankles—is absent, cheap and childish books of the "Tales about Trains" type, with sensational pictures of accidents and rescues, and books about the Wonders of Nature and that kind of thing are sufficiently represented. Altogether, there is scope here for some authority to explain. To the casual visitor, at any rate, this large and costly Government library seems managed remarkably ill.

The Theory of Evolution

University Correspondent, v4, no26, 26 May 1894, pp 339-340

Unlisted in the usual bibliographies, in this work Wells most clearly lays out the theory of evolution, providing a brief explanation of the "type" method used by T.H. Huxley. In his characteristically educational way, he concludes that the student learns more about life through evolution than through a model that creates a static system. The middle portion of the article appeared in his Text-book of Biology.

The word evolution meets the reader of books everywhere nowadays. Any kind of changes is labelled with this all too attractive name; we have the evolution of the solar system, the evolution of the chemical elements, the evolution of society, marriage, the alphabet, and what not. Yet though it is met with so frequently in these derived, and sometimes, it is to feared, depraved, uses, it is possible to imagine that many a "general reader" may still be willing to read a concise statement of the meaning which most rightly belongs to the phrase, "Theory of Evolution," when it stands alone. "Theory of Evolution" seems most commonly employed as an abbreviation of "the Theory of Evolution by Natural Selection," as it was propounded by Darwin, and that is what we have here briefly summarized. The theory is accepted by a great majority of naturalists, but not by all. The minority assert that species have intrinsic tendencies to alter, which do alter them even in spite of exterior conditions.

Two propositions hold true of the young of any animal: it resembles its parent in many points, and it differs in many points from its parent. The general scheme of structure and the greater lines of feature are parental, inherited; but there are also novel and unique details that mark the individual. The first fact is the law of inheritance; the second, of variation. How the variation arises is still a matter of controversy that need scarcely detain us now.

Now the parent or parents, since they live and breed, must be more or less, but sufficiently, adapted to their conditions of living—more or less fitted to the needs of life. The *variation* in the young animal will be one of three kinds: it will fit the animal still better to the conditions under which its kind live; or it will be a change for the worse; or it is possible to imagine that the variation—as in the colour variations of domesticated cats—will affect its prospects in life very little. In the first case, the probability is that the animal will get on in life, and breed, and multiply above the average; in the second, it is probable that, in the competition for food and other amenities of life, the disadvantage, whatever it is, under which the animal suffers will shorten its career, and abbreviate the tale of its offspring; while, in the third case, an average career may be expected. Hence, disregarding accidents, which may be eliminated from the problem by taking many cases, there is a continual tendency among the members of a species of animals in favour of the proportionate increase of the individuals most completely adapted to the conditions under which the species live. That is, while the conditions remain unchanged, the animals, considered as one group, are continually more highly perfected to live under those conditions. And under changed conditions the specific form will also change.

The idea of this process may be perhaps rendered more vivid by giving an imaginary concrete instance of its working. In the jungles of India, which preserve a state of things which has existed for immemorial years, we find the tiger, his stripes simulating jungle reeds, his noiseless approach learnt from nature in countless millions of lessons of success and failure, his perfectly powerful claws and execution methods; and, living in the same jungle, and with *him* as one of the conditions of life, are small deer, alert, swift, slight of build, inconspicuous of colour, sharp of hearing, keen eyed, keen-scented—because any downward variation from these attributes means swift and certain death. To capture the deer is a condition of the tiger's life, to escape the tiger a condition of the deer's; and they play a great contest under these conditions, with life as the stake. The most alert deer almost always escape; the least so perish. The most silent and powerful tigers are best nourished; those with duller senses, clumsier limbs, or more conspicuous markings, suffer most from any scarcity of food, and give way before their betters.

But conditions may alter. For instance, while most of these deer still live in the jungle with tigers, over a considerable area of their habitat, some change may be at work that thins the jungle, destroys the tigers in it, and brings in, let us say, wolves, as an enemy to the deer, instead of tigers. Now, against the wolves, which do not creep, but hunt noisily, and which do not spring suddenly upon prey, but follow it by scent, and run it down in packs, keen eyes, sharp ears, acute perceptions, will be far less important than endurance in running. The deer, under the new conditions, will need coarser and more powerful limbs, and a larger chest; it will be an advantage to be rough and big, instead of frail and inconspicuous, and the ears and eyes need not be so large. The old refinements will mean weakness and death; any variation along the line of size and coarseness will be advantageous. Slight and delicate deer will be continually being killed, rougher and stronger deer continually escaping. And so gradually, under the new circumstances, if they are not sufficient to exterminate the species, the finer characteristics will be eliminated, and a new variety of our old jungle deer will arise, and, if the separation and contrast of the conditions is sufficiently great and permanent, we may, at last, in the course of ages, get a new kind of deer specifically different in its limbs, body, sense organs, colour, and instinct from the deer that live in the jungle. And these latter will, on their side, be still continually more perfected to the jungle life they are leading.

Take a wider range of time and vaster changes of condition than this, and it becomes possible to imagine how the social cattle—with their united front against an enemy, fierce onslaught, and their general adaptation to prairie life—have differentiated from the ancestors of the slight and timid deer; how the patient camel, with his water storage hump, and feet padded against hot sand, has been moulded by the necessity of dessert [sic] life from the same ancestral form. And so we may work back, and link these forms and other purely vegetarian feeders, with remoter cousins, the ancestral hogs. Working in this way, we presently get a glimpse of a possible, yet a remoter, connection of all these hoofed and mainly vegetarian animals with certain " central types" that carry us across to the omnivorous, and, in some cases, almost entirely vegetarian, bears, and to the great and prosperous family of clawed meat-eaters. And thus we elucidate, at last, a thread of blood relationship between the, at present, strongly contrasted and antagonistic deer and tiger, and passing thence into still wider generalizations, it would be possible to connect the rabbit playing in the sunshine with the frog in the ditch, the dog-fish in the sea-waters and the lancelet in the sand. For the transition from dog-fish to rabbit differs from the transition from one species of deer to another only in magnitude: it is an affair of vast epochs instead merely of thousands of years. And in still widening circles we may at last link invertebrate with vertebrate, and see the boundary fade between the animal and the vegetable.

It would, however, be beyond the design of this article to carry our demonstrations of the credibility of a common ancestry of animals still further back. But we may point out here that it is not a theory, based merely upon one set of facts, but one singularly rich in confirmation. We can construct, on purely anatomical grounds, a theoretical pedigree. Now the independent study of the development of the young animal from the germ, the fact that it passes through phases resembling lower types—the human embryo, for instance, has fish and reptile-like stages—suggests exactly the same pedigree, and the entirely independent testimony of the fossils found in rocks is in very close harmony with the already confirmed theory arrived at in this way.

It is in the demonstration of this wonderful unity in life, only the more apparent the more exhaustive our analysis becomes, that the educational value and human interest of biology chiefly lies. In the place of disconnected species of animals, arbitrarily created, and a belief in the settled inexplicable, the student finds an enlightening realization of uniform and active causes beneath an apparent diversity. And the world is not made and dead like a cardboard model or a child's toy, but a living equilibrium, and every day and every hour every living thing is being weighed in the balance and found sufficient or wanting.

H. G. Wells, B.Sc.

Science Notes

The Journal of Education, vol XVI, no 299, pp 325-326, 1 June 1894

The items in these Science Notes are only loosely related. After mentioning the untimely death of Professor Marshall, Wells briefly explores the disconnect between good research, required of a professor, and good teaching. He then uses the Physiology examination at the Science and Art Department as an example of how vague questions can lead to poor results, and briefly comments on using poetry to elucidate science. The last section focuses on an article that had been published several years before in America.

The recent publication of a volume of Biological Lectures and Addresses reminds us again of the great loss zoological education has sustained in the unexpected accident of Professor Milnes Marshall's death[68]. He was, if not the most prominent, yet probably the most able and energetic, of all the newer generation of zoological teachers, and we find in this book fresh evidence of his unusual zeal in the educational part of his professorial position. Several of these papers were written for the students' societies connected with Owens College and were afterwards thrown aside, yet, now they are happily rescued and published, we find them none the less valuable and none the less balanced and charming on account of their comparatively modest destination. To Professor Marshall at least the student was an important charge, worthy of his best thoughts and work, and worthy too of his society. Would that we could say the same of all professors !

———

For after we have convinced the world that a schoolmaster should be required to know something of teaching, our proposition that the ability to teach is neither the common gift of humanity nor the necessary concomitant of knowledge, will bring us next to a consideration of professorial chairs. The filling of these is at present a very remarkable anomaly. Research makes the professor. An essential requisite in a professor of science is that he must have published "original work." To have made discoveries is everything; to make discoveries nothing. And as a consequence we find to-day entrusted with the care of the coming generation of investigators, nervous men who are afraid of their students, irritable men who detest them, philosophical men who treat them as a necessary evil, to be avoided as far as possible, and conscientious men who wake up too late

---

68. Zoologist Arthur Milnes Marshall was killed in a fall while photographing rocks on Scafell in the Lake District. He was 41.

to their responsibility, and— quite ignorant of any educational science—devise dismal cut-and-dried courses of instruction, in flat contravention of every sound pedagogic principle. Here and there is a Lord Kelvin, an Armstrong, a Huxley, a Marshall, or a Miall, but the brilliance of such teachers is a mere individual accident, and has little or nothing to do with their professorial distinction.[69]

How a most brilliant investigator—one, indeed, of the first half-dozen of our scientific leaders—may fall short of educational ideals, is shown very strikingly in the Science and Art Department Examination paper in Physiography this year. Here are two questions from the elementary stage, an examination which is supposed to test the knowledge in astronomy and physical geography attainable in eight-and-twenty hours with no previous foundation:— "How is the position of a heavenly body defined:—(a) In relation to the plane of the Equator ? (b) In relation to the plane of the Ecliptic ? State what you know of the equation of time:—(a) In relation to its amount at different times of the year. (b) In relation to its use in determining the moment of mean noon."

One might quarrel here with the phraseology. How will your average student interpret "define"? And one might paraphase almost every possible sentence by the introduction of that detestably vague phrase "in relation to." For instance : Good morning! have you been active in relation to the employment of Froth's soap? But, putting the phraseology on one side, let the experience of a teacher imagine the struggles of an elementary student trying to answer either of our two questions, the furious froth of words he will produce. Let the reader himself try his hand at the task of really answering this question as it stands. It is possible the examiner wants by way of answer the cabalistic words "(a) declination and right ascension, (b) celestial latitude and longitude." But this is not " in relation to" these two planes separately, since right ascension and celestial longitude measure from their intersection. And such an answer, like an old favourite, "Define energy," may be learnt by heart. It probes not at all into the realities of knowledge. It is the kind of question to find out a boy with a philosophical turn—and fail him.

The *Quarterly Reviewer* shows that Shakespeare "was curiously unobservant of animated nature"—though Beatrice seems animated enough—and "his works are most disappointing to lovers of nature by (their errors apart) their extraordinary omissions." Poor William! He should have read his Saunders and

---

69. Referring to physicist William Thomson (1st Baron Kelvin), chemist Henry Armstrong, biologist T. H. Huxley, zoologist Milnes Marshall, and educationalist Moses Miall.

his Kirby[70]. And Coleridge caught it in *Nature* some time since for putting a star in the moon's concavity.[71] All scientific people are surely not as bad as this? May we, in a column of Science Notes, gently insinuate that there must be something a little too specialized in a student who goes to Shakespeare for trivialities of observations about birds and beetles?

———

Mr. George Iles is not a professional teacher, but as an amateur he has something to teach us. He has been trying to make Euclid palatable to some little boys, and has hit upon some ingenious and original illustrations, many of which might be of considerable value for scientific object lessons.[72] From a chess-board and some problems in fence-making, for instance, he elucidates the fact that areas vary as the square of the linear dimensions, and from a pile of cubes that the masses vary as the cube. Thence he gets out the reason why small cinders go black quicker than large ones, why large bubbles race smaller ones, why big ships are the fastest, why coffee is ground for boiling, why all bridges are not built in one span, why dust and mist float, why rivers carry mud, why very small animals have no lungs, and why cacti are the shape they are. Altogether it is a very pretty and interesting list of deductions.

---

70. Edward Saunders and William Kirby were Fellows of the Entomology Society and wrote books on insects.
71. In a letter to *Nature* in March 1894, Edward Geoghegan lauded Tennyson's scientific accuracy, and said of Coleridge: "A little knowledge of astronomy would have led Coleridge's Ancient Mariner to know that he could never have seen 'The horned moon, with one bright star within the nether tip.'"
72. George Iles, "My Class in Geometry", *Popular Science Monthly*, vol 38, November 1890.

Science Notes

The Journal of Education, vol XVI, no 300, p 376, 1 July 1894

In these Science Notes, Wells again dismisses the idea that science is suitable for cramming and celebrates an article by his friend R.A. Gregory. He closes with another example of how loose categorizations make science examination difficult.

The report of the Committee on Army Examinations has given rise to some controversy. The most prominent suggestions are that Latin shall be transferred to the class of optional subjects, and that elementary chemistry and heat shall be made practically obligatory for Woolwich candidates. The *Times* has committed itself to a vehement denunciation of this change, inventing the proposition that chemistry is the most easy of all subjects to cram, and giving *Nature* an opportunity to convict the Thunderer of disregarding the evidence, misunderstanding the proposals, and ignoring the expressed opinion of the headmasters of public schools, on whose behalf its statement, that the recommendations "might have been framed by a committee of crammers," was presumably made.[73] It is scarcely a compliment to our public schools to confess that in the matter of sound science teaching, they are hopelessly incapable of competing with the outside coach, which persuasion is, apparently, the inspiration of the *Times* article. Yet, that such a belief may exist is a fact worthy of the consideration of all who are concerned in the efficient teaching of science.

———

One might have anticipated that the thing would be just the other way round. In preparation for a Latin examination all that is needed is a painstaking tutor—and the Army crammer is at least credited with a certain diabolical intelligence and industry—books, paper, reiteration. But for science, especially for physics and chemistry, there is practical work—or there ought to be—a large amount of apparatus, a suitably furnished laboratory, a teacher who can afford at least an hour's preparation before his class teaching, to prepare his experimental demonstrations. Are we to believe that the Army crammer can provide these things, and that the public schools, with their endowments and benefactors, cannot? If so, it would be a clear gain to scientific education if the public schools were at the bottom of the Pacific—even if their endowments were with them. However, the testimony of such witnesses as the headmasters of Rugby and Harrow shows pretty clearly that the *Times* must needs go to school again if it

---

73. The Report of the Committee on Army Examinations, *Nature*, June 7, 1894, pp 125-127.

would know how public-school science teaching has fared in the last few years. Dr. Percival, for instance, declared that any considerable school, large or small, is now sufficiently equipped to bring its candidates up to a fair level of science before entering Woolwich or Sandhurst. Only the Woolwich Professors can tell the benefit the insistence upon such a general ground-work would confer upon military education; though some other teachers may dimly imagine it.

———

Of course we assume that the examiner is efficient. Therein lies the defence of the *Times*. For if it be argued that sound science is one thing and examination science another, what can one say? But it is scarcely logical to object to a study because a certain proportion of our examiners do not understand the conditions of efficient examination. Yet it is a thing that eminent scientific people might give a thought to, this persuasion of the crammable nature of science subjects. The gravest obstacle in the way of scientific education in this country, we are assured, is the scientific leader who undertakes examinations and sets the papers in a hurry.

———

Of the other recommendations of the Commissioners, the most noteworthy is the addition of biology to the list of optional subjects. We may venture to doubt its value, either as discipline or knowledge. Theoretical biology alone is the purest of cram. Only so far as it is based on sound extensive (and time-consuming) practical work is this subject of any educational value. At its best— so far as school possibilities go—it is inferior to mediocre geology. Dissection in zoology is an art in itself, difficult to teach, gory and singularly repulsive in its earlier stages, and relatively costly. For efficient work on the botanical side of biology, every student must have a a microscope and numerous other costly appliances. At a later stage a museum is needed. The supply of teachers is small. The only favourable point is the fact that it is a necessary part of medical training, and pupils designed for the Army, and for medical study, would be able to work together.

———

Mr. R. A. Gregory, in his very luminous and suggestive papers, in *Nature*, upon the London polytechnics, points out the peculiar injustice and mischievous effect of estimating the merit of our polytechnic institutions by the standard of examination successes, and utters a well-deserved protest at the tendency to make these establishments mere evening playrooms, wherein young people may waste the little time they have for self-improvement.[74] He especially commends The Goldsmiths' Institute, wherein engineering and chemical societies grown up, in

---

74. R. A. Gregory, "Some London Polytechnic Institutes," *Nature*, vol 50, no 1283, pp 114–118, 31 May 1894.

which students read papers of real merit, and discuss important problems. The value of such discussion, as compared with solitary reading, can scarcely be over-estimated.

———

Here is the problem divided for the teacher of chemistry. In the current text-books bodies are divided into mechanical mixtures and chemical compounds. The former, it is stated, have their constituents in any ratios, and have properties proportionate to the ingredients; the latter have a definite combining ratio of their constituent elements, and have new properties which are not merely a mean of these ingredients. Now an intelligent boy asks if a solution of salt is a mechanical mixture or a chemical compound. What do you tell him? The fact of it is, this airy distinction is altogether misleading, and yet we venture to say that in nine cases out of ten it lies at the very foundation of the schoolmaster's chemical course.

Popularising Science

Nature, vol 50, no 1291, pp 300-301, 26 July 1894

In the prestigious journal Nature, *Wells here argues for the popularisation of the discipline as a way to increase support for scientific research and prevent what are today called conspiracy theories. In the transition from privately organized scientific communities to publicly supported research, people must be made aware of the benefits. He points out that many of the great scientists in recent years had addressed their work to a general audience. Wells extols the ability of the common man to understand science, and it should be presented seriously, coherently, and cater to the desire to solve problems and mysteries. Although written for a scientific audience, and concerned with the broader issues of educating the public, this advice is one of Wells's most direct pedagogical recommendations: "the final end of all science is to formulate the relationship of phenomena to the thinking man".*

"Popular science," it is to be feared, is a phrase that conveys a certain flavour of contempt to many a scientific worker. It may be that this contempt is not altogether undeserved, and that a considerable proportion of the science of our magazines, school text-books, and books for the general reader, is the mere obvious tinctured by inaccurate compilation. But this in itself scarcely justifies a sweeping condemnation, though the editorial incapacity thus evinced must be a source of grave regret to all specialists with literary leanings and with the welfare of science at heart. The fact remains that in an age when the endowment of research is rapidly passing out of the hands of private or quasi-private organisation into those of the State, the maintenance of an intelligent exterior interest in current investigation becomes of almost vital importance to continual progress. Let that adjective "intelligent" be insisted upon. Time was when inquiry could go on unaffected even by the scornful misrepresentations of such a powerful enemy as Swift,[75] because it was mainly the occupation of men of considerable means. But now that our growing edifice of knowledge spreads more and more over a substructure of grants and votes, and the appliances needed for instruction and further research increase steadily in cost, even the affectation of a contempt for popular opinion becomes unwise. There is not only the danger of supplies being cut off, but of their being misapplied by a public whose scientific education is neglected, of their being deflected from investigations of certain, to those of doubtful value. For instance, the public endowment of the Zetetic Society, the discovery of Dr. Platt's polar and central

---

75. Jonathan Swift satirized aspects of experimental science as impractical.

suns, or the rotation of Dr. Owen's Bacon-cryptogram wheel, at the expense of saner inquiries might conceivably and very appropriately result from the specialisation of science to the supercilious pitch.[76]

It should also go far to reconcile even the youngest and most promising of specialists to the serious consideration of popular science, to reflect that the acknowledged leaders of the great generation that is now passing away, Darwin notably, addressed themselves in many cases to the general reader, rather than to their colleagues. But instead of the current of popular and yet philosophical books increasing, its volume appears if anything to dwindle, and many works ostensibly addressed to the public by distinguished investigators, succeed in no notable degree, or fail to meet with appreciation altogether. There is still a considerable demand for popular works, but it is met in many cases by a new class of publication from which philosophical quality is largely eliminated. At the risk of appearing impertinent, I may perhaps, as a mere general reader, say a little concerning the defects of very much of what is proffered to the public as scientific literature. As a reviewer for one or two publications, I have necessarily given some special attention to the matter.

As a general principle, one may say that a book should be written in the language of its readers, but a very considerable number of scientific writers fail to realise this. A few write boldly in the dialect of their science, and there is certainly a considerable pleasure in a skilful and compact handling of technicalities; but such writers do not appreciate the fact that this is an acquired taste, and that the public has not acquired it. Worse sometime results from the persistent avoidance of technicality. Except in the cases of the meteorologist, archæologist, and astronomer, who are relatively free from a special terminology, a scientific man finds himself at a great disadvantage in writing literary English when compared with a man who is not a specialist. To express his thought precisely he gravitates towards the all too convenient technicality, and forbidden that, too often rests contented with vague, ambiguous, or misleading phrases. It does not follow that, because, what from a literary standpoint must be called "slang," is not to be used, that the writer is justified in "writing down" as if to his intellectual inferiors. The evil often goes further than a lack of precision. Out of a quite unwarrantable feeling of pity and condescension for the weak minds that have to wrestle with the elements of his thought, the scientific writer will go out of his way to jest jests of a carefully selected and most obvious description, forgetting that whatever status his special knowledge may give him in his subject,

---

76. The Zetetic Society was comprised of members who believed the earth was flat, Pratt was an anti-Newtonian who believed in divine forces influencing the solar system, and Dr. Orville Owen of Detroit spent his life deciphering secret codes in Bacon and claimed that Shakespeare and Bacon were the same man, the son of Queen Elizabeth.

the subtlety of his humour is probably not greatly superior, and may even be inferior to that of the average man, and that what he assumes as inferiority in his hearers or readers is simply the absence of what is, after all, his own intellectual parochialism. The villager thought the tourist a fool because he did not know "Owd Smith." Occasionally scientific people are guilty of much the same fallacy.

In this matter of writing or lecturing "down," one may even go so far as to object altogether to the facetious adornment of popular scientific statements. Writing as one of the reading public, I may testify that to the common man who opens a book or attends lecture, this clowning is either very irritating or very depressing. We respect science and scientific men hugely, and we had far rather they took themselves seriously. The taste for formal jesting is sufficiently provided for in periodicals of a special class. Yet on three occasions recently very considerable distress has been occasioned the writer by such mistaken efforts after puerility of style. One was in a popular work on geology, where the beautiful problems of the past of our island and the evolution of life were defaced by the disorderly offspring of a quite megatherial wit—if one may coin such an antithesis to "etherial." One jest I am afraid I shall never forget. It was a Laocoon struggle with the thought that the huge subsidiary brains in the lumbar region of *Stegosaurus* suggested the animation of Dr. Busby's arm by the suspicion of a similarly situated brain in the common boy. The second disappointment was a popular lecture professing to deal with the Lick Observatory, and I was naturally anxious to learn a little of the unique appliances and special discoveries of this place. But we scarcely got to the Observatory at all. We were shown—I presume as being more adapted to our intelligence—numerous lantern-slides of the road to the Lick Observatory, most of them with the " great white dome" in the distance, other views (for comparison probably) with the "great white dome" hidden, portraits of the "gentlemen of the party on horseback," walks round the Observatory, the head of an interesting old man who lived in a cottage near, the dome by moonlight, the dome in winter, and at last the telescope was "too technical" for explanation, and we were told in a superior tone of foolish things our fellow common people had said about it. For my own part, I really saw nothing very foolish in a lady expecting to see houses on the moon. My third experience was ostensibly a lecture on astronomy, but it was really an entertainment—and a very fair one—after the lines of Mr. Grossmith's.[77] "Corney Grain in Infinite Space" might have served as a title. It was very amusing, it was full of humour, but as for science, the facts were mere magazine *clichés* that we have grown sick of long ago. And as a pretty example of its scientific value I find a newspaper reporter, whose account is chiefly "(laughter)" with jokes in between, carried away the impression that Herschel discovered Saturn in the

---

77. George Grossmith was a popular actor, writer and comedian.

reign of George the Third.

Now this kind of thing is not popularising science at all. It is merely making fun of it. It dishonours the goddess we serve. It is a far more difficult thing than is usually imagined, but it is an imperative one, that scientific exponents who wish to be taken seriously should not only be precise and explicit, but also absolutely serious in their style. If it were not a point of discretion it would still be a point of honour.

In another direction those to whom the exposition of science falls might reasonably consider their going more carefully, and that is in the way of construction. Very few books and scientific papers appear to be constructed at all. The author simply wanders about his subject. He selects, let us say, "Badgers and Bats" as the title. It is alliterative, and an unhappy public is supposed to be singularly amenable to alliteration. He writes first of all about Badger A. "We now come," he says, "to Badger B"; then "another interesting species is Badger C"; paragraphs on Badger D follow, and so the pavement is completed. "Let us now turn to the Bats," he says. It would not matter a bit if you cut any section of his book or paper out, or shuffled the sections, or destroyed most or all of them. This is not simply bad art; it is the trick of boredom. A scientific paper for popular reading may and should have an orderly progression and development. Intelligent common people come to scientific books neither for humour, subtlety of style, nor for vulgar wonders of the "millions and millions and millions" type, but for problems to exercise their mind upon. The taste for good inductive reading is very widely diffused; there is a keen pleasure in seeing a previously unexpected generalisation skilfully developed. The interest should begin at its opening words, and should rise steadily to its conclusion. The fundamental principles of construction that underlie such stories as Poe's "Murders in the Rue Morgue," or Conan Doyle's "Sherlock Holmes" series, are precisely those that should guide a scientific writer. These stories show that the public delights in the ingenious unravelling of evidence, and Conan Doyle need never stoop to jesting. First the problem, then the gradual piecing together of the solution. They cannot get enough of such matter.

The nature of the problems, too, is worthy of a little attention. Very few scientific specialists differentiate clearly between philosophical and technical interest. To those engaged in research the means become at last almost as important, and even more important than the end, but apart from industrial applications, the final end of all science is to formulate the relationship of phenomena to the thinking man. The systematic reference of *Calceola*, for instance, *Theca*, the Lichens, the Polyzoa; or the Termites, is an extremely fascinating question to the student who has just passed the elementary stage, and so too is the discussion of the manufacture and powers of telescopes and microscopes; morphological questions again become at last as delightful as good chess, and so do mathematical problems. But it must be remembered that morphology, mathematics, and classification are from the wider point of view mere intellectual appliances, and that to the general reader they are only interesting in connection with their end. To the specialist even they would not be interesting if he had not first had their end in view. The fundamental interest of all biological science is the balance and interplay of life, yet for one paper of this type that comes to hand there are a dozen amplified catalogues of the "Cats and Crocodiles" description. I find again, presented as a popular article, a long list of double stars with their chief measurements. Now, to a common man one double star is as good as a feast. Again, the botanist, asked to write about leaves, will get himself voluminously entangled in the discussion whether an anther is a lamina, or in an exhaustive and even exuberant classification of simple and compound, pinnate and palmate, and the like, making great points of the orange leaf and the barberry. But the kind of thing we want to have pointed out to us is *why* leaves are of such different shapes and so variously arranged. It is a thing all people who are not botanists puzzle over, and a very pretty illustrated paper might be written, and remains still to be written, linking rainfall and other meteorological phenomena, the influence of soil upon root distribution and animal enemies, with this infinite variety of beautiful forms.

Enough has been said to show along what lines the genuine populariser of science goes. There are models still in plenty; but if there are models there are awful examples—if anything they seem to be increasing—who appear bent upon killing the interest that the generation of writers who are now passing the zenith of their fame created, wounding it with clumsy jests, paining it with patronage, and suffocating it under their voluminous and amorphous emissions. There is, I believe, no critical literature dealing generally with the literary merits of popular scientific books, and there are no canons for such criticism. It is, I am convinced, a matter that is worth of more attention from scientific men, if only on the grounds mentioned in my opening paragraphs.

H. G. WELLS.

Pestalozzi*

The Educational Times, vol XLVII, no 401, pp 393-395, 1 September 1894

In a complex bit of writing, Wells here critiques a book on Pestalozzi, but actually critiques the man himself and his role in the history of education. Johann Pestalozzi was a Swiss pedagogue in the early nineteenth century. His methods are discussed here as representing a failure, even though he is credited for practically eradicating illiteracy in his home country. Nevertheless, Wells sees his main achievement as a precursor to a later educationalist, Friedrich Froebel. Wells had written an essay on Froebel for his Licentiate of the College of Preceptors, five years before.

By H. G. Wells, F.C.P., B.Sc.

Of all educational writers we must frankly admit that Pestalozzi—saving, perhaps, Herbart—is the least educational. Here to hand is "How Gertrude Teaches her Children," now, for the first time, rendered completely into English—"an Attempt to Help Mothers to Teach their own Children," and, to be plain, a very unsuccessful attempt. Implicitly so much is admitted in the introduction, and in the editor's preface; we learn that Herbert Spencer has misrepresented him one way, Payne another, Quick a third, and we may presume that there is scope for others.[78] "His deep psychology has been the source of much error." We have got a little way forward with our knowledge of the infantile mind since this book was written, but our knowledge of its exposition by Pestalozzi is still very largely to seek. And yet this is to help mothers! Poor mothers, to have the mystery of the *Anschauung* added to their cares! As a matter of fact, Pestalozzi's efforts have never been generally appreciated as cradle-side literature by the married woman, though the ampler leisure and more ambitious intellectuality of the single has even found a certain fascination in his very intricacy. Once or twice he did himself sorrowfully admit this failure of his attempt, and post-dated again the consequent reorganization of humanity.

Now, whatever one may urge on behalf of Pestalozzi, it must be contended that to be obscure is the very negation of the art he would expound. If the teacher has an excuse for existing at all, it is because he comes between the multitudinous confusion of Nature and the learner. He selects and arranges. He makes his subject attractive and stimulating—psychologizes it. The very essence of the

---

78. Herbert Spencer was a positivist philosopher who wrote on education, William Morton Payne was an American social studies instructor and critic, and Reverend Robert H. Quick was a Cambridge-educated educational writer.

rottenness of the old education, against which the name of Pestalozzi is used as if it were a standard, was disorderly presentation. If the teacher does not select, arrange, and make acceptable, he is no true teacher, but a mere addition to the difficulty of the lesson. Judged by such a standard, we must submit that Pestalozzi does not rank at all as a great teacher—to use a popular phrase. He deliberately set out to teach mothers, it is true, but, so far as his own direct efforts went, he failed most signally.

By a more practical test, too, is Pestalozzi condemned as in any way a remarkably successful teacher. We may ask, what were the direct fruits in men and women of his own immediate instruction, and we should find that many a Dotheboys Hall could parallel the list of successes we should receive by way of reply.[79] His educational influence was, perhaps, more evident upon his assistants than upon his pupils, but even with them we have heresies, discussions, dissensions. Niederer takes the bit in his teeth and bolts with his director. Froebel comes open and appreciative, and goes away in a controversial spirit. "Each disciple interpreted the master's doctrine in his own way," and "ended by declaring that Pestalozzi had not understood himself." The local authorities cool towards his establishments, and none of these survive him. His life closes with "My Experiences," and a quarrel, all of personalities, with Niederer and Biber.[80]

Those who would present Pestalozzi as anything but a Great Failure are, in the face of these facts, forced into an attitude essentially esoteric. They resort to Kant and the like mysteries; they profess a belief in a great Pestalozzian theory of psychology that other eye than his hath not yet seen—a mystery, a miracle. They treasure his every word, and counsel us to read his books in the proper order, to
> "fast and pray
> That so perchance the vision may be seen
> By thee and thine, and so the world be healed."

"If we walk in his ways," says Mr. Cooke, the editor of this translation, "we may see what he saw." And the study of him thus becomes to a large extent an act of faith, an outward and visible labour undertaken to attain an inward and

---

79. Dotheboys Hall was a school in Charles Dickens' *Nicholas Nickleby*: "At Mr Wackford Squeers's Academy, Dotheboys Hall, at the delightful village of Dotheboys, near Greta Bridge in Yorkshire, Youth are boarded, clothed, booked, furnished with pocket-money, provided with all necessaries, instructed in all languages living and dead, mathematics, orthography, geometry, astronomy, trigonometry, the use of the globes, algebra, single stick (if required), writing, arithmetic, fortification, and every other branch of classical literature. "
80. Johannes Niederer, Friedrich Froebel, and George Biber were all associates of Pestalozzi.

spiritual and quite unknown benefit.

Now it may be that all the preceding will appear to the reader as an impudent attempt to belittle a great name. For all teachers are reputed to know and to respect the name at least of Pestalozzi. But these remarks are not offered in such a spirit. It has been denied that Pestalozzi was a Great—or, indeed, even a passable—Teacher, and it has been asserted that he was a Great Failure. Yet the greatest men have been failures. One might almost argue that failure is an essential of greatness. The battle of human progress is won by those who try and fail, as many another battle has been won by those who went forward to die. This theory of a transcendent Pestalozzi with an intellectual power that blinds and confuses a common man is, after all, far prettier than one which concedes his confusion, his gusts of temper, his vanities, and the deep and enduring sorrow and sense of defeat that rises ever and again through his self-assertion. To those who feel the pressure of work, responsibility, and their own limitations, Pestalozzi the Inspired Cryptogram is a poor substitute for Pestalozzi the man; more particularly of the man whom we discern between the lines of "How Gertrude Teaches her Children;" a man falling short in everything he essays, mainly because he aims so high, eagerly grasping at whatever is good, so eagerly that he overreaches himself; a man stung acutely by adverse criticism and jealousy, as only generous natures can be; by no means above self-assertion—Bell, by the bye, displayed that public nuisance of our profession, the system-monger, at his worst, when he prophesied that Pestalozzi's method would be forgotten in a few years, while "mine will be spread over the whole world"—and withal a man fundamentally honest and profoundly noble.[81] He struggled and he fell, and out of his fall there arose a great harvest of educational enlightenment.

Nothing could be finer, more generous, or more sorrowful, and nothing could be more adverse to the mystic theory of Pestalozzi than the Preface that he added to this book in 1820. Here he frankly discusses the Burgdorf failure. Herr Niederer, it was, who had the resplendent theory. "To my grave," says Pestalozzi, "I shall remain in a kind of fog about most of my views." The great matter with him was no "clearly defined or scientifically connected" view; it was an impulse "to seek and find for the people simple methods of instruction." This soon led to the perception that intelligible methods of instruction must, as a general principle, "start from simple beginning points," and be carried on "in a continuously graduated series." He was essentially an experimentalist; Yverdun,

---

81. The Bell-Lancaster method, also known as monitorial teaching, may not have immortalized Andrew Bell worldwide, but it did have an impact on Wells. The popularization of "mutual instruction" (using pupils to teach other pupils) made it possible for Wells to be a pupil-teacher for Horace Byatt at Midhurst Grammar School.

Burgdorf, Stanz are so many smashed crucibles and heaps of spoilt material.[82] "The crumb lying on the road arrested me if I thought it would afford the least bit of nourishment to my effort. I must stop and examine it, and until i know it thus I cannot possibly consider it critically in universal connexion and relation." But a "higher significance" was given to his views; he was "led away from" himself. At Burgdorf, this was the story (and parenthetically we remark that the translators' English might be a little more lucid);—

The cry "We can do it" before we could—"We are doing it" before we did it—was too loud, too distinct, too often repeated, partly by men whose testimony had a real value in itself, and deserved attention. But it had too much charm for us; we made more of it than it really said or meant. Briefly, the time as it was, dazzled us; yet we still worked actively, in order practically to approach our end. We succeeded in many respects in the way of bringing a few beginning subjects of instruction into better order and to a better psychological foundation; and our efforts on this side might have had really important results; but the practical activity, which alone could secure the success of our purpose, was gradually lost in our midst in a lamentable manner. Matters strange and far removed from our duty soon absorbed our time and powers, and gave a mortal blow to the simplicity, the progress, the concentration, and oven the humanity of our original efforts. Great ideas for improving the world, which arose out of elevated views of our subject, and which soon became exaggerated, filled our heads, confused our hearts, and made our hands careless of the needs of the Institute that lay before our eyes.

Nothing could more clearly vindicate Pestalozzi from the suspicion of being in any way the sphinx of a psychological riddle than these quotations. In brief, he wants to bring education to every man—as Comenius had desired before him—and he wants to find out the easiest way, and "the deductive view of our efforts, advancing in front of the practical performance, far surpassing it and leaving it behind, was Herr Niederer's view." He has no capacity for wide generalization, bitterly regrets it as the cause of his failure. "I ought," he says, "to pursue my way by *experiments*, which is the way of my life . . . without desiring the fruit of a tree of knowledge that for me and for the idiosyncrasy of my nature is forbidden fruit." And neither in the beginning nor the end do we find he has arrived at any comprehensive doctrine—the fog never lifts. But this "Anschauung" looms like a haze-girt lighthouse upon the explorer, a conception of the essential nature of a wide base of clear precepts to an orderly edifice of knowledge. There was something wrong with education he knew clearly enough from the start, a vice of wordiness, too wide a separation from common experience. The foundations of knowledge were left to chance; the schoolmaster

---

82. These are towns where Pestalozzi established schools at different points in his career.

came and talked, and if the child could not understand the talking, well—then it must be a very stupid creature. He spent his lifetime trying to bridge this gap, to understand the elementary preparation that the current education took for granted.

The figure of the elements of writing given with "The Method"—a translation of which is appended to the book we are considering—shows the necessary outcome of this idea. We are presented with certain curved and straight lines, and, if the child can master these, the rest of writing and drawing will be an easy synthesis. In the same way, language and number are analysed. At first it was inevitable that an unnatural synthesis would be attempted. The rest of his troubled life seems to have been devoted, so far as circumstances permitted, to experiments in the presentation of these elements—each experiment finally unsuccessful, and each rich with suggestion for the next attempt. The very title of "The Method"—like most of Pestalozzi's titles—is a misnomer. He was trying to discover methods all his life. His greatness is in this, that he kept on struggling even to the end.

Then out of his chaos of attempts and defeats, assertions and contradictions, there presently arose the clear theory and wise methods of Froebel. Without Pestalozzi Froebel could not have succeeded—could not possibly have been Froebel; without Froebel it may be that Pestalozzi had remained barren. So Pestalozzi has his place as the father of modern education, and exacts the reverence of all teachers, in spite of his essential failure. Yet whether we are indeed to blame for not giving Pestalozzi's works the exhaustive attention that Mr. Cooke claims, is another matter. To trace the turns and changes of his thought through the misleading confusion of his expression, in order to learn something of education, is merely the old bookish fallacy come again. Here are the children and their needs, and our present methods, to hand; that is our true problem, and not what was or was not intended by a man in a fog sixty-four years ago. The thing before the word. To quote Mr. Cooke—in a manner he will scarcely appreciate:—"We have not learned enough of his first principles to apply them to himself." Even with Pestalozzians, "the ideal of Pestalozzi remains to be achieved."

* "How Gertrude Teaches her Children." Translated by Lucy E. Holland and Frances C. Turner. (Swan Sonaenschein.)

Science, in School, and After School

Nature, vol 50, no 1300, pp 525-526, 27 September 1894

In one of his most thorough examinations of science teaching, Wells makes a clear distinction between education and instruction, between the teaching of adults and children, and between science as considered by educated people and that taught in schools. The Science and Art Department, based on the idea of the Mechanics' Institutes, was not intended to provide a model for lower schools; the adoption of that model brought school science teaching into ill repute. Wells also calls the bluff of the College of Preceptors, which teaches theory but practices traditional textbook and cramming techniques, even while better teaching models are available. This piece would be reprinted in a slightly modified form in The Educational Times *(November 1, 1894), introduced as "from the pen of H. G. Wells, whose essays on educational subjects are well known to our readers".*

It is an unfortunate accident of the conditions under which instruction in science has grown up, that in speaking of science teaching two essentially dissimilar things should be confused. This confusion has very seriously affected—and still affects—the development of method in this country. It arises from the fact that, twenty or thirty years ago at least, the ordinary schoolmaster was quite without the knowledge necessary to teach science, and that even when his scientific knowledge was a measurable quantity, that ignorance of psychology which was and which remains one of his most constant characteristics, rendered him incapable of innovations upon the tradition of mental training he cherished. Consequently what knowledge people obtained of the growing body of science came after the elementary stage of education was over, when their minds and senses had already received a considerable amount of cultivation and were, for good or evil, definitely developed in a prescribed way. The teaching given, therefore, did not aspire to be so much educational as *instructive*; it made the best of a bad job, and without any belated attempts to alter the fundamental intellectual mechanism, placed therein so much of the new facts and views as the circumstances permitted. It was addressed primarily to adolescence and to the adult, its methods were by lecture, diagram and text-book, and the written examination or a practical examination, turning chiefly on the identification of specimens or the interpretation of diagrams, was the adequate measure of its value. Such teaching can affect the taught only through their opinions and knowledge; it can discover scientific capacity, but it can neither develop nor very largely increase it, because it comes too late in the mental life. It is typically represented by the innumerable classes over which the Science and Art Department presides.

On the other hand, we have the science teaching that is *educational*, that takes the pupil still undeveloped and trains hand, eye, and mind together, enlarges the scope of the observation, and stimulates the development of the reasoning power. Such science teaching occurs at present most abundantly in theoretical pedagogics. It is, however, undoubtedly the proper science teaching for the school, if science is to have a place in the school. For it is universally conceded nowadays that the school is a training place, that there the vessel is moulded rather than filled, and that the only justification for the introduction of science is its educational value. Equally indubitable is it that it should be confined to school limits. An attempt to make the adult science teaching educational in the same sense, would be—to complete the image—extremely like putting a well-baked—if imperfect—vessel back upon the potter's wheel.

Now, hitherto the chief influence of this confusion has been to hamper truly educational science teaching in schools. Those who had as adults studied science under the Science and Art Department, or in University lecture theatres, took their text-books and the methods under which they had acquired their knowledge into the school, where the conditions were altogether different. The course of science lessons began as a lecture in which the class listened to colourable imitations at second or third hand of this or that eminent exponent of scientific theory. The more discerning teachers after a time realised the futility of requiring genuine lecture notes from such immature minds, and supplied the deficiency *by dictating* a colourable imitation. They also provided copies on the blackboard for such original sketches as were required, and indeed went to very considerable pains to keep the outward appearance of the lecture system intact. Examiners of schools—being selected without the slightest reference to their capacity to examine—fell very readily into this view, that school science-teaching was adult science-teaching in miniature; as some parents hold that infant costume should be a simple and economical adaptation of the parental garments. And so an elaborate system of lecturing, note dictating, "model answer" grinding, has been evolved, which is not only not educational and a grievous waste of the pupils' energies, but which seriously discredits the claims of science upon the school time, in the eyes of ordinary educated people.

This has been particularly the case in many middle class schools, though the recent abolition of the second class pass in the May examination has done much, as the Forty-first Report of the Department shows, towards mending the mischief. In connection with countless higher grade and small grammar schools, classes, containing as a rule only elementary pupils, and aiming really only at second class passes, have been organised from year to year. Not only was the science teaching given in the evening classes, but a considerable portion of the daytime was devoted to model answer drill and to mechanical copying out from the text-book. The minimum of apparatus required by the Department formed a picturesque addition to the schoolroom. This discipline resulted in remunerative grants for second class passes, but it resulted in very little else, except perhaps a certain relaxation of the pupil's handwriting and a certain facility in the misuse of scientific phrases. The certificates were framed and glazed, the teacher added a few modest comforts to his home, and there the matter ended.

The examinations of the Science and Art Department were scarcely to blame in this matter, although the blame has been generously awarded them. The Science and Art Department is a large and convenient mark, it is perfectly safe to throw at, and to attack it has something of the romantic effect of David against Goliath. But we must remember that its classes were primarily, as they are still in intention, continuation and adult classes, an outcome of the Mechanics' Institute movement, and it was an unforeseen accident, and one the full bearing of which only became apparent in the course of years, that they should so seriously affect the teaching of middle-class, and even of the higher standards of elementary, schools. For their proper purpose as a test of lecture teaching, the departmental examinations are generally efficient. Far more blameworthy are examining bodies whose work is specially directed to school needs. The College of Preceptors, for instance, while subsidising lecturers upon Educational Theory, has done nothing to promote practical work in schools, and many of its examinations set a premium upon that vicious lecture and text-book cramming which educational theory condemns. And in public schools over which the Department has no influence, young gentlemen from the older universities, beginning educators without of course the faintest knowledge of educational technique, set up precisely the same imitation of the professorial course. We have in consequence such a standing argument against science teaching as that naïve testimony of a prominent headmaster,[83] that he found boys who had followed the classical course for some years, and who then took up "science as beginners," speedily outstripped those who, to the exclusion of literary work, had been engaged during the same time in what he regarded as scientific studies.

So far the confusion between the two forms of elementary instruction has hampered science-teaching. But there can be no doubt that the educational reformer is abroad. A large, if somewhat inchoate, body of criticism has grown up, and good resolutions in the matter are epidemic. A really educational scheme of instruction in physics and chemistry now exists, having its base upon the Kindergarten, and developing side by side with elementary work in mathematics. Mr. Earl's recently published book upon Physical Measurements[84] is an admirable

---

83. The Royal Commission on Secondary Education, led by James Bryce, took testimony from bodies like the Headmasters' Conference.
84. Most likely Alfred Earle, *Practical Lessons in Physical Measurement*, London, 1894.

exposition of what is here intended by educational science-teaching. In this, information is entirely subordinated to mental development. His course is devoted to the measurement of space, mass and time, and to the observation and methods of recording various changes involving precise determinations. The first exercise requires the pupil to "measure the size or dimensions in inches of the paper on which you are writing, using for your standard a strip of paper one inch in length, and which you have divided into halves, quarters, and eighths"; and the book concludes with experiments upon torsion and the rotation of suspended bodies. The course must inevitably constitute a firm foundation of definite concepts, and develop a clear and interrogative habit of mind. It marks the line along which school science teaching must move in the future, if it is to attain that predominance which its advocates claim for it. Yet at the same time it may not be premature to notice that the new movement has its dangers.

These dangers arise from the confusion between the two distinct forms of science-teaching whose existence is necessitated by the present condition of things. In the past the error has been to treat children like adults; in the future it may be that adults will be treated like children. Such exercises as the one we have noticed, are excellent in developing concepts, but scarcely anything could be devised more irksome and exasperating to a mind already provided with a basis of definite ideas. Nothing, for instance, could be better calculated to discourage an intelligent student of eighteen or nineteen, curious about physics, than a day or so spent in manufacturing an unreliable millemetre scale. The problems of the science are already more or less vaguely in his mind, and there is every reason why these should be made the starting-point. To produce an intellectual parallel to the spiritual re-birth, is as impossible as it would be to refer an unsatisfactory chicken back to the egg to reconsider its ontogeny. We have now, and shall have for an indefinite number of years, to provide for the needs of a great number of people whose intellectual development is nearly or quite at an end, whose curiosity about nature is already aroused, and whose practical needs are also pressing for scientific information, and yet who are ignorant of any but the veriest commonplaces of science. For them the Science and Art Department classes were designed and are well adapted. It will be an unfortunate thing if the criticisms of the educational reformer should so far overshoot the mark as to affect their instruction. Yet one might suggest that a downward age limit, similar to that of the London University Matriculation, might save many a schoolmaster from the temptations of the possibility of grant-earning—a temptation, however, from which the abolition of the second class in the elementary stage has already to some extent relieved him.

H. G. WELLS.

A Specimen of American Pedagogics*

The Educational Times, vol XLVII, no 402, pp 432-434, 1 October 1894

This critique of a book by Frances Parker attacks Parker's claims to both innovation and scientific education. Transatlantic rivalry is evident. Parker wants to teach lessons to the "Old World", and claims that his philosophy of educational unification is new. Wells notes that such a scheme has been presented before, and relies on the principles of previous European educationalists. Parker's ideas are grandly presented and illustrated, but are just a jumbled American version of prior ideas about child behavior and holistic education. This piece was reprinted in The Public-School Journal *(Illinois) in December, where it was attacked by editor Dr. George P. Brown in a full-page critique. Brown called Wells a "feeble critic" who "cannot resist the temptation to exhaust his efforts in ridiculing the style of a book which contains so much that makes for the better teaching of the children".*

By H. G. Wells, B.Sc., F.C.P.

Here to hand is another large and imposing contribution to the educational library, in the shape of Mr. Parker's "Talks on Pedagogics." The suggestion of colloquial ease in the title scarcely does justice to the pregnant significance of the matter. But a clearer intimation is conveyed in the preface. There Mr. Parker tells us that "the doctrine of concentration in itself is a science of education that will absorb the attention of thoughtful teachers for centuries; it contains an ideal that is infinite in its possibilities"; and from the title page we learn that the book it preludes is the exposition of this epoch-making doctrine of concentration. We gather from this—though a becoming modesty prevented his saying so in as many words—that Mr. Parker stands towards education in much the same relation that Charles Darwin does to biological science or Clerk Maxwell to physics, or, if this should startle the sober reader, as Dr. Owen stands to Shakespearean research. Assisted by Miss Butt, Miss Montford, Miss Iredell, and other well-known educationalists, he has worked out a complete theory of education—making discovery after discovery—and here at last is the entire thing sent over for us, "the aristocracies of the old world," who, to quote Mr. Parker, "secure in palace and castle, fatten on the vitals of the people," to meditate upon. Coming as it does from a gentleman holding a position in Transatlantic educational circles which is the fair equivalent in pedagogics to a professorship in natural science, it is well worthy of our careful consideration. To refuse our admiration is impossible. In addition, we may draw some useful inferences concerning the quality and value of current educational science from a study of this book.

The cover bears a cabalistic design, an affair of mystic concentric circles and words mysteriously arranged, a thing that at the first glance might be a new kind of roulette wheel, or some sort of charm against evil spirits. But really this is a chart illustrating the theory of concentration. The hub is the child upon whom education is concentrated; around this comes a rim containing "energy" and "matter"; then another, "life," "physics," "chemistry." Then a wheel of radiating sectors, the circle of the sciences, displays "geology," "mineralogy," "history" as expansions of life, "ethnology," "anthropology," "zoology," "botany" as developing the idea of chemistry, and "geography," "astronomy," and "meteorology" as subsections of "physics." Then a narrow belt bears the inscription "modes of attention," and there are "observing," "reading," "hearing-language." The next zone, of "modes of expression," includes "gesture," "music," "making," "modeling," "painting," "drawing," "speech," and "writing." Then on to rim with "Form" and "Number," and no further remarks. This completes the platter. Like all great and novel discoveries, it is not without its element of simplicity. We are sure our readers will like to see it.

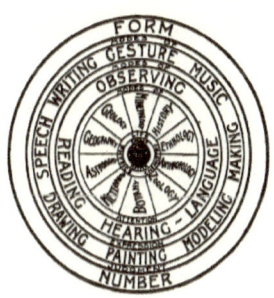

Mr. Parker begins at the centre and radiates. In reading the book we had first to traverse in Chapter I. a certain breadth of familiar matter, presented though it was in an unfamiliar style. "What is the child? What is the little lump of flesh breathing life and singing the song of immortality?" So Mr. Parker perorates. But this chapter comes to nothing more novel than that the spontaneous activity of the child determines method. Thence to Chapter II., to what Mr. Parker calls the Central Subjects of Study. These appear in the chart as the circle of the sciences. Here our author becomes more original. "The central subjects of study are but the main branches of one subject, and that subject is creation." It is curious how the Transatlantic writer loves "creation." "Creation" is eternal; it is the manifestation of invisible all-efficient power; therefore all study has for its sole aim the knowledge of the invisible. The highest, and at the same time the most economical, effort of the mind is the effective striving after the truth of creation; this action of the mind may be called instinctive—it is the shortest line of resistance between the soul and truth. The Central Subjects of Study represent that line, and point in that direction." A very good example is this brief passage of the Principal of Cook County Normal School in his more original mood. Read quickly over to a slow-thinking hearer, it sounds remarkably good. And he proceeds to exhibit his knowledge respecting these various sciences. Like many Transatlantic journalists, he frames his sentences very largely in the form of the epigram, and the reader is continually being confronted by the difficult problem whether any particular sentence is or is not amazingly smart or amazingly ignorant, or merely the contemporary platitude in an abbreviated dress. For example: "The study of soils is the study of mineralogy." "Weight, that mode of motion we call gravity, is another essential property of matter"; and, again: "The relation of mineralogy to geology is the relation of matter to motion." Then, again, this has a plausible air at the first encounter: "Creation is the order of progress, if we take the hypothesis of evolution that the energy which acts through the universe is being economised, that it acts against less resistance, and therefore accomplishes higher results." But examine it. "Creation is the order of progress"! Why not "Progress is the order of creation" or "Order is the progress of creation" or "Creation is the progress of order"? Ill-digested Herbert Spencer may account for the rest; its interest to us is that Mr. Parker is apparently not familiar with the hypothesis known as the Degradation of Energy. But we are wandering from the great theory of Concentration.

It comes to this—if we misrepresent Mr. Parker, it is because he has at least succeeded in imitating the impracticable obscurity of Herbart—that "the subject-matter found in the child's environment," the above selection of sciences, is to supply the entire interest of its studies, and that the "modes of attention" and of expression are to be developed on the way to the satisfaction of this interest. "The direct study of the central subjects of observation, investigation, imagination, and original inference, furnishes an inexhaustible means of educative mental action ... All study consists in investigation of the changes brought about by energy acting through matter, organic or inorganic." "Under the theory here presented, the power to read and to study text is acquired while used directly in the study of the central subjects." "The best possible physical development of the whole body as an instrument of thought and expression is brought about by continuous natural exercise of the body in the expression of thought." It is true that Mr. Parker, after the custom of the educational philosopher all the world over, garnishes his paragraphs with such stereo ornaments as "All true education is inherently moral and ethical," "the fundamental principle of Education is the altruistic motive," "hand in hand and heart to heart with the pupil," but they do not affect the body of his doctrine, which is that the entire education is to aim at a general knowledge of physical science, and that even music and physical training are to become incidental, as it were, to this pursuit.

Now, this, it must be remembered, is no ambitious but harmless rival of Bain or Spencer writing in his study, and spinning his little bit of imitation of "Great Thoughts." If it were, it would not be accorded this prominence. It is the book which expresses the views of a gentleman so prominent in theoretical education as to be entrusted with the duty of lecturing to teachers at what many people regard as the very centre of modern civilization. He has presumably studied pedagogic literature with care before being entrusted with this duty, and he must be aware of the various theoretical propositions of Spencer, Laurie, Quick, Meiklejohn, and the hundred other English contributors to the educational record. Yet, off he goes with his brand-new discoveries of all the old things we have been saying and re-saying for years, acknowledging nothing, criticising nothing, disproving no error, adding nothing to the body of our assured knowledge, presenting it all as a great discovery "which will absorb the attention of teachers for centuries." Yet, even his fundamental idea of a unified instruction has been amply dealt with in Mr. Courthope Bowen's "Connectedness in Teaching[85]." In pursuit of his conception of concentration Mr. Parker has omitted any proper consideration of language-teaching or of artistic design, and music becomes merely a mode of expression for geography, meteorology, botany, and the rest of them. And his mode of presenting that conception is far more suggestive of a revivalist preacher than a scientific investigator. He asserts with intensity; but for any skilful analysis or convincing exposition, for strength, breadth, or subtlety, the reviewer has sought in vain.

Of the reverse of these qualities there is evidence enough. Take, for instance, this leading educationalist's assertion that "up to the time of our Saviour each nation had its national God; everything outside of the nation was wrong and wicked; the gods of the nations were devils; the national God forbade intercourse with, and commanded extirpation of all people not under his immediate control." And he ascribes Lord Sherbrooke's statement that "there are no principles of education" to an aristocratic hatred of popular emancipation. But enough has been said to show the quality of this book.

The moral to be drawn is obvious enough. Mr. Parker in one place is very energetic in asserting that there is a science of education. His book is, however, a convincing proof that there is not, at least at Chicago. Possibly there might be. But for that the scientific spirit is wanted, and something of the scientific investigator's opportunity. The educational inquirer needs to free himself from cant, from that silly spirit of exaggeration that makes all his geese swans, all his

---

85. Bowen's work was subtitled "The School Curriculum as One Organic Whole". H. Courthope Bowen, "Connectedness in Teaching", *The Educational Times* XLIII no. 350, 1 June 1890, pp 243-246.

chance observations epochs in educational history. That spirit of careful inquiry, elaborate criticism, and guarded statement he has still to learn; that habit of earnest study and modest thoroughness that distinguishes the scientific worker. Until then, we fear—though we wish him well—that he must accept the popular estimate with such patience as he may.

* " Talks on Pedagogics." By Francis W. Parker, Principal, Cook County Normal School, Chicago.

The Problem of Sympathy

The Journal of Education, vol XVI, no 303, p 551, 1 October 1894

Similarly titled as "The Problem of Sympathy in Teaching" earlier in this volume, this work takes a different approach. Wells discusses the cultivation of both natural and unnatural sympathy in teaching children. He notes that in general, the developing young men who make up a significant portion of teachers are too self-centered to be suitable. Women, he argues, are automatically sympathetic by virtue of their capacity as mothers.

Nobody denies that the teacher must have "sympathy"; it is an absolutely essential condition to one's being a teacher, and nobody, alas! defines what sympathy may be. So that charges are made somewhat recklessly at times of the want of it, and sometimes there is a needless pride in its possession. For "sympathy" may be made as wonderfully mysterious and elusive as that strange thing "*chiaro oscuro*," of which no mortal man will confess either his ignorance or his interpretation; and the value of the proposition vanishes in the enhanced grandeur of the word.

What, then, is meant by sympathy in such use that a meaning attaches to it? The real intention of the word is a close parallelism of sensations and emotions, a feeling together, a likeness in thought, will, and sentiment. But it can never be really asserted that the teacher of children should have the mind of a child! Possibly the dictum is really meant to express the need of the harmony of unlike, rather than the unison of like, minds. The teacher and the child should agree, as Tennyson says of man and woman, "like perfect music unto noble words," and our "sympathy" means, not coincidence, but the capacity for co-operation.

Now, if we accept this looser interpretation as the one intended, the proposition that the teacher must have "sympathy"—ideally—comes without the need of any process of deduction, for there are no discords in the ideal. But in the world of realities we never get perfectly pure notes or perfect harmonies, and it becomes a matter of approximations. What kinds of mind then, we may ask, will be most and least fitted to the minds of children and boys and girls?

It would be a very wonderful thing if the best were not that of a mother. Nobody will deny this in a discussion, though it is denied abundantly enough in practice, for to deny it would be the denial of the consistency of nature and the general sanity of things. But how is it, if this is the case, that we find little children being taught everywhere by immature girls and hobbledehoys and young men?

The mental condition of the adolescent male may reasonably be expected to be at its very furthest from fitness to the needs of childish associates. Biologists assure us that every creature epitomises the story of its evolution in its development, and in the young man we have apparently attained to about the Viking stage of the human course. A healthy young man is essentially predatory and militant; in him the competitive tendencies are at a maximum; he is intolerant of opposition and impatient with weakness. Unless he is stupid or priggish, he is harassed by endless doubts about things and by contradictory persuasions, and full of vaguely noble and splendid aspirations that go ill with patient teaching. Egotism of a lively but not repulsive kind, vigorous self-assertion, are really becoming attributes of the young man. These attributes, however, are entirely out of place and sadly detrimental in the teaching of children.

A vast amount of irritation, a terrible destruction of good tempers, must go on in consequence of the pupil-teacher arrangement, which also obtains largely enough in middle-class schools, where, however, the pupil-teacher is called a "junior assistant." A vast amount of unnecessary punishment must be inflicted as a relief to the trammelled Viking's feelings, and in consequence of artless lapses that he does not understand. At no stage of life are the emotions of childhood more entirely forgotten than in adolescence; it is only when the civilized stage is reached and the wanderer settles down—a citizen, a man of formed opinions, and the head of a family—that he begins to recall those early memories. Then in the most natural way the broken link of sympathy is restored.

More or less obscurely, this discordance is perceived by many teachers, and their efforts to catch, or learn, or persuade themselves that they have, this needed talisman of sympathy vary between the pathetic and the ludicrous. They strain themselves to conceive what is going on within the curly pate, try and get at an emotion from the principles of psychology, and make every apparently spontaneous act towards a child the outcome of elaborate science. We get unnatural attempts at artless caresses and terms of endearment, and that ungainly lightness of demeanour that encounters only the grave-eyed scrutiny of children.

Who does not know the degraded assistant-master who has made his pious imitations of schoolboy slang a second nature, and proposes to the serenely-proud beauty of the ball to "come and have some of that swagger tuck in the supper-room"? Subsequently, when a curacy shifts the scene of his labours, he is obliged to read every word of his sermons in order to avoid any scandalous display of his fitness for boyish associates.

Sometimes we find young-men assistants getting hold of works generally recognised as good for "sympathy"—Dickens, for instance, or Rhoda Broughton—and reading the thing up: cramming sympathy most assiduously. And in this way, with the very best intentions in the world, they learn hypocrisy—"the crying evil of our profession." Much of the unreal maudlin talk we hear from schoolmasters, and too hurriedly condemn as "humbug," is born in this way from a most conscientious and genuine desire to remedy a deficiency.

There are happy ones, however, among men teachers. Pestalozzi's children rejoiced and wept with him, and the finest memory we have of Froebel is the picture the Baroness Bülow gives us of an old grey-bearded man ascending a steep hill, followed by a double file of children, who presently dance round him and sing and play one of those games that Froebel learnt from nature. But these are altogether exceptional men, while the commonest mother has a mind that is moulded to the mind of the child. A woman loves children not because it is right and proper, or by dint of high principles and virtuous resolves, or because the remuneration is adequate, but because she cannot help it. Dame Nature, the first and greatest educationalist, has kept the woman in compulsory attendance at a training college as long as humanity has endured, and all the regulations of the Education Department can create no diploma to equal hers.

From which considerations it follows that a male pupil-teacher as a teacher of children considerably younger than himself, or a man in a preparatory school, is at least as much out of place as a woman in a pulpit—which is sweetly reasonable and yet not likely to receive unanimous assent, at any rate from preparatory-school masters.

H. G. WELLS.

The Sins of the Secondary Schoolmaster:
I. His Technical Incapacity

The Pall Mall Gazette, vol LIX, no 9261, pp 1-2, 28 November 1894

In the first of a controversial series, Wells explores the schoolmaster untrained in pedagogy. Although unsigned, the work is claimed by Amy Catherine Wells as being her husband's work, as noted in Hughes and Philmus, The Early Science Journalism of H. G. Wells: A Chronological Survey. *The art of teaching, Wells notes, is known to few schoolmasters. In addition, many teach subjects they do not know. (Wells himself had experienced this when he studied for examinations at Midhurst.) He recommends that the Secondary Education Commission require that teachers be required to at least pass the Matriculation Examination at the University of London.*

In calling attention to the sins of the secondary schoolmaster, we write without animus. The schoolmaster is as his parents—that is to say, his scholars' parents—make him. Theoretically his is the noblest of all professions—except, perhaps, the journalist's. He makes children, who would else be savages, into civilized men. But practically he is the parents' assistant and the creature of parental demand. Whether he be a private or a public schoolmaster the ultimate test of his ability is the attendance at his school, and he cannot continue schoolmaster without a generous measure of support in the parental mind. His sins, therefore, are representative. His sins of commission are the outcome of parental urgency; his sins of omission reflect parental ignorance and neglect. We can even fancy him doing ill, when his heart is set upon good, and rejoicing in our attempt to enlighten his taskmaster.

In the first place—to put it frankly—the average schoolmaster does not know his trade. He does not, because he has no inducement to do so. Yet, obviously, there are right ways of teaching and wrong, and a knowledge of and readiness to employ the right ways is not a natural gift. There is no special variety of the human animal born possessing an inherent capacity for teaching. Teaching is an art with a technique that has to be acquired. One might therefore imagine that any one aspiring to be a schoolmaster or schoolmistress would devote a certain amount of attention to the study of right and wrong ways of teaching, over and above the study of subjects of instruction, and would be eager to exhibit proofs of this attention. As a matter of fact, this is not the case. In the public elementary schools, a certain portion of the teachers have gone through such a course of special instruction in "method," but the vast majority of middle-class, public, and high-school masters and mistresses are altogether without any evidence, documentary or practical, of such knowledge.

FIAT EXPERIMENTUM.

The practice in middle-class schools is to learn how to teach, experimentally, upon the pupils. The brand-new graduate who selects the scholastic profession goes into it, as a rule, absolutely ignorant of the art of teaching, as an art. He is pitchforked into a room full of boys, and "mucks about" as best he can. He has reminiscences of the ways in which he was taught, he has certain crude common-sense notions of his own, and the rest of his trade he has to pick up as he may by experimenting upon the vile body of the middle-class or upper-class boy. In a few years he acquires a certain rule-of-thumb skill; or his unconquerable incapacity cries even unto the parents' ears, he is complained of again incapacity cries even unto the par and again, "injures the school," and so drops out of the trade. At the best, the middle-class schoolmaster's teaching is extremely one-sided and unsystematic.

This is the case in all boys' and in the great majority of girls' schools above the elementary level. It is as if medical men were to begin their careers as assistants to practitioners with nothing more than a general education. And no doubt, were the legal restrictions to such a proceeding removed, and were the public to lose the healthy prejudice they have in favour of qualified men, the medical profession would speedily rot into a very similar state to that of secondary education at the present time, rot back to fading traditions, haphazard fluking, and old wives' expedients. So that it behoves the parent, in his individual and in his corporate capacities, to seek earnestly for evidence of knowledge of the art of teaching on the part of his schoolmaster and his staff, that this singular anomaly may be remedied.

At present the University of Cambridge, the University of London, and the College of Preceptors hold examinations in educational methods, of which the former two are dead failures—at least, so far as attracting men goes—and the latter awards less than thirty diplomas to men in a year, and these chiefly in the lowest of its three grades. These are the only examinations offered to secondary teachers in this country. It may be that a large number of the instructors of youth of the "classes" have studied the art of education, but disdained examination. If so, it would be no hardship for them if the parent were to urge them—for his own peace of mind—to submit to some such test at their earliest convenience. And if they know nothing of the art, and such an examination were insisted upon to their detriment, it would be, after all, simply weeding out so many quacks.

EVIDENCE OF FAILURE.

Now it may be alleged that in spite of the recognition accorded it by two English Universities, there is really no art of teaching—many middle-class and public school teachers do say so, speaking out of the omniscience of their perfect ignorance—or that what art of teaching there is needs no study, but is a commodity sold with the cap and gown. Against this we may urge one or two generally verifiable facts. The ordinary middle-class schoolmaster among other subjects, undertakes to teach every boy that comes to him the English language—so far as teaching is necessary—and French and drawing. Some old-fashioned schoolmasters, indeed assert that the latter subject is a "gift," but even then they are always willing to provide lessons in it as an "extra." They continue to teach these subjects throughout the school course, and by continuing to teach them they admit they are generally teachable. An instance is probably unknown of a schoolmaster discontinuing the lessons in any one of these subjects for any selected section of his boys because they proved incapables. Yet what has the average middle-class boy attained by the age of fifteen or sixteen? Can he write English with either grace, precision, or facility? Can he write French, or speak it, or even— which is the least of all—read it with any ease? Can he draw a passable rendering of anything that is in heaven or earth? The general experience will support us in saying that he cannot, and that his sister is in little better case. If that is so, his instruction in these subjects has been absolutely futile, and either the schoolmaster has been professing to teach what the boy was incapable of learning—in which case the schoolmaster is a knave—or the wrong way has been adopted because the schoolmaster is ignorant of the right. The reader may choose his alternative, but for our own part we incline to the least depressing conclusion— namely, that there is an art of teaching, which the average middle-class schoolmaster has not mastered, and which it therefore behoves him to master at the earliest possible opportunity.

It is not simply that he does not teach what he undertakes to teach skilfully. Through his—and the parents'—ignorance of what is possible in teaching and what is not, the time table of an ordinary middle-class school is a thing for gods to laugh at. He teaches impossible things. You will find the schoolmaster cheerfully professing to teach book-keeping, and wasting an incredible amount of the boy's time in a farcical rendering of a ledger clerk's employment; you will find him as cheerfully pretending to shorthand, when he himself could no more take a verbatim note than fly; he will teach chemistry without any apparatus, without even that fundamental chemical appliance, a balance. A huge proportion of the time and energy he has to dispose of is frittered away in the study of geography and history, subjects having, as he teaches them, absolutely no educational value and scarcely any subsequent utility. Then the waste of introductory Latin teaching that still goes on is enormous. Now the administration of obsolete and inefficient drugs by a medical man would, at the most charitable estimate, be taken as evidence that he did not know his trade, and when we find the schoolmaster and schoolmistress setting out to shape men and women by teaching an incongruous jumble of subjects—bookkeeping, history down to 1700, commercial geography, Latin (not including syntax), chemistry without chemicals, futile French, and English etymology—we are forced to an analogous conclusion.

HIS PERSONAL IGNORANCE.

The deficiency does not stop at an ignorance of the art of teaching. The general education also of the schoolmaster is sometimes more than doubtful. Even the headmasters of some middle-class schools have without that modicum of past knowledge indicated by a University degree. Some few are without any evidence of education, and are, indeed, in no sense of the term educated men; others are "members of the University of London"—that is to say, they have matriculated or taken their intermediate examination and then stuck fast. Of these latter, some delude the public by the specious title of "First B.A." Others admit their ignorance by obtaining such bogus diplomas as F.S,Sc.,[86] or such purely pecuniary distinctions as F.Z.S., F.R.G.S, or F.R.A.S.[87] To come to assistant masters in secondary schools, a very large proportion of these are below the rank of a graduate, as any one may see for himself in the "agency" columns of the *Educational Times.* A considerable proportion of the assistants who there advertise are without any evidence of education at all, and "Matric. London" —a quite elementary entrance examination imposed upon candidates for the London degree—is evidently regarded as a very satisfactory qualification for an assistant master. We are not speaking especially here of schools privately owned, though, no doubt, the worst schools in this country are private schools. Our strictures apply with almost equal force to the small grammar schools. There, quite as much as in the private schools, you find the illiterate assistant, the half literate headmaster, the insufficient appliances, the unreasonable medley of subjects. And from the top to the bottom of the present organization of secondary education—except in a few girls' schools— you may seek for any systematic knowledge of the art of teaching in vain. If a middle-class or upper-class teacher teaches well, then he or she teaches well by the mercy of heaven, or—speaking

---

86. Designation of a member of the Society of Science, Letters and Art, a self-proclaimed learned society joined by members desiring to wear academic dress.
87 Fellow of the Zoological Society, Fellow of the Royal Geographic Society, Fellow of the Royal Astronomical Society.

practically—acquires skill at the expense of the class first taken in hand. So many human beings hampered by needless misdirection, and with this and that possibility missed and wasted, go to the making of every skilful secondary teacher. As a rule, however, skill is not acquired.

THE FATAL RESULTS.

That the education of our middle classes is even to some extent in the hands of ill-qualified men and women is no light matter. If it were merely the pathetic struggles of a few hundred half-educated persons to seem wholly educated, and to gain a respectable living at the expense of their consciences, we might strain our charity and pass them by. "One must live," as the mosquito said. But they do such an infinite mischief in the lives they spoil. Our middle class is still shamefully equipped for the business of life; and is indeed now, relatively, the worst educated class in the community. More particularly is this the case of that section which comes below the professional class and above the patrons of the school—the class of respectable clerks and minor business men. But the upper-middle class is by no means exempt. The victims of the incompetent or dishonest schoolmaster enter life knowing no language but their own, and that imperfectly, dead to the beauties of literature or art, often incapable of using their hands skilfully, and indeed—unless the thirst for knowledge save them, that intellectual dipsomania that springs up at times so unaccountably in the minds of ill-educated youths—predestined to failure. They are condemned to live narrowly, work feebly, think darkly, and die with the best things in life still unknown.

Secondary education hitherto has advanced very slowly, but the wheels are running faster now. The Secondary Education Commission has sat and is meditating its report in an ominous silence. The clouds of gathering legislation darken above the schoolmaster while he is still in his sins. He will be well-advised to build himself the ark of technical qualification speedily. From the parents' point of view, and we hope from the point of view of the Commission, any legislation will be unsatisfactory that does not provide that every teacher—who is not merely the teacher of some special art—outside the ranks of elementary education, must be (a) at least as well educated as the common University graduate; and (b) acquainted with the principles of the art of teaching. This is a moderate, an extremely moderate, and perfectly reasonable demand.

In a subsequent paper we shall discuss certain significant features of the examination system of this country.

The Sins of the Secondary Schoolmaster:
II. His Remarkable Examination Results

The Pall Mall Gazette, vol LIX, no 9270, pp 1-2, 8 December 1894

Continuing from the first installment, Wells expands his complaints to the examinations system, and the way that pupils perform on them. This too is brought back to the schoolmasters, who know little of the subjects they are teaching. The education is inadequate for those who will have careers, govern, and run businesses. The Pall Mall Gazette *was a widely read magazine, unlike more formal educational periodicals, thus Wells's advice to the Secondary Education Commission would be more public.*

In a previous paper we pointed out that secondary schoolmasters—almost all of them—and, in lesser proportion, secondary schoolmistresses began and continued teaching without the slightest study of teaching as an art. But, after all, it may be asserted the proof of the pudding is in the eating, that these untrained and sometimes uneducated teachers answer their purpose, and that the pupil does, after all, get educated. That, we suggested, was not the case; and a little consideration of the real meaning of published examination results will prove this.

The largest exclusively middle-class examining body in this country is the College of Preceptors. Last year it examined 17,106 pupils from 5,000 schools. Some of these pupils were prepared by governesses and private tutors and should be subtracted, but we are prepared to give the schools the benefit of this, and indeed go further and, in order to avoid the inconvenient fraction of a person, to calculate the proportion of candidates as about 3½ per school per annum. Really the proportion of *new* candidates is much lower, as pupils may be entered again and again for this test, may be submitted first in the third-class examination, then in the second—a quite distinct stage—and then again in the first, and may pass in any stage over and over again. We have good reason to believe this reduplication would lower the average considerably below three, but we give the schools the benefit of this in consideration of an objection presently to be urged. Now, taking the ordinary course of a middle-class school to be seven years, this yearly output of less than 3½ boys gives us 24½ boys or girls educated up to the level indicated by entrance for—not passing, be it noted—the College of Preceptors' examination. Are we to assume that these 24½ pupils—of whom, by the bye, only nineteen pass*—represent the average attendance at these 5,000 middle-class schools? It is impossible to believe this, because a private school, depending upon fees, would not, at the ordinary middle-class rates, remain solvent with this attendance, and the ordinary endowed school certainly has an ampler turnover, Fifty is assuredly not too high a figure—indeed, it is charitably low. What becomes, then, of the balance of pupils unaccounted for?

THE MISSING PUPILS

Either they are educated up to the level of the minimum requirements of the College of Preceptors, or they are not. If they are they must either enter for some other equivalent or higher examination, or not undergo examination. Now we do not believe that any considerable proportion of boys or girls in these middle-class schools who are capable fail, to be presented. It would argue at least an unbusiness-like modesty on the part of the principal who did not present them. Doubtless here and there a careful parent forbids it, but we do not think such cases are frequent enough even to counterbalance the privately trained pupils of whom we have given the schoolmasters the benefit. With regard to other examinations, the only ones that affect this question are the University Locals. The reader may, of course, suppose that most or all of these 5,000 schools prepare half their pupils for the College of Preceptors' test and half for the Local Examinations, a proceeding which, among other things, would, since the requirements vary considerably, necessitate their teaching several subjects in duplicate. But if there were no other than our 5,000 under consideration, in the country, the entries to the Locals would still remain quite insufficient to account for the balance of boys and girls not examined. Furthermore, there are a large number of schools which confine themselves to the Locals, and in cases where the Locals and the College of Preceptors are both prepared for, the practice is towards duplicating, to send a boy or girl in for the lowest class of the College of Preceptors, and then to go to the Junior or Senior Local after the interval of a year or so. After the first examination a pupil is apt to drop out of the current of school work unless kept up to it by the stimulus of re-examination. We believe every one acquainted with middle-class schools will agree with us that the cases of re-examination of the same pupil by the College of Preceptor are more than ample to compensate for the cases of pupils who, while passing other examinations, are not entered for that most popular test.

THE VALUE OF THE EXAMINATIONS

These considerations point pretty clearly to the fact that more than half of the pupils of these five thousand schools which submit candidates to the College of Preceptors' examination never attain to the minimum requirements of the college. Now, to what do these minimum requirements amount? There is an easy paper in English grammar and one in elementary arithmetic; in addition either the geography of Europe and the British Isles or English history (names and dates) is compulsory, and both these subjects may be taken. Beyond this the pupil has a choice of book-keeping, the beginnings of Latin, French, without any severe translation and no oral test, the rudiments of algebra, Euclid (Book 1—the first twenty-six propositions), freehand drawing, and a few superficialities. He may take eight subjects altogether, but not more, and a quarter of the total marks, in any subject, pass him. This is low—amazingly low—no higher than the upper standards of the National and Board schools, which indeed are chiefly restrained from routing middle class schoolmasters in this their own field by a ten-shilling entrance fee. Nevertheless, it is to the credit of the College of Preceptors that it is no lower; and low as it is, it marks a level which, there is excellent reason tor believing, is not attained by half the pupils in these 5,000 schools.

DOWNWARD COMPETITION OF EXAMINING BODIES

We say it is to the credit of the College of Preceptors that it is no lower.

It must not be imagined for a moment that its examinations—or the Locals—are really independent exterior tests of a school's efficiency. These bodies are competing bodies, they exist upon the recognition afforded them by schoolmasters and schoolmistresses, and the College of Preceptors is a voluntary association, controlled by members who are mainly heads of, or assistants in, schools. If the college were to invent a fourth class examination below its third, of so rudimentary a character as to give every pupil in a secondary school the certainty of a certificate, it would no doubt clear a handsome profit. But in this respect the college has the best of the comparison with the University Local Examination authorities. Its third class is frankly third class, without subterfuge. The Locals resort to a misleading euphemism, similar to the Cambridge expedient with degrees; a really satisfactory pass is called honours, and a candidate who has failed in everything distinctive of secondary from elementary education is returned as having "satisfied the examiners." These examiners are "satisfied" by a rudimentary knowledge of arithmetic, reading aloud, and the answering of papers in religious knowledge and English. Such complacency would find in a glass of water and a crust, nectar and ambrosia. Even at that the "Local" examiners reject a quarter of the candidates, and their customers the teachers grumble. As a result a process of downward competition seems to be setting in, The pioneer body in this has been the Oxford delegacy, which has propounded a scheme of examination for children under fourteen, and we learn from the *Educational Times* that the College of Preceptors follows suit.

THE ROOT OF THE EVIL.

The general delusion about secondary teachers—especially in boys' schools—is that they "teach too much Latin," give "too much attention to pure mathematics," and so forth. The truth is, they do nothing of the kind. They do not teach too much anything, for the simple reason that they do not know the way. They fumble with Latin, fumble with mathematics, fumble with drawing, fumble with science, and with difficulty lift perhaps half their pupils above the level of the sixth standard of the Board schools. What a really independent examining board, which examined from the standpoint, not of what is done in schools, but of what might and ought to be done—what such an examining body would make of them is matter for the imagination. But we notice here that the old Matriculation examination of the London University, which was designed as a fair test of good all-round general education, proved altogether too much for the middle-class schoolmaster, and even now that the three languages required have been reduced to Latin and one other, and the range in science considerably restricted, still far above his head. To pass a boy or girl through this examination on the ordinary school teaching, instead of being a regular thing, is a huge triumph for the ordinary middle-class schoolmaster and schoolmistress, an occasion for vast astonishment and glory at the time, and a pleasant retrospect for their declining years.

Now this is surely a question of the greatest moment. Yearly something between thirty and forty thousand boys and girls, if not more, must be turned out of these five thousand middle-class schools of ours, who as a class should be equipped as officers of the social army, to manage businesses, factories, laboratories, to enter the professions, to practise the arts, to control households, and bring up a fresh generation of educated people. And half of them have not even the elements of an education. The gravity of the matter is scarcely realized by the public mind. We doubt if one middle-class parent in ten is even aware that the whole question is now being considered by a Secondary Education Commission. The Commissioners consult in obscurity, and without the sense and stimulus of public observation. The only signs of external interest are the vigorous efforts of the private schoolmasters to escape the fate they anticipate. And it must be admitted that the mere extinction of the private schoolmaster, which left the country "endowed schools" unreformed would be no satisfactory solution of the question. Yet we cannot expect anything but half-hearted measures from the Commission unless it is assured of a fair measure of public support. There is a real danger that the work of the Commission may run into a side issue, into quibbles of "organization," the endowment of new schools under county councils, the invention of inspectorships, and the general spending of public funds. Possibly teaching might be braced up by a vigorous, independent, and compulsory examination system; but the evils that cure would cause would be almost worse than the disease. School examination, unless it is absolutely brutal and unfeeling, must follow the teaching. The primary question, therefore, the big question that the Commission will shirk unless there is an inspiring support from the general public, is this: whether we are to permit the small proportion of uneducated men who conduct schools, and the large proportion of schoolmasters and schoolmistresses who with a general education have no more special qualification than they have to navigate ships or practise medicine, to continue plying their trade to the general injury.

* There were 6,490 entries last midsummer and 5,080 passes.

The Sins of the Secondary Schoolmaster:
III. His Absurd Technical Teaching

The Pall Mall Gazette, vol LIX, no 9274, pp 1-2, 15 December 1894

By the time he wrote the third installment in the series, Wells had already been criticized anonymously in an article entitled "An Unflattering Portrait" in The University Correspondent (15 December 1894). The author quoted extensively, and complained that according to the "Hon. Sec. of the Association of Assistant-Masters" the figures were "grossly exaggerated and inaccurate" and that the recommendations for the Commission were already known to everyone for years. Wells, as "The Writer of the Article", responded in the following issue (22 December). He had given no figures, he wrote, and referred the critic to Mr. Montgomery, who had shown that "about half of grammar-school masters are not graduates". Wells decries the poor quality of technical education in this scathing conclusion to the series.

In two previous papers we have discussed the scholastic insufficiency of secondary teachers, and pointed out how illusory, and, when examined carefully, how condemnatory their quasi-public examinations are. We wish now to draw attention to certain recent developments of secondary education, especially in boys' schools, that stand in urgent need of ventilation. Partly these developments have been forced upon the schoolmaster in spite of himself from without; partly their defects are due to his remarkable ignorance of his own art. We refer particularly to the teaching of the diverse subjects that come under the heading of technical education.

It is many years now since the public discovered that there was something wrong with ordinary school work, that it failed to equip the pupil satisfactorily for the business of life. One, Paterfamilias, was prominent. Something more "practical" was demanded, there was an outcry for science teaching, to which the powerful name of Mr. Herbert Spencer lent weight, and in those days was the genesis of the Science and Art Department; later came a fuss about "commercial education" and that terrible German clerk[88], and now we have the excitement about technical education—sedulously cultivated by certain eminent professors of technical science. The middle-class schoolmaster cheerfully acquiesced in all these proposals in turn, relabelled his establishment "Modern School," "Commercial Academy," or "Technical Institute," as the times required, reprinted

---

88. The German clerk was a caricature used to shame Britain into expanding commercial knowledge in competition with Germany, whose clerks were seen to be better trained.

his prospectus, and went on very much as before. The chief perceptible differences were the introduction of book-keeping and shorthand as school subjects, the invention of "commercial geography," the invention of school chemistry and school physiology, taught out of a text-book without experimental work, and recently the introduction of such technical subjects as the study of the diseases of plants, metallurgy, electrical engineering, the steam-engine, and sanitary science. It did not occur to the public that their sons and daughters were ineffectual citizens, handicapped rather than favoured against the board-school boy and the immigrant German, because the middle-class schoolmaster did not know how to teach anything; they considered—and still consider—that a change from the old curriculum of subjects, Latin and mathematics for instance, which he knows but teaches badly, to these new subjects, about which he is ignorant, and which he cannot teach at all, would remedy the matter.

Yet assuredly most of these technical and utilitarian subjects with which the time-table of the average middle-class school of to-day is invaded, and the prospectus crowded, are, as any one who has directed any study to educational methods knows, entirely out of place there. There is a certain natural order of studies which must be observed in genuine educational work, a point obvious enough, one might think, were it not disregarded so extensively. You cannot, for instance, teach algebra before arithmetic, or the second book of Euclid before the first, or statics before any geometry. You must begin teaching with simple and familiar things, and build up the mere complex and more abstract conceptions slowly and very carefully, if they are to last and give a basis for further advances in or after the school time. Of course you can make a pupil commit anything to memory, whether it be understood or not—all the more readily if it is not understood—but we are speaking now of real education, the building of a firm fabric of mental habits and co-ordinated ideas.

THE PRECEDENCE OF THE SCIENCES.

In such a subject as physiology for instance, even the introductory statements imply a fair knowledge of chemistry, and the main propositions of the physiologist necessitate a very sound knowledge of physical as well as chemical science. The action of the lungs, for example, involves knowledge of the composition of air, the principles of chemical combination, the diffusion of gases, their solubility and their pressure. Unless these things are first understood —and that means some years of study—a teacher's "explanations" of breathing will be mere empty gabble, and the pupil learning a miracle of faith and rote. Yet the middle-class schoolmaster and schoolmistress—and some elementary teachers, by the bye, who ought to know better—start off, with airy confidence and a cheap text-book, to "teach" physiology without any adequate grounding, without any grounding at all, indeed, in the foundation sciences. For any educational value or subsequent utility a pupil might just as well be learning a column of names and addresses out of the London Directory. This preposterous teaching of physiology before chemistry and physics, this beginning at the roof scientific fabric, may be taken indeed as a safe indication of the ignorance of the common sense of educational method. This kind of make-believe teaching of physiology however—since they can at present get no better—is recognised by various examining bodies, and countless little boys and girls who can call their insides "viscera," and know how many sympathetic ganglia they have, are awarded certificates, to the huge satisfaction of their innocent parents.

The same disposition to begin at the roof is manifest in almost all this technical teaching in schools. A sane and orderly knowledge of metallurgy, for instance, can only arise upon a broad and firm foundation of physics and chemistry, and practical rule-of-thumb knowledge only be acquired in seeing and practising actual metallurgical operations; and this rubbish of the schools is neither one thing nor the other. And so it is with almost all the technical teaching in middle-class schools.

We have no desire to depreciate science in comparison with classical or mathematical subjects, as matter for school education. Our contention is that the middle-class schoolmaster and schoolmistress do not know the order and method of science teaching, that in consequence they cheerfully undertake impossible things, and that to ask them to take up scientific and technical subjects is simply to add to the circle of their previous sins. On that account we consider the present tendency, on the part of the County Councils, to set a premium upon the introduction of technical subjects into the smaller grammar schools is an extremely unfortunate one, and likely to further diminish the already too slight efficiency of these schools.

HOW SCIENCE IS TAUGHT

Even when the secondary teachers take the fundamental science subjects, physics and chemistry, in hand, they teach them wretchedly. The whole benefit of science teaching consists in the gradual and systematic development of the general laws underlying phenomena. The law is of far less moment than the habit of mind induced by the investigation that led up to it. Not knowledge, but a critical and inquiring mental habit, is the aim of science teaching. Carefully graduated experiment and carefully elucidated reasoning is its essence. But your schoolmaster will set about teaching chemistry by telling boys that all matter is made up of molecules. He will give them scientific theories as if they were facts, explain the dogma first, and follow it with some specious examiner's proof that is no proof at all. In evidence of this assertion let any one look into a selection of school text-books in chemistry or physics. In these crystallized lessons one stark assertion follows another, and each chapter is rounded off with a selection of questions, demanding as little thought, and as much faith and memory, as the most dogmatic catechism that ever theologian invented. And clearly until the fundamental sciences are taught clearly and well, it is absurd for the public to demand, and still more absurd for the schoolmaster to pretend to supply, school teaching in technical and applied science, Where the foundation is bad, building is folly.

The schoolmaster's book-keeping is considerably more absurd even than his science teaching. It is really a farcical rendering of a ledger clerk's employment, resembling actual business routine mainly in its weary lack of interest, its paralyzing effect on the intelligence. A number of transactions are entered in a ledger, a balance-sheet is evolved, and then more transactions are taken in hand, and so on through a dismal waste of days. Then the victim also writes out a number of promissory notes and so forth, and occasionally exercises himself in "business correspondence," acknowledging "esteemed favours" from various Smiths, and informing needless Joneses that "we can do you an excellent claret as pr. sample at 12s." After all this a boy goes into a draper's counting-house, let us say. He finds in the desk a system of counterfoils quite new to him, an elaborate procedure called "dissecting" of which he knows nothing, bank pass books and so forth, and he never has to balance a ledger or write out a promissory note at all. If he succeeds it is because he is quick and observant, and if he is dull and mechanical he fails. And, apart from the time it takes from really quickening studies, nothing could be more exquisitely calculated to make a boy dull and mechanical than spending hours and days in entering "To wine, £350" in Smith's account, and then turning to Wine and entering "By Smith £350," and so on over hundreds of transactions. However, it satisfies the "practical" parent, justifies the prospectus, is little or no trouble to teach, and by means of it you can get certificates to the effect that the boy understands book-keeping from various examining bodies; and that is all the schoolmaster seems to desire.[89]

THE ROOT OF THE EVIL.

We have said enough to enforce our contention that the fundamental weakness of our present system is the general ignorance of the principles and

---

89. Wells was very familiar with this process, having been enrolled at Thomas Morley's Commercial Academy and passing the College of Preceptor's examination in book-keeping at the age of 13.

methods of sound education. The middle-class schoolmaster and schoolmistress notoriously do not know their trade, and several groups of equally ignorant and less experienced people, the London Chamber of Commerce, the Royal Agricultural Society, and the Society of Arts, for instance, have undertaken to teach them. It will do no good, we must insist, to devise new scholarship systems, to waste public money upon new schools of a new kind, to substitute Yiddish and other commercial tongues for Latin, to harry the last private middle-class schoolmaster into his grave, while no attention is given to the professional—as distinguished from the general—education of schoolmasters. The schoolmaster is still essentially an amateur; even in the public schools he teaches on his way to a bishopric or a deanery; and where he is not an amateur he is an unskilled workman. That is the source of all the trouble. Hitherto the various educational agitations have resulted in the lavish spending of money, but the lavish spending of money is not required here. The navy needs that. Here the need is not endowment but discipline. The schoolmaster will continue to muddle his work and waste human possibilities until he is persuaded or obliged to give the same amount of attention to the technique and theory of his trade as a physician does to his, or a solicitor to his. When he does that, the choice and arrangement of subjects will, of course, be recognized as his own affair, and the suspicious parent and public functionary will cease their interference. And in those days he will no longer feel that undeniable public contempt—the contempt he complained of some month or so ago in the *Spectator*.[90] Time was when the "leech" was despised equally with the pedagogue as a bungling pretender. The leech—urged by legislation—has risen out of the slough of patent incompetence to the respect of his fellow men. Let the schoolmaster take comfort. Yet a little time and he too will be gently (but, we hope, firmly) assisted out of his sins and lifted up to that place of honour to which his work—if he would but do it properly— entitles him. It is the feeblest and most cowardly thing in the world for schoolmasters to plead that the low state of their profession is due to the private schoolmaster. The profession, as a whole, is ignorant and incapable, and the profession as a whole must prepare for reform. If the body of secondary schoolmasters were fit to be trusted with secondary education it would long ago have cleared itself of the reproach of the private school. The private schoolmaster will not serve as a scapegoat now, and most assuredly the endowment of a few "technical" or "modern" schools will not redeem the schoolmaster from the burden of his sins.

---

90. In the 13 October 1894 issue, the *Spectator* published "The Standing of Schoolmasters", saying that although they did not agree that the English speak with contempt about schoolmasters, nevertheless "schoolmasters suffer in England from a certain slight sense of being disregarded" (p487).

The Sequence of Studies

Nature, vol 51, no 1313, pp 195-196, 27 December 1894

Expanding on his discussion in "The Sins of the Secondary Schoolmaster" for the Pall Mall Gazette, *Wells here uses a review to examine the order of subjects being taught.*

Physiology for Beginners. By Professor M. Foster, M.A., M.D., F.R.S., and Lewis E. Shore, M.A., M.D. (London: Macmillan and Co., 1894.)

Outlines of Biology. By P. Chalmers Mitchell, M.A., F.Z.S. (London: Methuen and Co., 1894.)

Practical Methods in Microscopy. By C. H. Clark A.M. (Boston: Heath and Co., 1894.)

The scientific precision and modernness of a book of elementary physiology, written by Dr. Shore, under the supervision of Prof. Foster, is scarcely to be called in question. This little volume is amply illustrated, and written with clearness as well as exactness. The authors are especially to be commended for laying stress in their preface upon the necessity of a preliminary acquaintance with Chemistry and Physics, and it is to be regretted that they had not the courage to insist upon this point. But here they are gravely open to criticism. "Knowing," they say, "how frequently a book on physiology is taken up without any such previous acquaintance, we have given a few chemical and physical facts as preliminaries in chapter i." A few, and quite too few, it is—six complete pages—expanding scarcely any of the principles which are involved in the simplest physiological explanation, giving, of course, no conceptions of the relations of chemical combination to energy, nor of osmose, diffusion, solution, isomerism nor the action of ferments, all of which come to the front directly one approaches respiration or digestion. We cannot but think that this concession to a common educational error is greatly to be deplored. The authors occupy a position of authority, and it was their privilege—a privilege they have neglected—to demand here, by assuming a sound basis of chemical and physical knowledge, the proper sequence of studies. As it is they have produced a little primer that by virtue of its clearness and attractiveness and the prestige of their names, will serve to uphold for a few years longer a fundamentally faulty system of scientific education.

The evil of a neglect of the rational sequence of studies becomes particularly apparent in the chapters upon the eye and ear. In the former of these an attempt is made to convey all the optical principles involved, in seven lines—"convex lens" is not even defined—and in the latter comes a series of dogmatic statements about sounds and noises, without a particle of that progressive reasoning process which is the very essence of genuine scientific study. Once the initial concession was made, however, this kind of thing was an inevitable consequence. In order to explain the science in hand, three or four others have to be compressed to the limits of a paragraph.

The same unfortunate disposition to begin the wrong way about is apparent in the little book by Mr. Chalmers Mitchell. But in his case there is even less excuse. His book is designed to prepare students for the Conjoint Boards Examination, and therein he is an examiner. Since he calls the tune he might have danced as he liked, and he has, we conclude, preferred of his own free will to contravene the common-places of educational science. We find such a proposition as the following, printed in spaced type; so that the medical student, preparing for examination by Mr. Chalmers Mitchell, who fails to learn it by heart will have only himself to blame for his failure. The earthworm, we are told,

"has reached the second stage of cœlomate development in that it is very highly segmented, and there is little or no trace of the third stage, the stage of the condensation of segments." . . . "Vertebrates are highly segmented animals, in which condensation of segments has become an important factor, resulting notably in the formation of a complicated head, and of kidneys formed by the aggregation of many nephridia."

Now these propositions are illustrated rather than supported by a brief description of the anatomy of the earthworm, dogfish, and frog, and we find that even in the case of these types the metameric segmentation of the cranial nerves is scarcely alluded to, and the homology of the mandibular arch with the branchial bars is not presented as a probability, but stated as a fact. And, in brief, Mr. Chalmers Mitchell, who is not a crammer, but a teacher, gives the medical student the impression almost in so many words—"cut and dried" and ready to be cast into the oven—that the vertebrate type is merely a concentrated derivative (concertina fashion) of the chætopod type, advancing this pure, and as he gives it, baseless, speculation, in the face of the absence of any chætopod stage in the embryology or palæontology of the vertebrates, in the face of the lesser metamerism in the vertebral column of more primitive fishes, and in the face of the declared opinion of many prominent anatomists. But whether the view he gives is right or wrong is, from our point of view, the smaller issue; the great and grave objection is the unscientific spirit of the presentation, the narrowness of the base of anatomical fact upon which this far-reaching generalisation is raised. We find this disposition to what is really the old theological trick of dogmatism, again and again in his book, and it is the evident and necessary consequence of an attempt to touch the far-reaching theories of comparative anatomy without a sufficient preliminary study of individual types.

It is odd that we should find another aspect of the same mistake cropping up in one chapter of Mr. Clark's extremely useful and well-arranged handbook for the beginner in microscopy. It is in almost every way a well-arranged and well-written work, and will be particularly a boon to the amateur to whom experienced advice is inaccessible. But before proceeding to the petrographical instrument, Mr. Clark has attempted a "concise description" of polarised light, which begins—

"The elasticity of the ether in space is believed to be equal in all directions. The same is true of the ether in non-crystalline substances and in crystalline substances of the cubical system. The particles of ether are consequently free to vibrate equally in all directions. In other crystalline substances the elasticity of the ether is modified by the crystalline structure. In some crystals there is one axis or direction about which the molecules are arranged in a uniform manner; such crystals are said to be uniaxial. In other crystals there are two such axes."

Now we believe a student who will clearly understand this will be sufficiently advanced not to require it, and that to the raw beginner, this passage, and its context, will be incomprehensible. Were it not for the actual evidence of these books it would seem the most unnecessary thing in the world to assert that a clear working idea of the *theory* of polarised light, or the general ideas of chemistry and physics, or a cyclopædia of the anatomy of the metazoa, cannot be imparted in half a dozen pages or so of text. If it could, our textbooks in these subjects would be unnecessary, for the ultimate aim of all intelligent research and teaching in pure science is broader and simpler general notions, and there can be no need for a volume if a handbill will suffice. Cannot the scientific writer insist upon the proper sequence of studies in his preface, and proceed on the assumption that his counsel will be observed? To positively encourage students to proceed to subjects for which they have not the necessary grounding, to proffer them snap-shot chapters upon these neglected preliminaries, is really, we are persuaded, to place a grave impediment in their way to genuine knowledge, all the graver because it seems a help, and to place one also in the way of our advance towards more efficient science teaching in the future.

H. G. WELLS.

The Biological Problem of Today

Saturday Review of Politics, Literature, Science and Art 78, no. 2044, pp703–4, 29 December 29, 1894

Frank Harris, who had printed Wells's "The Rediscovery of the Unique" in the July 1891 issue of the Fortnightly Review, *became editor of the Saturday Review in 1894. He called on Wells to write some articles as he livened up the magazine. Unsigned but claimed by Geoffrey H. Wells in his 1926 bibliography to be the work of H.G. Wells, this technical article explores the cytological science of the day. The cellular foundations of life were being explored, but there was a conflict over how traits were passed on to offspring. Here Wells critiques Weismann's ideas, which were popular, by countering with those of other scientists. In this instance, Wells was wrong. Wiesmann's ideas would develop knowledge of chromosomes and guide the future of genetics.*

Two hundred years ago interpretations of the embryological development of plants and animals frankly involved the miraculous. Naturalists found within the stem of a growing shoot of corn a miniature of the ear; or, breaking the shell of an egg incubated for a few hours under a hen, revealed therein a tiny organism, hardly visible, but pulsating with life. They were content with the conclusion that the process of development was the mere growth into visibility and then into adult size of a miniature of the adult. Following our human craving for a rounded interpretation of nature they held that, germ within germ, like a nest of Indian puzzle-boxes, all the descendants of each original animal and plant had been placed within each other by the Creator at the beginning of the world. The course of the generations of animals and plants was a true evolution, or unrolling of these series of miniatures; each generation was the blossoming into life of the outermost surviving member; each when it withered or died left behind the still surviving members folded one within the other in the seed or egg.

The methods and the habit of observation in those days alike were imperfect; yet in 1759 Caspar Friedrich Wolff, in his *Theoria Generationis*, confronted the prevailing doctrine with observations showing that young embryos were not miniatures of the adult. On the contrary, he asserted that young embryos were masses of tissue practically unformed, and that change after change was induced upon them until the characters of the adult were attained.

As is the habit of prevailing doctrines, this old theory of evolution did not succumb to observed truth: the generalization of Wolff found little favour among the biologists of his day. But, from then till now, a slow accumulation of observations has established his main contention, and, with our modern appliances, it could be demonstrated to any one within an hour that the successive stages passed through by embryos resembled neither one another nor the adult. Nowadays, every one knows that man, for instance, begins individual existence as a single cell of microscopic size; that this simple beginning on its upward path passes through stages corresponding first to the simplest and then to worm-like invertebrates, and that it puts on the vertebrate type in the guise of a lowly, fish-like creature. The gill-apertures close, the limbs appear, and it slowly creeps up through stages recalling the ranks of the mammals, until at birth scarcely has it concealed its identity with the man-like apes.

The microscope shows this slow metamorphosis to consist in the multiplication of cells—the living units of which all organisms are composed—and in the deploying of the sheets and masses of cells to their ordered places in the cell community. The recognition of the cellular nature of organisms, and of embryological growth as cell-multiplication and cell-arrangement, and of many diseases and abnormalities of organisms as vagaries of cell-growth, is not the least of the advances of the science of to-day. It has disposed permanently of the crude dogma of evolution that Wolff attacked; but it has merely changed the *venue* of the old controversy from the gross realities of visible matter to the invisible structure of living matter. Miraculous pre-formation of the adult in the egg, disproved for masses of cells, has betaken itself to masses of molecules.

Weismann[91] is the high priest of this temple rebuilded, and the only thing more astonishing than his theory is the vogue it enjoys. Correlating with the research of others some patient and beautiful investigations of his own upon the branching polyps of the sea, Weismann put forward the idea that seeds or eggs contained a peculiar substance, different in kind from the prevailing living protoplasm of plants and animals, and that they could arise only from those parts of the body in which resided a stock of the peculiar material originally derived from the parent. In its first inception this idea was neither novel nor unlikely; an increasing body of opinion in England and Germany supports the view that the resemblances of heredity are associated with the transmission from parent to child of a definite material substance. But the idea grew in Weismann's fertile imagination until it bore the exotic fruits with which his name is associated. First, he insisted on the complete separation between the hereditary material and the material of the tissues of the body. A portion was used in the formation of the

---

91. German evolutionary biologist August Weismann was one of the first to overturn Lamarckism, which had posited that acquired traits could be passed down to future generations. He developed the idea of germ-cells, those cells from the reproductive system that contain hereditary material, and soma cells, which may contain acquired traits. These cells do not interact (the Weismann barrier), so acquired traits cannot be passed on.

new organism; the remainder was secluded in the tissues of the organism undisturbed and uninfluenced by all the shaping and moulding influences that affected the organism during life, and was handed on unaltered to the next generation. Translated into intelligible terms this metaphysical conception implied that acquired characters are not inherited; that, for instance, however a man's habits and vices and education may write their marks upon his bodily frame, his children come into the world exactly as if his experiences had been the stuff that dreams are made of. But a development still more surprising was to come. It is agreed that the material bearer of inherited qualities (named by Weismann the germ-plasm) resides in cells, almost certainly in the special organ of the cell known as the nucleus. Weismann would now have us suppose that the germ-plasm is composed of a number of separate pieces, each piece being a veritable microcosm corresponding to some separate ancestor, and each being composed of innumerable particles. These are the ultimate living units, and they are arranged in a definite and extremely complicated architecture. The mystery of development is that as the organism grows by the division of cells, these cells arrange themselves in the proper places and assume the proper characters. "It is no mystery," says Weismann, "for I have imagined my architecture of the pieces of the germ-plasm to be such that at each cell-division the architecture partially disintegrates, and to the cells resulting from the division there are handed on different and appropriate groups of particles corresponding to different qualities. When the organism is fully formed, the architecture of the germ-plasm is disintegrated completely, and each cell contains only the particles corresponding to its individual characters." Naturally such cells are incapable of giving rise to anything but cells of their own order. New organisms can arise only because a number of the complete ancestral pieces of the germ-plasm were preserved with their architecture untouched.

It is a charming instance of the invention of a tortoise to support the elephant that carries the earth. But, apart from its purely imaginative character, it rests upon a supposition regarding cell-division which Oscar Hertwig[92], than whom no one living knows more about cells, has recently shown to be unproved and improbable. The supposition is that there exists a kind of cell-division in which the qualities of the parent cell are distributed unequally between the daughter-cells. In the stages of division of cells, as seen under the microscope, nothing is more striking than what one may call the elaborate precautions taken to secure that a fair half shall be handed to each daughter-cell. In the vast assemblage of organisms the bodies of which consist each of a single cell, the most

---

92. Hertwig was a German zoologist who studied the cell nucleus as the site of transfer of hereditary characteristics, which would be proven 50 years later. He is considered the founder of cytology.

familiar method of reproduction is by simple division. Yet in these the daughter organisms become like each other and like the parent cell. Among higher animals and plants there are known innumerable instances showing that each cell or group of cells contains the characters of the whole organism, although only such characters are active at any time as are required by the situation of the cell or group of cells. Many plants may be chopped in pieces, and each piece, placed in damp earth, will reproduce the whole. A piece of begonia leaf, part of the twig of a willow, pieces cut out of many worms and polyps, under suitable conditions, will reproduce the whole organism. But still more definite are some recent experiments upon the early stages of developing embryos. Hertwig and Driesch and Wilson[93] have succeeded in shaking apart the cells of young embryos; upon which the separate cells did not give rise to parts of the embryo but, recommencing from the beginning, proved that they contained the qualities of the whole by giving rise to the whole. It were tedious iteration to detail these facts which are known to every biologist. But it is worth while to point out that while the public have been devouring the fruit of the tree of Weismannism, spite of the warnings of Herbert Spencer[94] and Romanes[95] that it is bitter, Dr. Oscar Hertwig has cut the tree across.

---

93. Hans Driesch's work on sea urchin embryos showed that whole larvae could grow from cells separated during division. Edmund Wilson, American zoologist, was an expert in internal cellular organization.

94. Herbert Spencer was continuing in the tradition of Lamarck, promulgating the idea that conditions can influence the inheritance of physical features.

95. A colleague of Darwin and of Huxley, George Romanes had died earlier in the year. He worked with the idea that more highly evolved organism display higher functions. The Romanes Lectures are still held at Oxford.

The Darwinian Theory*

The Pall Mall Gazette, vol LX, no 9289, 1 January 1895

Claimed in David Smith's bibliography as being the work of Wells, this unsigned review critiques the printed lectures of the recently deceased zoologist, Milnes Marshall.

This book reminds us again of the untimely, perhaps the irreparable, loss that British zoology suffered in Milnes Marshall's death.[96] For he was of that type of man that science can least spare, a two-sided man: on the one hand an investigator of eminence, but on the other, and it is the rarer distinction, a pre-eminent teacher and a skilful popular exponent of scientific principles. And in these days, when zoology inclines more and more to the academic and obscure, when it is steadily reverting, with its "ids" and "asters" and "chromosomes"[97] to the unmeaning complexity of the old transcendental anatomy, and when a distinguished politician can deny its fundamental principles without a word of capable protest from its younger investigators, such a man is surely the last that could be spared. His science was without pedantry, the greater issues he had ever in mind, and though, like Francis Balfour, he actually belonged to a younger generation than Huxley and Darwin, like Balfour he belonged in spirit to that splendid group, and like Balfour, too, he has died untimely.

His book is rather the makings of a book than a finished work. In 1893 he delivered a course of lectures upon the Darwinian theory, in connection with the Victoria University; some of these he wrote out, some he delivered from notes, and his MS., revised and a little amplified, constitute the book. Uneven and imperfect as it is, it is yet a remarkably full and explicit exposition of the theory of Natural Selection, embodying the gist of the splendid edifice of confirmatory evidence of embryology and palæontology that has arisen since Darwin's time. No doubt the book is inadequate in some respects as it stands. It is scarcely possible that in his lectures he could have so disregarded the objections of Wallace to the hypothesis of sexual selection, as the mere mention of them here seems to imply, and the editor might well have noticed the remarkable observations, linking that earliest bird Archæopteryx with the flying reptiles of the Jurassic period, to which Marshall's colleague, Dr. Hurst, called attention last year. Moreover, the singular

---

96. As noted in *Science Notes* (1 June 1894), 41-year-old Arthur Milnes Marshall died was killed in a fall while photographing rocks on Scafell in the Lake District.

97. These complexities are explored in *The Biological Problem of To-day*, previous in this volume, likely written at the same time.

fossil remains found at the Cape of reptile-like creatures linking the mammals on one hand with the amphibia on the other go unnoticed. But in spite of such possible criticisms the book remains decidedly the clearest modern exposition of the Darwinian theory for the general reader, and in these pitiful latter days, when such dark speculations as those of Weismannism, or such criticisms upon points of detail as those affecting the theory of coral reefs, are eagerly seized upon by the small fry of science to belittle his name, a noble and, unhappily, a needful tribute to the memory of the greatest biologist that the world has ever seen.

* "Lectures on the Darwinian Theory." By A. Milnes Marshall, M.A., D.Sc, F.R.S. (London: David Nutt.)

Science Teaching—An Ideal and Some Realities

The Educational Times, vol XLVIII, no 405, pp 23-29, 1 January 1895

In this speech to the College of Preceptors on December 12, 1894, Wells ties together many of the threads of his thought about science teaching: the conflict of subjects, the poor training of teachers, the reliance on examinations, and the idea that if done poorly, science should not be taught at all. He also emphasizes the idea that equipment and pedagogy need not be overly complex, and that large reference works in the school library are better than small textbooks privately owned. In his biography of Wells, H. G. Wells: Another Kind of Life (2010), Michael Sherborne considers this speech to indicate a recognition of Wells as an expert and his increasing importance in public life.

It was commented on in the "Notes" column of Nature:

"Much attention is now being given to the methods of science teaching in our elementary schools and colleges, and Mr. Wells's views on the subject are sound enough to be taken into consideration. In the course of his lecture, he pointed out that a rational course of science should grow naturally out of kindergarten. This should lead to object-lessons proper, and demonstrations in physics and chemistry may be made to grow insensibly, without any formal beginning, out of such lessons. The best, about the only permanently valuable, preparation for a scientific calling that can be given to a boy in a secondary school, is the broad basis of physics and chemistry led up to in this way."[98]

THE TWO POINTS OF VIEW.

There are two chief aspects from which we may survey almost any question of human interest—or, at least, almost any question outside the domain of theology. We may regard things as they are, or we may regard things as they might be; we may grope among thorny tangles of facts in search of truth, or we may wander free and unconfined in the wide and beautiful domains of the ideal. This second standpoint, the poetical, the idealistic standpoint, is—for excellent reasons—the one most frequently adopted in educational discussion, and it would be presumption on my part if, in the earlier portion of this paper, at least, I did not follow so honourable a precedent.

To begin with, I shall consider the position and procedure of science teaching in an ideal secondary school, and then I shall take into consideration

---

98. *Nature*, 20 December 1894, vol 51, no 1312, p 182.

certain qualifying complications, certain little matters that have no place in that better and altogether handsomer and simpler world. I shall begin with what one might call pure or theoretical pedagogics, and come round at last to mixed or practical pedagogics, to some of the actual needs, I hope, of everyday teaching.

These two points of view, by the bye, have exactly the relationship existing between theoretical and practical mechanics. We have all heard, I expect, of the celebrated examination question involving a man, a lever, and an elephant, and requiring certain practical estimates, "neglecting the weight of the elephant." Well, that, of course, is purely theoretical mechanics. In much the same way we tackle our problems in theoretical education, "neglecting the weight of the examiner," or the parent or the expense, as the case may be. The system has the cardinal advantage of convenient simplification. We take an abstract case first of all, and afterwards we can introduce, one by one, our modifying considerations.

PECULIARITIES OF THE IDEAL SCHOOL.

But first a word or two concerning the peculiar conditions of the ideal school. The ideal school, I take it, exists entirely to complete the development of the pupil, to take the wholesome little child in hand, manipulate it, and turn it out as perfect and civilized a man or woman as its intrinsic possibilities admit. No secondary considerations of profit or competition complicate the direction of the ideal school. The parent, the wayward, necessary parent, ladies and gentlemen, is a negligible quantity there, simply a benevolent source of children. Governors, managers, do not trouble you. There is, therefore, no need of the prospectus, of the newspaper paragraph, of the deliberate advertisement, of the cheerful, hopeful, buoyant report. There is no need, unless there be educational advantages in these things, of the examination, and the published examination results. So that the ideal schoolmaster can give his whole time to education. And his physical constitution, too, we may remark, educational theory requires to be exceptional. In the ideal school there is no fatigue among the staff, no sense of boredom at the patient duties that recur and recur, no wandering, regretful glances at the great eventful drama of the adult world outside the school-house. The ideal teacher's digestion, physical and spiritual, like all the rest of him, must be ideal. He must never feel those awful qualms of doubt, that horrible sense of one's own insufficiency, and the insufficiency of one's persuasions, that comes at times to the best of common men—most frequently, perhaps, to the best of common men. Moreover, to the exclusion of all other passions, he must be consumed by the pedagogic passion. And all that I have said of the ideal schoolmaster applies with equal force to the ideal schoolmistress.

In a third respect, too, possibly the most serious exception of all, the ideal school of theoretical pedagogics is unique and unattainable. It has no past. It is unhampered by any tradition of method, by any previous organization. All its staff comes to it equally untrammelled, and well trained and fully equipped for their work. Unlike the common workaday school, it is not evolved from anything lower and less perfect. It is a thing *created* brand-new and immediately complete, as all things are in the ideal world. It flashes forth, one may say, full-grown and in all its panoply, from the head of the educational reformer, as Minerva came from the head of Jove.

THE IDEAL SCIENCE COURSE.

In preparing this lecture, I was, I regret to say, tempted, at this point, to proceed to a general consideration of the curriculum of such an ideal school, in order to define the position of science with precision, but, in doing so, I found that so many side issues were opened that I had to abandon that discussion. I shall assume that a course in science has a part in such a school, and go on at once to the arrangement and methods of that course. That done, I shall consider the educational value of this ideal, and that will involve some passing notice of the counter-claims of certain competing disciplines.

To begin with—but, as a matter of fact, a rational course in science has no beginning—it grows naturally out of kindergarten, as kindergarten grows out of the inherent educational activity of a child. In the kindergarten the child has already begun its mathematics with bricks or cubes, and its physical science with colour observation; its drawing and modeling, in part manual training, is also in part a training in physical observation, and it has already got some way on in its training in the perception of geometrical form. Out of this we may and should pass insensibly through arithmetic towards formal mathematics on the one hand, and on the other to the orderly study of science.

At first this science will scarcely be separable from the typical kindergarten disciplines, a mere handling, naming, modelling, and drawing of objects. From thence we come to object-lessons proper. Of course every efficient teacher constructs his own object-lesson as his command of material admits, but, if models are required, those of Miall, Todd, and Murché may, perhaps, be mentioned as being in various ways extremely suggestive and useful.[99]

---

99. Moses Miall published *Practical Remarks on Education* in 1822, advocating personal attention to the individual circumstances and abilities of each child. American astronomer David P. Todd of the Amherst Observatory published books on popular astronomy, including *The Total Eclipse of the Sun* (1888), with diagrams and viewing instructions. In 1897 he would publish his own astronomy laboratory manual, having found none suitable for teaching. Vincent T. Murché was the author of two science readers for children in 1895. According to a review in *Nature*, he made the subject clear

These lessons may range widely, but as the education advanced attention would be directed especially to the chief properties of matter and, by lessons upon coal and coal gas, upon carbonic acid and so forth, to the beginning of chemistry. Indeed, demonstrations in experimental chemistry and physics may be made to grow insensibly, without any formal beginning, out of object-lessons.

A word or two may perhaps be given here to the method of object-lessons. They present considerable scope for the teacher, and their success depends far more on his or her individual skill than is the case with any other kind of lesson—except perhaps language lessons. They degenerate very easily into mere lore or useful information lessons upon the reverend pattern of the "Child's Guide to Knowledge."[100] To get a brick, a lump of mud, and a flower pot, for instance, and to proceed to tell a class of children about Israel in Egypt, and the pottery district, is not all that an object-lesson upon clay might be, though it will give an idea of what such lessons may become in unskilful hands. The first object to be attained is, by suitable questions, to make the children see certain visible facts as connected with certain other visible facts. How to do that the three writers I have named show very ably. But that by no means exhausts the possibilities of an object-lesson—though the tendency of English teachers is to make it stop at this stage. In America, Miss Burstall tells us in her able Gilchrist report, far more attention is given to elucidating from the child an oral description of the facts observed, and I believe that in this country we might with advantage consider this aspect of object-lessons as a means of training in expression, and link with them the drawing and modelling, and even the composition of short accounts of, the objects studied.[101]

Gradually the object-lessons will develop into a systematic course of experimental demonstrations. *Concurrently with the later object-lessons*, beginning perhaps as early as the seventh year, is an expanding discipline which, using the term of Mr. Earl (who, following out the suggestions of Professor Armstrong, has done some excellent work in the development of this factor in science teaching),

---

and interesting.

100. *The child's guide to knowledge: being a collection of useful and familiar questions and answers on every-day subjects adapted for young persons, and arranged in the most simple and easy language* by Fanny Umphelby was in a question and answer format, and was first published in 1825 as *262 Questions and Answers*. By 1895 it was in its 58th edition.

101. In 1893 the Gilchrist Trustees had sent five British teachers to America to study and report on schools and colleges for women in the United States. Sara A. Burstall, of the North London Collegiate School for Girls, published her report in 1894.

I have called Physical Measurements.[102] This, indeed, in the stricter sense of the word, is the beginning of the science teaching. Hitherto we have been naming things, framing propositions about them, gaining an empirical knowledge of form by drawing and modelling. Now we begin to be exact.

PRACTICAL WORK.

This discipline of physical measurements will at first be intimately associated with the arithmetic. Both arithmetic and this discipline are indeed the true offspring of the counting and grouping of blocks and so forth that constitute an integral part of the kindergarten exercises. The discipline of practical physics begins with the measurement of certain linear dimensions by means of paper scales, and would then best proceed to the measurement of surfaces, to a kind of practical mensuration. It will also at first be closely linked to geometry; the commoner geometrical figures would be cut out of paper, and some of their chief properties practically and very strikingly demonstrated. Such things, for instance, as the equality of parallelograms on equal bases and between the same parallels may be shown very convincingly in this way. From surfaces we may proceed to an elementary consideration of volumes, by comparing the contents of vessels by a standard, two beakers, for instance, by means of a test tube, or cubes of various edges by the kindergarten blocks. It would also be possible to study volume by means of such an inelastic plastic substance as clay, but I know of no exercises in this. Concurrently, abundant arithmetical problems upon standards, areas, and contents may be worked and verified by measurement. A few cheap scales and spring balances, or the new letter balances with a counterpoise, are all that is necessary to open the question of masses, and from that we proceed to the experimental determination of specific gravity. We move slowly through this, with an abundance of experimental and arithmetical illustration. The subject now opens out. Along the geometrical line we proceed to consider the determination of the position of bodies in space, and this takes us to the beginning of general geography, latitude and longitude, and the interpretation of the movements of the stars. Along another we come to the measurement of time, the record of observations, and so to experiments upon elasticity and heat. And all this, be it noted, is possible with simple and fairly inexpensive apparatus: a scale or so, some balances, a globe for demonstration purposes, the sky—which

---

102. Alfred Earl was the author of *Practical Lessons in Physical Measurement*. Henry Edward Armstrong was a chemist; in September 1894 he had published an article on scientific education in *Popular Science Monthly*, which began "English boys and girls at the present day are the victims of excessive lesson learning, and are also falling a prey, in increasing numbers year by year, to the examination-demon..."

costs nothing.

And, incidentally, may I call your attention to the way in which the sky is wasted by schoolmasters? You have, in the motions of the sun, stars, and planets, the possibility of a beautiful exercise in observation and reasoning. All these things which are taught dogmatically, the roundness of the earth, its motion in its orbit, and the like, may be seen and thought out by boys suitably directed. You want Foucault's pendulum—which may be improvised in any high room with a thread of cotton and a lump of lead—a few marks on the floor and wall of the school room where the shadow of the sun has reached, a white globe, and the simplest theodolite it is possible to obtain. You do not want a telescope to observe and explain these celestial motions. The results of telescopic and spectroscopic astronomy, the writings of Herschel and Lockyer, are no doubt very marvellous and inspiring, but they have certainly served to obscure the educationally more valuable astronomy of Galileo and Kepler.[103] The up-to-date schoolmaster has hastened to tell the schoolboy that the sun was ever so many thousand times the earth's mass—I don't remember how many times, and I doubt if many people do—and that it contains free hydrogen and an element *helium*, and similar results, long before the boy is in a position to appreciate these facts, and so when he gets to that age when they might appear wonderful they are merely trite. But this about astronomy is an interlude, as the astronomy itself should be in the school course.

So, standing on these two supports, object-lessons and physical measurements, we come to the body of our scientific course. The chemical balance and the thermometer come into play in the object-lessons—I am afraid it is too much to expect that every boy may have his own three-guinea balance to spoil—and so the object-lessons become science demonstrations, first, perhaps, in heat only, and then heat and chemistry. The physical measurements are conducted no longer to solve simply geometrical problems, but problems arising out of the demonstrations, and graduate into the laboratory accompaniment of the demonstrations.

Instruction in physics and chemistry should finally take the form of lessons in explanation of an experiment or group of related experiments, and exercises upon the lessons. The full importance of these experiments should be elucidated by questions. The pupils should draw the apparatus and describe the experiment orally, and should set down precisely what has been seen and what is to be inferred. They should also perform experimental work, involving measurement and computation, and further illustrating the principles evolved. and should be

---

103. William Herschel theorized about nebulae, and Joseph Lockyer discovered helium and founded the journal *Nature*. Presumably the earlier work of Galileo and Kepler provided better foundations for students to learn.

called upon to imagine and describe the laws they had already become familiar with under new conditions. Only incidentally would a valuable knowledge of chemistry and physics be acquired; the main object of the teacher would still be to teach his pupils to observe, to measure, to infer, and to verify. Above all except in the upper forms, there would be no text-book. Each pupil would build up his own in his note-book as he proceeded.

THE USE OF BOOKS.

In the upper forms there would still be no text-book, if by that we are to understand the little abstracts of the sciences that now prevail. But the ideal school should have a good library—I must confess I consider it disgraceful that so few existing schools in England possess this essential appliance—and therein would be all the big science text-books—the real text-books: Michael Foster's "Physiology," Deschanel's and Ganot's "Physics," the "Dictionary of Chemistry," Newth and Bernthsen,[104] foreign text-books, too, perhaps, as a whip for the language teaching, and to these the boy or girl in the higher forms would go for facts and discussions, guided at first by references provided by the teacher. In this way the ability to use books intelligently and to work alone would be acquired. They do this in America, Miss Burstall tells us, but over here, even in theorizing, we disregard this important factor in education. The consequence is that the English boy or girl of sixteen or seventeen has only one use for a book—to grind slowly, painfully through it from end to end—and is altogether without the initiative to get what he or she requires out of a big book. The average University student of eighteen or nineteen—and I have taught some hundreds—has to be nursed at his work like a child, told just what to read and just what to omit, have everything put into his mind, spoon-meat fashion, just as it is to remain there. This "cut-and-dried" teaching is sometimes spoken of as the peculiar vice of coaching institutions, but that is really quite misleading. This book [the lecturer showed one] is the note-book used in teaching morphology in the University of Cambridge, and is intended for students who have passed the Little Go.[105] Every page contains explicit instruction for the work to be done upon that page; the student is not even trusted with the lettering of the sketches he makes. These students, I presume, are, if anything, rather above the average products of secondary education. Nothing could show more clearly the helplessness that results from our small text-book system. It is the gravest defect of our science teaching. And, to put the matter plainly, I very much fear that the real cause of

---

104. G. S. Newth and August Bernthsen both authored textbooks on chemistry, inorganic and organic, respectively.
105. The second-year university examination.

the preference in England for small science text-books, individually owned, is a consequence of the commercial spirit that animates our schools.

However, I am getting away from the ideal school.

By-Products of Science Teaching.

The peculiar advantages of this course of work in chemistry and physics, considered as the main part of an ideal school course, are these. It calls in eye and hand to aid in the intellectual development; it draws together to one head the entire educational process, as no other discipline can. If you make your staple language-teaching or mathematics, then you will need to give a larger share to manual training, drawing, wood-work, and so forth, and these courses will lie disconnected in the school scheme; your drawing will be a mere reproduction of copies, and not a mode of expression, your other manual training a making of unmeaning and useless pails and pen-trays which your pupils will, with the hastiness of youth and the prejudice of their class, be decidedly inclined to despise. And you will still have science invading your curriculum, on the plea of practical necessity.

And science study affords a discipline in the use of language such as direct language-teaching fails to give. That must be insisted upon. The pupil is throughout attempting to express thought; he describes, and later he draws inferences. Almost unconsciously he will acquire the power of writing and expressing his thought clearly. And that is only to be acquired unconsciously. The study of grammar and of style will no more lead to easy and natural composition than a study of the muscles of the foot will enable a child to walk. As you know, overmuch attention to the details of walking will cause a man to stumble, and consciousness of style is one of the greatest obstacles that a literary aspirant can have. Moreover, you must in teaching the use of language have some subject to talk or write about. The custom is to teach essay writing and other forms of composition by requiring abstracts of stories or essays upon such vague topics as Kindness to Animals, the English Constitution, Poetry, or True Politeness. In such topics there are few facts to be arranged, and no scope is offered to close reasoning; they are mere exercises in platitude. The pupil learns insensibly to be sonorous, antithetical, and insincere; to wrap up nothing in an elegant and attractive parcel. We can have no exact writing without exact thinking, and we can have no exact thinking without an ample background of inductive study. But a properly organized course in pure science would, I am convinced, involve the acquisition of a clean clear English style, just as it would involve the acquisition of facility in sketching, of considerable manual dexterity, and of a methodical and yet thoughtful and originative way of dealing with business affairs. Your language master must in fact be a consummate critic, and, when he is a consummate critic—there are editors who demand his services, and he ceases to be a language master.

Then only by mathematics is experimental science excelled in certainty as an exercise; as in mathematics, an error anywhere in the working, or reasoning, or the arrangement of the experiment, vitiates the conclusion. So errors detect and even correct themselves. But, with exercises in languages, a slip here does not affect a point there; the teacher need be always wakeful, and acute, and stupendously industrious to let no mistakes escape him. And in translation there is always a best and a second best and a third best, and so on down to slovenly interpretation, inaccuracy, and, at last, absolute incorrectness, and it is the hardest thing in the world, sometimes an impossibility, to say why this rendering is to be preferred to that.

PHYSIOLOGY AND PHYSIOGRAPHY.

Chemistry and physics form the backbone of our course. Of physical geography and physiology, two very popular subjects, I have so far said nothing. Physiology might perhaps come in in the last year, but I doubt whether it need come in at all. No doubt that, if we could give every child a sufficient knowledge of his physiology to save him from the snares of the patent medicine vendor and from various other dangers, it would be well; only *can we?* The fundamental problems of this science can scarcely be approached in a scientific spirit until we have a sound and rather broad foundation of physics and chemistry. For instance, how can we explain digestion until the action of a ferment, or starch, the difference between crystalloids and colloids, is understood? How can we even explain the necessity for digestion? Then, again, to understand muscular action, it is absolutely necessary that we should understand the relationship of chemical change to energy. In another direction, genuine teaching in physiology is impracticable—dissection is so unpleasant. I have tried it with boys, and they are, I suppose, less sensitive than girls, and I am convinced that it is an unwholesome thing for them to witness. The large amount of physiological teaching done in our schools, I fear, is done in vain. We can, of course, give a child certain ideas about its internal geography, replace the mystery of its interior by a blue stomach and a red heart and pink lungs, but I do not see the value of that even as knowledge. We can lead his memory with empty gabble about flesh-forming foods, heat-forming foods, corpuscles, and phagocytes, but such lessons are really mere exercises in credulity, and, so far from saving a child from quacks, give him just the conceit of knowledge that makes him an easy victim to a plausible fallacy. The most valuable part of physiology, from the point of view of everyday needs, the physiology of the nervous system, is just the most obscure and difficult to teach. And before animal physiology the far simpler problems of vegetable physiology, where you have no nervous or muscular system, but simply an organization for nutrition and reproduction, should first be considered. This can be reached experimentally and inductively as a natural development of the chemical course.

Similarly, to properly understand physical geography is not nearly such a light matter as those who place this subject early in the school course must imagine. You can, of course, teach a boy or girl to say acceptable things about the winds and ocean currents—they did that in the days of Mangnall and Brewster—but to grasp the true bearing of these phenomena is an altogether different matter. For that at least a sound knowledge of the science of heat is required, and a sound knowledge of heat implies experimental work. Take one commonplace of physical geography, the change of temperature with altitude. Ask yourselves: Why is the summit of a mountain covered with snow under a hot sun? Because it is nearer the sun—is, of course, no reason at all. You will, of course, know the true explanation; but, I ask you, is this a thing you can easily explain, without a previous study of physical science, to a boy or girl? Then, in the attempt to adapt the general atmospheric circulation to the schoolboy mind, a long-exploded and very illogical explanation still does duty in schools—and did duty in a Government examination too, by the bye, only last year.

Possibly some of the problems of physical geography are admissible as illustrations and special applications of the principles of physics, but I must insist upon it that chemistry and physics form the backbone and the essential part of an ideal course in science. And the central law to which these studies tend, which holds them all together, and the perfect comprehension of which is the intellectual crown of the school-work, is that splendid generalization known as the conservation of energy.

BOTANY, ZOOLOGY, AND GEOLOGY.

I have not mentioned systematic or descriptive botany, hitherto, because it can have little or no share in the main process of experiment and induction. But I have assumed that the drawing of leaves, the modelling of fruits, the naming of leaves, even the description, would come at the kindergarten end of the course, and that some object-lessons would be devoted to the purport and chief forms of flowers. At a later stage botanical physiology would be studied experimentally and inductively. Still later biological botany might be attacked, the interpretation of structure as the outcome of necessity acting upon inheritance, and the struggle for life and the modification of species.

I can find no excuse for including the formal study of zoology in a school course. It is interesting work, but it has no educational advantages over any other science subjects. Neither has geology such qualities as justify any claim for it to hold a primary place in the intellectual scheme. In a secondary position it is worthy our consideration. It is cheap to teach, but that is no recommendation in the ideal school. Coming late in the school life some study of geology would broaden the horizon behind historical studies. But such a lot of things do that. That claim alone may be satisfied by a few special lessons on the model of Seeley's well known lecture-excursions,[106] directing the attention of boys to such geological phenomena as occur in the neighbourhood, and to such books as Hutchinson's "Extinct Monsters" and "Creatures of Other Days," and Bonney's "Story of Our Planet."[107] Certain elementary conceptions of geology are also necessarily involved in any sound geographical teaching. But more advanced geology, systematic palæontology, and detailed stratigraphy, if only on account of the competing claims of history and literature, and apart from their inherent dulness, must be omitted from the ideal school course.

This, then, is the ideal school course which is also formulated as a main course of mental training. So far as I am aware, it is generally in harmony with the proposals of authoritative writers upon scientific education, except perhaps with respect to the animal physiology, a subject Mr. Herbert Spencer, writing many years ago, advocated. But his advocacy did not go to the extent of proposing it should be the first science studied, as is actually the case in many schools.

CERTAIN REALITIES—THE OVERCROWDED TIME-TABLE.

We have now to take up certain hitherto neglected considerations, certain sad realities, that stand between us and the adoption of such a course in schools. And foremost amongst these obstacles is the overcrowded state of our school time-tables. Thirty or forty years ago the middle-class and upper-class curriculum was objectionable because it was antique; now the objection is that it is chaotic. Time was when in the higher boys' schools Latin and Greek were almost exclusively and very thoroughly studied, and in the middle-class—well!—history, English language, and geography were studied. But new ideas have been propagated, the educational merits of this, that, and the other subject have been urged upon the public, and the private schoolmaster and the boards of governors, anxious to oblige, have tried to include them all. The result is an indigestion of subjects, a miscellany. In some middle-class schools you will find boys learning

---

106. H. G. Seeley was a geologist who conducted excursions each summer for over two decades, based on his lectures for the London Society for the Extension of University Teaching. His *Handbook of the London Geological Field Class* was published in 1890.
107. Rev. H. N. Hutchinson, *Extinct Monsters: A Popular Account of Some of the Larger Forms of Ancient Animal Life* (1893) and *Creatures of Other Days* (1894); T. G. Bonney, Story of Our Planet (1893).

Latin, French, German, the English language and literature, freehand and model drawing, mathematics, a subject called chemistry, of which more anon, another called electricity, agriculture or metallurgy—if the local parent demands technical education—universal geography, English history, mechanics, mensuration. Sloyd,[108] bookkeeping, shorthand, patriotism, commerce, perhaps Yiddish, possibly other subjects.

It is altogether too much. I doubt if any teacher who has thought at all has not at some time thought that the modern curriculum is getting overcrowded. Yet only in the last few years we have had commercial geography thrust upon us, and this present demand for technical education is raising new spectres for the teacher. It is not simply that the pupil suffers directly. He suffers indirectly through the teacher. I suppose a very large majority of middle-class schools in the country number below one hundred pupils, very many below fifty. In these you will have a staff of two or three masters at the outside, and it is quite impossible to expect that on such a staff science, mathematics, commercial experience and method, literature, two foreign languages, and classical learning can be represented. Do we not all know the consequences?—The young men and young women of the "educated" classes who have forgotten their Latin for the simple reason that they have never learnt it, who cannot even read a French, much less a German notice board, who can solve a simple equation after a little thinking, provided it is presented as an equation and not as a problem, whose reminiscences of chemistry are chiefly of the type that O for some mysterious reason =16, who know the principles of shorthand and cannot use it; and so all round the circle. They cannot think clearly or consecutively, much less present their thoughts in writing; they cannot make the slightest use of drawing, and they find no delight in any literature but the shallowest fiction; on the business of life they find themselves inefficient competitors against the enterprising product of the Board school.[109]

The only remedy is to throw some of this multitude of subjects overboard. I sometimes think there is a trifle too much mutual consideration in pedagogic discussions. It is no good admitting that there is much to be said for this subject and much to be said for that. The point is that there is not time enough to teach them all honestly, that some have to be thrown overboard, and that until this matter has been thoroughly discussed we shall have no guiding principle to go upon in dealing with secondary education.

Now, for my own part, I should propose to throw overboard Latin and Greek altogether, English history and geography, except for the last two or three

108. Handicraft, usually for the purpose of educational and personal development, rather than educational training.
109. State-funded school.

years, shorthand, bookkeeping, and all special business training of that type altogether. I also propose to bundle out almost all technical teaching from the secondary school—the exceptions I will specify. A foreign language or two must be retained as an atonement for the Tower of Babel, rather than as a necessary part of an ideal education.

Geography and history tend far more than science, when ill taught, to degenerate into memory subjects, lists of names, altitudes, and dates. The enormous sale of a certain little hand book of dates and enactments and chief events[110] shows pretty clearly the disposition of history to become mere cram. And the really essential facts in these subjects are naturally attractive, most boys and girls will read eagerly books of travel and adventure and historical fiction. If we have a school library, containing such works, and if, in addition, good vivid wall maps and not too encyclopædic chronological charts waylay their attention, a great deal of the formal teaching in these subjects might be dispensed with. Towards the end of the school course, perhaps, it becomes necessary to systematize the shapeless mass, to drill the mob of ideas they will have acquired by reading. However, I must not expatiate on the teaching of geography and history. I have said enough to show some considerations in favour of their omission, say up to thirteen—because there is not the same need of the stimulus of a developing presentation, the same progressive discipline, that there is in science teaching, and because in dropping them out of the school course there is no serious danger of their dropping out of culture. I believe that most cultivated people will admit that little of their historical knowledge was obtained in school, in spite of the hours devoted to it. What they have is mainly the result of private reading.

LANGUAGE *VERSUS* SCIENCE.

To come now to the great omission of the classical languages. With these, it must be insisted, it is a case of all or nothing. There is no room for the teaching of classics and of science, as I conceive it, side by side in the same school. All other considerations apart, the time will not admit of it.

Professor Laurie, in a short essay, has concisely stated the case of language *versus* science, and I cannot do better than consider his argument, so far as I have been able to elucidate it, at this stage. It is a highly academic argument, as you

---

110. Likely this refers to *A Handbook in Outline of the Political History of England, Chronologically Arranged* by Arthur H. Dyke Acland and Cyril Ransome, in print since 1882 with updated and revised editions, or its abridged version, *A Skeleton History of England*.

will see, and runs as follows.[III]

First, that the teaching of Latin, *mensa*, *dominus*, and so forth, presents the *realities of ma's nature* to the student, and that science presents only the *realities of physical nature*. This he asserts as a fact that he knows, without any appeal to evidence. He asks you to think that the study of language brings home the realities of man's nature to the student—whatever the realities of man's nature may be.

Secondly, comes a proposition about which I am still in doubt— it really seems, if you will pardon my applying the expression to Professor Laurie, so incredible. It is this, that language study deals with all words, science only with words denoting the objects of external perception; that, therefore, science, according to Professor Laurie, only teaches us to use the "language of a single department of knowledge," whereas "linguistic training by teaching the value of words *as such*, to whatever department of human knowledge they may belong, educates the intellect to precision in the use of them generally." In other words, the outcome of a scientific training is that the pupil can talk about what he knows, and of a classical education that he can talk about things—generally. Does this argument need rebutting?

Thirdly, Professor Laurie tells us that, "language being the body of thought, the student of it is studying concrete mind." This should console the small boy struggling with his irregular verbs. As a matter of fact, there is a kink here in Professor Laurie's argument, a twisted simile. Language is the body of thought— language the body, thought the soul. Now, if it follows that the study of language is the study of the concrete mind, whatever that may be, then the study of anatomy is the study of the concrete soul, whatever that may be. If the student of language is unconsciously a student of logic, as Professor Laurie avers, then your anatomist is also unconsciously a student of psychology. But that is absurd, and its absurdity reflects upon the claim Professor Laurie puts forward to a superior precision and clearness of thinking on the part of the classically educated.

Fourthly, Professor Laurie lays stress on the excellence of the discipline of language teaching. "What higher discipline of intellect for your pupils," asks Professor Laurie, "than to lay before him a mass of words, apparently dead and disjointed signs, and to require that, from a steady consideration of these, the living organism of speech shall be built up?" Now, ladies and gentlemen, you know that no teacher of language ever did "lay before his pupil a mass of words, apparently dead and disjointed signs, and require that, from a steady consideration of these, the living organism of speech should be built up." Professor Laurie has here simply evolved these impressive qualities of linguistic

---

III. S. S. Laurie, "Remarks on School-Instruction in the Classical Languages—especially Latin—as compared with Instruction in Science", reprinted in *Lectures on Language and Linguistic Method in the School* (1893).

teaching from his imagination in order to suit his arguments, as the German philosopher evolved his camel.[112] And they help him forward about as much as that transcendental animal. He further implies that Latin cannot be crammed and that science can—that science can be presented as tabulated results and acquired by the exercise of memory. Now, in the first place, Latin and Greek can be crammed, and are crammed, for examination purposes just as easily as science—French gender grinding is the quintessence of cramming—and in the next place the science teaching which aims simply at the formulation of natural laws is on a level with the linguistic study that aims only at a translation into English, and grammatical questions, and considers one of Bohn's excellent series of cribs and a handbook on accidence legitimate means for attaining these ends.[113] But evidently Professor Laurie compares the worst of existing methods of teaching science with a kind of language teaching that exists only in the mind of the philosophical methodologist.

Finally, Professor Laurie appeals to what he considers to be notorious facts. "Setting aside men of genius"—that is to say, excepting any exceptions that may occur—"the man of one science or even two is about the narrowest and most hopelessly barren of educated men." That is Professor Laurie's opinion—he makes no attempt to prove it, or to define the singular phrase "the man of one science or even two," and I do not see that it requires any disproof, or has indeed anything to do with the matter under discussion. It is just abuse, an appeal, an undignified appeal, to the narrow prejudice of those who have been mainly educated in linguistic studies, and who have not corrected their deficiencies by subsequent reading. It would be quite hopeless to argue with them, and quite needless to argue with any one else that the average scientific man is neither narrow nor hopelessly barren.

That completes the case of language *versus* science. I must confess I do not think it is a very strong case, and, were it stronger, you must remember this is a question of language teaching *or* science as mental training—there is no room for both —and I fancy the case for science would still carry the verdict.

"TECHNICAL" SUBJECTS.

With regard to recent developments in the direction of technical teaching, the objection I have raised to physiology comes in with renewed force. You must have a complete and strong basis of physics and chemistry before you can approach applied science in anything but an empirical way. And in addition the

---

112. The first of Nietzche's phases of childhood.
113. Bohn's Libraries, first published in 1846, were editions of *Standard Works of European Literature in the English Language*.

body of technique changes rapidly. New improvements in method often bring in applications of scientific principles which hitherto have not been applied in a particular technique. A metal which has hitherto been obtained by a purely chemical reaction is obtained, let us say, by the action of an electric current. A man who has studied the old technique on a narrow basis of chemistry, finds a great gulf, his ignorance of electricity, fixed between himself and the scientific comprehension of the new process. This danger of new methods vitiates all teaching of applied science without a broad basis of pure science. The pure science is relatively unchanging; it develops but it does not alter; industrial methods simply fluctuate. The best, about the only permanently valuable, preparation for a scientific calling therefore that we can give a boy in a secondary school is this broad basis of physics and chemistry.

This is a fairly obvious consideration, and yet it has often been very conspicuously overlooked in the distribution of the technical education funds. If an exception is to be made to that exclusion, it is certainly in favour of that branch of technical education which comes under the especial protection of the Royal Agricultural Society. The systematic study of the bird and insect, friends and enemies of our crops, giving an hour a week to it, say, except during the winter, would, with a due encouragement of the collecting spirit, be an excellent training, in country schools attended chiefly by day-boys, of the observation, and would certainly prove of subsequent service to those who took to farming. I think, too, an exception might be made in favour of the principles of education and the methods of kindergarten in the upper forms of girls' schools. But that is the only exception that has occurred to me. Beyond that I fail to see how applied science can be brought into a secondary school—unless, in a diplomatic mood, as a concession to the foolish parent, we label mixed mathematics, physics, and chemistry "technical," in order to satisfy his craving.

THE WANT OF TRAINED TEACHERS.

There are yet other impediments to sound science teaching. As I reminded you at the beginning, we cannot start off with brand-new schools, and teachers to pattern; we have a great number of children under education with whom it would be foolish to tamper; we have a great number of teachers, some of whom can teach Latin efficiently, and some of whom cannot, but who are agreed in knowing no science worthy of the name. Then the details of the science course must be worked out practically in a few schools before the many are touched, and at present we have no supply of trained science teachers at all. When I say "trained" I mean teachers who have given any sustained thought and study to scientific method. The Royal College of Science turns out a number of students yearly who are labelled trained science teachers, but—it seems almost incredible—they receive no instruction or training in teaching whatever, and are merely provided with an advanced knowledge of some one or two isolated sciences, geology, mechanics, and physics, perhaps; occasionally you meet science teachers from South Kensington, with the highest certificates in zoology or agriculture or astronomy, who have never done an experiment in chemistry in their lives. Altogether you perceive, ladies and gentlemen, our ideal science course is very much in the air; and, until the experiments of Earl and Gordon and others have been carefully revised and criticised, until the supply of trained teachers has increased, I believe it will be well that, for a little while longer, it should remain there.[114]

EXISTING TEACHING.

Finally, standing in the way of the ideal course of science teaching is the actual teaching of science in schools. This is a very considerable reality. As a rule, an isolated *subject* is taken; human physiology has considerable vogue, botany, especially in girls' schools, inorganic chemistry and perhaps theoretical mechanics in boys'. An hour or so a week is a fair allowance of time, and the work is either done by one of the staff (who may also perhaps undertake foreign languages and shorthand, drawing, and any odd duties of that sort), or a visiting master— sometimes, I believe, a visiting professor—attends. An objection to the latter system is the difficulty in discipline. Not uncommonly the science is charged for as if it were a luxury, like parlour boarding,[115] or a crime, like leaving without notice. Some times there are no appliances whatever; sometimes one has to manage with a compass diagram and a model pump; sometimes there is a certain amount of apparatus—the disintegrated remains of Messrs. So & So's two-guinea set, perhaps. I have heard of girls' schools that put aside as much as ten shillings a term for new scientific material, but this lavish expenditure is exceptional. The private schoolmaster, I hope, will take no offence here. I am not speaking here specially of private middle class schools. There is not a pin to choose between science teaching in the smaller grammar schools and company schools and in private schools of the same size, except that many of the grammar schools absorb grants from the County Councils. In neither case does the teaching grow, as it should, out of the preliminary kindergarten training.

---

114. Hugh Gordon was science demonstrator to the London School Board and author of the guidebook *Elementary Course of Practical Science*. Alfred George Earl, educated at Cambridge, was Science Master at Tonbridge school, and had published *Practical Lessons in Physical Measurement*.
115. The practice of an elite child's family paying for them to have their own room at boarding school.

Commonly the teaching centres entirely upon a text-book, especially when the subject is taken by a member of the staff—the English master, say—as an odd subject. The worst case is when this sacred text is studied without comment. This science teaching cannot, so far as I can see, develop directly into that propounded by educational idealists. It will have to go. Gradually I hope to see science object-lessons introduced into the lower forms of middle-class schools, and science spreading upward. We cannot hope to see this upper-form science teaching spreading downward. Its methods are entirely wrong from the school point of view. As soon we might think of beginning a house at the roof and ending it with the foundation.

It does not follow that we are to ignore this upper-form science. We are now down among practical considerations, ladies and gentlemen; our scheme has receded into its proper atmosphere of hopes and dreams, a thing to be hoped for, worked for, and, if we are wise, waited for. At present, and for some years, it cannot be. In the meanwhile, whatever its relations with the ideal may be, the parent, and the committee-man who is only a kind of representative parent—old parent writ large—will demand this top-dressing of science, and the middle-class schoolmaster and schoolmistress will have to supply it. It has no place in the ideal, but that is no reason why we should not make the best of it.

In these finishing courses in science we cannot hope to adequately cover the fundamental principles of any science, though that is what is attempted. The experimental possibilities and the time allowed forbid. I would suggest that, instead, only a portion of some one of the sciences, as ordinarily defined, should be treated as a problem; that we should do as the Extension people do, and limit our field. Instead of the whole of botany, it would be far wiser to deal with leaves, say, dealing with their forms and the physiological import of these forms, or with flowers and fruits only. From such a readable work as Kerner's "Botany," a teacher would be able to obtain all that was necessary for such a course.[116] Or the motions of the stars or the chemistry of combustion would form very excellent short courses in science. In such courses it is possible to work inductively from observed facts towards generalizations, and to give at least a taste of the scientific method. But that is impossible if the entire field of such a science of chemistry or geology is to be covered, however thinly, in a course extending over one or two years for perhaps a couple of hours a week, birthdays and examinations permitting. But at present no school examinations recognise this partial science teaching, or indeed any science teaching except the cramming of little text-books, and this for schoolmasters and schoolmistresses, competing against each other for a living, is a very grave consideration. Examiners in science might very easily do something to help forward genuine teaching of this type, by demanding fewer facts and

---

116. Anton Kerner von Marilaun, *The Natural History of Plants* (1894)

closer reasoning, and giving such a wide choice of questions as would place those who had studied a part of the field with some thoroughness upon a level with those who had a smattering of the entire subject. Unhappily too many of our science examiners do not appreciate their opportunities. On the contrary, they are too often mere scientific experts, and quite unable to discriminate between what is crammable and what is the distinctive outcome of sincere teaching. Take, for instance, that recent London Matriculation question: "Write a little essay about oxygen." Cannot you imagine that little essay about oxygen? "Oxygen is a colourless, inodorous, tasteless gas," it would begin, "having a density of 16, and constituting $\frac{23}{100}$ by weight of air, and $\frac{16}{18}$ of water. It is also an important constituent of the earth's crust." And so on. Just the kind of thing the honestly taught boy would not be able to do, and which the crammed boy would reel off like a phonograph.

CONCLUSION.

But I draw towards the extreme limits of my time. I have a painful sense of many omissions, but I hope I have made it clear that a scientific course of great, and possibly pre-eminent, educational value is possible in schools, and that it would consist essentially of chemistry and physics; that among the chief impediments in the way of this course being universally realized is the lack of appliances and teachers, which can only slowly be remedied, and that, therefore, its introduction must be slow; that the ideal course must come to us as an upward development of the kindergarten, and not as a modification of the ordinary text-book science work of our schools; that the immediate work before those who would extend science teaching is not to effect any extensive revolutionary changes in the school curriculum, but to assist in the criticism and development of such tentative work as that of Messrs. Earl and Gordon, and to stimulate, in every way, the discussion and criticism of methods among science teachers and science examiners; and that, so far as existing science teaching goes, it might be much more efficient if the science examiner properly understood the responsibility and the possibilities of his position.

But more immediate than any of these things is the overcrowded state of our time tables. That is a matter for consideration at once. It is impossible to go on professing to teach everything, as too many secondary schools do—classics, modern languages, science, mathematics, and office routine. Yet we cannot begin to throw things overboard until it is decided what must be thrown overboard. I have said what I can for science, and have proposed to exclude the Latin and Greek languages and classics, commercial and technical subjects, and most geography and history, and I naturally believe in my own case, but I would rather see science absolutely swept from our schools than the present aimless miscellany remain as a curriculum.

I trust that there at least I have afforded scope for discussion. We hear very much of the conflict of studies, but it is a protracted, a guerilla, warfare. I should be glad to find that I had done something to bring about a decisive engagement.

The Science and Art of Education*

The Educational Times, vol XLVIII, no 406, pp 67-68, 1 February 1895

Here Wells returns to the importance of the sequence of studies, by reviewing books on psychology. In general he compares them unfavorably to the Teacher's Handbook of Psychology by James Sully, which had been published almost a decade before. What may be a good book for a scientist may not work well for education, and all four are reviewed solely in light of their educational value. In one he deplores their lack of engaging writing, in another the lack of solid theoretical conclusions. The review, as Wells himself notes, is a handy reference to the state of educational theory at the time.

By H. G. Wells, B.Sc., F.C.P.

It has ever been a matter of controversy whether a science of education exists. The matter turns upon the question—as they say in debating societies—of "your definition" of science. Assuredly, there is a science of education if there is a science of engineering or a science of hygiene. No one, I presume, will claim for it anything more than that, and if engineering is merely a series of special applications of the general principles of physics, and hygiene merely a conference of physiology, bacteriology, physics, and chemistry, then there is also no distinct science of education. From that standpoint the true science of education is psychology—is, indeed, merely the application of psychology and logic to certain special cases. And, undoubtedly, as an engineer or physician must approach his practice through a preliminary study of pure science, so the teacher who wishes to be something more than a mere stoker of minds, a mere bottlewasher in the educational laboratory, must approach his art through the study of psychology.

It is a favourable sign of the growing recognition of this truth that Professor Sully's remarkably clear little handbook, which has hitherto had almost a monopoly in this department, should now be challenged by two rivals.[117] Professor Lloyd Morgan, the Principal of the Bristol University College, is perhaps the ablest English exponent of psychology from the biological side, the author of an unrivalled text-book of biology, and, now that Milnes Marshall has been lost to science, perhaps the foremost among living biological teachers. In the treatment of the infra- and sub-conscious elements in psychosis this book is much more modern than that of Sully, and, as an introduction to the science of

---

117. James Sully was the author of *Teacher's Handbook of Psychology* (1886), a book detailing the psychological development of the child.

psychology, it appears, to the present writer at least, to be preferable on that account. But the analytical treatment, which Sully has, at times, in his pursuit of clearness, carried to the pitch of caricature, has yet its peculiar advantages when we consider the science with especial reference to educational theory. The presentation that makes so many sensations make one percept and so many percepts one concept, whatever its value or truth, brings out, at least, the developmental aspect of the mind, the aspect that appeals most to the educator, and so very convincingly establishes the idea of a sequence of studies in a curriculum.

We do not find a sufficient stress laid upon the progressive phases of the mental life in Professor Lloyd Morgan's work. Indeed, though his references to teaching are abundant, we cannot regard his book as having that particular adaptation to educational requirements that the title might lead one to infer. And there is a certain lack of strength and sequence in the volume, a tendency to wander into irrelevant anecdotes, to give amateurish dicta upon method (a province in which Professor Lloyd Morgan can claim no authority), to drag in literary criticism, and generally to fall away from the subject in hand. A whole chapter is devoted to "Literature," a chapter of snippets from the poets, interspersed with sere commonplaces—this kind of thing:—

He must remember, too, that his aim is to minister to all-round mental development. He should endeavour to cultivate an appreciation of literary excellence in all its phases. The majestic verse of Milton and of Wordsworth at his best; the polished excellence of Tennyson, and the concentration and dramatic power of Browning; the broad humanity of Shakespeare and of Scott; the humour and pathos which find such different expression in Thackeray and Dickens; the strength of George Eliot and the delicacy of Elizabeth Browning; the word-painting of Ruskin and Carlyle; the wit of Tom Hood and the delicate humour of Charles Lamb—all these should have their chance of appealing to a mind that has had an all-round education in appreciation. And since we must distinguish between our lower and our higher interests; between the pleasures which are mean, trivial, or sordid and those which are ennobling and appeal to what we feel to be the better side of our nature; so we should encourage our pupils to appreciate best that literature which appeals to lasting and enduring interests, to those pleasures which are ours in virtue of our distinctive humanity.

Now it is an excellent thing to find that a distinguished interpreter of science reads his Milton and Tennyson, and has an eye to their distinctive merits, but, when he pads out a work on psychology with twenty-six pages of the mental *sequelæ*, the teacher may reasonably complain. A lack of pithiness is a failing common to most psychological text-books, but Professor Lloyd Morgan has exemplified this common failing in a very uncommon measure. Far more scientific in its plan and development is the little primer of Ladd's, a book which, although it is not deliberately addressed to teachers, should yet prove a more serious rival to the "Teacher's Handbook." Yet it certainly does not possess the admirable, the almost dangerous, lucidity of Sully's work, and though we welcome both these new-comers gladly, if only as evidence that a growing number of students renders their publication possible, we may doubt whether they really add anything of importance to our educational resources.

The point to which we would most particularly draw attention is this, that a small book of psychology cannot be made "psychology applied to education," by peppering its pages with fragmentary applications to, and illustrations from, school practice, any more than geology could be applied to the theory of education by constant appeals to the playground gravel, the slates, and the front steps. In Dr. De Garmo's "Herbart and the Herbartians," we find evidence of far wider possibilities. A triple problem is presented—the selection of the subject-matter of education, the rational articulation of that subject-matter, and the development of sound *principles* of method; and that is the triple problem to which Professor Lloyd Morgan should have applied his psychology. Particularly interesting is the portion of Dr. De Garmo's work dealing with the efforts of Ziller and Frick to construct a theoretical curriculum.[118] There cannot be the slightest doubt that such a curriculum is the immediate problem before the educational theorist, and that, until some generally satisfactory solution has been established, there will be to applied science of education worthy of the name, nothing more than an aggregate of wise saws and interesting instances, and a museum of discordant views.

The very question of what is to constitute the backbone of the course remains unsettled. Ziller advocates a core of history and literature, about which the whole of the teaching is to be "concentrated"—a mysterious word, by the bye, that has also fascinated Colonel Parker, of the Cook County Normal School, Chicago.[119] Dr. Frick objected to "concentration," and has built up a "co-ordinated" educational scheme to embrace most geography, the history of the world, geology, zoology, botany, physics, chemistry, Latin, French, Greek, German, literature and grammar, mathematics, and religion. No mention is

---

118. Johann Friedrich Herbart was a German educational philosopher of great renown who had died in 1841. Tuiskon Ziller was a German educationalist who applied Herbart's ideas to elementary school. Otto Frick applied a number of Herbart's ideas to secondary education in Halle.

119. Francis Parker, an American educationalist, created a child-centered progressive approach to teaching.

made of music or drawing in the scheme presented. Finally, Dr. De Garmo proposes what is not so much a new curriculum as a suggestion of a new standpoint upon which a new curriculum may be planned. He distinguishes three "cores," the humanistic, the scientific, the economic, roughly equivalent to the historical and literary, the scientific, and the "technical" elements in our English view of education, and proposes to group all the teaching about one or other of these. But in the exposition none of these various schemes remains in close touch with psychological generalization, and there is a singular absence of any attempt to establish the necessity of the diverse constituents by appeals to psychological principles. In this book, as in too much of our educational theorizing, when we come to the question of subject-matter, the writer lets himself go. We begin soberly with an excellent account of Herbart and the German Herbartians, and end with a new bubble of theory, quite unfounded opinions, advanced with a quite unwarrantable enthusiasm that reminds one almost of Colonel Parker. "A New Era in Education" one chapter is headed. It contains Dr. De Garmo's own views.

These three books show only too plainly the state of educational theory at the present time. On the one hand is psychology, which still remains applied no more directly than Froebel applied it; and on the other, theories of curricula and concentration, feebly luxuriant for the lack of the pruning influence of such an application. The study of history and literature, on the one hand, and the study of science, on the other, differ so fundamentally that we are forced to conclude that either Ziller, who prescribes the former as the educational core, or Parker, who prescribes the latter, must be wrong, if not both. But there is nothing in the science of education—nothing having any authority higher than individual opinion, nothing threshed out and permanently established—upon which to go in arriving at a decision. Yet professors of education exist, and it is curious to speculate how they regard this unprogressive condition of educational theory. Professor Meiklejohn, for instance, recently told the world that there was no special science of education, and one is tempted to think he is right.[120] But whether there might not be one is an altogether different question. The only direction in which we can hope for progress is in the promotion of discussion, and at present there are absolutely no facilities for conclusive discussion in this country, and no tribunal to test our theories. From one lecturer in education comes one assertion and from another another, and the algebraic result of it all is scarcely a matter for boasting.

But, though the general theory of education remains at a standstill, the devices of methodology advance, as Mr. Cowham's excellent "School Method"

---

120. J.M.D. Meiklejohn, "Is Education a Science?", *Journal of Education*, March 1,1894, pp. 155-156.

witnesses. He assumes the Code subjects as though they were as undeniable as the forces of nature, and is, apparently, under the impression that any science "subject" is as good as any other for school work; but upon arithmetic, drawing, writing, and reading, he is as sound, and more practical, if far less scholarly, than Landon. The use of his book by those who are beginning educational work in secondary schools would save an infinite amount of time, energy, and temper, and one turns to it with something of relief from the more theoretical works. He may not make an artist, but he will help to equip a very serviceable pedagogic artizan.

* "Psychology for Teachers," by Professor C. Lloyd Morgan (Edward Arnold); "Primer of Psychology," by George Trumbull Ladd (Longmans); "Herbart and the Herbartians," by Charles de Garmo, Ph.D. (Heinemann); "A New School Method," By Joseph H. Cowham (Westminster School Book Depot).

A Man of Science
(1895-1897)

Bye-Products in Evolution

The Saturday Review of Politics, Literature, Science and Art, vol 79, no 2049, pp 155-156, 2 February 1895

In one of his few early works connecting factual science with human culture, Wells here suggests that human attributes which produce and appreciate culture are simply side effects of natural evolution. Using the analogy of accidental impacts that happen on the way to accomplishing something else, Wells explains that evolution itself will necessarily produce seemingly useless impacts that are nevertheless necessary to the process. These "bye-products" are often the subject of fruitless efforts at explaining them, and may be used as an excuse to dismiss the idea of natural selection. For mankind, there is no obvious utility to music or art. Although unattributed, this piece was noted by Gordon Ray as on the lists of Amy Catherine Wells.[121]

The evolutionary bye-product is a thing that still awaits appreciation even by some who profess science. It may even be that the phrase needs explaining here. Yet there are those who believe that all the best things in life are evolutionary bye-products. A concrete instance may serve to make the thing clear to any reader to whom the phrase is new.

A man, we will suppose, looks out of a window in the ground-floor of a house and sees a pillar-box opposite. In his hand he holds a letter of vital importance, and which he must post forthwith. Clearly he has to go through the front door, and over to the pillar-box and there post the thing. But the door of the house is locked and the key is upstairs, and he cannot take the letter until he has gone upstairs and obtained the key. Now to an observer who did not appreciate the locked door, his journey upstairs would be absolutely unmeaning. Suppose, too, that the key is covered with wet paint and enclosed in a sealed envelope. Then we find, as an outcome of the necessity to cross the road to the pillar-box, not only that the road is crossed, but that the man makes a journey upstairs, gets a certain amount of paint on his fingers, and breaks the seal of an envelope. The journey upstairs, the discoloured fingers, the broken seal, are as much bye-products in the process of crossing the road, as slag and various gases are bye-products of the reduction of iron. Or to put the thing in an abstract form, an end A can only be attained by a process that simultaneously produces B, C, and D, results not needed and yet inevitably involved.

The reader will perceive at once how this will apply to organisms. Let us say

---

121. Gordon Ray, "H. G. Wells's Contributions to the Saturday Review," *The Library* s5-XVI, no. 1, March 1, 1961, p 33.

that a species under the pressure of changing conditions must either modify some organ in the direction A or perish. But that modification, we will presume, involves a disturbance in the whole physiological balance, more of this product and less of that, and so in parts of the body quite remote from the organ involved in the change A, other consequent changes are set up, and the directly unserviceable and yet absolutely necessary modifications B, C, and D ensue. For example, a species is under stress through the need of a certain pigmentary modification. The elaboration of the new pigment, or an increased elaboration of an old pigment, involves certain chemical bye-products which cannot be allowed to remain in the blood, and yet are products which the excretory apparatus of the animal is ill adapted to remove. It may be they are deposited about the body at points where they are least injurious, or even where they acquire a slight utility. For instance, for all we know to the contrary, the change of this or that animal from grey to drab may involve the appearance or disappearance of fleshy excrescences or horny out-growths, and the development of hoof or horn, the profoundest changes in colour or kidney. Yet people who understand a little of the theory of evolution but not very much of it, will attempt to explain every feature of the structure of a living thing, down to it minutest curves, as the reaction of that organism to it necessities, and to an enormous majority of educated people, the instance of a perfectly useless organ would be considered an adequate objection to natural selection. But obviously, until we can be assured of every phase in the processes of physiological chemistry, such a objection is altogether beside the mark. It may be, that a large number of inexplicable colorations, inexplicable wattles, horns, manes, skeletal bars, and the like, will ultimately prove such evolutionary bye-products.

In the case of man particularly is such a speculation suggestive. His appreciation of musical harmony, his sense of visual beauty, are things that invariably puzzle the logical student of evolution, whose attention has been confined to immediate utility. But with regard to the subtle mechanism of mind, we are even more in the dark than when we deal with the chemical equilibrium. It may be true that we cannot show that the capacity for pleasurable emotion at the event A is inseparable from pleasurable emotion at the event B, but to prove the negative is equally impossible. You cannot make a hay-cart that will refuse to carry roses. Every new need may necessitate, not merely its satisfaction, but some collateral enrichment of life; and hunger, thirst, and lust, working upon our plastic specific substance, have truly engendered all the nobler attributes of the human soul. Our mother Want may have made the spiritual not because she sought it, but because it was inseparable from the maternal security she sought. And so the world of art and the body of literature become explicable among the bye-products of the evolutionary worker. Heaven forbid that we should say that actually the thing is so. All we would point out is that so common a difficulty may be at least plausibly explained.

The Palmy Days of the Universities

The Saturday Review of Politics, Literature, Science and Art, vol 79, no 2052, pp 259-260, 23 February 1895

This is one of the only analyses Wells ever made of the university structure's historical roots, since the book being reviewed presents the topic. The Wellsian themes of the "unending conflict between legitimate mediocrity and the brilliant outsider", the contrast with "text-book" cramming, and the inability of the university to respond to change, all appear here, but in the context of the educational system of the Middle Ages. The conformity of the medieval teaching degree suppressed original thinking. Wells's own sympathy is clearly with the renegade "brilliant outsider" Peter Abelard, considered only briefly in the book being reviewed.

"Abelard and the Origin and Early History of Universities." By Gabriel Compayré. London: William Heinemann. 1893.

The copy of Compayré's Abelard, that Mr. Heinemann has sent us, belated though it be, yet comes apt to the movements of the time. Abelard, indeed, is but a figurehead. His connection with the Paris university is chiefly geographical, he taught in Paris before the university came into being, and it is a graceful compliment to ascribe that body to his distinguished parentage, as Virgil traced his Cæsar to the gods. Yet surely—as M. Compayré admits—the university grew out of schools that existed long before Abelard's time, and the less picturesque Alcuin is robbed by this arrangement. Or if the university did not exist until it began in university form, then it began nearly sixty years after Abelard's death, and was by all that his posthumous child. In many ways, indeed, Abelard was antithetical to the true university spirit. His beginning was as an intellectual freelance; he was reproached "for teaching without a master, *sine magistro*." "When he presented himself at the school of Anselm at Laon, his fellows reproached him with having as yet been initiated only into the natural sciences." His attack on the legitimate teachers, upon William of Champeaux in particular, was in the character of an external teacher, an irresponsible detractor, an unqualified and impertinent assailant. He opened a private adventure college at Melun in 1102, and then another at Corbeil, and from thence passed to supersede his victim of Notre Dame. It is all very well for M. Compayré to say: "This single episode in Abelard's life is, as it were, the symbol, the striking image of the relations subsisting in general between the episcopal schools and the universities, the latter supplanting the former and installing themselves in their place;" but it is far more symbolical of the unending conflict between legitimate mediocrity and the brilliant outsider, of that continual process of destruction and reconstruction that is an inevitable condition of human progress. The wheel of thought advances only by revolutions, and it is in the growth of the mediæval universities that we find the influence that stifled the intellectual impulse of Abelard. Yet, as we say, he makes a picturesque, if inappropriate figurehead to M. Compayré's book, and after the first three-and-twenty pages we hear very little of him. The rest is a brilliant, scholarly, and most suggestive account of the earlier phases of these institutions.

The great discovery, the essential fact, of the mediæval university was the degree, the license to teach, and, as Professor Laurie has shown, the spirit that inspired the limitation of teaching to graduates was closely akin to the spirit of the trade guild.[122] True, Valentinian had attempted something of the kind in the fourth century, a sort of sophist's license; but, as our author says, "it is none the less true that it was the Middle Ages that really inaugurated a system of graduation, conferring the right to teach after a certain term of studies and appropriate examinations." Previously whosoever could teach had taught; now only those who were "qualified" to teach might have that privilege. The value of this in preserving intact a body of doctrine, of weeding out conceited innovators and ill-disciplined characters, will be at once obvious, and it largely explains the otherwise unaccountable fact that the body of European thought and knowledge remained practically unchanged, a profound and stagnant pool of learning, from the twelfth to the dawn of the fifteenth century.

The latter-day university reformer must look back with a certain regret to these palmy days of university teaching. No objectionable system of text-book cramming prevailed then; indeed, there were scarcely any books at all available, and whatsoever poor man would have learning, went and sat at the feet—literally at the feet and in straw—of the happy *idoneus et litteratus* who had the license to teach, the earthly added to the heavenly gift. "The teaching was altogether oral," and our hour-lecture system, like our academic costume, dates from those days. And though examinations existed, were indeed a mediæval invention, there was nothing of that unreasonable impartiality and severity that has made the London University of our own times a bane to true university teaching. The Chancellor made "inquiries of the professors of theology and other serious and instructed persons," and no doubt if the candidate was of a passable presence, of respectful demeanour, and had refrained from differing from or ridiculing these "serious and instructed persons," his degree was a safe enough thing for him. But would Abelard have got his degree from William of Champeaux? Moreover, the candidate had to be "neither a bastard nor deformed"—for of such was not the

---

122. S. S. Laurie, *The Rise and Early Constitution of Universities*, with a Survey of Medieval Education, New York: D. Appleton & Co., 1887.

kingdom of learning according to mediæval wisdom. And "to arrive at the doctorate particularly one needed to be actually rich, rich in money still more than in knowledge. At Salamanca, to intrigue for the honours of the doctorate one of the formalities required from the candidate was to defray the expenses of a brilliant *corrida de toros*. Here again, consider Abelard. At Bologna, one had to clothe a large number of persons. Savigny says that when Vianesius was refused his degree "he had already spent five hundred livres in buying scarlet cloth for pelisses." Banquets were the rule everywhere, and Ramus complained that "of the nine hundred livres which medical studies cost, three hundred were devoted to banquets.... Sometimes wines and spices were distributed to the examiners." "It must not be for gotten that the degrees were one of the principal sources of revenue to the professors," and "not a single case of a candidate who failed is found on the register of the Paris Medical Faculty from 1395 to 1500.... Abuses were increased by the multiplication of universities; they became each other's rivals and sold diplomas at a discount.... The examiners willingly displayed a certain partiality toward the nobles and the great."

This was, of course, the logical outcome of the *idoneus et litteratus* idea, an idea which eliminated from teaching all those stiff-necked rebels who fell into trouble with their professors. The very qualities of mind that would make a rising student pleasing to his professor and successful in his career, a teachable, uncritical, dexterous turn, are just the complaisant qualities that will make a dishonest ruler; it is the unruly will that even an eminent professor cannot tame that matures to be proof against the temptations of material bribery. This was the inherent weakness in the organization of mediæval universities—they were fenced about with an elaborate system of courses and degrees against new ideas and new and independent types of men—and this weakness will recur again in any university of the future in which the teachers of one generation select unchallenged the teachers of the next. It was to the intellectual outcome of this process that M. Birt alluded to when he said that "the ancient universities were in the eighteenth century several centuries in arrears of all that concerns sciences and the arts. Peripatetics when all the world had renounced the philosophy of Aristotle with Descartes, they became Cartesians when the rest were Newtonian. This is the way with learned bodies. They do not make discoveries."[123] M. Compayré would have us believe that this stagnation ensued "by virtue of that fatal law which forbids old institutions to reform themselves." We do not believe in that fatal law, and we have no such pessimistic view of the destroying of old institutions. It appears to us that by an appeal to the inevitable consequences of

---

123. This is an error in the original printing. It should refer to Jean-Baptiste Biot (1774-1862), a physicist, astronomer, and historian of science. The quotation attributed to him is from page 304 of Compayré's book.

an unfortunate system by which the teachers granted their own students degrees, that incapacity to advance, that dry-rot of the mediæval universities, is adequately explained.

The South Kensington Revolution

The Educational Times, vol XLVIII, no 407, pp 150-152, 1 March 1895

This optimistic report on the recent changes to dedicated science schools is unusual. Wells celebrates not only the reforms, but also the freedom of the teacher to choose what is best for his particular students. He is particularly happy about the emphasis on practical work in laboratories, which in chemistry at least has been detailed. The more frequent school inspections, and reductions in grants that encourage cramming, are also noted as positive achievements. The payment by results system, from which Wells had benefited as a younger man, is replaced by grants upon inspection. The result will be State responsibility for all secondary schools that privilege the sciences. As for the effectiveness of inspections, Wells reasserts his arguments for inspectors with teaching experience and a broad view of science, extending it to secondary schools.

A leader-writer in one of the London daily papers, some years ago, laid it down as a truism that, though Latin and Greek could be crammed, science obviously could not. The full force of the unconscious sarcasm of that remark can only be appreciated by those who have known the wholesale possessors of the old "E2" certificates of the Science and Art Department. To say that the older regulations of the Department absolutely compelled the teacher to cram would possibly be too severe an accusation; but assuredly the method of allotting grants, ignoring, as it did, all differences in local circumstances, in the purpose of the teaching, and in the individual capacity of students, put a premium upon cram such as only a local committee both wealthy and wise could resist. Step by step, reforms have been made in the regulations; but it has been left to Mr. Acland to attempt a revolution.

It is an innocent-looking revolution—on the face of it. Form No. 201 looks much like any other one among the scores of these blue papers in which South Kensington is so prolific; nor is the accompanying white-paper circular, No. 174, dated 23rd January, 1895, any more revolutionary in its appearance. The copy that lies before the present writer is further accompanied by a little explanatory note, summarizing the main alterations effected by Form 201, and stating that it will affect some one hundred and twenty organized science schools throughout the kingdom.

THE ORGANIZED SCIENCE SCHOOLS.

What is an "organized" science school? It is a school—either day or evening—at which a Department-organized "thorough, and progressive course of education in science, *combined with literary or commercial instruction,*" is given to "students who have received an education equivalent to that set out in Standard VII. of the Code for Public Elementary Schools." The clause italicised above is a recent innovation in the definition. To many engaged in education even, it will be a surprise to learn that there are one hundred and twenty such schools in the kingdom: but this is a small number compared with what we may expect in a few years, if Mr. Acland's new scheme works smoothly. Practically any school, at which boys or girls from thirteen or fourteen year on are educated on a science basis, can become an organized science school by simply submitting to the not very excessive amount of State regulation and inspection at present required in return for the State grant. We will consider the case of day schools most fully, as it is these that will be most affected.

Up to and including the present school year, which will end on the 31st July next, the science teacher in such of the one hundred and twenty as are day schools (we do not know what proportion that may be) has had laid down for him a rigid course for the first two years. In the first year he must teach the first stage of the Department syllabus in Mathematics, in Practical Geometry, in Inorganic Chemistry (Theoretical and Practical), and in either one of the two recognised branches of Physics or in Physiography; all these having to be taught with an eye to the examinations in May. To these subjects have recently been added certain elementary drawing subjects, and some provision has been made in the regulations for literary and manual instruction. The only differences between such a school and one which merely sends up its pupils to get what grants they can at the May examinations are: firstly, the restrictions as to the subjects to be taught; and, secondly, the payment by the Department of a capitation or "attendance" grant on students who have made more than a certain number of attendances. In the second year a similar course is followed, the second stage being taken in the chief subjects, and Elementary Mechanics and Physiology being added. In the third year the course is practically left to the teacher's discretion, a number of possible alternative courses being suggested.

REFORMS IN THE SCIENCE TEACHING.

Now for the new alterations. In the first place, allowance is made for inequalities in students' capacity, and the personal ideas of the teacher, by the abolition of the rigid arrangement of the course in "years." An elementary course is laid down containing the subjects of the old first-year course as obligatory, but allowing the teacher freedom as to additional subjects, and the option of spreading the course over one or two years without any financial pressure curtailing his freedom. A special course is also suggested for girls, with some domestic subject included, but here again it is left to the teacher's discretion to adopt it or not.

Secondly, a determined effort is made to get rid of cramming, by abolishing the entry of students in the elementary course for the May examinations. They are not forbidden to enter, if they care for it, but no grant is to be gained by so doing, and even the indirect compulsion of the rule that no grants will be paid for successes at advanced examinations, unless the elementary stage has already been passed, is greatly mitigated by allowing students of the advanced course to enter for either of the three stages at the May examinations.

Thirdly, what new method is to replace the system of examination and "payment by results"? The method already adopted in public elementary schools is now to be extended to these secondary schools—a staff of inspectors and assistants has been appointed, whose duty it will be to visit and report upon the classes in session, the laboratories, apparatus, &c. For the present they are to make a fixed annual inspection during May, June, or July. In consideration, no doubt, of the complaints that have been sometimes raised against the strain caused by the rigid annual inspection in elementary schools, provision is made for the possible future replacement of this system by more frequent visits. The nature of the annual inspection is also left to the discretion of the inspector—it may be *vivâ voce* or by written papers, or both; and, in respect to the subjects outside the scope of the Department, he may either examine in person, or request the help of one of his Education Department colleagues (H.M. Inspectors of Schools), or he may accept the report of some public examining body.

On the report of the inspector grants are to be made as follows:—(1) The old "attendance" grant on students who have made over 250 attendances, is raised from £1 to about £1 10s., a modification being introduced into the way of calculating it that will make it vary somewhat in amount. (2) A new "variable" grant paid on each student who earns the previous grant, but on a scale determined by the report on the school as a whole: £2 for "excellent," £1 10s. for "good," and £1 for "fair." (3) A grant in addition to the latter, for practical instruction, based on the report upon the efficiency of the teaching and of the laboratories— £1 10s., £1, or 10s. for Chemistry and Physics for elementary students, and £2 10s., £2, or £1 10s. for Physics and Biological Science per student in the advanced course. (4) The May examination grant, abolished in the case of elementary students, as already explained, is reduced about thirty per cent. in the case of advanced students, and, moreover, will not even then be paid on more than five subjects.

Lastly, to come to the details of the subjects taught, we are tempted to refer to the snakes of Iceland, but that will not do, for although the absence of detailed regulation of the courses is one of the main features of the scheme, in one subject at least specific instructions as to the nature of the practical instruction are given. This is in Chemistry, in which subject the first year's practical work is no longer to consist of mechanical "test-tubing"; instead, the use of apparatus, measurement of mass and volume, gas-preparation, and the like, is to be substituted. This alone is a splendid advance. The other obligatory subjects are much the same as formerly, but full freedom is allowed to the teacher within the limits that sound methods of teaching allow. Several possible advanced courses are indicated, but it is difficult and unnecessary to summarize them.

ANNEXATION OF LITERARY SUBJECTS.

So far, we have reforms, possibly with drawbacks, but still reforms: the revolutionary change consists in definite provision being made for the inclusion in the school course of subjects outside the scope of the Science and Art Department. Every school must submit for approval a time-table, which, if approved, must be hung in a conspicuous position in the class-room; and this must allow for not less than thirteen hours per week for "Department" subjects (which, it must be remembered, include Mathematics and Drawing), and not less than ten hours per week for other subjects, including (after 1896) two hours for manual instruction.

The "variable grant" will only be paid on students who have studied, in addition to the obligatory Science and Art subjects, at least one language, and some other literary or commercial subject set out in the time-table. When the advanced course is reached, the hours devoted to subjects outside the Department's scope may be reduced to six per week. These are the essential features in the new scheme, as it applies to day schools. As summarized by Mr. Acland himself in the explanatory note, they are: substitution of payment on inspection for payment by results; greater freedom to the teacher; and recognition of subjects outside the scope of the Department.

INFLUENCE UPON ORDINARY SECONDARY SCHOOLS.

Two important questions at once suggest themselves: Is the substitution of inspection for examination likely to have its desired effect in the rise of the standard of science teaching in institutions under Department control; and, What will be the effect of the provision for the teaching of extra-Departmental subjects? Let us consider the latter question first.

Practically the scheme invites secondary schools, willing to give to science a large share of their school-time, to come in under the protection of the

Committee of Council on Education, not only in regard to their science-teaching, but in regard to the whole of their teaching. Pending any steps that may be taken on the recommendations yet to come from the Royal Commission, we have here a very definite step towards State organization of secondary education on a science basis. That, under any circumstances, the State control could long remain in the form established in the scheme, is improbable. The provision that the Science Inspector may call in one of his Education Department colleagues gives to that Department for the first time a definite standing with respect to secondary schools—a standing that is too informal to remain unchanged, and which is plainly but the thin end of the State-organization wedge.

If the scheme works smoothly, and even if no steps are taken save such as follow inevitably on the present one, the Science and Art Department—alone, or jointly with its Whitehall ally—will before long, either by the absorption or by the replacement of existing institutions, control a large proportion of our secondary schools. Assuredly, such a revolution was never before begun with so little ostentation.

THE INSPECTORS.

In discussing the second question—the effect of the new regulations on the efficiency of science-teaching—we must include evening as well as day schools. The chief points in which the rules as applied to the former differ from our summary are the time-table arrangements and the value of the grants. The essential change consists in the replacement of the old uniform mechanical examination system of measuring efficiency, by a system of personal inspection of the actual teaching, combined with a less formal personal examination. The success of the new method must evidently depend on the choice of inspectors. What are the requirements of the ideal inspector? He should himself have taught, and taught more than one kind of student, for the man who has been teaching in one groove only will judge of teaching by a very narrow standard. He must have a clear idea of the relative positions in education of the three important, but quite distinct, purposes for which science teaching is of value—cultivation of observation and judgment, discipline in habits of thought, and acquisition of knowledge—a failure to understand which is at the root of much of the failure of science teaching. He must be, not a narrow specialist, but a man of wide sympathies, and a capacity for placing himself in the teacher's place.

Pending the advent of a sufficient number of these ideal men— in a chariot of fire or otherwise—we must be content with the best that can be got, and do what we can to manufacture better ones for the next generation. In view of the utterly slipshod method of "training " its science teachers which the Department adopts, we must not be too sanguine of obtaining many ideal inspectors from among the fruits of the South Kensington hot-house. Nor are the Universities any more promising in this respect, seeing that early specialization for "research" is the ideal held up for students of science there.

Until a system is adopted of training science teachers to *teach* and not merely to *know*, such as is already adopted for elementary teachers, the obtaining of really qualified inspectors must be a mere matter of luck.

In spite of these drawbacks, one may be sanguine enough to think that inspection will prove a distinct improvement on formal examination as a test of the efficiency of science teaching.

If the inspector is only willing to learn, his work cannot fail to educate him. Just as the best way to learn a subject is to have to teach it, so the best way—or, at least, a very good way— to learn how to teach is to study how others teach. Though, as an examiner, the educational capacity will show itself in the setting of questions, yet as a mere corrector of papers the best of educators can do no more than the worst. Think of the examiner dividing, with blue pencil, sheep No. 57,341, who has written that oxygen is a colourless, tasteless, odourless gas, from goat No. 57,342, who has perversely managed to state something different; and then think of the inspector to whom 57,341 and the rest of the numbers are replaced by living boys or girls, and together forming, not a bundle of blue papers, but a class living and learning in a definite town or county with its own particular natural features, industries, and traditions. While the work of the former must ever grow more mechanical, that of the latter must be a constant stimulus to better work in the future.

Unless an inspector happens to be exceptionally faddish and prejudiced, he can hardly interfere with the work of a competent teacher, even though he may allow an incompetent one to pass muster. And a state of things which merely secures "equality of opportunity" for all teachers (which the old examination system did not) must, in the end, mean the "survival of the fittest"; for only by artificial support can a bad teacher flourish long.

There is a certain type of science teacher, for whose existence the Department is essentially responsible, who will not take kindly to the new conditions. Years of grant-earning by preparing candidates for the May examinations cannot have had any but a withering effect on the originality and sound educational notions which will be required under the new scheme, if the inspectors do their duty. When we consider that the Department has always acted on the principle that for science teachers the only training required is a study—more or less severe—of the subjects they will have to teach, we cannot but expect that a large proportion of existing "qualified" science teachers have nothing but rule-of-thumb notions of education. The teacher of this sort, probably crammed into his qualification originally, accustomed to drill his students year after year for the same examination, in entire disregard of the purpose for which they were intended to be taught, will simply find himself at a loss when he has to teach without a view to any examination. Perhaps the art of inspector-pleasing may come to replace that of examiner-dodging, but, on the whole, it is not likely to be so successful an art.

And, at last, the real teacher, who has groaned under his conditions in the past, who is capable of something far higher than mere exam.-cramming, may look forward with hope. He can now arrange his teaching in accordance with his own ideas, ignoring examinations completely; and his capacity for discriminating between student and student, hitherto wasted, will be turned to account.

The immediate benefit of the change will of course depend largely on the proportions which crammers and educators actually bear to one another in the existing body of teachers. That the experiment alone can show. The crammer no doubt will feel himself cruelly treated by the Department that has called him into being, and with a certain show of justice, and he will do his best to maintain the "ancient use." But he is doomed. Last year the *Educational Times* spoke of the writing on the wall.[124] Here it is again, but this time on what is much more significant in these days—blue paper.

---

124. This was an item on the Report of the Science and Art Department, from page 381 of the September 1, 1894, issue. It referred to the impact of the decline in exam passing rates on grant earning as "the writing on the wall".

Scientific Research as a Parlour Game

Saturday Review of Politics, Literature, Science and Art, vol 79, no 2060, p 516, 20 April 1895

In this particularly vicious review, Wells makes clear the distinction between formal scientific study and popular science.

"The Source and Mode of Solar Energy throughout the Universe." By I. W. Heysinger, M.A., M.D. Philadelphia: J. B. Lippincott. 1895.

It is not all of us who can give our time exclusively to scientific investigations, and join in the great game of scientific research. Yet as one sits by the fire of a winter evening and reads of this great discovery and that, and the praises of this or that great leader, the itch of speculation is apt to be aroused. And as a result we now have to consider seriously a new species of books that will no doubt in time have its own specialists and collectors, and which to an irresponsible reviewer reads delightfully enough, books which embody the results of this new amusement for the more serious classes: "research-elle," we might call it on the analogy, which will at once occur to every one, of bagatelle, or, perhaps, more correctly, "researchette."

It seems a fascinating occupation; though at present, of course, many of its discoveryettes are crude enough. There seems to be a need of sympathetic criticism ; and its workers—excluded by the narrowness and prejudice of legitimate scientific investigators from making use of the ordinary channels of communication—might very well consider the advisability of having a Royal Society of their own, a kind of Britannia metal Royal Society, with Proceedings and all complete. Then they could meet together and perfect one another in the new amusement; there would be Doctor Platt, who discovered the "central sun" last summer, and Mr. Hovenden, F.L.S., F.G.S., F.R.M.S., who first saw molecules through a microscope—you can see a picture of them on the last advertisement page of *Nature*—and the various schools of Shakespearian cryptogramists and all the rain-makers, and the Transatlantic pedagogic people, and the Zetetics—who indeed do possess a Society already—and perhaps one or two real scientific investigators *ex officio*, as "psychical" amateurs. Then there is theosophy—and the pyramids. It would be a delightful gathering, quite as nice to look at as a Royal Institution soirée, quite as rich and quite as contented with itself. But we wander away from Dr. Heysinger and this matter of solar energy. For which we crave his pardon.

Dr. Heysinger, like Newton, is a thinker rather than an experimentalist. His facts are none of them new— indeed, some of them are a trifle *passé*—and they have been extracted mainly from Appleton's Cyclopedia (a most invaluable source), the more popular works of the late R. A. Proctor, and Lord Salisbury's address to the British Association.[125] Yet, just as Newton in the (quite incorrect) nursery story, discovered gravitation in a windfall, where most of us find only maggots, so Dr. Heysinger has discovered in these simple and quite popular works "a simple, all-embracing cause, a few simple and uniformly operative principles . . . which, once thoroughly comprehended and rigidly applied, will be found to elucidate all the multifarious phenomena of siderial space." Of course, it is electricity. It always is. It is simply wonderful what insight unhampered by excessive knowledge can manage. The sun is a kathode, and the planets anodes, and so the attenuated water vapour (you know) between us and the sun is electrolized, and the hydrogen goes to the sun and the oxygen comes to the earth, and the sun is luminous because the positive pole of the arc light is. And what more do you want? It seems to us a very pretty piece of researchette, and we offer Dr. Heysinger our congratulations unreservedly. Very pretty and quite characteristic of this kind of thing is the treatment of Lord Kelvin and Sir William Thompson as separate persons, the omission of any allusion to Clerk Maxwell, the complete ignorance evident of Lockyer's Meteoric Hypothesis, the incidental discovery of a populous other side to the moon, with air and water complete, the introduction of the supposed and exceedingly doubtful connection of sun-spots with magnetic storms as "established fact," and the concluding rehabilitation of the Mosaic cosmogony.[126]

Now, jesting apart, we think this book—a by no means ill-written one—is well worthy the consideration of scientific men, though perhaps scarcely in the way its author meant. On that account we have given it this much space. It is pretty clearly the result of an indigestion of certain very popular astronomical writers; and especially of Proctor (who is quoted forty-three times) and Appleton's Cyclopedia (thirty). The author is certainly not a fool; he writes neatly and sometimes strongly, and he has a vivid but by no means fantastic imagination. If he is a young man he may even have a future before him—though not as a

---

125. Appleton's Cyclopedia was a collection of biographies of people in American history, which contained entries that were likely unreliable; Richard A. Proctor was an astronomer who mapped Mars and published *Old and New Astronomy* in 1892; Salisbury addressed the British Association of the Advancement of Science as its new president on August 4, 1894 and reviewed recent advances in science.
126. William Thomson was 1st Baron Kelvin; physicist James Clerk Maxwell had created a theory of electromagnetic radiation; the Meteoritic Theory was developed by Lockyer and hypothesized about the origin and prevalence of meteors in space; Mosaic cosmogony is the explanation of the creation of the earth from Genesis.

philosopher. But his ideas are loose, because, as his quotations show, he has read nothing but a loose type of scientific book, books that aim to give startling and picturesque results rather than to demonstrate and educate. It is perfectly open for him to plead that they came to him as the work of responsible investigators, and therein lies our moral. He has caught their style, their trick of seeming to reason—and behold this contribution to pseudo-scientific literature! These "research-ette" results undoubtedly increase and multiply, and they are, we fear, the direct outcome of a well-meant study of these all too popular popular scientific books. And a considerable number of persons with the leisure to write, the means to print, and (in this case at any rate) considerable ability, are lost to science thereby. Yet they might do something as a kind of scientific militia. Is it not worth the while of those interested in the advancement of science to consider this question of the Utilization of the Waste Amateur?

Variorum: Of the Fallacy of Museums

The New Budget, no 3, 25 April 1895, p18

In his quick criticism of teaching through a school museum trip, Wells continues his disdain of disconnected knowledge as being worse than not helpful. This piece also includes a portrait of the assistant schoolmasters self-consciously conducting their charges, a situation with which Wells was all too familiar from his time at Henley House School.

There are those who regard a Museum as the place to spend a happy day. There is no accounting for tastes, and I would not stand in the way of such people. I have even heard of a couple who spent their Bank Holiday at the Parkes Museum in Margaret Street—an extensive collection of specimen food-stuffs and hygienic window-shutters, and that kind of thing. It is, to my sense, a strikingly disagreeable and most instructive display of the appalling repulsiveness of a really wholesome life. You should see it. But that is a digression.[127] I have, I say, no quarrel with people who go to a Museum for pleasure. They will not get it, I think; but that is their affair. My concern is for those who go there for knowledge, or—which is commoner—send other people. What I want to point out is the patent, yet widely disregarded, fact that the very last place in the world where we can really learn anything is in a Museum. I really would not trouble the reader with a thing so obvious, were it not for the fact that I came upon no less than four schools entangled in the labyrinthine interstices of that place in Cromwell Road.[128] Odd as it may seem, from what I overheard I have not the slightest doubt that these boys and girls had been brought there with the idea of improving their minds. So, though I feel that I write platitudes to the general, there are assuredly quarters where a lucid explanation is needed.

Do not imagine I wander from the subject if I remark that the boys' school undergoing the process of being taken out is a common but interesting spectacle about the fringe of London. The young pupils do not wear tall hats and shell jackets now as they used to do, but they look as wretched as ever, and the assistant-master even more so. Assistant-masters in boys' schools appear to be selected entirely on account of their self-consciousness; they are invariably at that acutely sensitive age when one is neither youth nor man, and seem absolutely

---

127. Wells would continue this digression in the amusing story "The Parkes Museum" in *Certain Personal Matters*, his 1897 "Collection of Essays and Short Stories, some autobiographical". He called the museum an "armoury of hygiene".
128. The South Kensington Museum.

unable to shake off or conceal the persuasion that some unseen parent is ever watching their very souls. So they go along, acting a part, painfully conscious of the ever-present spirit of insubordination, and the puerile intensity of original sin, being "fatherly," or "elder brotherly," or "kindly instructive," or "manly," or "sympathetic," or "jovial"——but never, never at their ease. You should look out for them. They will take you for an uncle, and it will make them worse. However, this certainly has nothing to do with the fallacy of Museums, about which I was speaking, except that in a Museum the young assistant-master becomes more self-conscious than ever. He assumes the garment of omniscience——horribly aware the while of gaps and tatters therein——he feels that the watchful parent requires him to improve the occasion, and—there are so many strange things he cannot explain!

But in his trouble is really the clue to the fallacy of the Museum. He sees row upon row of the skeletons of birds, case after case of chunks of mineral, here a multitude of Etruscan vessels—an archaic crockery warehouse, and there an arsenal of mummies. If, for instance, he wanted to point out what feathers any bird wore outside its skeleton, he would have to go into another room, where the taxidermist has arrayed a regiment or so of them stuffed and staring. If he wishes to explore the interior of the bird there is possibly a displayed dissection downstairs. If he wants to show what the bird eats, what enemies it has, how it flies, how it lives, then, perhaps, there is a nest somewhere, and perhaps not, and for the rest he has to go ignorant. You see, the Museum people have simply taken the bird away from its proper surroundings, torn it to shreds, put its bones here and its beak there, lost its eggs in a set of drawers, and generally made a puzzle of the thing. The specimen becomes the answer to a riddle without the question, a mere recondite allusion to the life it led, a quotation without its proper context, a dead pendant to a dead label bearing a dead name. The excellent assistant-master takes his boys to the Museum and points to the pieces of the corpse of the bird and mispronounces its name, and thinks now that the boys know the bird. But they don't, any more than if they had been shown a picture of it. It's merely the old folly of fetichism in a modern phase——that ancient and hardy delusion that puts into the hand of the clairvoyant some personal possession of the person you wish her to see. The Chila Indians think that to be given a lock of a man's hair is as good as being given the man, and everyone has heard of the presentation of earth and water as the act of submission to a conqueror. Yet, in our practical affairs at least, we have got beyond this stage, and a London hostess would think herself insulted if, in a tidy bundle, you sent your morning coat, silk hat, umbrella, hair clippings, false teeth, and visiting card to make a call upon her.

You see, a Museum is just a collection of scraps, a re-warehousing, as it were, of the furniture of creation, putting all the skeletons here and all the feathers there, the flowers in one room and the roots in another. Even the Museum custodians begin to recognise this, and at that Natural History Museum South Kensington you may see they are trying to replace things in their natural relations again—the bird to the nest, the manufactured article to the raw material. But thereby they give themselves away. Clearly it's a step back towards leaving the things alone, and giving up collecting. We begin to recognise that the Universe is the Universe, and the Museum only an odd corner of it; that we can no more condense and abstract the material poem of the world than we can condense Milton into a key-word, or philosophy into an epigram. The Museum is at most a clumsy mnemonic; convenient, perhaps, as a summary, after one has learnt something of the world outside. But to take little boys to these neatly-packed mortuaries, or to go there oneself, to *learn*—really it's absurd! It's part of the educational foolishness that makes teaching history a business of dates, or morality a matter of maxims. A Museum, at best, is nothing more than a place where one can acquire the simulacrum of knowledge from the disarticulated vestiges of things—just as much as a "cramming" institution as the establishment of an army "coach". And to send little boys there of a bright afternoon, under the plea of improving their minds, is saved only by its utter foolishness from being absolutely a crime.

H. G. Wells

The Threatened University

Saturday Review of Politics, Literature, Science and Art, vol 80, no 2094, pp 803-804, 14 December 1895

Beginning with this article, Wells exhibits great confidence in attacking not only methods and institutions but individuals, and causing controversy in the process. Wells's career as a fiction writer had finally begun with the publication of The Time Machine *earlier in the year, and his critical voice was becoming more direct. In this vociferous protest to a previous column on the University of London, Wells defends external students and the correspondence tutors supporting them. His own experience with both the University Correspondence College and the Normal School of Science (by this point the Royal College of Science) gives weight to his argument. He claims that the common perception of external student efforts as "cram" is false, and the public assumption that a top teaching university provided individual attention is also false. He points to the excellence of tutors by correspondence, and the divided attention of university professors whose main goal is research rather than teaching, causing the students to be taught by assistants. In addition, university instructors also teach cram courses, and assistants mark papers just as they would if they were doing it by post. Wells also attacks directly the cramming engaged in at Finsbury College, run by Professor Silvanus Thompson. He closes with an eloquent defense of educational access for the original and energetic working-class student.*

This letter was so controversial that it was printed with an editorial comment (Frank Harris was editor of the Saturday Review *from 1894 to 1898). This asserts that Wells is confusing the current proposal, which supports external students, with the Gresham Scheme of 1892, and that Finsbury College papers are supplemental to laboratory work and constitute "the anti-thesis of tuition by correspondence" This comment has been included below, and the conversation continues with the next item in this volume.*

To the Editor of the Saturday Review
10 December, 1895

Sir,—It is impossible for one who is so deeply indebted to the present London University as I am to pass by the misleading article in your last issue, "The Duke and the Crammers," without a protest.[129] The question is a special one, and

---

129. "The Duke and the Crammers." *Saturday Review of Politics, Literature, Science and Art* 80, no. 2093 (December 7, 1895): 755. The opinionated article claimed that crammers and correspondence schools were immoderately profiting because London University

overmuch left to those immediately interested. The Duke of Devonshire has shown in this business an unexpected breadth of sympathy. Like Sir John Lubbock, he has evidently studied the matter broadly and carefully, and the advocates of one of the most tawdry of all the cheap and nasty reform movements that Liberalism has produced in its decay, may count upon one more honest and enlightened opponent to their persistent enterprise. The ill-informed reader would imagine from the tone of your article that the new scheme proposed some splendid addition to the teaching facilities of London, and that a dishonest crew of "crammers" obstructed this for their own ends. As a matter of fact, no new teaching body, no new buildings, no new professors, are to be provided. I challenge your contributor to state any definite enlargement that would certainly ensue if this Gresham scheme operated. The point at issue is not enlargement, but contraction—a monopoly of teaching. The essence of this precious "reform" movement, apart from the demand for an easier medical degree, is to exclude the non-collegiate student, to force such non-collegiate students as have the means into the empty class-rooms of those whom your contributor calls the "ablest men in the educational world," the energetic movers in the matter, and to prevent altogether the poor self-educated man from obtaining the worldly advantage, the honourable hallmark, of a London degree. To do that your representa-tive of these "ablest men" sticks at nothing, not even at the assertion that a majority of the country graduates are favourable to the scheme, not even at the self-contradiction of invoking heaven and earth to deprive Convocation of the right of vetoing a plan which he asserts Convocation has already approved.

Then this attack upon the University by Correspondence. What does it really mean? The ill-informed reader will imagine, on the one hand, some seedy rogue "cramming"—what a magic word that is!—his gaping, strenuous customers, and on the other the wise, grave professor, like a father in the bosom of his family, giving individual attention to his select following, saying this apt memorable thing and that, cherishing, developing. But the facts! I chance to know two typical establishments passing well: one a University by Correspondence, a cramming shop, the other a great scientific school—the Royal College of Science to be explicit, College elect of the wonderful University that is to be, if the public conscience permit it. Take the mathematical instruction. In the former you have actually teaching such brilliant and original investigators as Mr. Bryan, a Smith's prizeman, one of the youngest of the Fellows of the Royal Society, and Mr. Barlow, as scholarly if less original a mathematician. In the latter the bulk of the actual teaching is in the hands of (comparatively) unknown men. In the latter establishment, too, the professors, as your contributor probably knows as well as

was solely an examining body, and that Lubbock and the Duke were duped into opposing the proposal that it become a teaching institution.

I do, being preoccupied by the keen competition in re-search, lecture a minimum of lectures, talk a text-book that is, and never come into personal contact with their students at all. During my three years of instruction, save for a rare "good-morning," I never spoke to my professors at South Kensington—Professors Huxley, Guthrie, and Judd—except in the case of the latter. And most of my conversations with Professor Judd were devoted to points of discipline. This is the usual experience of South Kensington students, and it is probably the general rule in college teaching; you cannot expect celebrated men to spend their lives teach-ing the rudiments. The personal teaching in the College is almost entirely in the hands of men not a whit above the "crammers," and in many cases the College instructors eke out their incomes by "cramming" of an evening. In the University by Correspondence you have teaching now, a former Demonstrator of the Royal College of Science, and another of its outlaw teachers has recently passed on into "genuine" teaching in a university college. Again, a Royal College professor was formerly a Correspondence tutor. You have one and the same man, here a heaven-sent teacher, and there a scoundrel crammer. And as for a University by Correspondence, I can assure you that, save for the intervention of the postman, they teach geology by correspondence at the Royal College of Science; assistant teachers at a guinea a week give out instruction papers, and the students work accordingly. The stress is sustained by frequent and stringent examinations. There is not a pin to choose between the two methods. I have, too, the note-books of the Cambridge Morphological Laboratory, in which the same "cut and dried" method is carried far beyond the University-by-Correspondence system as it is known to me. And when as Doreck Scholar I inspected and reported upon the school of Professor Silvanus Thompson in Finsbury, a couple of years ago, I found the same mechanical cramming, by instruction papers and class examination, in full operation in that institution. Yet he is one of the leading "ablest men" in this movement. Where more than two or three students are gathered together there are necessarily instruction papers and delegated teaching in the midst of them. And the proposition that private teachers are necessarily dishonest teachers and endowed professors the reverse, is certainly not the axiom your contributor would have your readers suppose.

But apart from the natural indignation excited by the pot calling the kettle black, I have little interest in defending the University by Correspondence. All teaching in big classes must necessarily make against originality, and Mr. Blank's class in matriculation Latin and Professor Judd's class in elementary geology are mechanical for much the same reasons. The point upon which I am more concerned is the closing of the worldly advantages of the degree, the withdrawal of the encouragement to self-help it offers to the outside man, the cobbler's 'prentice who reads of an evening, the literary bricklayer, the ambitious shopman and their class. That is a type of energetic man the country cannot afford to stifle down in the interests of the reputedly able and certainly very self-assertive professors of London. It is, to mention haphazard the names that come first to hand, the class of Dalton, Joule, Miller, and William Smith, the founders of modern chemistry, modern physics and geology, of Shakespeare, Burns, and Blake, and a host of lesser but still honourable citizens. Scholarship is an admirable thing in its way, but the greater need of science and literature alike is energy and originality. After all, the finest scholar in the world is but a parasite upon originality. And London University, with its hard examinations to all-comers, has been for many years now an open, a stimulatingly difficult, but a possible and encouraging way from down below there, to a position as teacher, as journalist, or what not, to a breathing space wherein a young man of this type may find his possibilities. So long as *his* way keep open, open beyond any risk of tampering, the "reformers" may, for all I care, tinker as they like with the rest of the University structure, organize boards of fellows and high professors, reconstruct the charter to give one another honorary degrees, put an easy medical degree upon the market, and enrich this great Metropolis with a University worthy of its County Council. Other graduates perhaps are more squeamish, but, whatever else they oppose, the exclusion of the rank outsider is the vital objection in their opposition.—

    Yours, &c.,   H. G. WELLS.

[It seems to us that so much of Mr. Wells's letter as is not devoted to a puff of one particular set of "correspondence classes" is based on a complete misapprehension of the proposed changes in the London University. He muddles up the present scheme for reconstitution of the University by Royal Commission with the proposal of three years ago to create a Gresham University, which should exclude non-collegiate students. So far from this, the scheme of reconstitution which was, urged upon the Duke of Devonshire specially provides for maintaining intact, and even for extending, the feature of admitting non-collegiate students. This is evident from Clauses 7, 42, and 48 of the Report of the Royal Commission, which deal with regulations for external students. From our knowledge of the leading men who have been moving in the matter, we can state that there is not one of them who is not heartily in favour of maintaining this feature.

We have also ascertained that Mr. Wells's assertion as to tuition by correspondence at the Cambridge Morphological Laboratory and at the Finsbury

College is entirely incorrect. Printed papers are in these establishments handed to students working in the laboratories as instructions about particular experiments. This is a totally different matter from sending them by post to absent students as a substitute for genuine laboratory practice. It is the antithesis of tuition by correspondence. —ED, "S. R."]

The London University Question

Saturday Review of Politics, Literature, Science and Art, vol 81, no 2097, p 17, 4 January 1896

The previous letter set off a heated exchange that continued into the new year. Silvanus P. Thompson, a member of the Royal Society and a member of the Royal Commission proposing to make London University a teaching institution, would respond with a letter with his own. He claimed that there would be no exclusion of the non-collegiate students despite "Mr. Wells's barefaced assertion", and called it "pure fiction" that there was cramming going on in places like his own Finsbury College. Wells persists, showing how lightly the reformers take the plight of the ex-collegiate student. Frank Harris again found it desirable to add his own comment, reprinted below.

To the Editor of the Saturday Review.

Sir,—Professor Thompson repeats the statement already made by you in an editorial footnote, flatly contradicting my assertion that the exclusion of the private student from the degree examinations is the root idea of the present London University "reform" movement. If this movement is not to exclude the private student, what *is* it to do? I challenged your contributor to state any positive addition the reformers would make to the teaching facilities of London, and that challenge is, of course, open to Professor Thompson. The reform is to annihilate the "crammers," I learn from your article, and how it is proposed to close the way to the pupils of the guerilla teachers, while leaving it open to the untaught private student, I cannot conceive. Professor Thompson writes gaily of the proposed scheme of reform making "elaborate provision for including" these private students. The elaborate provision consists in creating a special board for their benefit, a board largely under the control of the London professors, to whom the "crammers" and those stubborn originals who prefer self-education are absolutely antagonistic, and endowing this board with practically unlimited power of regulating the ex-collegiate pupil's courses of study. The fact that the Gresham scheme, excluding the ex-collegiate students, and the Cowper Commissioners' scheme, including them, have been supported in their turn by practically the same body of advocates shows how much good faith there is in this proposal. We who oppose these schemes, therefore, simply decline to believe in that "elaborate provision," and as our only security for the better definition of these vague promises of consideration, we insist on the right of Convocation to veto any scheme unsatisfactory upon this point. But however else the "reformers" change, they are resolutely determined that the veto must not be exercised. How can we trust them? There is nothing to prevent the ex-collegiate student being "included," much as a bear includes a casual antagonist. So far from convicting me of a "good downright thumping—misuse of language"—as Professor Thompson puts it in his animated way—I think his letter will, in the judgment of every thoughtful and impartial reader, simply illustrate the levity with which the interests of the ex-collegiate students are treated by him and his fellow-movers in the matter.

My statement that the Finsbury College is, educationally, on a level with any "cramming" establishment he deals with in a similar fashion. It is, he says, "pure fiction" that the teaching is by mechanical instruction-papers under stress of frequent and stringent examinations. "Examinations are held as seldom as possible," he says; and adds, in his airy way, "once only in each term." Yet surely it is possible to be less frequent than that—the "crammers'" pupil is examined once a year or so. On the score of "stringency" he does not add, as well he might, what percentage of the students entering his college successfully complete their courses. Do sixty per cent. survive? Of instruction papers he almost seems to say "there is none." There were. The instruction-papers in his college, unless they have been destroyed since my inspection, are simply printed demonstrations, and can only be intended to economise personal teaching. If the use of them was not necessarily cramming, then I submitted that correspondence teaching was not necessarily cramming. That was my position, and Professor Thompson's denials do not touch it.—Yours, &c. H. G. WELLS.

[Mr. Wells must be aware that the promoters within the University of London of the present scheme for reconstruction, as proposed by the Cowper Royal Commission, were the parties most strenuously opposed to the creation of the Gresham University as a second and rival University for London. He must also be aware that, of the numerous projects of reform to remedy the Present crying injustice to the collegiate students, the only one which proposed a Board specially to look after the interests of non-collegiate students is the Royal Commission's scheme, which he described as excluding such! We do not know why Mr. Wells should claim to know more about the Finsbury College than Professor Silvanus Thompson, who is its responsible head.— Ed. S. R.]

Elementary Science Teaching*

The Educational Times, vol XLIX, no 418, pp 76–77, 1 February 1896

In reviewing the new form of the Department of Science and Art, Wells bemoans the continued emphasis on memorization of scientific facts from textbooks, without a larger understanding of nature. The South Kensington system, and the set examinations, determines what is taught. Practical chemistry and physics remains difficult to teach because there is little equipment available at a price schools can afford. The new form, however, indicates that good recommendations on teaching are being adopted. In briefly reviewing his friend R. A. Gregory's new exercise book, Wells ties the work into the bettering of science teaching.

English schoolmasters and schoolmistresses have been teaching natural science—we judge by the prospectuses extant —for the better part of the century. But it was—save for the globes —a bookish thing, that led to the consciousness of knowledge rather than to knowledge, and had an infinitesimal educational value. And in spite of several generations of educational reformers, it remains curiously bookish still. Under the writer's paperweight now there is a pile of examination answer papers in botany, written by a class of girls in a country place, where vegetation must be positively tapping at the windows and clamouring for attention. And these papers testify beyond dispute that these little girls have been studying not botany so much as Professor Bayley Balfour's book—they know that "cells" contain "raphides," they know that there is a "nucleus" in every cell, and they have heard of exogens; but they do not know that plants feed by their leaves, or that the stem is anything more than a sort of bears' pole for "the sap to go up and down."[130] No one who has given any attention to the facts of contemporary teaching, as well as to contemporary theories, but will admit that this is by no means an exceptional sample of how not to teach. And in the case of botany it is difficult to explain the persistence of the vicious old method. The right way is easier for teacher and pupil alike, and no costlier. It has the objection that the individual pupil does not require a text-book; but then, by serving out special note-books, the subject may be made not absolutely unremunerative. It has the advantage of being not only the right way to teach botany, but also a pleasant contrast with and relief from severer studies. Its preservation is probably due more than anything else to the persistence of bookish examiners, and the want of a convenient teacher's handbook. The South Kensington system of written examinations has stimulated the production of text-books written to a syllabus,

---

130. Isaac Bayley Balfour was a Scottish botanist.

which, intended primarily for adolescent students, have, by the cheapness which resulted from the large sale, crushed out any suitable school-book on the subject. Yet these causes alone seem insufficient to account for the defect. The want of technical training is probably the major influence in the matter. The bare idea of practical teaching has, even in the year of grace 1896, still to reach the remoter practitioners of the noble art of making men and women.

It is easier to see why the practical teaching of chemistry and physics has still to conquer the great majority of schools. Added to the other influences against progress, there is the far more important one of expense. The need of apparatus blocks the way. On the one hand you have the parent jealous of "extras," and on the other the scientific instrument maker, a typical British manufacturer, turning out the most costly and beautifully finished appliances, and resolutely refusing to study the great market he might foster among school teachers.[131] One essential in teaching chemistry, for instance, is a cheap strong balance. At present, in dozens of schools, practical chemistry is still a hunt through test tubes and tables, after acids and bases, for the want of that one requisite. Yet I have on my table a little eighteen-penny thing used for weighing letters, a counterpoised lever with a curved scale; and similar ones are used by stationers for weighing sheets of paper. The man who would put upon the market a refined form of this model for a few shillings would remove one of the gravest obstacles in the way of a rational teaching of chemistry. The admirable suggestions of such reformers as Professor Armstrong[132] are largely vitiated by the costly apparatus demanded. So long as schoolmasters are asked to put a three-pound balance in the hands of ordinary schoolboys, so long will the proper practical teaching of chemistry remain—theory.

Undoubtedly the Science and Art Department is awaking to its responsibilities in the matter of practical instruction, and the new Form, No. 74, S. gives a very hopeful sketch of a suggested Elementary Course. It has the old South Kensington vice of being too full, and the old hard-and-fast distinction of subjects—Sound, Light, Heat, Magnetism, and Electricity. But the earlier lessons show that the work of Worthington, Armstrong, Gordon, and Earl[133] has really

---

131. This will develop into a fiercer argument about microscopes, featured near the end of this volume.

132. Chemist Henry Armstrong, also mentioned in "Science Teaching — An Ideal and Some Realities", above.

133. These would be Arthur M. Worthington, Henry Armstrong, Hugh Gordon, and Alfred G. Earl. Armstrong lauded Gordon's *Elementary Course of Physical Science*, Worthington's *An Elementary Course of Practical Physics* and its updated *A First Course of Physical Laboratory Practice*, and Earl's *Practical Lessons in Physical Measurement* for helping students learn the essential skills of science rather than cramming. See Henry E.

got home to the Departmental intelligence. It is divided into eighty-four lessons, and, spread over about 120, it will serve as a very excellent guide to teachers. When the College of Preceptors takes up, as it must do sooner or later, the work of stimulating practical teaching on science, it will find in this document an admirable example of how to direct instruction. Simultaneous with it, and perhaps not altogether unconnected with it, there comes to hand a brilliant and valuable little book by Mr. R. A. Gregory. It is not a text-book at all—the days of the text-book draw near an end. It is an exercise-book. Instructions head each page, and beneath is a space for drawings or calculations, as the case may be. The arrangement of the matter, as a glance at the list of contents will show, follows the best models.

Observations on the flotation of solids in various liquids (such as saturated brine, water, and turpentine), involving the determination of the extent to which they become immersed, and a comparison of their weights with those of the amounts of liquids which they displace. Application of knowledge thus gained to the explanation of ships floating. Comparisons of the apparent loss of weight suffered by solids of known volume when weighed immersed in different liquids with the weight of volumes of the liquids equal to the volumes of the solids. Determinations of relative densities by this method. Use of hydrometers.

Observations of the level character of liquid surfaces, except near to the walls of the containing vessel and in narrow vessels (tubes)—capillary attraction. Observations of counterbalancing pressures in communicating vessels or tubes containing a liquid (hydrostatic pressure), and of the effect of varying the width of the one tube. The hydraulic press. Observations of the pressure exerted by air—the barometer as a measurer of this pressure. The construction of curves showing variations in barometric pressure. Weather charts as illustrating differences in pressure in different places, and the influence of such differences in giving rise to winds. The determination of mountain heights by means of the barometer.

Observations on the expansion and compression of air; use and construction of the air pump. The Sprengel pump....

Experiments with levers. The construction of a "balance"—its resemblance to a simple lever or see-saw with equal arms. Determinations of weights by means of a lath or rule used as a "balance"; the use of levers with arms of various lengths in weighing. The various forms of "balance" in use—their construction. The mode of action of the different classes of levers and the mechanical advantage gained by them. Simple machines. The wheel and axle regarded as a form of lever. The use of the pulley. Combinations of pulleys as used in cranes, on ships, &c.—study of the manner in which they act....

The effect of change in temperature on the weight of air; ventilation. Determination of the capacity for heat of common solids in comparison with that of water. Observations on the heat of fusion. Heat of vaporization of water. Cooling as a consequence of evaporation—use of the wet and dry bulb thermometer. Determinations of the extent to

Armstrong,. "Research in Education." *Nature* LI (March 14, 1895): 463–67.

which water evaporates under different ordinary conditions. Determinations of the daily change in weight of a piece of seaweed or blanket—the airing of clothes.

But Mr. Gregory is no mere intelligent dispenser of other men's prescriptions. His book is essentially original. He has one of the most valuable qualities in a teacher—a ready invention. This, for instance, is a remarkably clear and convincing way of getting over the difficulty of proving that the area of a sphere $=\pi r^2$.

Procure a wooden pulley-end of a blind-roller, and a piece of thin sheet india-rubber, like that of which toy balloons are made. Place the india-rubber over one of the faces of the pulley, and fix it on by means of string tied around the groove of the pulley. Draw a square centimetre upon the india-rubber. Now fit a glass tube about a foot long into a cork which will fit tightly into the central hole in the pulley. Introduce water into the tube until the india-rubber upon the pulley has bulged out so as to form one-half of a globe, as nearly as you can estimate. You have now a hemispherical dome, the base of which is the pulley. It can be proved that such a dome has twice the area of the circular base upon which it rests. Test this statement by finding, while the india-rubber is stretched, the area of the square drawn upon it. If this area is about twice that of the original square, you may conclude that the dome surface of the india-rubber is twice that of the flat circular surface, and, therefore, that the whole surface of a sphere has four times the area of the flat part obtained by cutting the sphere into two halves.

But the book is full of such clever attacks on standing difficulties in teaching. Put by the side of the text-books of even five years ago, it justifies, after all, an optimistic view of the prospects of science teaching, in spite of the prices current of balances, and the fact that a teacher of botany down in the country has been teaching in the year of grace, 1895, as though no one had ever given five minutes' thought to teaching since the world began.

H. G. WELLS.

* (1) "Department of Science and Art, Form No. 74, S." (2) "An Exercise-Book of Elementary Practical Physics." By R. A. Gregory, F.R.A.S. (Macmillan.)

Mr. Gregory's "Physics Exercise-Book"

The Journal of Education, vol XVIII, no 319, p 105, 1 February 1896

This is a response to an unfriendly review of the recent book by Wells's friend R. A. Gregory, a book favorably reviewed by Wells in The Educational Times *(see the previous article in this volume). Wells believes the reviewer's objections are unfounded, and that the strength of the book is that it "is not slavishly written up to a syllabus", but rather focuses on sound ideas of teaching physics. Wells thinks the book excellent on several levels. The reviewer responded in the same issue, saying that not covering the topics dictated by the Department of Science and Art is a weakness, that the book is too basic to be helpful, and that Wells is not the only one who reads books carefully and studies educational method.*

To the Editor of The Journal of Education.

Sir, —Your Journal is so influential among teachers, and commonly so impartial, that I may perhaps be permitted to protest against the short and misleading notice of Mr. Gregory's new book in your last issue. Apparently, your reviewer's objections to it are:—

(1) That, though it runs on the same lines, it does not blindly follow, a syllabus issued, after its publication, by the Science and Art Department—a syllabus published expressly to suggest and not to prescribe what form teaching may take in Departmental classes.

(2) That the first half is too elementary for an organized science school, and that 167 experiments, of 206, are not on "physics proper" (Science and Art Department Syllabus physics?), but are concerned with form, volume, mass, and other such indispensable preliminary matters.

(3) "Sound, light, magnetism, and electricity" are absolutely neglected.

(4) "It is not a satisfactory book at all."

(5) The preface is not to your reviewer's taste.

Yet surely the *Journal of Education*, of all papers, should be the first to welcome a book that is not slavishly written up to a syllabus, that aims at simplicity and easy graduation, and wherein the necessary introductory exercises upon spatial ideas and the general properties of matter are not shirked in order to cram "sound, light, magnetism, and electricity" into 206 experiments. Your reviewer must surely have the imagination of a hardened "grant-earner" to raise that last objection. The teaching of physics in schools should aim at discipline surely, not at a scrappy omniscience. As a contributor to a weekly review and as a student of educational method, I have had to read Mr. Gregory's book very carefully. It appears to me to be one of the best adapted to school work that I have ever seen. It seems equally commendable on the score of high aims and of good sense. On the one hand, it follows the principles of Froebel, and, on the other, the apparatus is studiously kept within the narrow financial possibilities even of the private school. It is a noteworthy, genuine, and very hopeful attempt towards practicable practical science teaching. I certainly anticipated better treatment for it in the organ of the party of educational advance.—I am, Sir, &c.,

H. G. WELLS.

Cheap Microscopes and a Moral

Saturday Review of Politics, Literature, Science and Art, vol 82, no 2133, pp 277-279, 12 September 1896

Having previously mentioned the disadvantage to practical science teaching caused by the expense of equipment, and the competition in science posed by Germany, Wells expands his argument to include protectionism and business practices. In this piece Wells takes his attack directly to the British instrument makers and merchants. Several would respond to this article, insisting that their microscopes of a few years before qualified as both good and cheap. Henry Crouch, whose higher priced microscopes had been recommended by Wells in "Biology for the Intermediate Science and Preliminary Scientific Examinations" (1893), earlier in this volume, would be one of these respondents. Wells's answer, a challenge for any British maker to identify a good microscope that could be had for three and a half guineas or less, was responded to by several makers claiming they offered one.[134] There would be no comparable response to the issue of balances or scales for learning chemistry.

The story of the cheap microscopes, to be presently followed, no doubt, by the story of the cheap chemical balance, and, it may be, by the story of the American bicycle, is, the writer submits, at the very centre of this trouble about German competitors. It displays you the British merchant and his methods very purely: his curious contempt for the common man, his regal incapacity for considerations of small change, his autocratic bearing, his love of a bouncing overcharge even at the cost of business. The writer is clearly no Protectionist. He submits the trouble is barely at all a question of tariffs, and not essentially a question of technical education. It is something wider. To use an admirable phrase, made in Germany by one Herbart, the British merchant needs an enlargement of his "circle of thought," and only financial stresses will do him that service.[135] Then he will take to technical education as a matter of course. But to the story.

Seven years ago there were, I suppose, very nearly as many medical students and science students and amateurs of botany, biology, pond-life studies, and so forth, as there are to-day. They all needed microscopes, and those who had from five guineas upward to spend upon an instrument got them from English

---

134. See Wells, H. G. "Cheap Microscopes." *Saturday Review of Politics, Literature, Science and Art* 82, no. 2139 (October 24, 1896): 444.

135. Early 19th century educationalist Johann Friedrich Herbart has been mentioned in several previous articles.

manufacturers. Those who had not, coveted, and for the most part went without. Seven years ago there was no compound microscope worthy of the name upon the market at a less price than five guineas. Of that the high power was very unsatisfactory; it was good only for elementary work. Even to buy one at that price involved humiliations, just as buying the lowest priced article at a respectable English shop does always involve humiliations. The buyer was shown a fifty-guinea instrument some opulent amateur had ordered, and was left to infer he was certainly no gentleman to be buying this cheaper stuff. Many of the cheaper English microscopes were made of a nasty looking white metal, and delivered in cardboard boxes— it would seem just to teach the mean creatures who bought them a lesson. And the higher-power lenses seemed to have been ground at times in an exceedingly offhand spirit. "Cheap goods," quoth the manufacturer. A really efficient microscope was, in fact, so costly and so difficult of access that one can understand many were deterred from biological studies by their use, and students, to their infinite annoyance and detriment, clubbing to share one. The general practitioner as a rule sold his, at the end of his student days. But to any demand for a cheaper instrument the British manufacturer replied in his stereotyped formula—and, were the industries of this country protected, he might be doing so to-day. "Can't be done," said the British merchant, and to point the moral would produce a "toy" or a "junior" microscope at thirty shillings or two guineas that was a downright insult to a modern nursery.

And then came the cheap and nasty German microscope—one of which has been my good friend and companion for the last five or six years. The cheap and nasty German microscope was made of brass, pleasant to see and handle, strong, easy to work, with an astonishingly good high power, and neatly packed in a stout box of polished wood. It was in the very best style; it had all that was necessary, and nothing superfluous. And the price of this cheap and nasty German instrument to the English purchaser was three and a half guineas. It simply kicked the contemporary British five-guinea instrument out of the market. In the high power, particularly, there was no comparison between the two. At the time it came over—things have altered since—it was the equal in efficiency of any English instrument at double the price. And I have no doubt the dealers won a fair profit. At that time I was engaged in teaching biological science to candidates for London degrees, and I saw it arrive. Most of these candidates were school teachers and medical students, and anything but opulent. To begin with, the want of microscopes was the curse of their work. In a class of a score, there would be perhaps eight or nine students too poor to own instruments, one or two with worn-out secondhand things, and for the rest an ancestral oddity or so, a maddening toy caricature, and perhaps four or five really efficient eight or ten guinea ones, hired or owned, round which the class clustered like a swarm of bees.

Now in the classes I used to teach the German maker reigns almost alone, and every student has his microscope. And the Germans are using their small microscopes as a means for the introduction of more complicated instruments of undeniable cheapness and efficiency. They must be selling hundreds of microscopes in this country. The English manufacturer has come down to the German prices, but a market once lost takes years of recovery. Not that the English manufacturer ever had the market represented by the poor modern student. He was simply too high and mighty for such middle-class traffic. That must be borne in mind. His business method for years had been the stupid one of trying to force his customers to purchase goods beyond both their requirements and means, or letting them go without. And doubtless under his ascendency dozens of English students went without this most necessary appliance for scientific study. It is not only a question of lost trade, but also one of intellectual hindrance—a far more serious national impoverishment in the long run.

That is the story of the cheap microscope. There is another story I am fairly certain some will be writing in five or six years' time—the story of the cheap chemical balance. It is now generally recognized as a matter of urgent public importance that a considerable number of people should be practically and efficiently taught chemistry. There are classes in chemistry enough in this country, Heaven knows! but for the most part they engage in learning to gabble text-books or watching their lecturer's experiments from the remote recesses of a class-room. Laboratory work in nine cases out of ten means a kind of work fudged by teachers to fill up time, and called qualitative analysis. All authoritative writers upon the teaching of chemistry agree that chemistry cannot be properly taught unless each student can work extensively at a balance. Since no teaching can be cheap that is not worked in classes, it is eminently desirable that there should be at least one balance to each couple of students. Now at present there is no efficient balance sold at such a price as will admit of chemistry being taught in the prescribed and efficient way in middle-class or continuation schools; a balance, that is, at about twelve or fifteen shillings. From any practical scientific instrument maker the reader consults he will learn that it "can't be done"—just as he would have learnt the impossibility of a three-and-a-half-guinea microscope seven years ago. Yet, nevertheless, that balance will be done in the next five years—a practicable weighing machine, possibly on the lines of the counterpoise letter balances that have nearly swept the good old costly brass scale and weights out of existence. It will be done because this particular market cannot possibly take anything higher. And the odds are that it will be done in Germany. And from Germany too, in the wake of the balance, will come, sooner or later, intelligently arranged cheap sets of apparatus for the teaching of chemistry.

I could enlarge upon the amazing want of enterprise of the English scientific instrument maker, so far as the cheaper, but in the end—if he would only test them—more lucrative branches of his business go. He is particularly opposed to science teachers and science students, insisting upon a dilemma of exquisite finish and impossible price, or—trash, and "I told you so." For years it was impossible to get a box of biological dissecting instruments under a guinea; in most shops they would have asked thirty-five shillings or two guineas. For the classes I have already referred to this price was too high, and certain enterprising booksellers arranged and sold a quite sufficient box for ten and sixpence. These we got in before the Germans, and in a year or so the scientific implement dealers had learnt their lesson. Now you can get an admirable box for that price in quite a number of shops.

But enough of these anecdotes: one carries the moral as well as a hundred. I have no doubt the little peculiarities I have developed are not confined to scientific instrument makers. Protection in the cases I have stated could only have worked to protect the British merchant from the stimulus he has received and to prolong his really stupid obstruction of the important national work of education. And technical education would scarcely have remedied the matter. The defect was just sheer want of business capacity, that unpatriotic serenity that seems inevitable in a generation following a period of undisputed prosperity. We want, in fact, a mission to our merchants and manufacturers to enlarge their circle of ideas. That enlargement attained, they will see to technical education as a matter of course, and they will require no other protection.

H. G. WELLS.

The Root of the Matter: Some Reflections on the British Schoolmaster

(London) Daily Mail, p4, 18 November 1897

As Wells began to rely more on his income from writing fiction, his commentary on education broadened. While he continued to write about science in the journals, more of his pieces undertook a national and international perspective. The Daily Mail was founded by Alfred Harmsworth, who had founded the Henley House School Magazine, *for which Wells had written as a much younger man. Since then Harmsworth had become a vigorous supporter of the British Empire and the* Daily Mail *was considered a mouthpiece for imperialism. Here Wells connects the paper's focus to his own interests. Wells notes the success of Germany in the marketplace due to their superior education system, with which he had been familiar for some time. His call was, as many of his calls would be, prescient.*

(By H. G. WELLS.)

"The economic battle of Waterloo was lost on the playing fields of Eton."

The greatest, perhaps, of all the evils of a morning paper is the provocation to stop work and manage the affairs of other people that it brings with it into a household. And in the matter of the national prosperity, this has clearly been irresistible to all sorts and conditions of men. So much in extenuation. And further—to be vivid one must be brief and a little emphatic, for it is surely better to seem cocksure and impertinent and carry a meaning than to be the most refined and considerate figure of ambiguity it is possible to conceive.

Now, Mr. Steevens[136] and Mr. Williams[137] have combined to give your readers the clearest and most indisputable picture of our country's steady loss of industrial pre-eminence that it could be possible to have. The response in suggestions is abundant enough. The most noticeable thing is that in this case, and putting aside what is obviously foolish, these suggestions of why we are defeated do not seem to be traced to any one fundamental inferiority. They lie in groups mutually contradictory, and so soon as action is proposed along the line

---

136. George W. Steevens was one of the Daily Mail's main journalists and later a war correspondent.

137. E. E. Williams was a protectionist who engaged in several debates in the newspapers about the decline of British industry. He had published a series of articles entitled "Marching backwards" in the Daily Mail.

determined by any one group of suggested causes, some one is bound to

RAISE ANOTHER GROUP, AND PLEAD,

"But what good would that possibly do in this case?" Suggest that Free Trade, though an admirable principle; requires, like all admirable principles, an intelligent qualification for daily use, and a voice replies that the mischief lies in our want of technical education. And any demand for an intelligent system of technical education is immediately met by instances of extraordinary stupidity in the British methods of sale. Attack the British merchant with a charge of inflexibility and stupidity, and he points at once to a Trade Union delegate, as an adequate excuse for his neglected duties. The Trade Union delegate hands you on to a greedy, unpatriotic railway company, to a pig-headed quarry owner, or to a grasping landlord, whose prompt and effectual answer is—this pedantry of Free Trade.

So we drift, and every year gives Mr. Williams more striking figures for his articles. So we drift, voluble and inconclusive, in our parliamentary English way, doing nothing, and cursing the prophets of evil. So we drift, trusting, it seems, to the remote chance of a Continental war and the "silver streak" to save us from disaster. Though the fear of our impending defeat becomes conviction—saving such nursery expedients as the "Made in Germany" invention—we do nothing. We do nothing, from, no lack of will, but because the public mind seams to lack the necessary clearness to know what to do.

Now in that last sentence is the first intimation of the present argument. The

PUBLIC MIND IS NOT CLEAR ENOUGH

to meet this reverse. In other words, the public mind is not sufficiently well educated to meet this reverse. And if we take each of the alleged causes of our defeat and examine the way in which that cause operates, we shall find this general proposition either wholly confirmed or repeated in a particular instance. Why do a large number of people, myself included, deprecate any present abandonment of the principle of Free Trade? Because they do not believe that British merchants are sufficiently intelligent, broad-minded, and far-seeing to resist the immediate opportunity to rob their fellow-country men by tariff manipulation. Each trade would intrigue for protection in order to raise prices to the home producer, and the national advantage of that alone would be a negative quantity. There is in that matter the object lesson of America. And further, these doubters have no confidence that the other influential classes of the community are intelligent enough and well informed enough to prevent British merchants doing this. Want of education again—or real, efficient education, that is. Why are British merchants old-fashioned, unenterprising, and extravagant in their methods of sale? Why do they send circulars to foreign countries in the English tongue? Why do they support the compulsory advertisement of all German goods? Why do they persist in not making the sort of goods their customers require? Why, for instance, do our microscope makers obstinately refuse to produce the microscope English students require until a German firm picks up the derelict custom, and our publishers and booksellers

DEVISE THE MOST IDIOTIC COMBINATIONS

to discourage the few people who still buy books from doing so? Either because they are naturally fools or because their early training has not developed them to meet the. demands of their position. Since previous generations of British merchants have certainly not been fools, we are forced to conclude that here, again, the general explanation holds—that a want of adequate education is the root evil of the matter.

And, again, coming to the working man. Why do we hear so much for his insubordination and disloyalty? Mainly because his employer is not capable and intelligent enough to inspire his confidence, and because he himself is just educated to the pitch of reading a Labour paper, and not educated to the pitch of understanding it. The working man is so ill-educated and so bitterly aware of the stupid selfishness of the managing classes that he even sets his face against labour-saving appliances. They throw him out of his immediate employment, the merchant is incapable of helping him, and too short-sighted to help him if it were possible, and the flexibility of mind necessary for him to readjust himself to fluctuating conditions has not been developed. With man, as with master, the trouble is—inadequacy of education.

So it shapes itself to at least one observer, this figure of depression, this network of statistics, is merely the immediate aspect, the curtain of the reality. Lift the curtain, and behold! The dull, pretentious, classical examinee, head master of the upper-class school, boring away with his obsolete sham learning of Greek and Latin, his pure, his scrupulously pure, mathematics, his unspeakable French, and his

ISOLATED BITS OF BOOKISH SCIENCE.

He knows about as much of expert teaching as a mediæval medical practitioner knew of anatomy and physiological chemistry. The only real education the public school provides is found in its games, and in its tradition of "good form." His privilege it is to "educate" our great captains of industry, our rich; from him many of them proceed directly to face the young German. I know something of his work, for I have in my time coached public-school boys for military examinations. Even for them to pass examinations conducted by an examiner of his own class they have to be taken out of his hands. When I think of the pleasant, stupid, young men who passed even, when I think of them as possibly leading our unlucky Tommiea against educated Germans—I must confess I shiver. But my concern at present is not with those who passed, but with those who failed. Do you know what became of them? They went into business.

And below the public-school master, comes the middle-class schoolmaster, endowed or private—dealing in a sort of cheap imitation of the public school course, Greek omitted and the Latin rarely rising even to the pitch of translation at sight, truncated beginnings of mathematics, a chip of cheap science (the laboratory, a cupboard), and lessons in misunderstanding English literature. His "good form" is a training in snobbishness, and his games a system of advertisement. He educates the smaller capitalists, the bulk of our military officers, most of our navy men, he lays the foundation for our professional experts.

HE IS WHY, FOR INSTANCE,

it becomes necessary to import technical chemists from Germany.

And, lastly, the elementary schools. I could point to one gleam of hope in certain higher-grade schools, but I write not of hope, but of repentance. And a glaring placard flouts across my memory: Vote for Diggle and Economy." Wonderful economy, heedless of race or Empire, so long as we keep down the Rates.

And what of Germany? Three generations ago, was Germany's time of humiliation; the Germans were a beaten people at the feet of Napoleon. A generation already passing has seen thirty years of strength. What was that strength? Bismarck and drill, you may think. But neither Bismarck nor drill account for this amazing efficiency of the common German. For that you must seek some other influence. You will find it in the history of German education during the first half of this century.

The simple, brutal truth is—the English ironmasters admitted it, bitterly, only the other day—the Germans are now better educated—more efficient, that is—than the English. By virtue of that, in spite of their crushing military burthen, they are beating us. They will go on beating us for some years, whatever we may do in the way of tariffs and trade marks to prevent them, because, at this game, the more intelligent people is bound to win But their educational system is no longer progressive, and their autocratic Government is a perpetual uncertainty. A vigorous reorganisation of our secondary education would begin to tell upon this struggle in a few years' time—and in the course of a generation we might even recover the old predominance. It is our only chance in this long-drawn battle of commerce. Protection, Technical Schools, Labour Legislation, and so forth, are incidents, details. The German schoolmaster made Germany possible. The inefficiency of the British schoolmaster is the root of all our inefficiencies.

H. G. WELLS.

1

2

Sums: The Fine Art of Not Teaching Mathematics

(London) Daily Mail, p4, 24 December 1897

Although not directly a criticism of science teaching, this column notes the difficulties in funding a proper mathematics instructor in middle-class schools where the emphasis on classics continues. Wells also takes a swipe at commercial education in mathematics, which he experienced as a boy at Mr. Morley's Academy.

In certain papers that have appeared in the "Daily Mail" it has been suggested that the prominence of Latin and Greek in our middle-class schools is extremely bad for these schools; that the middle-class boy never masters these subjects, and obtains little or no benefit from their half-hearted and incomplete study.

But that is the least evil in the matter. The teaching of these classical subjects not only involves a monstrous waste of time and energy, but it acts in the most disastrous way upon the teaching of other subjects that are of the highest value and that might be done very thoroughly in the middle-class school.

Now the way in which this second and greater consequence of the classical incubus obtains is easy to understand. When Latin, with or without Greek, takes precedence among the school subjects, it follows that the head master of a middle-class school is usually a classical scholar, or at least the holder of a degree in classics—a man, that is, who has' studied these beautiful useless languages to the exclusion of other subjects. The mathematical accomplishment exacted from the graduating classical man at the English universities is severely elementary, and he is already

BUSILY FORGETTING THE LITTLE

he knew long before he takes his degree and begins to teach. Applied mathematics, the exemplification of the import of mathematical exercises, he barely touches, or touches not at all. But since the latter-day parent, in spite of Professor Mahaffy, insists on mathematics, and so forth, he permits these things to be taught under him, and will even in a manner teach them himself.

Now, as things are at present, the financial arrangements of the ordinary middle-class school do not permit of an unlimited staff. The average middle-class school of about 100 boys cannot afford three highly qualified and able men. The market price of highly qualified and able men is one of those things that are likely to remain high. Consequently, if the chief position and the chief salary go to a man erudite in the dead languages, and if it is also necessary to have at least one athlete on the staff, and if men conversant with French and German are needed, and if, moreover, an able scientific man has to be tempted for the lucrative opportunities of technical physics and chemistry, the chances of a really thorough mathematician on the staff of the secondary school are very remote indeed.

So that, & priori, the probability that mathematics will be well done in middle-class schools is very small. And how badly mathematical subjects are done let Professor Oliver J. Lodge, one of the ablest teachers of physics in this country, witness. Reading a review by him in "Nature" a few days ago, I came across a few pregnant allusions. "Alas!" he writes, "many of us know boys of sixteen who have been for years at *what schoolmasters call mathematics,* and who

HAVE HARDLY YET

arrived at quadratic equations. In many a British, school trigonometry forms a sort of goal." And again: "When feebleness of this kind .... is believed to represent mathematics, no wonder that practical men regard that subject with aversion thinly veiled by contempt."

If anything, Professor Lodge understates the case. So far from "trigonometry" being a goal in middle-class schools, the bulk of the boys never do more than hear of it, as the wonderful exercise of gifted beings. If the reader consult the requirements of the London University Matriculation or other high-class leaving school examinations, he will find the mathematical high-water mark is such a smattering as Professor Lodge ascribes to the average boy, and that that instructive and representative body, the College of Preceptors, does not even set papers beyond the Fourth Book of Euclid and the easiest trigonometry.

Yet it is impossible to go very far with physical science, to master anything beyond the barest principles of those commercially and educationally most important subjects, electricity and chemistry, without mathematical attainments far beyond this level.

Now are the attainments of our boys in these subjects so low because the average boy is a blockhead, or is the teaching to blame?

We have seen why It is that the chances are against the man who teaches mathematics in a middle-class school knowing very much about his subject. But that defect of equipment is only part of the evil. There is now, one must premise,

A DISTINCT ART AND SCIENCE

of education, just as there is a distinct art and science of surgery. But, amazing as it may seem, the middle-class schoolmaster do as not study this science and art. He is not required to study it, and, when he is a classical man, cannot, as a rule, even be made to see the necessity of studying it.

And as a consequence of this ignorance the middle-class schoolmaster sets about his mathematical teaching in obsolete and stupid ways. If he had planned most carefully how to keep boys back, while seeming to be urging them forward in mathematics, he could not have more effectually attained that end than he does at present. Let me ask the reader to recall his own school experiences, and he will begin to see how ingeniously the schoolmaster wastes time and brain labour and human lives.

The child of middle-class parents usually learns to count before five, to add, subtract, multiply, and divide by six, or, at latest, seven. In these things he gets a start of the lower-class child, because of his better home conditions, and that start he ought to keep. At seven he is quite ripe and ready for the study of fractions and the beginning of algebra, easy and attractive subjects when they are intelligently taught. Geometry follows, and by eleven trigonometry, and by twelve geometrical conics may well be under way. I am not writing without experimental

PROOF OF THESE ASSERTIONS

The thing has been done, not with exceptional boys, but with an entire class, simply by setting about it the right way. But the middle-class schoolmaster, instead of going on to fractions and algebra, sets the unhappy little boy, so soon as he has learnt to add, subtract, multiply, and divide, at a solemn tomfoolery called "money" and "weights and measures" sums, practice," "bills of parcels," "rule of three," "interest," "discount," and similar trash, upon which his victim, so far as concerns mathematics, wastes sometimes six years of his school life, and loses all the start his more stimulating home conditions gave him.

The reader wall remember these wasted years, the worry of learning the mysteries of "carrying" the complex intellectual torture of having to "reduce" terms to the same name, the thousand and one reasonless mechanical processes that had to be learnt. Even now as I write comes back the sense of stupefaction, of wandering in a great desert of unreason, the mental stress and perplexity with which, under the guidance of a middle-class schoolmaster, I confronted "sums" in "cube-root"—a matter which, taught as an incident of algebraic study, presents not an atom of difficulty.

A pretence of utility—for the "commercial" education fallacy is, at least, two hundred years old—is the excuse for this disastrous waste of time. And for the general badness of our middle-class mathematical teaching, of which this is a part, we have to blame chiefly two things—the predominance of Latin and Greek in education, the lowness of the average schoolmaster's mathematical attainments and his obstinate refusal to study the science and art of his calling. Of how greatly it must work to the national enfeeblement—for in Army and Navy, in almost every great manufacture, sound knowledge of applied mathematics is an essential conduct of efficiency—it is surely unnecessary to write at length.

H. G. WELLS

"Stinks." The Cheerful Game of Teaching Science Without a Balance

(London) Daily Mail, p4, 28 December 1897

By this point, Wells had published The Time Machine, The Wonderful Visit, The Island of Dr. Moreau, The Wheels of Chance, *and* The Invisible Man. *But he couldn't resist another swipe at the appalling state of science education in Britain.*

By H. G. Wells

When the English middle-class schoolmaster was first confronted with science, he called it "Stinks," and considering that he had disposed of the matter, went on teaching the dead languages.

But Mr. Herbert Spencer, and a number of other authoritative persons, and the rebellious, but none too rebellious parent finally prevailed against this attitude, and science teaching entered the middle-class school.

Science teaching entered the middle-class school, but the science teacher did not do so, for the simple reason that in those remote early Victorian times there were very few teachers of science. The common practice was for the French master, or the drawing master, or some such handy man, to "take science."

One imagines the schoolmaster, hot for interviewing an exacting parent, popping his head into the assistant masters' room. "I want one of you to take science," one conceives him saying. That was not so very long ago, and though every school nowadays flaunts "science" on its prospectus, a school with a teacher who has a science degree is still the exception.

The science thus taken, was, of course, handled in striking and original ways. The middle-class school had not only no science teacher, but no apparatus and no laboratory. No middle-class teacher knew how to teach, save by way of book, oral repetition, and exercise—even the public elementary schools had scarcely discovered object-lessons. Naturally, the middle-class schoolmaster got a book, a cheap book, with definitions at the beginning, and scientific facts arranged as much like rules and paradigms as possible. So that, instead of teaching things, he merely crammed his boys with phrases and sentences about things. The science VARIED WITH THE SCHOOL;

some schools "took" chemistry, some electricity, some physics, some geology. It scarcely mattered—the books were in a series, and all the same price. The boys toiled at the text-book for, perhaps, an hour a week, and in that way science was taught. If they were in doubt upon some passage in the book they consulted the gentleman who "took" science upon the meaning of that passage. His decision was final.

In addition there were such experimental demonstrations of chemical facts as did not require too costly, difficult, or dangerous an apparatus. A diffident and dubious young man would perform upon a kitchen table with a pneumatic trough and a retort, often consuming several pennyworth of chemicals in one experiment, while the whole school (collected from motives of economy) witnessed his unaccountable marvels. So chemistry, the chief school science subject, was made manifest to middle-class youth, and so it is still taught in the majority of middle-class schools professing science. The boys would, of course, be far better employed at any wholesome game, or even cleaning windows à la Squeers—that pioneer of sound practical instruction[138].

No doubt the middle-class schoolmaster will deny the truth of this picture. But, happily, the parent has an efficient means of testing that denial. Professor Armstrong, and all other authoritative writers upon the teaching of chemistry insist upon

THE PARAMOUNT IMPORTANCE

of one piece of apparatus, without which chemistry cannot be taught. That is the chemical balance. In any place where chemistry is honestly and properly taught there must be either sufficient balances for all the pupils to use, conveniently and without haste, or there must be one balance, so fine and big that all the details of the weighings done therewith may be visible to the entire class under instruction. Therefore, let the parent see to that chemical balance. He must understand by balance a beautifully delicate weighing machine—not a mere pair of scales. If that balance cannot be produced the chemical teaching of that school is not what it should be; is saved, indeed, from being a deliberate fraud only by the plea of ignorance on the part of the head-master.

But if the school can produce adequate balances, and if the teacher of chemistry—whom the parent might also see for himself—is a university graduate in science, the chances are that chemistry is thoroughly taught in that school.

That balance cannot be too rigorously insisted upon. It is the parent's only guarantee. For here, again, the examining bodies that should protect him, betray him.

The Science and Art Department (which ought to know better) and, of course, such schoolmaster's examining bodies as the College of Preceptors, will cheerfully give certificates, witnessing to

A KNOWLEDGE OF CHEMISTRY,

to boys who have simply crammed one of the dreadful little text-books to which allusion has been made. The examiners must know quite well that half the boys they pass have never seen a quantitative experiment in their lives.

---

[138] Cruel headmaster Squeers is featured in Dickens' *Nicholas Nickleby*.

The complaisance of these examining bodies is, indeed, one of the most serious problems in the complicated question of middle-class education. The ideal examining body will stimulate and control efficient teaching by insisting on genuine attainment in the examinee, and refusing any eulogious equivocations on the pattern of the Cambridge Local "satisfied the examiners" for an unsatisfactory scramble through a mere preliminary test. To do that it must be absolutely beyond the influence of the less-capable schoolmasters. The various middle-class examining boards at present compete against each other, and for one to raise the standard in any subject is simply to send school after school, each with its dozen or score of fees, to a more obliging rival. And until human nature alters, or the strong arm of the exterior authority, backed by public opinion, intervenes, this state of affairs will continue.

Not only do these examining bodies give certificates in science on the strength of

A WRITTEN EXAMINATION ONLY,

but they also meet the demand of the market, and supply any examination in "practical" science—"Practical Chemistry," for example, of the most unreal and dishonest description. To describe this sort of examination in detail is impossible here; suffice it that it is quite possible for a candidate to pass the ordinary middle-class examination in "practical" chemistry, and that candidates have passed it, simply by learning by rote a dozen pages of a book of analytical tables, without doing any practical work at all before entering the examination room. But at present our concern is with science teaching, and not with this wide issue of facile examinations.

For school purposes the twin subjects of chemistry and physics are all the science that has educational value. A little gossip about animals and the names of plants for little boys, a little optional botany and geology in connection with walks and holidays, and a good book or so on natural history lurking in the school library to catch the boy with a taste that way, will do all that is required of the rest. Physiology, the science of health, is recommended by various authorities. It is extremely plausible to say that schoolboys should learn something about their own bodies. But, as a matter of fact, the subject is quite unteachable to ordinary schoolboys. Physiological processes demand an understanding of a trained sort, and costly appliances, dissections of animals, skeletons, microscopes, and so forth, beyond the means of any but the richest school. What is called "teaching" physiology in most schools is merely the cramming of specious gabble about diagrams, eminently calculated to beget the illusion of knowledge. And chemistry and physics, mathematics

UP TO THE CALCULUS,

English and drawing, a glimpse of history and a foreign language are quite enough, and more than enough, even for a clever boy to master between six and sixteen. There are dozens of things it would be nice for a schoolboy to know. But the price to pay for all these nice things is that the boy should be an all-round smatterer, the most useless sort of human being it is possible to imagine. The Middlesborough Chamber of Commerce amused itself the other day in writing down a list of *nineteen subject*—nineteen!—for the instruction of boys leaving school at fifteen. One of these was "natural history applied to British industries." Wonderful people!

Physical science—chemistry and physics, that is—may be, and in some places is, thoroughly taught in middle-class schools. Taught thoroughly, in laboratory and class-room, it has indisputably the very highest educational functions; not only is it of extreme value as knowledge, but it creates a comprehensive habit of mind, a real power of meeting occasions, and the inestimable qualities of accuracy and mental honesty. It is not in most cases taught thoroughly, chiefly for five reasons—(1) the school time-table is crowded with the impossible attempt at classical learning, or the trash and cram known as "commercial subjects"; (2) the mathematical teaching is too feeble to assist in its development; (3) its teachers are often

IGNORANT AND INEFFICIENT;

(4) the equipment of apparatus is wanting; and (5) the ordinary middle-class examination discourages the honest teacher, and endorses the crammer. The extreme importance of having these things set right cannot be too vigorously insisted upon. The encylopædic proposals of Middlesborough, were they realized in a school, would produce boys as chock full of information as educated Hindoos, and as incapable of independent thought and action. We don't want to teach boys what they can get at any time out of "Whitaker's Almanac," a cyclopædia, or a gazeteer; we want to teach them far-reaching principles, to train them to think and act. No subject within the possibilities of middle-class education can compare in educational value with science when it is taught in properly-equipped schools by men who have also made a study of education, and who are supported by efficient co-operation in mathematics and drawing. And let the reader make no mistake about specious "commercial" subjects and all the fancies of the impracticable "practical" man. It is on the teaching of science in our middle-class schools that our ultimate victory or defeat by the United States and Germany in the great commercial war mainly depends.

H. G. WELLS

Bibliography

Hughes, David Y, and Robert M Philmus. "The Early Science Journalism of H.G. Wells: A Chronological Survey." *Science Fiction Studies* 1, no. 2 (1973): 98–114.

Parrinder, Patrick and Robert M. Philmus, eds. *H.G. Wells's Literary Criticism.* United Kingdom: Harvester Press, 1980.

Philmus, Robert M, and David Y Hughes, eds. *H. G. Wells: Early Writings in Science and Science Fiction.* Berkeley: University of California Press, 1975.

Sherborne, Michael. *H.G. Wells: Another Kind of Life.* London: Peter Owen Publishers, 2010.

Smith, David C. *H.G. Wells: Desperately Mortal.* New Haven and London: Yale University Press, 1986.

———, ed. *The Correspondence of H.G. Wells.* Vol. 1. London: Pickering & Chatto Ltd, 1996.

Wells, H G. *Experiment in Autobiography.* New York: The Macmillan Company, 1934.

Acknowledgements

Special thanks to:
> Sara Cassetti, the tireless interlibrary loan librarian at MiraCosta College.
> Sarah and Taylor, who helped with transcribing.
> Jenny, for unwavering, enthusiastic support.
> Patrick Parrinder and the H.G. Wells Society.
> The Yale University Library, Bromley Library, Bodleian Library, and British Library, for access to the articles and assistance.
> Stewart Gillies of the British Library Newspaper room, for finding an article for me during the pandemic.
> The Internet Archive and Hathi Trust, for online resources.
> David, for listening to it all.

Title page image by H. G. Wells, from *Text-book of Biology* (1893)

The typeface used for this book is Cormorant Garamond by Christian Thalmann, Switzerland. Provided by Google Fonts. Cover design: Sarah Lane Daymude.